D0742619

WHEN THE TEXANS CAME

When the
TEXANS *Came*

MISSING RECORDS FROM THE CIVIL WAR IN THE SOUTHWEST

1861–1862

JOHN P. WILSON

UNIVERSITY OF NEW MEXICO PRESS

ALBUQUERQUE

Library of Congress Cataloging-in-Publication Data

When the Texans came : missing records from the Civil War in the
Southwest, 1861–1862 / [compiled by] John P. Wilson.— 1st ed.
p.   cm.
Includes bibliographical references and index.
ISBN 0-8263-2290-5 (alk. paper)
1. Southwest, New—History—Civil War, 1861–1865—Sources.
2. United States—History—Civil War, 1861–1865—Sources.
3. Southwest, New—History—Civil War, 1861–1865—Campaigns.
4. United States—History—Civil War, 1861–1865—Campaigns.
I. Wilson, John P. (John Philip), 1935–
E470.9 .W47 2001
973.7'3—dc21
2001002483

Design: Mina Yamashita

Contents

Illustrations

Maps

Figures

Abbreviations

A.&I.G. / A.&I.G.O.	Adjutant and Inspector General / A.&I.G. Office.
A.A.A.G. / A.A.A.Ge. / A.A.A.Gen. / A.A.A.Genl / A.A.A. General.	Acting Assistant Adjutant General.
A.A.C.S.	Acting Assistant Commissary of Subsistence.
A.A.G. / A.A.Gen.	Assistant Adjutant General.
A.A.Q.M. / A.A.Qr.Mr.	Acting Assistant Quartermaster.
A.C.S.	Assistant Commissary of Subsistence.
Act.	Acting.
A.D.C. / Aid D.C.	Aide de camp.
Adj. / Adjt. / Adj^t.	Adjutant.
Affs. / Affrs.	Affairs.
A.I.	Acting Inspector [General].
A.Q.M.	Assistant Quartermaster.
Arz.	Arizona.
Asst.	Assistant.
A.T. / Aza. Ty.	Arizona Territory.
Batt^n.	Battalion.
Bt. / Bv. / Bvt. / Bv^t / B^{vt}.	Brevet.
Cal. / Cala.	California.
Cap. / Capt.	Captain.
Cav. / Cvy. / Cav^y.	Cavalry.
Co. / Comp.	Company.
Col. / Colo.	Colonel.
Com.	Commissary.
Comdg. / Comd'g. / Comg. / Commg. / Commdg. / Cmg. / CM.	Commanding.
C.S.	Commissary of Subsistence, or, Confederate States.
C.S.A.	Confederate States of America.
C.S.P.R.	Confederate States Provisional Regiment?
D / D^r.	Dear.
Dept. / Dep't / Dpt. / Dp^{mt}.	Department.
Dis. / Dist.	District.
D^n.	Don.
Drag^s.	Dragoons.
Esqr.	Esquire.
Ft.	Fort.
Gen. / Genl.	General.
G.O.	General Order.
Gov. / Govr.	Governor.
Hd. / H^d.	Head.

Hon.	Honorable.
Ind.	Indian.
Inf. / Infty. / Infy. / If.	Infantry.
Inspr. / Inspt. / Inspec.	Inspector.
Inst.	Instant (i.e., the present month).
Lieut. / Lt.	Lieutenant.
Lt. Col.	Lieutenant-Colonel.
Maj.	Major.
Memᵒ.	Memorandum.
Mil.	Military.
Mntᵈ / Mtd. / Mᵗ.	Mounted.
N.M. / N. Mex. / N. Mexᵒ.	New Mexico.
N.M.V. / N.M. Vols.	New Mexico Volunteers.
ob. / obd't / obedt. / obedᵗ / obt. / ob't / obᵗ.	Obedient.
Off.	Officer.
O.M. Co.	Overland Mail Company.
Par.	Paragraph.
Prox.	Proximo (i.e., the coming month).
Q.M. / Qʳ Mʳ / Qur. Mr.	Quartermaster.
Qrs. / Qʳˢ / Qurs.	Quarters.
Recᵈ.	Received.
R. / Regt. / Rgmt.	Regiment.
Resp. / Resply. / Respy. / Respectʸ.	Respectfully.
RMR / R.M.R.	Regiment of Mounted Riflemen.
S. Bde.	Sibley Brigade.
Secʸ.	Secretary.
Senʳ.	Señor.
sgᵈ.	Signed.
S.M. District.	Southern Military District.
S. / So. / Soutⁿ.	Southern.
Sp.	Special.
Subs.	Subsistence.
Sup. / Supt.	Superintendent.
Servt. / serv't / servᵗ / Sevt. / Svt. / Svᵗ.	Servant.
T.M.R.	Texas Mounted Rifles.
T.M.V.	Texas Mounted Volunteers.
Ty.	Territory.
Ulto.	Ultimo (i.e., the past or previous month).
Vol. / Vols. / Volts.	Volunteers.
W.M.	Western Military [District].
Yr. /Yrs.	Your / Yours.
&c.	Et cetera.

Acknowledgments

MANY PERSONS HAVE HELPED to make this volume possible. I first want to thank Dr. Robert W. Frazer for lending me two custom microfilms that included selected correspondence from Fort Union, N.M. letter files, reproduced here in chapters 3 and 4. Staff members at the National Archives in Washington have arranged for photocopying and microfilming many records over the years, and I particularly appreciate the advice and suggestions of Elaine C. Everly and her finding the casualty lists for Valverde and Glorieta (chapters 13 and 14). Equally welcome is the aid given by DeAnn Blanton, Stuart L. Butler, Ann Cummings, Dale E. Floyd, Robert B. Matchette, Michael P. Musick, and Michael E. Pilgrim of the Old Military and Civil Records office and its predecessors, and Janet L. Hargett of the former General Archives Division. Dr. James H. Hutson sent a copy of the Library of Congress Manuscript Division's unpublished guide to the Records of the Confederate States of America. From this, microfilm reels were requested on interlibrary loans.

Dr. Martin H. Hall's references to unusual sources led me to documents used in chapters 1 and 12. Mrs. Margaret McLean, former Newspaper Microfilms Librarian at the Amon Carter Museum of Western Art in Fort Worth, loaned me the *Alta California* and other newspaper films. Later, Sheri Tufts at the Amon Carter helped reconstruct the published Confederate casualty list from the Battle of Valverde. Mr. Ed Simonich of Pueblo, Colorado found John Miller's long letter about the Battle of Apache Cañon in a 1907 issue of *The Pueblo Chieftain* and graciously sent me a copy. In Las Cruces, the New Mexico State University (NMSU) Library's Interlibrary Loan office arranged many loans of books, articles, and microfilms. I wish to thank them and everyone else named here.

Dr. Rick Hendricks checked and corrected my transcripts of the letters written in Spanish and improved my translations as well. Any lapses from attempting to retain the convoluted structure of Spanish sentences are my own fault. To David V. Holtby, my editor at the University of New Mexico Press, my gratitude for making this manuscript into a book. I have tried to comply with suggestions made by Dr. Jerry Thompson.

This project sought out previously unpublished photographs, sketches and paintings as illustrations. Some success was had, but it was not possible to locate images of Captains Saturnino Barrientos and Isaiah Moore; prints or negatives of the photos that accompanied newspaper accounts of the 1993 Confederate reburials; or a Confederate flag captured at Valverde. Mr. Bill Diven, now of Albuquerque, helped with the search but no one could find photos of the reburial ceremony.

On the other hand, Mr. Henry C. Sibley, Jr. owns the Sibley's Brigade banner presented to his great-grandfather, Brigadier General Henry Hopkins Sibley, and he allowed us to reproduce a photograph of it taken by Roger Sibley, great-great-grandson of the general. Mr. Arthur H. Bergeron, Jr. owns the original image of General Sibley used here. Other illustrations or permissions for their use were received from the Arizona Historical Society, Colorado Historical Society, Missouri Historical Society, Museum of New Mexico, the University of Texas Center for American History, and the Superintendent of Fort Union National Monument. My wife Cheryl, head of the NMSU Library's Special Collections, arranged for some photographic work, while Mr. Jack Diven made improved prints of the 1993 Confederate reburials, the Colorado Volunteers' flag, and the Sibley's Brigade banner. Ms. Dawn Santiago did an outstanding job creating the index.

The acquisition of some twenty-two photographic prints and agreements for their use was financed by the Historic Preservation Fund, National Park Service, U.S. Department of the Interior, administered by the Historic Preservation Division (HPD), State of New Mexico, 228 East Palace Avenue, Santa Fe N.M. 87501. This support was part of an HPD Small Projects Grant. The source of each illustration is cited in its caption. I drafted the New Mexico and Arizona maps and touched up the printout of Captain Moore's sketch of the country about Abo Pass. Ms. Anne Fox first alerted me to Sergeant Graves's drawing of the skirmish at Mesilla, and ten years ago I made a sketch of it at the University of Texas Center for American History. The redrafted version is much more legible than the photostat negative on file there, and the HPD grant paid for a print of the drawing. This financial assistance is most sincerely appreciated.

This program received Federal financial assistance for identification and protection of historic properties. Under Title VI of the Civil Rights Act of 1964, Section 504 of the Rehabilitation Act of 1973, and the Age Discrimination Act of 1975, as amended, the U.S. Department of the Interior prohibits discrimination on the basis of race, color, national origin, disability or age in its federally assisted programs. If you believe you have been discriminated against in any program, activity, or facility as described above, or if you desire further information, please write to:

Office of Equal Opportunity
National Park Service
1849 C Street, N.W.
Washington, D.C. 20240

The title *When The Texans Came* derives from a hearing on the western boundary of the Hugh Stephenson or Brazito land grant, held at Las Cruces in 1908. The hearing transcript is now part of Record Group 49 at the National Archives. Witnesses included residents of the Mesilla Valley who were young children in the 1840s and 1850s. They could neither read nor write, and calendrical dates or placing events in sequential order were mostly beyond their experience. The examining attorneys resolved these problems by asking whether something happened before or after the big flood by the Rio Grande, or in relation to the year the Texans came up? For example, Anastasio Montoya was asked in his cross-examination about his visits to Los Pencos, a little settlement below Mesilla, N.M.:

Q. How many times did you go down there?

A. About three or four times together with him [a guardian named Maese] going down to El Paso.

Q. Was that before the Tejanos came up or afterwards?

A. In the same year that the Texans came up.

Q. You are talking about the civil war, are you not?

A. Yes sir.

More than forty-five years afterwards, persons who were small children at the time had not forgotten this episode.

INTRODUCTION
The Civil War in the Southwest

The American Civil War, 1861–1865, was fought primarily on battlefields east of the Mississippi River, on lands belonging to the seceded Confederate States. Southern historian Douglas Southall Freeman characterized this as "the most thoroughly studied military conflict of modern times," but only since the late 1950s has the far western branch of the war received much attention.[1] In the Southwest, fighting began when a regiment of Texas volunteers invaded New Mexico Territory and sought to make it part of the new Confederacy. New Mexico at that time included all of modern Arizona.

Brevet Lieutenant-Colonel Edward R. S. Canby, commanding the Military Department of New Mexico since June 11, 1861, could call upon less than twenty-five hundred Union infantry, dragoons, and cavalrymen dispersed in small posts across hundreds of miles. The great majority of these Regular Army men would remain loyal to the United States. Orders had already come to send two regiments east and replace them with locally raised volunteers. Soon all of the regulars would be ordered out of the department.[2]

In the end they stayed in New Mexico, but the Union commander's troubles were only beginning. Canby prudently began to concentrate his forces and he strengthened Fort Fillmore, just south of Las Cruces, New Mexico, with most of the Seventh Infantry regiment and two companies of the Regiment of Mounted Riflemen. Rumors of a Confederate invasion became a reality when companies of the Second Regiment, Texas Mounted Rifles, reached Fort Bliss, Texas, in late June and early July. On July 24 their commander, Lieutenant-Colonel John R. Baylor, led 258 of these men up the Rio Grande. They occupied Mesilla, New Mexico, and skirmished there with the federal troops from nearby Fort Fillmore, led by Major Isaac Lynde. The Confederates held the town and Major Lynde, having lost the skirmish, decided to abandon the fort and lead his troops toward Fort Stanton, some 130 miles to the northeast. Baylor quickly followed and captured virtually the entire garrison without a fight. This debacle cost Canby nearly six hundred officers and men, one-quarter of his fighting strength. Although released on parole, these men were ordered east and remained out of action until exchanged.[3]

Under orders from the departmental commander, soldiers in southern

Arizona had already abandoned the two posts there, Forts Buchanan and Breckinridge, to return to the Rio Grande. They narrowly evaded Baylor's men and hastened on to Fort Craig, the nearest post in New Mexico. This left Ammi White's store and gristmill, at the Pima Villages on the middle Gila River, as the only remaining outpost of Union sentiment in southern New Mexico or Arizona. The Pima Villages lay a good 350 miles west of the Mesilla Valley, outside the immediate reach of the Confederates. Already a southern mail contractor named George Giddings had revived his old San Antonio and San Diego Mail Line as a new stage and mail service that stretched from San Antonio all the way to Los Angeles. He operated this for several months, under the nose of California authorities.

Lieutenant-Colonel Baylor proclaimed a Confederate Territory of Arizona that comprised all of New Mexico Territory south of the thirty-fourth parallel, with himself as governor. Eventually the Confederate Congress passed a bill to establish Arizona as the South's only territory.[4] Baylor also sent one of his companies to occupy Fort Stanton in what is now Lincoln County, New Mexico. For about a month their presence there created considerable anxiety in northern New Mexico, where a parallel Confederate advance up the Pecos River was half-expected. Baylor cleverly exploited these fears and even sought to use what would now be called disinformation to subvert New Mexicans' belief in the patriotism of their own leaders.[5] Several companies raised in Arizona and the El Paso area joined Baylor and raised his strength to about eight hundred men; too few to capture the next obstacle, Fort Craig. Through the fall and early winter the Southerners scouted and occasionally skirmished from their base in the Mesilla Valley, while they waited for reinforcements from Texas.[6]

All of the North-South fighting in the Southwest took place between late July in 1861 and early July 1862. The contests here involved many fewer men than on eastern battlefields, while distances were vastly greater. The absence of railroads and a scarcity of good roads made transportation a major consideration, while communication depended entirely on couriers. In addition, the Rebels found themselves ensnared in an ongoing Indian war. From Dragoon Springs in southern Arizona to Pinos Altos in southwestern New Mexico, and as far as the Gallinas Mountains north of Fort Stanton, Apaches and even Kiowas took a toll on the invaders. On their part, the Rebels controlled the new gold camp at Pinos Altos and the Santa Rita copper mines.

Baylor as a civil governor grew increasingly despotic. He shot the editor of *The Mesilla Times* newspaper, threatened to hang Ammi White, and later seized the property of one John Lemon while putting him in fear of his life.

White and Lemon survived, but the newspaper editor and one person taken prisoner at the same time as Lemon did die.[7]

Farther north, Canby and his officers had begun to raise and equip several regiments of volunteer soldiers and a number of independent companies. The New Mexico commander received some material support from the eastern United States, but no reinforcements. During the months of recruiting, organizing, and training the volunteers, he also sent scouting parties to watch for another Confederate force that might come by way of the Pecos River Valley or across the Texas panhandle. The rumors and conflicting information passed on to him, some of these no doubt planted, kept the Rebel intentions unclear. Not until February 1862 did the Union commander concede that the next invasion would come via the Rio Grande Valley from southern New Mexico.[8]

In the meantime, Confederate President Jefferson Davis ordered Brigadier General Henry Hopkins Sibley to seek volunteers for a mounted brigade of Texans who would occupy New Mexico and perhaps even advance to California. Sibley hurried back to Texas and organized three regiments, some twenty-seven hundred men in all. He marched them to New Mexico and assumed command over all Confederate forces there, designating them the Army of New Mexico. Baylor, whom Sibley promoted to a colonel, continued as the civil and military governor of Arizona.[9]

Canby had almost twice this number of men under arms, but the majority were poorly trained New Mexico Volunteers and militia who would likely prove unreliable under fire. On February 7, 1862, Sibley finally ordered his brigade and part of Baylor's regiment, about 2,590 men, north along the Rio Grande toward Fort Craig and the Union army. Approximately thirty-eight hundred federal troops, more than two-thirds of them volunteers and militia, waited there. These small armies met February 21 at the Battle of Valverde, above Fort Craig. At day's end the Confederates had gained a tactical victory while Canby's forces sought the shelter of the fort. The actual battlefield casualties on both sides are published here. Sibley's troops, having lost part of their transport, now suffered from a serious shortage of clothing and supplies as well. They had little choice but to continue north and hope to find food and forage at Albuquerque, Santa Fe, or the principal Union depot at Fort Union.[10]

Sibley largely failed in this quest, but his troops did occupy the two cities and even Galisteo briefly. One attached company, appropriately known as the Brigands, was the first to ride into Santa Fe. Canby, who stayed at Fort Craig, had long since asked the governor of Colorado to raise volunteers as reinforcements. Now their commander, Colonel John P. Slough, led his First Regiment of Colorado Volunteers south more than four hundred miles in thirteen days, arriving in time to block the Confederate advance on Fort Union. One of Slough's senior officers, Major John Chivington, met the Rebels in Apache Canyon on March 26 and turned them back with a dramatic cavalry charge. This dash through the canyon has not been well documented until now.

Chivington's action did not involve the main forces on either side. Two days later, Slough's Coloradoans met the Texans a few miles farther east. Here, at the Battle of Glorieta, the invaders forced Slough back and held the field at the end of the day. On his part, Major Chivington led some 430 men of the federal force through the mountains to the western end of Apache Canyon. There they completely destroyed the Confederate supply train and freed its draft animals, retaining a few. The Rebels, already low on food and ammunition, stumbled back to Santa Fe and began confiscating whatever they could lay their hands on. The Confederate battlefield deaths at Glorieta are known from both their official casualty list and the recent discovery of their grave site, while the most complete list of Union casualties is one compiled by Major Chivington, given in chapter 14.[11]

Baylor, who had been left behind in the Mesilla Valley, led two hundred to three hundred of his men on a raid through southwestern New Mexico and down into Mexico as far as Corralitos. While he claimed this was in retaliation for Indian atrocities, his swashbuckling conduct sparked diplomatic protests by the Mexicans to Sibley, who forwarded these to Richmond. Until now this invasion, which apparently left three Indian servants dead, has been known principally from Hank Smith's anecdotal account and a passing reference in Baylor's long letter in defense of his murderous policies.[12] Because of this episode and for other reasons, Jefferson Davis reduced Baylor to the rank of private. He continued to hold the title of governor of Arizona.

A few weeks earlier, Baylor had ordered Captain Sherod Hunter and his Company "A" to occupy western Arizona, maintain law and order there, and keep watch for any enemy movements from the direction of California. Hunter arrived in Tucson at the end of February and one week later rode up to the Pima Villages, where he seized Ammi White's goods. He captured a Union advance party under Captain William McCleave and sent both the trader and the captain back to the Rio Grande as prisoners. Part of Hunter's company continued west for another one hundred miles, as far as an old Overland Mail Co. stop at Stanwix Station on the lower Gila River. This station, scarcely ninety miles from California, became the setting for the westernmost skirmish of the Civil War.[13]

Fig. 1. Albuquerque, New Mexico, Plaza and Church (Perry Coll. No. 65).
Photograph by Alexander Gardner, 1867. Missouri Historical Society,
St. Louis, negative no. OutSTL 201.

Hunter abandoned his "Post at Tucson" on May 14, 1862, and returned to the Rio Grande. A small army of Union cavalry, sent to relieve New Mexico, entered Tucson unopposed on May 20. Six weeks later the first units of this Column from California arrived on the Rio Grande, just above old Fort Thorn. By this time Edward R. S. Canby had been promoted to brigadier general.

As the Rebels began their demoralized evacuation of Santa Fe, Canby moved north from Fort Craig and engaged the small Confederate force at Albuquerque in an artillery duel. Sibley continued withdrawing and the two sides had a much sharper exchange at Peralta, eighteen miles south of Albuquerque. Canby then let the worn-out Southerners resume their retreat, and when they arrived in the Mesilla Valley they had little more than their weapons and the clothes on their back. With provisions, forage, and ammunition exhausted, the Army of New Mexico found itself in desperate straits. Sibley led his weary men back to San Antonio, leaving behind his sick and wounded. As they left, the Texans again turned to confiscation, but now the citizens fought back. While poorly documented, the casualties on both sides appear to have been substantial.[14]

In letters to Texas newspapers, two of the Rebels called the entire New Mexico campaign a "wild goose chase" and a series of "blunders and mishaps."[15] Sibley's own officers in the Fifth Regiment, Texas Mounted Volunteers, were scarcely kinder. More than five hundred of the approximately thirty-five hundred Texans who set out to conquer New Mexico a year earlier had died from disease or in combat. Another five hundred were missing in action, left behind in hospitals, or had been taken prisoner.[16] Elsewhere the Civil War would continue for another three years, but in New Mexico it was over. The territory would revert to campaigns against hostile Indians plus a massive effort to resettle the largest such group, the Navajo. That story too was chronicled in part in the *War of the Rebellion . . . Official Records* volumes.

Compiling the Official Records

The principal source for contemporary documents about the American Civil War has always been the 128 volumes of the *War of the Rebellion: A Compilation of the Official Records of the Union and Confederate Armies.* Preliminary efforts to compile war records, sponsored by the government, began as early as 1864 and serious work about 1878. The first published volume appeared in July 1881 and additional volumes, each ranging from 600 to almost 1,700 pages in length, came from the press at an increasing tempo through the early 1890s. The pace then slowed a bit until the 1,286-page General Index, published in 1901, concluded this project. The total cost, not including the pay of army officers detailed for duty in connection with the work, came to $2,858,514.67.[17] This was somewhat more than the cost of the battleship *Maine* commissioned in 1895 but doomed to a much briefer service life.[18]

The background to the publication of the *Official Records*, or *OR* as they are commonly cited, is given in the Preface section to the General Index.[19] The undertaking was an immense one for the time, not only in the locating, copying, compiling, and collating of documents, but in rendering the decisions as to what should be included. Perhaps the greatest stumbling block was how to organize the thousands of records, winnowed from the millions that were reviewed. Two preliminary editions, one of eight volumes and a seventy-nine-volume series known as "preliminary prints," were prepared but never distributed because of deficiencies in these pilot projects.[20]

In 1880 a plan of publication was decided upon and subsequently adhered to through the entire program. There were four series, instead of a single one. Series I, the longest, contains 111 volumes of Union and Confederate reports arranged by campaign and theater of operations and then generally in chronological order. This series is now used almost to the exclusion of the other three. Series II (eight volumes) concerns prisoners of war. The third and fourth series (five and three volumes, respectively) include correspondence, orders, and reports not related especially to the subjects of the first and second series. The secretaries of war, beginning with Edwin M. Stanton and continuing through Elihu Root, exercised overall direction of the project. Congress funded the work with annual appropriations or as funds were required, beginning in 1874. Between 1889 and 1899 a Board of Publication, consisting of a military officer who served as president and two civilian members, supervised preparation and publication of the volumes issued during that decade.

In describing the plan of publication, volume 1 in Series I asserted that "this compilation. . . . will embrace all official documents that can be obtained by the compiler, and that appear to be of any historical value."[21] Consistent with this, the last volume of text stated that "Nothing is printed in these volumes except duly authenticated contemporaneous records of the war," and that the compilers' work had been to decide upon and arrange for the materials to be published, correct spellings, and add footnotes of explanation when necessary.[22]

The Preface to the General Index volume elaborated at some length on the editorial policies, including considerations in the decisions as to what to include and what to exclude. One important factor was that the material must be contemporary, thus excluding recollections and supposed corrections of errors, as well as papers that could not be authenticated. As early as 1882 Lieutenant Colonel Robert Scott, who supervised the project until his death in 1887, commented that "The experience of this office has demonstrated the utter unreliability of recollections of the war."[23] In an interview he cited some examples, including the following:

One day an old officer came rushing in, and, in an excited tone, exclaimed:

"Have you said I was not in the second battle of Bull Run?"

"No, not exactly that," I said.

"Well, Bob Scott, I was told you said so, and I came in here to put daylight through you if you stuck to it."

"Oh, no," I replied, laughing, "I never said you were not in that battle. What I said was that you yourself, in an official report dated the day of the battle, had said you were in the Cumberland Valley, a hundred miles from Centerville and Bull Run."

His eyes looked dizzy and his face was a most amusing picture of consternation. What I said was true. I tapped a bell, called a clerk, who brought the officer's official report, and there in his own hand-writing, over his signature, in black and white, was his own word that he was not at Bull Run. He read the report through twice in silence, so solid you could slice it. Then he took his hat, and without a word, arose and left the building.

A prominent officer of my acquaintance has described often in my hearing with great minuteness, the battle of the *Monitor* and the *Merrimac*. He told the story as an eye witness, described his field glass and the point of observation. I paid no attention to the matter until I had heard the tale told twice. Then I became curious, and hunted up the official reports made by this officer. I found that if he saw the *Monitor* and *Merrimac* in that battle his field glass was a most powerful one. He never saw the *Monitor* and *Merrimac* fight, but was at Falls Church the day of the battle, if his own reports are to be believed. There is a good deal of fiction in our war stories.

A Major-General is not often any more sure of facts twenty-five years ago than a private.[24]

The *OR* project did make a conscious effort to balance accounts by actively seeking Confederate records, which were understandably fragmented and scattered. One secretary of war commented that "It may be well to observe in this connection that all Confederate matter is, and for some time has been, inserted in the volumes." Douglas Southall Freeman wrote that this compilation amazed the South by its impartiality.[25] Organization within some of the volumes may be less than ideal, an understandable shortcoming in light of the amounts of material.

In retrospect, this was a monumental publication effort and scholars have generally regarded it as exhaustive, showing little awareness that unpublished official records might exist. With this series and the parallel *OR* ... *Navies* series concluded, publication of new primary sources on the Civil War during the twentieth century has emphasized personal documents—letters, diaries, and journals, as well as recollections and reminiscences. Writing and editing continue unabated, and a claim that publications about the Civil War have appeared at an average of one per day since the war ended is probably as valid as ever.[26]

The National Archives and Civil War Records

Occasional footnotes in the *OR* volumes are explanatory (for example, "Not found") and say nothing about the location or source of individual documents. At the time of their publication, 1881–1901, such citations would have been unnecessary. The War Records Office, directly under the secretary of war, had custody of the original papers or copies of all available federal documents. Another branch, the War Department's Archive Office, had responsibility for the Confederate records. The War Records Office evidently borrowed these as needed, copied and returned them, while placing the copies in a "Publication File" in order of their publication. Except for private papers and historical society collections, most Confederate records would now be at the National Archives in Record Group (RG) 109, the War Department Collection of Confederate Records.[27] Some documents may be in other Record Groups. The best available finding aids are a preliminary inventory for Record Group 109,[28] a book-length guide to Confederate archives,[29] and National Archives guide pamphlets to various microfilm publications of Confederate records.

Other Confederate War Department records are among the Records of the Confederate States of America, also known as the Pickett Papers, in the Manuscript Division of the Library of Congress. This entire collection is on seventy microfilm rolls, of which rolls 63 through 68 are War Department reports. An undated finding aid provides some guidance to this collection.[30] The U.S. Treasury Department received most of these records in 1872 and used them in settling war claims. Some of the diplomatic correspondence appeared in *OR, Series IV Vols.* 2 and 3.

Federal records for the Civil War period are more dispersed. One large collection, now Record Group 94, Records of the Adjutant General's Office, was transferred to the National Archives in March 1947. Approximately one-quarter of that body of material has since been split off as Record Group 393, Records of U.S. Army Continental Commands 1821–1920. There are preliminary inventories for both Record Groups, the inventory for RG 393 consisting of four published volumes plus a fifth one that remains in manuscript.[31] Both inventories are indispensable to finding groups of records ("Entries") within these two Record Groups. For federal records there is also the Munden and Beers guide, which is very useful for its descriptions and explanations.

A circular stamp "War Records, 1861–1865, Copied" on a Civil War letter means that the document was selected for possible publication in the *OR* series and returned to its file location after a copy had been made. The copy will probably be in the "Publication File" but the stamp does not guarantee that the letter was published. While all of the Confederate records made available to the War Records Office were returned, that office retained many other borrowed documents and intermingled some of these with letters or reports contributed from private sources.[32]

Some of the unpublished federal records from the Southwest have been microfilmed. The Letters Sent and Letters Received by the Headquarters of the Department of New Mexico for the Civil War years are included on Microfilm Publications M-1072 and M-1120, both of which are available at major university libraries in the state. Many New Mexico documents published in the *OR* series can also be seen here. Letters contained in the much larger (828 rolls) Microfilm Publication M-619, Letters Received by the Office of the Adjutant General, Main Series, 1861–1870, were probably more important in compiling the *OR*, but the documents within it were filed chronologically and then alphabetically, so that those originating in New Mexico were interfiled with letters received from all other states and territories.

These micropublications either make available directly or index much material for the history of the Southwest. That the films are not used more widely is probably because of the expense of purchasing them (currently thirty-four dollars a roll) or unawareness that two series are held at university libraries within New Mexico. In addition to these stock microfilms, private parties and institutions have ordered custom microfilming of a few categories, or "entries" as they are called.

Most of the microfilmed records do not bear a "Copied . . ." stamp, which means that they were not selected for publication. Despite the prefatory statements in the *OR* volumes that everything had been seen and the records of historical value were published, many contemporary papers without a stamp are more than routine acknowledgments or personnel actions. Perusal of even the stock microfilms of Letters Received shows that much material may never have been examined, and that official records equal to or greater in value than those chosen for publication lie waiting to be discovered.

Over time, my own research has brought an increasing awareness of how much information was not in the *OR* series. Command documents constitute most of the *OR* series, but in the Southwest the official records are at least equally valuable for their portrayals of what went on outside of the battle lines. The *OR* series published only the most general casualty listings, which was understandable a century ago. A broad policy of exclusion is less justified where relatively few battles were fought over the course of a year, in a small theater of action. The battlefield casualty lists may now hold considerable interest for historians and genealogists.

The Missing Records

Where are the unused records? Nearly all of them are in the custody of the National Archives. When the work of compilation and copying was going on in the late nineteenth century, some files of Civil War records evidently still remained with the U.S. Army's military departments and divisions and even at individual army posts. The adjutant general received the records of discontinued military commands, but the District of New Mexico maintained its identity until August of 1890. The "Unregistered Letters Received," by the Military Department of New Mexico during the Civil War and before, was actually the departmental commander's confidential file. As will be seen, many of these unregistered letters are very interesting. None bear a "Copied . . ." stamp.

The bulk of the Union correspondence from August 1861 included in chapter 4 is from a custom microfilm of Headquarters Records, Fort Union, New Mexico, made by the National Archives for Dr. Robert Frazer in 1967. None of the filmed letters have the "Copied . . ." mark. Similarly, the Letters Sent and Letters Received for the Central District, Eastern District, District of Fort Craig, and District of Santa Fe, New Mexico, were microfilmed by my own requests, and a few of these did have the "Copied . . ." stamp. Additional documentation on the surrender of the Union garrison at Fort Fillmore, New Mexico, in 1861 is found in two files on Major Isaac Lynde, the unfortunate federal commander.[33] As for Confederate records, Boyd Finch's discovery of about fifty documents in Captain Sherod Hunter's jacket at the National Archives was indeed a small treasure.[34] Thirteen of these fifty have been selected for inclusion here. The original compilation for the *OR* series was extensive but not exhaustive, and it left many files untouched.

Newspapers of the period were particularly useful for their printing of official casualty lists and reporting of events outside of military confrontations. Occasionally they printed records that have not survived otherwise. Papers in both the North and the South published war news virtually without censorship. Selection of a few personal letters has a precedent, in that the *OR* series occasionally printed such letters. One document from the Juárez, Chihuahua, archives is included; undoubtedly more correspondence could be found in Mexico. Henry P. Beers has cited other locations of contemporary records in his guides.

The Preface to the *OR, General Index* tells us that a uniform style of spelling, punctuation, abbreviation, and capitalization was adopted for the series while errors or discrepancies in the original papers were not changed. Headings were reduced to a standard and signatures generally printed as written, while guarding against changes in the language or meaning. These standards were consistently followed and spelling corrections are the most striking difference between printed documents in the *OR* and the originals.

Other editorial changes or deletions may not be acknowledged, as with omissions from Major Isaac Lynde's report of July 26, 1861, and Captain James Graydon's May 14, 1862, report. Users of the *OR* series should be aware that such silent editing exists, although in most instances the printed record is a cleanly edited version of the autograph original.

A New Volume of Official Records

After reading hundreds of unpublished official records, I decided that wider availability of a generous selection from these could provide a better understanding of events during the Confederate invasion. This book is the result. One goal has been to document the presence and activities of individuals such as Kit Carson, Lawrence G. Murphy, and William Brady, whose roles in the Civil War have been incompletely known. Another is to provide all known documentation on lesser-known aspects of the war, for example Colonel Baylor's incursion into northwestern Chihuahua, the Confederate occupation of present-day southern Arizona, and the month when the Rebels held the Rio Bonito (Lincoln, New Mexico) country. An anonymous report dated August 15, 1861, portrayed a grim picture of what happened there. The author of that report is identified here.

More light can be shed on such intriguing episodes as the operations of volunteer companies during the early months of Confederate occupation, Baylor's role in the arrest and near-hanging of John Lemon at Mesilla, Ammi White's activities on the Río Gila, and the battles between retreating Rebels and Hispanic residents at Mesilla, New Mexico, and below El Paso, Texas. Conflicts with the Navajo, Apache, and even Kiowa Indians had largely died away by the summer of 1861, but Texas troops fought with them on several occasions.[35] Dr. Martin Hall originally found Alexander M. Jackson's appraisal of New Mexico.[36] It is given here as the lead document.

There were sophisticated Confederate attempts to subvert the loyalty of Union troops and sow mistrust among New Mexicans in their leaders. Baylor led these disinformation efforts in the summer of 1861, and he had some local help. Hugh M. Beckwith's letter of August 18, 1861 (chapter 8), was probably written with the intention that it be intercepted and (hopefully) would create distrust of Major J. Francisco Chaves, a loyal Union man. This was a transparent effort that Chaves immediately disowned. Colonel Henry E. McCulloch's alleged letter of July 21, 1861 (chapter 7), in which he offered to join Baylor, received a wide circulation but McCulloch at the time was back in San Antonio commanding the Department of Texas.

Lieutenant-Colonel Benjamin S. Roberts at Fort Craig, in his own letter of August 21, 1861 (see chapter 6), considered the McCulloch letter a forgery "intended to intimidate this region." I am inclined to agree. Strangely enough, Colonel Roberts in the same letter accepted as genuine one written by William Pelham, a former New Mexico surveyor general and Southern sympathizer. From Roberts's description (the letter itself has not been found), it would appear to be just as spurious in its contents as the McCulloch letter. The colonel's dilemma shows how easily Confederate disinformation could sway federal decisions as to who was loyal and who was not. Sibley wrote in his May 4, 1862, report that "One thousand dollars is all I have been able to procure for the use of hospitals and *for secret service*" (emphasis added).[37] Canby, who saw through these efforts, must have been thankful that it wasn't more.

Other reports may offer leads for future research. The eastern theater in New Mexico, from Manzano east to the Pecos River and also along the Canadian River, was a principal concern for the Union commander. The little-known post of Hatch's Ranch, fifty miles south of Fort Union by road and on the west bank of the Gallinas River, assumed major importance as a base for scouting parties. During January 1862 Colonel Canby sat in Belen, New Mexico, receiving intelligence reports and trying to determine whether Sibley, in southern New Mexico, was only a distraction from the real Confederate advance via the Pecos River Valley. At the end of the month Canby made up his mind and moved down to Fort Craig to wait for Sibley.

The role of native New Mexican officers such as Captain Saturnino Barrientos in leading their companies on scouting and spying missions has been almost unknown. During the fall of 1861, Barrientos's company of spies and guides formed part of the eyes and ears of the Union forces. Their reports, in Spanish, escaped the *OR* series. On the Confederate side, there are hints that Pablo Alderete led a locally raised company that was never mustered into service. Could the Captain Phillips mentioned in Union dispatches dated August 24, 29, and 30, 1861, have been John G. Phillips, subsequently the leader of Sibley's notorious "Brigands?"[38]

The proceedings of the officers in Sibley's Brigade, Fifth Regiment T.M.V. [Texas Mounted Volunteers] dated May 15, 1862, is one of the more poignant documents (chapter 16). It offered a completely honest appraisal that the Confederate Army of New Mexico had no recourse but to return to Texas. This dose of reality survived in the printed pages of the Houston *Tri-Weekly Telegraph*. This document and the report of Captain Isaiah Moore on his abandonment of the Arizona posts and retreat to Fort Craig, New Mexico, were made available previously.[39] Boyd Finch first published Baylor's orders to Captain Sherod Hunter and Hunter's report on the Battle of Picacho Pass.[40]

In selecting the 282 documents presented here, the policy has conformed as closely as possible to that of the original *Official Records*. The entries chosen must be contemporary with the events and emanate from authentic sources, which may include civilians. All of the Unregistered Letters Received, the documents from New Mexico subdepartmental commands, two files on Major Isaac Lynde, and the cited service records were reviewed. Most of the Letters Received, Department of New Mexico, have been seen. Selected articles from surviving runs of the Civil War–era newspapers in New Mexico, Texas, and California are used as well.

The autograph original documents are given in entirety, aside from three that supply only the missing paragraphs from Major Lynde's July 26, 1861, report; Captain Graydon's May 14, 1862, postscript; and Major Chivington's list of casualties at the Battle of Glorieta. In a fourth document, the May 25, 1862, Proceedings at Fort Barrett, testimony of the single eyewitness to destruction at Ammi White's mill is transcribed here. Minor spelling errors in some words and proper names have either been corrected or are indicated by a [*sic*]. The Confederate casualty list for Valverde is partially restored from the only known copy of the May 3, 1862, *San Antonio Herald*, which unfortunately was damaged and not 100 percent readable.

Materials are limited to the period of the Confederate invasion and immediately preceding and following it. A total of sixty-seven new Confederate records is included; many came from compiled service records, but nine were drawn from the letterbook of Colonel William Steele, the last Confederate commander of Fort Fillmore. The original *OR* published only four of Steele's letters, from the total of twenty-one relating to the New Mexico campaign in this letterbook. The remaining eight are of little historical value or concerned with personnel matters.[41] The overall compilation is approximately equal to the number of documents covering the New Mexico campaign published in the *OR* volumes.

The matter of organization greatly troubled early workers under Lieutenant-Colonel Scott. The arrangement by action or theater of operation, Union or Confederate, and then chronological order was a reasonable one, although there were many lapses in implementing this. Preliminary sorting of the entries in the present volume resulted in sixteen chapters, whose contents range in date from February 1861 to August 1862. The invasion itself extended from July 24, 1861, to July 8, 1862.

Because this is primarily a scholar's tool, the chapters and individual letters are given no special introductions. All of these were selected because they had a potential contribution to offer. The value of action reports on the battles of Valverde, Glorieta, and Peralta is sufficiently obvious, but the reasons for choosing other records may be more subtle. For example, Baylor's cryptic note of January 19, 1862, more than implied that Crittenden Marshall of Mesilla was hanged at the instigation of Baylor and with the active involvement of the Captain Phillips mentioned earlier, while the list of John Lemon's property suggests that he danced at the end of his rope until he revealed where his money was. This case was more complex than either W. W. Mills or Hank Smith thought.[42]

Similarly, Lieutenant-Colonel George Andrews's letter of August 9, 1861, was ample evidence to condemn Ammi White as a spy. White should have destroyed it. Lieutenant-Colonel Benjamin Roberts showed equally bad judgment in naming the Union spy in Las Cruces (Father Manuel Chavez) in a written communication of September 7, 1861, to Colonel Canby. Baylor's interception of that message would undoubtedly have led to the priest's death. The incident of the horse race at Fort Fauntleroy, New Mexico, that nearly precipitated another war with the Navajos is relatively well known, but the report by post commander Lieutenant-Colonel Manuel Chavez has not been available until now. Captain James (Paddy) Graydon's postscript to his report of May 14, 1862, mentioned what was possibly the last issue of *The Mesilla Times* newspaper. Unfortunately there is no extant copy and its date is not known.

The point was made earlier that there is more to Civil War history than battle reports and personal narratives. Healthy signs of broadened interests are seen in the recent publishing activity on Confederate financing[43] and the war's effects on civilian sufferings.[44] The war affected everyone, north and south, particularly in areas where the armies helped themselves to the few available resources.

An independent means of judging a war's impact is through the music of the time. Songs in the Southwest were probably no different than those sung elsewhere. Music can tell a lot about what people thought they were fighting for, how they regarded their leaders, the strength of family bonds felt by those at home as well as by absent husbands and sons, interspersed with occasional mocking of the enemy or the hardships of army life. There were profound expressions of patriotism, on both sides. Amateur and professional lyricists wrote verses that they sometimes adapted to already familiar melodies.

Many Civil War lyrics would be meaningless to modern readers, but a few still give enduring impressions of wartime experiences. At least two— "The Battle Hymn of the Republic" and "John Brown's Body"—have uniquely powerful phrasings. In a six-stanza rendition of the latter found in an Illinois newspaper, five of the stanzas have not been seen elsewhere.[45]

The language strongly suggests that the author may have been Julia Ward Howe, already famous as the lyricist of "The Battle Hymn of the Republic." Each chapter in this book ends with three stanzas of a song, chosen to help illustrate the impact of the Civil War on the people of those times.

We hope that the range of documents will appeal to the interests of everyone who studies the Civil War in the Southwest. Not least will be a confirmation that we still have much to learn about this tragic conflict.

"Another Yankee Doodle"
(after melody—"Yankee Doodle")

Yankee Doodle had a mind
To whip the Southern traitors,
Because they didn't choose to live
On codfish and potatoes.
Yankee Doodle, doodle-doo
Yankee Doodle dandy,
And so to keep his courage up
He took a drink of brandy.

Yankee Doodle made a speech,
'Twas very full of feeling;
I fear, says he, I cannot fight,
But I am good at stealing.
Yankee Doodle, doodle-doo,
Yankee Doodle dandy,
Hurrah for Lincoln, he's the boy
To take a drop of brandy.

Yankee Doodle soon found out
That Bull Run was no trifle
For if the North knew how to steal,
The South knew how to rifle.
Yankee Doodle, doodle-doo,
Yankee Doodle dandy,
'Tis very clear I took too much
Of that infernal brandy!

CHAPTER ONE Prelude

A Confederate Assessment
of New Mexico in 1861

<u>No application for office</u>
Enclosure to be answd.   referred to Dept. of State
J. D.
Ripley, Apl. 6th 1861.

Hon. Jefferson Davis
Sir:

I take the liberty of trespassing for a moment on your time, by inclosing for your perusal a letter which I received a short time ago, from Capt. A. M. Jackson, Secretary of State of New Mexico.

It contains, in my opinion, valuable information, on the state of public affairs there, from a source entitled to the highest credit, which ought to be in the possession of our Government.

I will only add, that the letter was written in reply to one from me inclosing him our ordinance of Secession, immediately after its passage, suggesting to him the propriety of taking prompt steps to bring New Mexico into our Confederacy, as a State.

Hoping that God may preserve your life and health, for the good of our holy cause—

I remain
very respectfully
Your obt. Svt.
<u>O</u>. [Orlando] <u>Davis</u>

P. S. Since writing the above, I see it announced in a late St. Louis paper that a revolution has occurred in New Mexico, headed by Gov. Rencher, who has taken possession of Fort Marcy in the name of the Confederate States. Capt. Jackson's letter fully explains the necessity for this course.

O. D.

Santa Fe, New Mexico, Feby. 17, 1861

O. Davis Esqr

My Dear Sir!

Only today am I in receipt of your interesting and important letter of Jany. 10th from Jackson. Of course I had earlier information of the glorious action of our State—which, indeed, I have confidentially anticipated for six months and more. I congratulate you, personally, most heartily on your participation in a deed which will preserve your name in honor and respect to all posterity. A seat in the Mississippi Convention of 1861 is the only political position I have ever really coveted for its own sake—but thank God, Mississippi has many a worthier son than I.

Having for several years looked forward to the action now being taken by the Southern States, I fully appreciated the importance, on my arrival in this Territory, of legislation by the Territorial Assembly for the protection of slave property—less in view of any immediate want of such property than of the ultimate position of New Mexico in the Confederacy. Therefore, I have steadily concentrated and directed all the influence I could acquire to the enactment and maintenance of our present law upon that subject. I am happy to say to you that "it still lives." At the adjournment of our late Assembly, on 31st of Jany. last, I wrote to Govr Brown & Col. R. Davis, informing them of that fact—which letter, thinking it likely that postal connections were disturbed, I forward under cover to B. F. Dill at Memphis. I stated to them that this legislation perfected the title of the South to New Mexico, and her cession ought to be insisted on.

Your letter, however, seems to contemplate voluntary action by this Territory in regard to her future connection with the States. I am sorry to say that I do not think this is to be hoped for. In her Territorial condition, she is incapable of expressing a choice, and it is impossible to persuade her people to assume the robes of a State's Sovereignty. In our late Assembly a Bill was introduced to call a Convention for this purpose, but the ground swell from below was too much for it, and it failed, not to be repeated, probably for some years. The opposition, however, had not the slightest connection with the "nigger question" nor with the momentous events transpiring in the States. It consists purely in the terror of "taxation," which the natives of this Territory have inherited from their fore-fathers who suffered three hundred years under the impositions and Military extractions of old Spain and Old Mexico. Since their acquisition by the U.S., their Exemption from these oppressions has been all that has reconciled them to the change; and when taxation is mentioned to them or any project invoking it, the picture of these old evils returns with all the force of the defunct reality. No countervailing advantages have any charms for them. The South, there-fore, had better at once renounce any hope of summoning a State Sover-eignty into existence out here, which shall cast in its lot with hers.

But, this is by no means to be regarded as any obstacle to the acquisition of this Territory, as a Territory, by the Southern States—always supposing that a separation takes place without war. I do not mean to rehearse to you the obvious claims which they have to an equitable division of the public domain—claims, which as applied to this Territory, should be considered incontestable in view of her adoption and maintenance of the institutions of the South. The assignment of New Mexico to the Southern Confed-eracy will certainly be in consonance with the wishes of a majority of her people—but, in my opinion, no action tending to that result, except by the American Settlements in Arizona, is to be expected. The position which Missouri shall assume will have more effect upon the native population than all other considerations combined. Their commercial connections are almost exclusively with that State. I speak of New Mexico <u>proper</u>, above the Mesilla Valley.

But it is of the very first importance that the South should demand the release of this Territory <u>without</u> <u>the</u> <u>slightest</u> <u>delay</u>. Upon all questions of extra-territorial import, Territorial politics are but the reflection of Federal power. I do not hope that our law for the protection of Slave property will survive a day beyond the assembling of a Territorial Legislature convened under the auspices of an Abolition Administration—unless, it shall in the mean time become certain or probable that this Territory will be assigned to the South. The repeal of that law by the Territorial Legislature will interpose a serious, if not insuperable, impediment to the cession of the Territory by the Old Confederacy. It was this consideration which made me so apprehensive of its repeal by the late Assembly, which I feared might be infected with the contagion of Abolitionism disseminated by its success in the Presidential Election. And but for careful and strenuous effort on my part, I think the law would have been repealed so far as the Assembly could have repealed it without the concurrence of the Governor—whose veto could not have averted the main evil. The mass of the Mexicans, I feel certain, and more particularly the wealthy and intelligent classes, are decid-edly in favor of the institution of Slavery, and this sentiment has been steadily growing ever since the enactment of our Slave Code. Still, this will not suffice to preserve the institution in this Territory in opposition to the influences of Federal power and patronage. Therefore the South should fix the status of this Territory before the meeting of the next Legislative Assembly on the 1st Monday in December.

A torrent of "Pike's Peakers," ninety nine hundredths of whom are from the free states, are pouring into the northern portions of the Territory. They will constitute the only considerable body of people who would be averse to the Southern connection. One of them will make more noise than a hundred Mexicans, and before the year is out their lawless and contentious clamor will be considered in the States the voice of New Mexico. Before this Class succeed in obtaining by fraud and violence the influence they got in Kansas by the same means, the future destiny of New Mexico should be determined—otherwise it is determined already.

These considerations will convince you and all other Southern men of the vital importance of early, immediate, action.

The resources of this Country are immensely underrated in the States. I risk nothing in asserting that, excepting the mountain ranges, it is a country of infinitely more value, agricultural and pastoral, than Kansas, or even those portions of Texas not adapted to Sugar or Cotton. Its mineral wealth will prove inexhaustible—protected from Indians, its stock raising capacity is unsurpassed on the face of the earth—and from fifty miles south of this city, the valley of the Rio Grande is the Paradise of the Vine, the culture of which can be made greatly more profitable than that of any staple in the Southern States, though its aggregate value might not approach to that of cotton.

Southern Statesmen must realize the fact at once that if New Mexico is to be acquired for the South, it must be done by the South in her settlement with the balance of the late firm. Reliance on these people further than their good-will, notwithstanding their present proclivities, will be misplaced. It is this fact which I wish to impress upon you, and, if you esteem my views to any consideration, I hope you will use them to impress this fact upon the men who are shaping the future of our Country. But it is best that at least that portion of them which discloses the feeble foothold and tenure which Southern interests have in this Territory, should be kept out of the newspapers. The Northern Journals are eager, I observe, to impress this idea on their people, and a Southern authority even as obscure as myself would not be despised.

In bringing about the present pro-Slavery status of New Mexico, everything is done that can be done here. I could agitate the question, but it would only be productive of evil. These people are fully prepared to go South, provided Missouri so goes; but in advance of Missouri, no expression could be obtained from any respectable body of them. I am posting them as extensively as possible, upon the hostility with which they and their religion, their race, and their own social relations, are regarded by the Black Republicans, as evidenced by the New York Tribune and its congeners in Congress. But having no press at my command, I cannot expect to effect a great deal.

Regarding every thing here to be in as favorable a condition as possible, and averse to holding position under the Abolitionists, particularly after the secession of Mississippi, I am closing my official business as rapidly as possible, and intend to resign my commission in the course of next month. Early in April I expect to start with my family for San Antonio, Texas, where, if that State secedes, I shall probably pitch my tent for life.

But if, contrary to my almost certain hopes, Texas shall succumb to the Federal Despotism, I shall go back to Mississippi. Individually, my choice is Mississippi before Texas or any other State or Country; but a sad experience has proven that my wife could scarcely hope for health upon her soil, while I think that the climate of Western Texas is exactly what she needs.

I have written you an unconscionable letter—but you may take the blame to yourself. I am rejoined to shake hands with you over old political differences, and proud to witness the patriotic unanimity with which the sons of the South have risen to repel the oppressor. I do not begrudge you the high privilege which Old Tippah conferred upon you, and which will forever associate your name with the proudest deed that illustrates the untarnished fame of Mississippi; but I shall never outlive the regret that I could not sit by your side.

But I must close. Remember me to all friends, if any there are who remember me. My family are all well, except my wife—and she is improving. I have another addition to my family, a little girl two weeks old.

Present my respects to Mrs. D.

> & believe me
> Yours truly,
> A. M. Jackson

Learning from the papers that the postal system is still maintained in Miss. I direct this straight to you.[1]

"The Bonnie Blue Flag"
(Harry Macarthy, 1861)

We are a band of brothers, and native to the soil,
Fighting for our liberty, with treasure, blood and toil;
And when our rights were threatened, the cry rose near and far,
Hurrah for the Bonnie Blue Flag, that bears a single Star!
Chorus: Hurrah! Hurrah! for Southern Rights Hurrah!
Hurrah! for the Bonnie Blue Flag, that bears a Single Star!

First gallant South Carolina nobly made the stand,
Then came Alabama, who took her by the hand;
Next, quickly Mississippi, then Georgia, Florida;
All raised on high the Bonnie Blue Flag that bears a Single Star!
Chorus: Hurrah! Hurrah! &c.

Then cheer, boys, cheer, raise the joyous shout,
Arkansas and North Carolina now have both gone out;
And let another rousing cheer for Tennessee be given,
The Single Star of the Bonnie Blue Flag has grown to be Eleven!
Chorus: Hurrah! Hurrah! for Southern Rights, Hurrah!
Hurrah! for the Bonnie Blue Flag has gain'd th' Eleventh Star!

CHAPTER TWO

Southern New Mexico, June–July 1861

UNION CORRESPONDENCE

Fort Fillmore N.M.

June 17th 1861

Sir

To enable me to make purchases of subsistence stores for the posts in Arizona, to advantage, it will be necessary for me to have some specie, especially in the purchase of <u>beef</u>, as that article is very scarce here & some money will be required to buy what there is. I went down the country the other day below Ft. Bliss, Texas, in search of cattle, & found a few, but could not buy them with [?], & I have nothing else. I can buy flour with drafts to supply this post & Ft. McLane. I will buy tomorrow about sixty head of Beef Cattle but will be compelled to pay nine cents per pound, when I could get it for eight if I had the cash.

It is now very uncertain about getting mails to or from Forts Breckinridge & Buchanan, as it has now been a month since I have written to find out what amount of stores were on hand at these posts, & I have received no reply from either place, & it may be a month or more yet before I hear. In consequence of this, I think I will give the A.A.C.S. at each of these posts instructions to buy Flour, Beef, & Beans, to supply them up to the last of Dec. I have learned that these articles can be bought in the vicinity of these two posts cheaper than they can here, & of a better quality. I will give instructions that the articles be bought in open market, or by contract, as is most to the advantage of the government.

I am Sir, very respectfully

Your obt. Servt.

Capt. J. P. Hatch	W. B. Lane
Chief C.S. of the Dept.	1st Lt. Rifles
Santa Fe, N. M.[1]	A.A.C.S.

H^d Qrs. Dept. New Mex°

Fort Fillmore 22nd June 61

To the Asst. Adjt. Genl. Dept. New Mex°

Sir,

I have the honor to acknowledge the receipt of your communication enclosing me the Order for mustering into the service of Volunteers &c. I

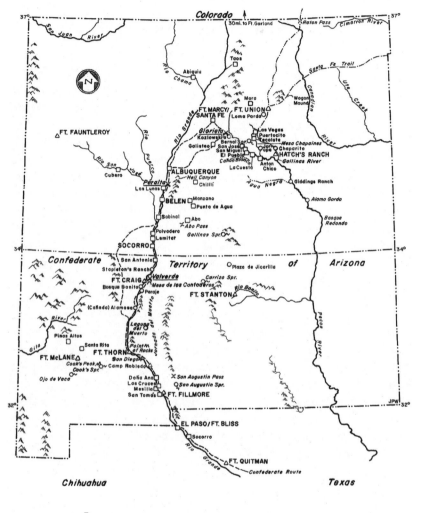

Map 1. New Mexico in 1861–1862.

wish you to give instructions to Col. [Edward R. S.] Canby to give all the necessary orders for the carrying into effect the orders & all other instructions that may arrive & deem this the best course, as the acceptance of my resignation will in all probability reach here by the next mail. A few days since, the horses belonging to A. Co., Rifles, while near this Post, were run off by a band of robbers. They overpowered the guard & carried them into Texas. There was no mounted force left of strength to pursue. The Texas authorities at Fort Bliss have disavowed the act and are exerting themselves to have them returned. I shall do all I can to effect it & I am not without hope of succeeding.

> Respectfully
> Yr. obt. svt.
> W. W. Loring
> Bvt. Col. U.S.A.[2]

Make copy of this letter
to be forwd. to President
W. P. D.

Indian Superintendency
Santa Fé, N. Mex. June 22nd 1861

Sir,

I have the honor to inclose for your consideration the copy of a letter received this morning from Agent [Lorenzo] Labadi, who left here some two weeks ago for Tucson to take charge of the Indian Agency at that place, recently under the control of Col. John Walker. The letter will explain itself.

It is perhaps unnecessary for me to trouble you with comments upon this case, nor would I do so but for the reason that you may not be fully advised of the true condition of political divisions in Arizona. The large majority of the population there are Mexicans, who with few exceptions are loyal to the Government. The disaffection is confined to a few Americans who have assumed to control the affairs of that part of the Territory. These Americans are Southerners, mostly from Texas, and have been in open disobedience to the laws for several years; and now it seems have determined to drive all Federal authority from the Territory.

I inclose two slips cut from the paper published at the Mesilla, *The Times*, which will give you some idea of the hostile feeling that exists there. To attempt to reconcile these men would be absurd, nothing but force and that immediate can save that part of our Territory from becoming the strong hold of secessionism. It is doubtless at the instance of those few factionists that the troops mentioned in the inclosed slip have been ordered to Fort

Bliss. That point is the key to both New Mexico and Arizona. They know and understand its importance and have doubtless urged its occupation by a strong force. I regard it of the highest importance, if the Government desires to maintain the integrity of New Mexico and Arizona to the Union, that our troops should be ordered to take and hold Fort Bliss.

In New Mexico there is very little disaffection to the Government, especially amongst the Mexicans, but if our authority is allowed to be openly disregarded and insulted, as in the case of Agent Labadi, it will most surely lead to disrespect, and perhaps insubordination amongst that part of our population, and may in the end give us trouble. In view of these facts, I would most respectfully suggest that the two Regiments of the Regular Army, the 5th and 7th Infantry, that have been ordered out of this Territory, be allowed to remain, and that steps be at once taken to repossess Fort Bliss, and to hold it.

This movement can now be accomplished without difficulty or loss as there is only about 70 Texas troops there. But if the additional companies that have been ordered to that point are allowed to reach the fort, it will of course give us more trouble to recover possession. This movement would have the best possible effect upon the Mexicans, not only in this Territory and Arizona, but upon those living upon the border of Mexico, adjacent to Arizona.

Judge [John S.] Watts, since his arrival here, has been urging the importance of this step, and has hopes that it will be done, and if it should be, before an order can be sent from Washington, he trusts that your influence may be used with the President and Secretary of War to ensure its approval.

Agent [Michael] Steck reached here last week and left on the 18th inst, to resume the duties of his Agency, but of course he will not be allowed to remain there, and will most likely return to this place. I have written to Agent Labadi to return for the present, and until matters are more settled in that section.

The suggestions which I have here made do not properly come under the supervision of our Department, but a residence of more than thirty years in this Territory and a very general knowledge of its people must be my excuse for this troubling you.

Very respectfully
Your obt. sevt.

Hon. Wm. P. Dole   J. L. Collins
Commissioner of Indian Affairs   Sup. Ind. Affs. N. Mex.
Washington City

Translation from the Spanish [note on original]

Las Cruces New Mexico
June 16, 1861

Sir;

I have the honor to report to you that upon the 14th of the present month, I was astonished to find myself waited upon by a Committee from Mesilla with the object of showing me a certain Resolution passed in a Convention held at that place—which resolution I enclose for your information.

They have desired to compel me to depart from within the limits of the Territory of Arizona, and have given me to understand that if I do not comply voluntarily they will drive me out by brute force—that they have at hand a fine barrel of tar, into which they will put the first officer appointed by President Lincoln, feather him, and start him out to fly. They have had some consideration, however, for me, on account of my friends and because I am a Mexican.

I replied to the gentlemen of the Committee that I recognized no authority in them to compel me to desist from the performance of my official duties in this Territory—that my instructions required me to proceed to Tucson, and that thither I should go unless prevented by force. I have also thought it proper to place this circumstance before you, in order that I may await your decision.

On yesterday I visited Fort Fillmore and conversed with Major G. R. Paul, commanding, upon this subject, and with much good will he told me that he would be ready to resent [*sic*] any attack which should be made upon me, at any time when notified by me, and that he was there for the purpose of causing the laws of the country to be respected.

I am in momentary fear of an attack upon my person by this band of desperate men, if not here, at more advanced stages of my journey—for it is said that matters are worse there, and on that account I consider myself to be in great danger of losing my life.

I have put myself in readiness to depart on the 25th or 28th with a train of wagons which is going to Guaymas.

The occasion for writing this will be excuse sufficient for the length of it.

Respectfully Your ob[t] Sv[t]

(Signed)   Lorenzo Labadi
Indian Agent N.M.

Mesilla 14 de Junio de 1861.

The 6th Resolution of a Convention held in the City of Mesilla Arizona the 16th day of March 1861 is as follows

x x x

Resolved that we will not recognize the present Black Republican Administration and that we will resist any officers appointed to this Territory by said Administration with whatever means in our power.

A True Copy   Ja[s]. A. Lucas
                                               President of the Convention
Attest
Chas. A Hoppin Sec[y]
To D[n] Lorenzo Labadi
Las Cruces N. M.[3]

                                               Fort Fillmore New Mex[o]
To the Asst. Adjt. Genl.   23rd June 1861
Dept. of New Mexico
Santa Fe
Sir,

As the acceptance of my resignation has undoubtedly reached New Mexico before this, and is on its way here, I think it best for all concerned that I should turn the command over to Colonel Canby, 10 Infantry, my next in rank. Another consideration which is important is that there are instruction(s) requiring the immediate action of the Comd'g. Officer of the Dept. at Santa Fe, and for the reasons above stated, it will be impossible for me to reach there before my term of service would be at an end.

I shall give myself a leave until the acknowledgement of my resignation has been received. You will therefore direct Colonel Canby to take command of the Department.

Respectfully
Yr. obt. svt.
W. W. Loring
Bvt. Col. U.S.A.
Comd'g. Dep't.[4]

Fort McLane N. M.
June 24" 1861

Dear Colonel

Your letter of June 16" and instructions of same date were received yesterday by express from Fort Craig. At the same time, an express from Fort Fillmore brought from Col. Loring copies of General Orders of May 17" from the Headquarters of the Army, and Special Orders No. 85 from Head Qrs. Dept. of New Mexico, addressed to Forts Breckinridge and Buchanan. These two Orders have not been received at this Post and are supposed to have been stolen from the mail by Sergeant Allen of "A" Co., 7th Inf. who was sent express from this Post to the Mesilla Post Office, and who deserted from that point. If he took them, I presume his object was to publish them in Texas.

I do not think it at all probable that a force from Texas will pass Fort Fillmore to attack any Post west of that point. In fact they could not do so unless they marched through Mexico, without the Commanding Officer at Fort Fillmore being made aware of it. There are not inhabitants enough in Arizona west of Mesilla to be feared at all, as the Indians have driven most of them from the mines. What there are left, however, are not to be trusted. I think your plan of concentrating troops at Fort Fillmore much the wisest, for the safety of the whole country. I have now two Companies of the 7" Inf. on a scout after Indians, and most of the mules that are not with escorts and expresses are with them. It will be some days before they can be brought in. I shall detain a Government train of twelve wagons from Albuquerque to Fort Buchanan, which is expected back daily, to assist in moving the public property from this Post.

I shall proceed to Fort Fillmore and establish my Head Quarters at that Post as soon as transportation comes in.

I will keep you informed of anything of interest that may transpire, but I have heard nothing that I consider reliable of the reported movement of the Texans.

A Copy of Gen. Order No. 1, published on receipt of your instructions, goes by this express to your staff officer.

Yours truly,
I. Lynde

To Lieut. Col. E. R. S. Canby
Comdg. Dept. of New Mexico
Santa Fe N. M.[5]

Copy
Confidential   Head quarters Dept of New Mexico
                                                    Santa Fe N.M. July 6th 1861.
Sir,

I am instructed by the Lieut. Colonel Commanding to say that the communications from this office of the 23", 24", 29" & 30" Ulto. will have advised you of the state of affairs on the Texas frontier, which does not appear to have been realized by the officers on duty at Fort Fillmore at the date of the last reports from that post. The evidence in his possession is conclusive as to the existence of a plot to seize Fort Fillmore, and the attempt will be made the moment that the conspirators think they have a reasonable prospect of success. If not strong enough to carry out their plans to their full extent, they are prepared to avail themselves of any opportunity to cripple your command or embarrass your movements by stealing your horses or means of transportation, or by assailing any interest of the United States that may for a moment be left unguarded.

The State of Texas, by her Acts and the proclamation of her Governor, is openly at war with the United States, and Colonel Canby cannot comprehend how any different state of affairs can for a moment be recognized by any authority of the Government. And any faith that may have been placed in the professions of [Simeon] Hart and his associates will inevitably be re-paid by treachery.

He considers it highly important that a volunteer force of loyal men should at once be organized in the Mesilla Valley, and that effective measures should be taken to protect the Union men in all their rights. And to repress any measures that may be undertaken against the interests of the Government.

But these and all other measures that may be necessary, are entirely committed to your judgment, as he wishes to leave you entirely untrammeled by instructions that might, under circumstances that cannot be foreseen, conflict with your opinion of what may be necessary and proper to protect the interests and guard the honor of our country.

                                         Very Respectfully, Sir,
                                           Your Obed^t Servant,
                    (Signed)   A. L. Anderson
Major I. Lynde 7" Infantry,   2nd Lieut. 5" Infantry.
Com'dg. Southern Mil. District.   A.A.A. General.
Fort Fillmore N. M.
Headquarters Dept. of New Mexico }   Official
Santa Fe Oct. 1st 1861.   }

A. L. Anderson
2nd Lt. 5th Infantry,
Act. Asst. Adjt. Genl.[6]

———— ✦ ————

(Confidential)   Head Quarters Fort Stanton
July 7th 1861

Colonel:

I have the honor to acknowledge the receipt of your confidential communication of June 30th, and to say that the information it conveyed was not unexpected. That officers of the Rifle Regiment who have resigned, tampered with the loyalty of their men, long before leaving, was known to me; and constrained by a sense of duty, I reported it at Department Head Quarters. I know that it was in contemplation to march the entire Rifle Regiment into Texas, and turn it over to the Army of the Southern Confederacy.

I have so far progressed with the defenses of this Post, as to feel secure against any attempts upon it by the Texans, unless they attack with artillery. The place cannot be held against shot and shell, as it is commanded on all sides by high hills within 1000 yards. The Quarters are of bad stone, without cementation; and would yield at once to heavy ordnance. I keep one of my mounted companies all the time in motion toward Fort Fillmore, and the other toward the Pecos to observe that route and protect the settlements.

Your directions to reinforce my command came so soon after I had expressed to you my views of the necessity, that I have deemed it proper not to detach one of the mounted companies to Fort Fillmore, unless the troops you have ordered to this Post shall reach it. The services of every man, in scouting on the two threatened routes, and in fatigue strengthening the Post, was of urgent necessity. I have spies in at Fillmore and down the Pecos, and hope not to be taken by surprise.

It has seemed to me best to conciliate the Mescaleros, and I have kept two of the principal chiefs, Cadette & Manuelito, near the Post. They inform me that Manco and the other Captains will come in by the middle of the month, bring with them and deliver up to me the thieves, and the horses they have stolen. The forces that are expected here, and my defenses, will have their influence in restraining these Indians.

I have pleasure in reporting my convictions of the loyalty of my entire command. All the officers have renewed their oath of allegiance, and there is universal cheerfulness and contentment at the Post. There are a few secessionists and bad men in the settlements below, and I shall be glad of your directions either to cause their arrest, or remove them from this Indian

Territory. They are trespassers here, and may do mischief. I have already destroyed several whiskey establishments, and sent off the Indian dealers and traders in that staple of the country.

I am Colonel, Very Respectfully

Yr. obt. servt.

Lt. Col. E. S. Canby   B. S. Roberts

Comdg. Dept. N.M.   Lt. Col. U.S.A.

Santo Fe[7]   Comdg. Post

Fort Fillmore N. Mexico

July 7th 1861

Dear Sir;

    I take the liberty of writing you a few lines privately about a certain Mr. [W. W.] Mills who passed by this post on his way from El Paso to Santa Fe last week. I understand that on his way up the Country, that he spread some erroneous reports in regard to officers at this post, and in regard to me which I wish to correct, as on his arrival at Santa Fe these reports may reach your ears. Lt. [C. H.] McNally, RMR, who on his way from Craig met Mr. Mills, says that Mills told him that I had expressed an opinion to him (Mills) of the disloyalty of the officers at this post, & had said that if I was a line officer I would depose Lt. Lane from the Command, arrest him & take command myself; that I also expressed to him Mills doubts of Dr. [James Cooper] McKee's loyalty, and other remarks of like nature. I wish to assure you, sir, that I never expressed to any one an opinion that Mr. Lane or any other officer here was disloyal; much less would I do so to a man who I never saw before and whose real views I had no means of knowing. Any statements which Mr. Mills may make, which would imply such a course of conduct on my part, are malicious falsehoods. They are as absurd as they are false, and I do not deem it necessary to go into any detailed denial of any remarks he has made. It does not become my position to criticize the actions of other officers, but it may not be improper now to state that, as far as I know any thing about the matter, every disposition is shown by the authorities here to defend the public interests.

    All I know about Mr. Mills & all I had to do with him I can state in a few words. This Mr. Mills was introduced to me by Dr. McKee, and when I was alone asked to see me in private. I of course granted his request, and then he told me some remarks which he said he had heard Col. Loring make in El Paso reflecting upon some officers here. He said he was directed to me by Dr. Steck, Indian agent in Mesilla, that he was going to Santa Fe expressly to give his news, and asked me to give him a letter to some one there. I refused him this, and charged him to be careful what rumors he spread on his way up. He left immediately for Mesilla. I had occasion to go up there before the stage left for Santa Fe, & it occurred to me that it would be well [to] write a private letter to [2nd Lt. A. L.] Anderson, stating what I had heard from Mr. Mills, my chief object being to give Anderson the rumors in regard to this post being attacked, giving Mr. Mills as my authority on the subject and giving them only on Mr. Mills authority, not on my own. In that letter I expressly disclaimed any knowledge of anything reflecting on the officers here, or any desire to insinuate anything against them. I met Mr. Mills in Mesilla and gave him the letter, as it was currently reported that the mail would be attacked on its way up and I thought it would be safer in his hands. This is all I had to do with Mr. Mills. I know now that I was deceived in the man. I saw he was excited & inclined to exaggerate, but had no idea he was capable of a malicious falsehood.

The officers here were naturally much annoyed when they heard of Mills' statements, and none more so than myself. By the advice of some of them I have written to you. I never had any desire even if I had the power to injure any one here, and I feel confidently nothing I have said, will be or can be used to place me in any unpleasant position with the command here.

Hoping you will pardon this long letter & knowing that your own judgment will be our best defense against Mr. Mills' absurd reports.

I am very respectfully
Yr. obt. servant
C. H. Alden

[to Lieut. Col. Ed. R. S. Canby][8]

Head Quarters Fort Fillmore N. M.
                                July 14, 1861.

Sir:

The State of affairs is much the same at this Post as when I last reported. It is rumored that they have raised a company of volunteers at Fort Bliss, as spies for the purpose of stealing the animals from the different Posts in this Department. Strength about 40 men.

They bluster very much about attacking us here, but have made no effort to do so as yet.

I received your communication by Mr. Mills. He has rendered himself so obnoxious to many of the officers here, that he declines taking any part with the volunteers. I have employed him as confidential agent to El Paso. I think by the time the arms arrive from Fort Union, I can muster at least one company. Am I authorized to mount one company? They will be very useful here.

I have heard nothing of the company of Rifles ordered here from Fort Stanton.

Very respectfully
Yours &c
(Signed)   I. Lynde
Major, 7th Infantry.

Lieut. Col. E. R. S. Canby, U. S. A.
Santa Fe, New Mexico

Hd. Qrs. Dept. New Mexico   A true copy
Santa Fe, Septr. 28, 1861.   A. L. Anderson
                                       2^d Lieut. 5th. Infantry
                                       A.A.A. General[9]

Copy.
Confidential.

Head Quarters Dept of New Mexico.
Santa Fe N.M. July 14, 1861

Sir,

Instructions were received by the Mail of yesterday directing the withdrawal of the remainder of the regular force in this Department. This determination will necessarily involve the abandonment of Fort Fillmore as soon as the regular troops are withdrawn, as no volunteer force from New Mexico can be raised for a position that will put them directly in opposition to the Texan troops.

Under these circumstances both policy and humanity dictate that no measures should be taken that would involve the Mexican inhabitants of Doña Ana and Arizonia [sic] Counties, and inevitably subject them to retaliation the moment the regular troops are removed. Any efforts to raise volunteers in the neighborhood of your post will accordingly be suspended for the present, and any operations for defense or offense will be made by the regular troops.

The force now at or ordered to Fort Fillmore will be kept at that post to prevent any aggressive movement on the part of the Texans, and to cover the operations necessary in withdrawing the troops from the interior posts in Arizona.

It is of course important that the knowledge of these intended movements should be confined to yourself until the arrangements for carrying them out are completed. You will be advised in this respect by the next mail, and you are desired to take in the meantime such preparatory measures as you may consider necessary, availing yourself of return trains or other public transportation coming North, to send to Albuquerque, any stores or property that will not be needed by your command at Fort Fillmore or on the march to the upper posts. Property not worth transportation will be inspected and disposed of as the interests of the service may require, care being taken that nothing shall fall into the hands of the Texans, or other disaffected individuals, that can be of any possible service to them.

This communication will be sent by mail and a duplicate by express from Fort Craig.

Very Respectfully Sir,
Your Obed^t Servant,
(Signed)   Edw. R. S. Canby
Major 10" Infantry +
Commanding

Major I. Lynde 7' Inf.
Com'dg. Southern Mil. Dist.
Fort Fillmore, N.M.

H^d Qrs. Dept. of New Mexico. }
Santa Fe Oct. 1st 1861   Official,

A. L. Anderson
2nd Lieut. 5" Infantry
Act. Asst. Adjt. Genl.[10]

-------------- ⊷ --------------

Las Cruces New Mexico
July 15th 1861

Dear Sir,

I am still at Las Cruces, but as I wrote you by the last mail, I am unable to do anything and, in these exciting times, it may be many months before the presence of an agent will be needed here. I have therefore concluded to come to Santa Fe by the next mail.

We have many rumors here of war preparations by our friends in Texas, and it is believed here generally that an attempt will be made to take Ft. Fillmore. I have just conversed with two reliable men who left Ft. Bliss yesterday and they say that it is publicly talked about and that they are only waiting for the infantry troops to leave to make the attack. That it is the intention I have not the least doubt. They have now at Bliss about 500 men. They have just organized a spy Company whose publicly avowed object is to steal Govt. property. Most of the Sessionists [*sic*] from Mesilla left there for Ft. Bliss last night & today, about 20 in number. They are also looking for a reinforcement of two Companies from Texas. If the infantry troops leave here & the Fort is not strongly reinforced, it will certainly be attacked and taken.

Capt. [Robert R.] Garland deserted from Fillmore last night; gone to Bliss. The sympathies [of] the Mexican population is with the Govt. Reports are also current here that a party has gone to Stanton to steal the horses, and another and believed by all Sessionists that Ben McCulloch is now on the plains to intercept supplies & money destined for this territory. That his intention is to winter in Ft. Union. I have not the slightest doubt that an attempt will be made to take Fillmore. It is thought by those who have just returned that they will wait until the infantry leave. Some say the attack may be made within a few days. Mesilla will be occupied by two or three companies [of] troops today or tomorrow.

If it is the intention to hold this valley, reinforcements should reach here soon and the presence of some volunteers from N. Mex. and Col. Chaves (Manuel Chavez) would stimulate the Mexican population. Their sympathies are with the Govt., but want encouragement. Yesterday the Texans stole some cattle from near Las Cruces. The mail is about to leave.

Respectfully your
Obt. Servant
M. Steck

James L. Collins
Supt. Ind. Affrs.
Santa Fe N. Mex.[11]

Fort Craig N.M.
July 15 1861

Colonel
D Sir.

There is nothing new from below. My expressman who returned from Fort Fillmore says that they are entrenching that Post, and that the Fort is filled with soldiers and families. I have strengthened the weakest points of this post with sand bags, repaired two old mountain howitzers, and am making cartridges for them today. I have twenty-four spherical case shot. They the pieces are not of much service, but may serve a purpose.

Very truly Your friend
R. M. Morris[12]

Copy

Head quarters Department of New Mexico,
Santa Fe, N.M. July 20th 1861.

Sir,

Your communication of the 14" instant has just been received. My letter of that date will have advised you of the intention to withdraw all the regular troops from this department, and consequently the impolicy of compromising any of the inhabitants of New Mexico at points where they cannot be protected. Those in the neighborhood of your post who have already committed themselves by volunteering must be taken care of in some way. If they elect to enter the service, they may be sent to Fort Craig, which will be kept up if a volunteer force can be raised to hold it. In any event, you will please make the best arrangement that you can to prevent them from suffering for the part they have taken.

It is not improbable that the orders for the withdrawal of the troops may be modified to some extent, and Fort Fillmore or some point in its neighborhood still be kept up, but no assurance of this kind can be given and it will be best for the people in your neighborhood to avoid committing themselves.

In consequence of the necessity of abandoning Fort Fillmore, I have suspended the transfer of all supplies to that post, except such as would be needed while your command remained there.

Should there be a change of orders, all necessary supplies will at once be forwarded. In the meantime, the Commanding Officer at Fort Craig will be instructed to supply any thing on hand at his post that you may call for.

Lieut. [Asa B.] Carey has just relieved Captain [Alfred I.] Gibbs in order to enable me to send "I" Company Rifles to your post. There is no officer to relieve him, and it will probably be necessary to put two Companies temporarily under the command of the same officer.

Nothing was heard by this mail of the command at Breckinridge and Buchanan. If you have received any information from them, will you please advise me by the earliest opportunity.

Very Respectfully, Sir,
Your Obt. Servant

(Signed)   Edw. R. S. Canby.

Major 10" Infantry + Commanding.

Major I. Lynde 7" Inf.
Com'dg. Southern Mil. Dist.
Fort Fillmore N.M.

Head Qrs. Dept. of New Mexico, }
Santa Fe October 1ˢᵗ 1861   } Official.

> A. L. Anderson
> 2ⁿᵈ Lieut. 5th Infantry.
> A.A.A. Genˡ.¹³

Copy

Head quarters Dept. of New Mexico.
Santa Fe N.M. July 20 1861.

Sir,

In carrying out the instructions from the Head Qrs. of the Army in relation to the withdrawal of the regular troops from this Department, I am instructed by the Lieut. Colonel Commanding to indicate in general terms the course that will be pursued, leaving the details of the movements necessary in your district entirely to your judgement.

The garrison of Fort Fillmore will be retained at that post long enough to cover the movements of the troops withdrawn from the interior of Arizona, and the removal of the supplies from your post. These troops, unless you should need them at Fort Fillmore, will take the direct route to Fort Craig, and in this case you will please communicate your orders to them before they reach the point at which the roads separate.

The removal of the supplies from Fort Fillmore should be completed, if possible, by the time the troops from Arizona have passed up, in order that the abandonment of the post may succeed that event as soon as possible. The trains employed for that purpose will take the route by Fort Craig under such escorts as you may consider necessary. Instructions in relation to the transportation will be given by the Chief Quartermaster.

Should you deem it advisable, a part of your command will march for Fort Union by the way of Fort Stanton. This command and the force that marches from Fort Fillmore after the abandonment of the post, should be of sufficient strength to defend themselves against attack, and be encumbered with no more baggage than is needed for the march. There will be subsistence at Forts Stanton and Craig to renew the supplies if necessary.

If Captain [Joseph H.] Potter's company can be spared, the Lieut. Colonel Commanding desires that it may be sent to Fort Stanton, as he wishes to relieve Lieut. Col. Roberts in order that he may go to the Head Quarters of his Regiment at Fort Union.

The regular troops will not be withdrawn from Forts Stanton, Craig and Albuquerque, until after the troops from the South have reached these posts, when they will join or follow the movement.

The Companies from Stanton, Craig and Albuquerque that have been ordered to report to you, will be sent out by the way of the posts from which they came, in order that they may get their baggage.

Captain Gibbs, Mounted Rifles, has been ordered to escort some beef cattle to your post and to report to you for any duty you may assign him, in keeping open the communication, escorting trains &c.

Very Respectfully, Sir.
Your Obed^t Servant

(Signed)   A. L. Anderson

Major I. Lynde 7' Inf.   2nd Lieut. 5th Infantry.
Com'dg. Southern Mil. Dist.   A.A.A. General
Fort Fillmore N.M.

Head Quarters Dept. of New Mexico } Official.
Santa Fe October 1st 1861.

A. L. Anderson
2nd Lieut. 5" Infantry,
A.A.A. General.[14]

H^d Qrs. Fort Fillmore N.M.
1½ A.M. July 25" 1861

Captain,

The Major directs that you move your Command to this post with the least possible delay. Information just received from a Prisoner captured by the Pickets, that a large body of mounted men are in our immediate vicinity. You will leave everything the men cannot carry.

I am Sir

Very Respectfully
Your obedt. Servt.

Capt. Joseph H. Potter   (Signed)   Edward J. Brooks
Comdg. San Tomas N.M.   1st Lieut. 7th Infy.
                                      Adjt.

A true copy
F. J. Crilly
Lieut. & R. Q. M. 7th Inf.
    Acting Adjt.[15]

[Section omitted from published report of Major I. Lynde to A.A.A.G., Santa Fe, in regard to the skirmish at Mesilla, N.M., July 25, 1861 (*OR, Series 1 Vol. 4*, pp. 4–5)]:

Head Quarters Southern District N.M.
Fort Fillmore N.M. July 26, 1861.

Sir: . . .

List of killed

Private	[John] Lane	Company "F"	R.M.R.
"	Jenkins	" "I"	7th Infty.
"	Sherwood	" "G"	7th "

List of wounded

Lieut.	[Edward J.] Brooks	7th. Infty.	Slightly
"	[Christopher H.] McNally	R.M.R	Severely
Sergt.	[James] Callaghan	Co. "F," Rifles	Mortally.
Private	Meyers	" "E,"7th Infty.	Slightly
"	[Jacob] Farber	" "I," "	"
"	[James] Goss	" "D," "	"

"F" Co. R.M.R. 4 horses wounded
"B"   "   "   1 horse wounded[16]

Head Quarters Fort Fillmore N. M.

General Orders   July 26, 1861.
N° 37

I . . . By authority from Department Head Quarters, this Post will be abandoned.

II . . . In consequence of the limited transportation at the Post, all property of whatever description, public and private, that cannot be transported will be destroyed as far as practicable.

III . . . The Command will be supplied with Five days rations (to include the 31st).

IV . . . The Men will be permitted to take but one blanket, and no extra clothing, except what they carry on their persons.

V . . . 40 rounds of ammunition will be carried in the boxes, and each Company will take 1000 rounds in the Wagon.

By order of Major I. Lynde
Edw. J. Brooks
1st Lieut. 7 Infty.
Adjutant[17]

Copy

Fort Craig, N. M.
July 30th 1861

Dear Mrs. Gibbs:

In the first place, I wish to write that your husband is well, but is a prisoner of the troops of Texas. I met him at the point of rocks on the "Jornado," but the night before I received an express from Ft. Fillmore, saying that the Texas troops had arrived in Mesilla. He then turned off the road and struck across the country to the road leading from Ft. Fillmore to Stanton. On reaching this road he met Major Lynde's command from Fillmore en route for Ft. Stanton. The major, two days before, had attacked the Texas troops in Mesilla & got whipped, or at least he went back to the post. Soon after the Captain joined Major Lynde's command, the Texas troops were seen coming up the road. The Capt. formed to fight them, but was prevented by Major Lynde. The Major soon after surrendered with his whole command to a force not equal to his.

I got the information of the surrender from two soldiers of the Rifles that escaped from the Texans the night before last. Capt. Gibbs was then in Las Cruces and well. I suppose he will be allowed to join you; if not, please command me in any way that I can be useful—please don't hesitate. I leave here to day as an escort to a train for Albuquerque. Mrs. Lane is with me and I intend to take her to Fort Union. She joins me in kind regards to you & yours.

Your friend, (sg^d) W. B. Lane[18]

Statement of Capt. F. J. Crilly, A.Q.M. U.S. Army, relative to the evacuation of Fort Fillmore N.M. July 26th 1861, and the surrender of the troops at San Augustine Springs on the 27th of July 1861, made at the request of the friends of Major I. Lynde, late of the 7th U.S. Infantry.

The surrender of the troops at Fort Fillmore was one of those unaccountable events, resulting from a combination of circumstances happening in quick succession, until the unfortunate affair itself was the climax.

I was the Junior Officer of the Command and never knew what were the orders of Major Lynde relative to the evacuation of the Post. The order for it promulgated by him stated that it was in accordance with authority received from the Head Quarters of the Department. I believe

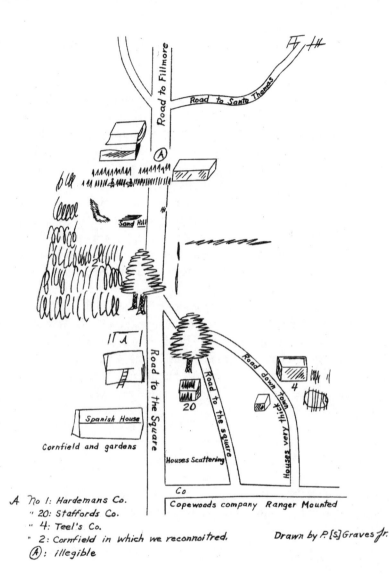

A   No 1: Hardemans Co.
" 20: Staffords Co.
"   4: Teel's Co.
"   2: Cornfield in which we reconnoitred.
Ⓐ: illegible

*Fig. 2. Sergeant Peyton Graves, Jr.'s untitled sketch of the skirmish
at Mesilla, July 25, 1861, as redrawn by John P. Wilson.
From a faint photostat copy with the Nathaniel Wyche Hunter
and Malcolm Kenmore Hunter family papers at the Center for
American History, University of Texas at Austin.*

all the orders and instructions sent to Major Lynde were confidential; at least none of the officers, as far as I am aware of, knew anything of their contents.

The order was published about sundown of the 26th of July, 1861, and the garrison marched out and abandoned the Post about one A.M. next morning. The time allowed was so short that few stores could be destroyed, except the ammunition, which was entirely destroyed. The hospital stores were partially destroyed; some of the liquor got among the men and there were a few instances of intoxication, but it was not by any means general, probably not so much as would be ordinarily among troops changing their station.

I have no personal knowledge of the amount of Q.M. or Com. Stores destroyed; my impression is that no effort was made to do so, on account of the short space of time. The officers left their personal property in their houses; very few of the officers knew of the destination of the command, and no particular preparation was made by the Company officers for a long march without water.

The Command marched along the Rio Grande about four miles in the direction of the town of Las Cruces, when the head of the column was turned to the right and marched in the direction of the Organ Mountains, about twenty miles distant. The amount of transportation was I think about one wagon to a company, in which to haul four or five day's rations, company property, camp women (four to a company), and officers' baggage. The wagons were naturally overloaded, and moved very slowly. There was, I think, no supply train. The total number of wagons was about twelve.

The sun rose early and hot, the road was heavy and sandy; it ran over the Organ Mountains to San Augustine Springs. The distance from river to Springs was fully twenty-five miles. The ascent of the mountain was long and in some places very steep. As early as nine o'clock the extreme heat of the sun, made doubly hot reflected from the sand, and want of water, caused many of the men to fall out of the ranks, exhausted, to seek the shade of the bushes, which were so small as to cover scarcely their heads. About this hour a rear guard of three Companies was detailed, with what orders I cannot say; it was under the command of Capt. M. R. Stevenson, 7th Infantry, since deceased.

About 12 N. the whole Infantry Command can hardly be said to have had an organization; it was stretched for miles along the line of march, each man trying to save himself from the terrible heat. It was beyond anything that it was possible to imagine; many of the men became absolutely insane. Some wandered off the road and died; one party killed a dog and drank his blood. Major Lynde kept at the head of his Command. I do not think that he left that place until he arrived at the Springs. The wagon teams broke down in ascending the mountains. I think only two or three got to the Springs. My Company was detailed to stay with the wagons to help them along.

The head of the command got to the Springs about three o'clock in the afternoon. A detachment of the Mounted Rifle Regiment, numbering probably about fifty men under Capt. Alfred Gibbs, joined about two o'clock in the afternoon. I was about that time halfway up the mountain. Capt. Gibbs went forward and reported to Major Lynde, and shortly returned, with what orders I do not know. He joined the squadron of the Rifles, under Lieut. E. P. Cressy, which formed part of our Command, Capt. Gibbs assuming command of the whole. I saw little or nothing of what transpired in the rear, and knew nothing personally of what reports were sent in to Major Lynde by Capt. Gibbs. While on the Rio Grande side of the mountain, to the best of my recollection now, I saw nothing that looked like the approach of an enemy, but there were some reports to that effect. I joined with Lieut. D. P. Hancock in trying to halt some of the men and form them as they straggled up, but the extreme heat had made them so weak that they could not stand in ranks. I concluded that it was best to let them get into Camp as best they could, to obtain water.

I did not at that time feel that there was the slightest danger of an attack, or that if one was made, but what there were sufficient men in camp to repel it.

I omitted to state that there were four small Mountain Howitzers, fastened behind the wagons, and dragged in that way. Finding that the teams were completely broken down, and that it was impossible to get them any farther, I pushed forward into Camp to get the mules from the wagons that had already reached there, and had been watered. I started them back, and also had all the canteens and kegs filled that I could carry, which I took back with me in a light wagon to give to the men lying along the road. I met Lieut. Geo. Ryan (since killed in battle) about halfway up the mountain, on the side towards the Springs. I had great fears of his recovery. I gave him some water. I also gave some to Lieut. [David P.] Hancock, also still in the rear, and to what men I met. I shortly afterwards met Capt. Gibbs with his command of the Rifles. They advised me not to go back any further, as the Texans were but a short distance in [the] rear on the other side of the mountain.

I kept on, however, until I saw the head of their Column at the summit. I then turned round and came into Camp; the Texans, who were mounted, coming after at a gallop. On arriving at the Springs, I found so much of the command as was there formed in line of battle. The officers' wives and camp women, such as had gotten in, were also there. One of the howitzers had also been hauled in. I placed it on the left of the battalion and had it ready to fire. The balance of my company were formed in ranks. There were about one hundred men formed in the infantry battalion.

The men had become refreshed on reaching the water and were eager and ready for a fight. No one as far as I am aware of felt differently, except Major Lynde himself and perhaps his adjutant, Lieut. Brooks. Lieut. Brooks went out and conversed for a few minutes with the commander of the rebel Cavalry. The rebels advanced. Major Lynde, on the return of Lieut. Brooks to him, addressed the battalion to the effect that to prevent the effusion of blood he had determined to surrender the command. Capt. J. H. Potter and Capt. M. R. Stevenson, the two senior officers, advanced from their companies to Major Lynde and protested. Major Lynde said that he was in command and that he assumed the responsibility. By this time the Texans were in our midst and further parley useless, and the surrender of seven Companies of U.S. Infantry and I believe one hundred and fifty men of the Rifle Regiment was complete.

How many men the Texans had, I never accurately knew. I have given the foregoing statement purely from memory after a lapse of four years; it is correct in all the main particulars. Some minor matters may have escaped my memory, which I would recollect if my attention was called to them. My opinion relative to the surrender and the causes that led to it are the same as they were then. Fort Fillmore was an untenable position, being over a mile from water, surrounded by hills which were within easy cannon range of every spot in the garrison. The fort consisting simply of adobe houses, the troops were worn out by details for guards to the water wagons, and by trying to intrench.

It was known that the rebels had several pieces of artillery, six-pounders. This being the case, if operations in other parts required that the position near them should be held, there were strong defensive points along the river to which the Command could have been removed and from which four times their number could not have driven them. There was plenty of time for this, as also to have sent off the women and children. The presence of these at the Springs was on the grounds of humanity the only extenuation for the surrender. If it had been determined to abandon the position entirely, the march should have been conducted in such a way as to have had the troops ready for action at any time. Major Lynde knew that the Texans had advanced in force, and were only waiting for a favorable opportunity to attack.

The Infantry Command on leaving Fort Fillmore was fully five hundred men. When it arrived at San Augustine Springs, it had been reduced to one hundred men, in line of battle. Even with these, a few hundred irregular Cavalry should have been driven off. There were two routes to take the Command to the nearest U.S. Mil. post; one across the sandy plains and steep ascents of the Organ Mountains to Fort Stanton, the other along the Rio Grande to Fort Craig. Many of the officers at the time and all of the men ascribed the surrender of the troops to the treachery on the part of Major Lynde. I did not think so then, nor do I now after a careful review of all the circumstances.

The actions of Major Lynde to my mind were those of a man who had become superannuated in service. I have no reason to doubt the courage or nerve of Major Lynde, for on the day previous to the evacuation, in a slight engagement with the Texans near Mesilla, he was personally into the Texan pickets where any novice must have expected to find them. His escape from being wounded must have been purely accidental. His handling of the troops at Mesilla and on the march to San Augustine Springs showed the actions of a man superannuated and unfit for active command of so many troops in the field.

The foregoing statement may seem uselessly long, but as the whole affair has never been made the subject of official investigation, and as this statement is made at the request of the friends of Major Lynde, in justice to myself I feel that I could give nothing less than a complete narrative of the facts as they appeared to my mind.

F. J. Crilly

Capt. A.Q.M.

U.S. Army[19]

The following is a brief statement of the facts preceding and attending the surrender of a body of U.S. troops at San Augustine Springs, New Mexico, on the 27th day of July 1861, by Major I. Lynde, 7th U.S. Infantry.

On the 5th of July 1861 I assumed command of Fort Fillmore N.M. with instructions from the Commanding Officer of the Department of New Mexico to concentrate at that post as many of the troops stationed in Arizona as possible, to protect that post. I soon discovered that the Fort was so placed as to be indefensible against artillery, being commanded on three sides by sand hills within easy range of a six-pounder, and the only water for men and animals was at the river a distance of one and a half miles. These facts I immediately imparted to the Head Quarters of the Department and recommended that the post be abandoned and a more eligible point be selected.

I received no answer to this report as it was not received at Head Quarters, that as well as many communications having been abstracted from the mails. I soon discovered that the greater part of the inhabitants of the Mesilla Valley were secessionists and that I could gain no information that I could rely upon from Texas. I also became aware that an influence was being exerted upon the enlisted men to render them dissatisfied and disaffected towards the Federal Government. A number of the officers of my command were Southern men who did not conceal their sympathy with the seceded States and one (Captain J. M. Jones) had sent on his resignation.

About the 15 of July, Captains Jones and Garland left the post without permission and proceeded to Texas, and I had good reason to suppose, with the knowledge and assistance of one or more of the officers at the post. They were beyond my reach before I had any intimation of their intention to desert. This created much excitement among the enlisted men and tended to shake my confidence in the troops under my command, and this excitement was much increased by a report which was spread among the enlisted men that two more officers would desert on a certain night stated, but which proved false, or was prevented if ever intended.

This was the state of my command when the Texan troops approached Fort Fillmore. On the morning of the 25th of July, a deserter from the Texans was brought in by one of my pickets, who reported that a force of about 300 mounted Texans were approaching to attack the post. The command was immediately formed and scouts sent out to ascertain the whereabouts of the enemy. After considerable time, it was discovered that they had passed up the opposite side of the river about three miles from us and had gone to the town of Mesilla, six miles above, where they had been joined by 150 men of that place and vicinity. I then feared that they would pursue and capture a train loaded with commissary stores that had left for Fort Craig a day or two before, escorted by one company of Regiment of Mounted Rifles on foot.

To prevent this and to try the strength of the enemy, I determined to make a demonstration in the direction of Mesilla, and on the afternoon of that day I proceeded with a part of my command (leaving one Company and the Band 7th Infantry to guard the fort) to the vicinity of the town and fired a few shots from 4. four-pound Mountain Howitzers, the only artillery that I had at the post, and receiving some rifle shots from a house in our front. As night was coming on and the main object of the demonstration accomplished, and being convinced that we could only drive the enemy out of the town if we persevered, and if driven out, that they would either pursue the train or turn our flank and capture the Fort in our absence, I determined to return to the Fort with my command. My calculations all proved true, for I was afterwards informed that when I approached the town they were just starting a part of their command to pursue the train and their plan was, if they were driven from the town, to make a dash upon the Fort, which they might have done as they were all mounted and I had but about 50 mounted men. As it was, the train escaped.

The next day I continued the work of strengthening my defenses and, as the enemy had no artillery up to this time, I was confident of my ability to defend the post, though from some circumstances that had transpired I had not full confidence in my troops. On that morning, I was informed that 100 Infantry had joined the enemy the night before from Texas. From the best information I could obtain, this was all the force they had in that part of Texas, but on the afternoon of that day I had reliable information that a battery of artillery guarded by 300 Infantry was approaching and would be with the enemy that night. If I detached a sufficient force to have any hope of capturing this artillery, I should weaken my command, so that the enemy at Mesilla who were watching us would be able to capture the Fort. They were at least 550 strong at Mesilla, while I had only about 500 all told. If this artillery joined them, they would have about 850 men and a battery of artillery of heavier guns than mine—they were represented to be 12 pounders. On consultation with my officers most of them agreed with me, that if we remained we must eventually be captured, but by abandoning the Fort we might reach Fort Stanton, and by forming a junction with that command we might assist to protect that post, which was reported to be threatened.

A few days previous to this, orders had been received from the Head Quarters of the Department to abandon Fort Fillmore as soon as certain arrangements could be made, and at any rate I considered that, as the commander of the Southern District of New Mexico, I had full authority by my instructions to abandon the post if I thought it for the good of the country. If I remained, the troops and the public property would fall into the hands of the enemy. If I abandoned the post, the troops, it was hoped, would escape capture and the public property be destroyed.

I issued an order to my command to destroy all public property that could not be carried with the limited means of transportation at the post, and at 1 o'clock on the morning of the 27 of July took up my line of march for Fort Stanton. I had never been over the road myself, but it was represented to me by officers acquainted with the road that it was about 22 miles from Fort Fillmore to San Augustine Spring, the first water on the road, and that at that point there was plenty of water. We proceeded very well on our way until the sun rose, when it became excessively hot, and soon after the men and animals began to show signs of fatigue and suffering from the heat and want of water. When within about 5 miles of the springs, I determined to push forward with the mounted force and procure as much water as they could carry and bring back to the Infantry in the rear. At this time there was no indication of pursuit.

On reaching the Springs, I found that the water was in limited quantities and not sufficient for my whole command. After filling all the vessels, I started back and had proceeded but a short distance when I met Capt. Gibbs, Regiment of Mounted Rifles, who reported to me for duty with his Company from Fort Craig, and also that his men and horses had had no water for 24 hours. I directed Captain Gibbs to take command of all the mounted troops, about 70 in all, and to protect the train in conjunction with the rear guard of three companies of the 7th Infantry.

I had not proceeded far beyond this point when I became so much exhausted from fatigue and excessive heat that I could sit on my horse no longer, and I had to stop and dismount, sending on the mounted forces. After sitting by the road side for some time, I was able to return slowly to the spring, but suffering from such intense pain in my head as to be almost blind.

Reports came in repeatedly that the men were giving out, and every effort was made to send water out to them. An express came in from Capt. Gibbs and reported that eight companies of mounted Texans, supported by a large body of Infantry and something that looked like Artillery, were approaching our rear. I sent him an order to protect the train by all the means in his power. I immediately had the command formed and could not bring more than 100 men on the ground. Many were lying under the bushes near the Spring, totally unable to rise, and a large proportion of the Infantry were lying by the road side unable to get in to the Springs. Soon Capt. Gibbs galloped into Camp with his command, having been driven in without firing a gun. He then reported the enemy to have eight companies of mounted troops supported by a Regiment "more or less" of Infantry and some Artillery. He then applied to me for permission to try to escape, saying it was impossible to contend against such odds; that he thought he could escape with the mounted men, but the Infantry could not. I refused the permission as I did not then think of a surrender.

A body of mounted Texans soon made their appearance in our vicinity, when I found that 3 out of 4 of our Howitzers had been captured with more than half of our train and all of our men who were in the rear, amounting to from 150 to 200, and that I could not bring more than 250 men all told on parade and most of those nearly worn-out. If Captain Gibbs reports were true, and I had no reason to think them otherwise, it was hopeless to resist longer. A parley was held and terms of surrender agreed upon.

I. Lynde

Late Maj. 7. Infy.

Note. It was well known that the Texan organization was 100 men to a Company.[20]

The Surrender of Fort Fillmore, New
Mexico—The Treason of the Officers

We give below the statement of a soldier who arrived here on Wednesday from Fort Fillmore:

On the fifth of July, Major Lynde had command of seven companies of infantry and two of cavalry (F and B of the Mounted Rifles), in all about 700 men. The next officers in rank were Capts. Potter and Stevenson and Lieut. McAnnelly [McNally]. On the 24th [*sic*; 25th] of July, at 3 o'clock P.M., 480 men, with four pieces of artillery, started for Mesilla; arrived there at dark, were drawn up in line of battle between two cornfields; there were no flankers and no skirmishers out; the cavalry were within 85 yards of the ambuscade laid by the Texans, who numbered less than 200 and were poorly armed. Shots were fired out of the cornfield, one of them taking effect on Lieut. McAnnelly, a true Union man. Major Lynde was behind a wagon. A perfect cross-fire was opened on the cavalry, and no officer now being in command of them, they retreated. No order had been given them to dismount, fire or charge, and they retreated "on their own hook" to the rear of the infantry, in order to give the artillery a chance to fire. Our own infantry opened a perfect volley on our own cavalry—by mistake, it was said. A few shots were fired by the artillery, when the whole command was ordered to retreat back on the post. Arrived there at 9 o'clock.

Next day all were engaged in fortifying. At half past ten an order was given to evacuate that night. The Commissary was ordered to roll out the whiskey, and the infantry were allowed to drink it and fill their canteens. No water was furnished for the hot march before them. The march was undertaken in the most irregular manner, and before we had gone ten miles, men were dropping from the ranks and falling down drunk.

At two in the morning [*sic;* afternoon], Texan troops were seen advancing on the Las Cruces road. Our Adjutant, on being informed of it, made no preparations to resist an attack, but said "They have nothing to fear from us."

Of the seven companies, so many had been left drunk and captured that no more than two companies went into camp.

The officers left us and held a long council of war. The men of the rifle command decided among themselves to fight. Just as they were ready, Capt. Gibbs came up, ordered a retreat upon camp, saying: "We will fight them there." As soon as we reached there, we were formed into line and told to dismount for the last time: "You are turned over as prisoners of war." All our arms and supplies were given up, the oath was administered, and next day we were released on parole.[21]

No. 212 F. St. Washington
December 6th, 1861.

Major General George B. McClellan
Commander in Chief. &c.
General

An official order has been published by which Major Isaac Lynde is "dropped" from the rolls of the army without trial on the charges preferred against him by Capt. J. H. Potter, 7th Infty., and Capt. Alfred Gibbs, 3d. Cav[y]., and as I learn, it has been decided not to grant the request for a Court of Inquiry on their own conduct, preferred by them and other officers included in Major Lynde's surrender. At the same time, I see that a member of the House of Representatives has introduced a resolution of Inquiry as to what punishment has been inflicted on these officers, as well as on Major Lynde.

That blame if not disgrace will be imputed to Major Lynde's subordinates unless some steps are taken either to clear them, or allow them to clear themselves, appears to me certain. As it is not supposed that the President, in reply to the inquiry of the house, can render such information as will exonerate them, they must either submit to this in silence or be driven to the columns of a newspaper in self-defense, unless they are allowed the privilege usual in such cases.

I am General
Very respectfully
George Gibbs[22]

"A John Brown Song"
(*Quincy Daily Whig and Republican*, March 5, 1862)

Old John Brown's body lies a mould'ring in the grave,
While weep the sons of bondage, whom he ventured all to save;
But now although he lost his life while struggling for the slave,
His soul is marching on.
Chorus: Glory, Glory, Hallelujah! Glory, Glory, Glory, Hallelujah!
Glory, Glory, Hallelujah! His soul is marching on.

He captured Harper's Ferry with his nineteen men so few,
And frightened 'Old Virginny' till she trembled through and through;
They hung him for a traitor, themselves a traitor crew,
But his soul is marching on.
Chorus: Glory, Glory, Hallelujah! &c.

John Brown was a hero, undaunted, true and brave,
And Kansas knew his valor when he fought her rights to save;
And now although the grass is growing green upon his grave,
His soul is marching on.
Chorus: Glory, Glory, Hallelujah! &c."

CHAPTER THREE
Headquarters and Northern District Correspondence, June–July 1861
UNION CORRESPONDENCE

H^d Q^{rs}, Northern District of New Mexico
Santa Fe N. Mex. June 13, 1861

Colonel,

Second Lieutenant [Ira W.] Claflin R.M.R. with 25 effective men and horses will be detached from Ft. Union for special service connected with the recovery of the public herd, stolen from the neighborhood of the Galisteo on the 4th instant. The Command will take 10 days rations and move with pack mules with as little encumbrance of baggage as possible.

The Chief Quartermaster at Dp^{mt}. Head Quarters will furnish such information as may be in his possession in relation to the present locality of the stolen animals, and send with the command one or more persons who are able to identify them.

Lt. Claflin will be instructed to use every exertion to recover the stolen animals and, if they are found in possession of private individuals, to secure their restoration by peaceable measures if possible, and by force if necessary. This duty will be exercised with judgment and discretion, but with determination, and if resistance is offered, the persons engaged in it will be regarded and treated as enemies. Should he deem it necessary, Lt. Claflin will be authorized to call upon Lieut. [Charles J.] Walker for assistance in carrying out these instructions, but no time must be wasted in endeavoring to find Lt. Walker's Command.

The deputy U.S. Marshal who accompanies the bearer will represent the Civil Authorities and will be respected and supported accordingly.

Very respectfully, Colonel,
Your obedient servant
Ed. R. S. Canby
Maj. 10 Infy. & Bt. Lt. Col. Commg.

To Bvt. Lt. Col. W. Chapman
Major 10th [sic] Infy. Commanding
Fort Union N. M.[1]

Confidential
Head Quarters Northern District
Santa Fe, N.M. June 19th 1861

Sir:

The Lieut. Colonel Commanding desires that you will organize a small party of spies for the purpose of watching the road from Fort Smith to Anton Chico, and another to watch the country east of Fort Union and south of the road to the Crossing of the Arkansas. These parties should be composed of Mexicans or Indians, if reliable men can be found, as under the ostensible purpose of trading with the Indians, they would attract less attention than parties of troops. They will be required to furnish their own animals and arms, but will be furnished by you with subsistence and ammunition. The compensation will be the same as has heretofore been allowed by Department Orders for similar services.

It is important that these parties should be organized as quietly as possible and that the real object of the service should be concealed under some plausible pretext. They should be advanced so far in both directions as to be able to give you timely warning of any movements being made in the direction of the frontier or against the trains on the road.

Arrangements are being made by the War Department for guarding the line of communication from the Missouri frontier to this country. The extent of these arrangements is not fully known here, but no apprehensions are entertained except for the trains that may now be between your post and the Crossing of the Arkansas. If you should apprehend any danger for them, you will without waiting for instructions make the best arrangement that may be in your power for their protection. If it be necessary in order to replace any portion of your command that may be detached for this purpose, you are authorized to call into the public service two or more companies of volunteers to strengthen your command. These companies if called for will be regarded as part of the two regiments to be raised in New Mexico, and their organization will conform to the minimum organization prescribed in War Department General Orders No. 15 of 4th ult.

On the 14th inst., two companies of the 5th Inf. were ordered from Fort Fauntleroy for the purpose of strengthening the depots at Albuquerque and Fort Union, but it will be some time before the company destined for your post can reach it, and in the mean time the Lieut. Colonel Commanding does not wish the strength of the garrison at Fort Union to be reduced below 200 men without calling for the volunteers.

You will please report as early as possible any information that you may obtain of the state of affairs of the country east and south of your post.

Three or four Indians will be sent from this place to Lieut. Walker at Hatches Ranch to be used for the abovementioned purpose. Instructions for their employment similar to the above, will be sent from these Head Quarters to Lieut. Walker.

Very respectfully Sir
Your obed^t serv^t
A. L. Anderson

To Bvt. Lieut. Col. Wm Chapman   2nd Lieut. 5th Inf.
Comdg. Fort Union N. M.   A.A.A. Genl.

[Jacket]   List of Mexican Spies employed on the 25' of June 1861, agreeably to the within instructions.

1. Julio Martin
2. Juan Martin
3. Antonio Salasar
4. Anastasio Truxillo
5. Benito Martin
6. Cristoval Santistevan
7. Antonio Mascareños
8. Decidereo Garcias
9. Jesus Laiva

Rationed to include the 14' July commencing on 25' June 1861 (20 days).

Wm Chapman Bt. Lt. Colo. Comg.

———————— ➤ ————————

Head Quarters Northern District
Santa Fe N.M. June 23 1861

Sir:

I am instructed by the Lieut. Colonel Commanding to inform you that Col. [Céran] St. Vrain will leave this afternoon for the purpose of hastening the organization of the volunteer companies that are to be mustered into the service of the United States. The Governor of the Territory has delegated to Col. St. Vrain the selection of the companies that are to be presented to you for muster, and upon their arrival at Fort Union, you will please muster them into the service of the United States in conformity with the regulations of the War Department of June 12, 1848 and War Dept. General Orders No. 15 and 25 of 1861.

If Mr. Stanton, the agent of the War Department, should reach Fort Union before the companies are mustered in, you will please communicate to him the steps that have already been taken for organizing the companies.

A copy of the regulations of 1848 is enclosed herewith, but as it is the only copy in the office, you are requested to return it as soon as you are through with it, or immediately if there is another copy at Fort Union.

As soon as the companies are mustered in, they will be armed and supplied with the necessary camp and garrison equipage, upon requisitions approved by you. No clothing will be issued.

The oath of allegiance will be required of all who enter the service, and the refusal to take it will be an absolute cause for rejection.

Very respectfully Sir
Your obt. servt.
A. L. Anderson
2nd Lieut. 5th Inf.
A.A.A. Genl

To Bvt. Lieut. Col. Wm Chapman
Comdg. Fort Union N. M.

Fort Union N.M.
June 26th 1861

Sir

In obedience to the letter of instructions dated Santa Fe N.M. June 13th 1861 I proceeded to Hatche's Ranch, and in as secret a manner as possible, obtained all the information in my power concerning the duty with which I was charged.

Very little was elicited, as I am satisfied from having served with but short intervals of absence for over two years in the Gallinas and Pecos Valleys, that those inhabitants who are not associates of a regularly organized band of robbers are compelled by motives of safety and interest to refrain from exposing those who, for years, have been engaged not only in preying upon their fellow citizens, but also upon the Government they have so long and loudly called upon to protect them.

I examined all the herds in the valley, but succeeded in capturing only six of the cattle which had been stolen ~~with~~ three of Mr. Taylor's & Mayberry's herders. One of these men it is said was one of the parties who drove the cattle from Galisteo. I trailed about twenty of the oxen into the mountains above Mr. Taylor's house, and all the information that can be obtained shows that Mr. Taylor is the leader of the band who have so long infested that country, filling it with rumors of Indian depredations that were only instigated by themselves and executed by their peons and partners.

It may be remembered that last fall the herd of the Commissary Department was driven off. A party of troops were [*sic*] sent in pursuit to chastise the "Comanches" for this daring robbery. I had at one time a man (a peon of Taylor's) who confessed that the Indians did run the herd off, but only received about twenty of them, and Mr. Taylor and Mayberry the balance.

May I be allowed to add, that the rumors of Indian depredations are industriously started and kept in circulation by persons whose pecuniary interests require that troops should be stationed in that country, and if at any time it is necessary to have some robbery or murder as a show for the justice of their demands, they have the creatures around them to whom either would be a pleasure.

Every report of Indian depredations has been by Lieut. Walker proven to be totally false, and when large bodies of Indians were reported in the immediate vicinity, I with a small party on two occasions by actual examination found them to be totally false; also the Indians who infest the valleys of the Gallinas & Pecos are white men and Mexicans.

	Very Respectfully
To Lt. John F. Ritter	(Signed) Ira W. Claflin
Lt. 5" Infty. U.S.A.	Lt. Rifles U.S.A.
Acting Adjutant	
A true copy	
Wm Chapman Major 2' Infty.	
Lt. Colo. U.S.A.	

Head Quarters Dept. of New Mexico
June 29th 1861

Sir:

I am directed by the Lieut. Colonel Commanding to acknowledge the receipt of your communication of the 26th inst.

He considers the report of Lieut. Claflin to be very interesting and the result of his operations very satisfactory, as it will no doubt lead to the breaking up of the bands of robbers that have infested that part of the country.

If the Comanche women cannot be made useful in furnishing information, they will be released and permitted to return to their tribe. Colonel Chapman will please tell them to say to the Comanche Chiefs that the Government of the United States has no wish to make war upon the Comanches, but that a large force is now being collected and will be sent into their country to punish them if they fail to keep the promises they made at Alamo Gordo.

The form for the muster roll will be sent by the next mail.

	Very respectfully Sir
	Your obt. servt.
To Bv^t Lieut. Col. Wm Chapman	A. L. Anderson
Maj. 2nd Inf.	2nd Lieut. 5th Inf.
Comdg. Fort Union, N.M.	A.A.A. Genl

Head Quarters Dept. of New Mexico
Santa Fe N.M. June 30, 1861

Sir:

I am instructed by the Lieut. Colonel Commanding to say that as soon as the companies of New Mexico volunteers to be mustered into the service at Fort Union are equipped, you will organize a command of at least 100 mounted men and two companies of New Mexican volunteers—the whole to be under the command of Capt.[Thomas] Duncan, R.M.R., for the protection of trains on the road from the Crossing of the Arkansas to Fort Union.

The command will move as lightly equipped as possible, and will take with it rations for thirty days. As the service will be performed on or near the road, wagon transportation will be used, but a few fresh mules should be taken to meet the contingency of temporary detachments, if it should be necessary to make any.

A party of ten spies and guides will be attached to the command, and particular care should be taken in selecting them.

You will please indicate to Capt. Duncan that the Lieut. Colonel Commanding trusts entirely to his discretion for the protection of the trains, and that he will take such measures as may in his judgment be most necessary to accomplish this object. He thinks it proper to suggest, however, that the command should be kept as compact as possible: that no detachment should be made if it is possible to avoid it, and that the country on his front and flanks should be thoroughly searched by the spies attached to his command.

The Commanding Officer at Fort Larned has been requested to advise trains passing that post to keep up the Arkansas and come into New Mexico by the Raton route.

Capt. Duncan's command will be relieved in season to return to Fort Union at the expiration of the thirty days for which he is provisioned, if it should be found necessary to keep out a command for a longer period.

It has been found necessary to send the company of the 5th Infantry intended for Fort Union to Fort Stanton, and a company of the 10th Infantry has been ordered to report to you in its place.

Very respectfully Sir
Your obd't. serv't.
A. L. Anderson
2nd Lieut. 5th Inf.
A.A.A. Gen'l

To Bv't Lieut. Col. Wm Chapman
Maj. 2nd Inf.
Comdg. Fort Union, N.M.

H^d Q^{rs} Departm^t of New Mexico
Santa Fe N. Mex. July 6, 1861.

Circular.

Sir,

The reclamation of Peons who have been enrolled in the volunteer Companies mustered into the service of the United States will no doubt be raised at your post, and I am instructed to state for your information, that no discharges for this cause will be ordered at Department Head Quarters. Consequently, that the only resource of the persons claiming such service will be by the writ of habeas corpus, from the United States Courts in the Territory. The local Courts of the Territory have no jurisdiction and their writs will not be respected.

Very respectfully, Sir
Your obedient servant,
A. L. Anderson
2nd Lieutn. 5th Infy.
A.A. Adj^t Genl.

Commanding Officer Fort Union

H^d Q^{rs} Department New Mexico
Santa Fe N. Mex., July 7, 1861

Sir:

The Lieut. Colonel Commanding has advised the Governor of the Territory that the Companies necessary to complete the 1st and 2nd Regiments of New Mexican Volunteers will be accepted and mustered into the service as soon as they are presented, and he instructs me to say that, accordingly, you will please muster into service any Companies of the 1st Regiment that may be properly presented to you at Fort Union.

As soon as mustered in, a Camp will be established at Fort Union for instruction and discipline, and you are desired to give such directions and take such measures as will advance these objects as rapidly as possible.

Very respectfully, Sir,
Your obedient servant,
A. L. Anderson
2nd Lt. 5th Infy. A.A.A. Ge.

To The Commanding Officer
Fort Union, N. Mx.

Fig. 3. Major General Edward R. S. Canby.
Courtesy of Museum of New Mexico, negative no. 54169.

[Jacket]   Rec^d Fort Union N.M. July 8, 1861. Sent an express to
             Captain Duncan with a copy of this on 8' July 1861 at 8 P.M.

My dear Colonel:
    I have just heard from a private source that the Government trains are
taking the route by Fort Wise. This relieves my anxiety on their account, to
a very considerable extent, as no force that we can spare at present would be
sufficient to guard them against a large, organized force from the frontiers

of Arkansas or Texas. The most that I expect from Capt. Duncan's command is to protect them from the Indians and marauding parties, and I do not wish to place his command in a position from which he cannot make good his retreat to Fort Union.

The organization of the volunteers is progressing very slowly. I am hastening it as much as possible, in order to get the regulars in where they can be concentrated to meet any contingency.

Very truly
Yours &c.
Ed. R. S. Canby

I have no special news from the East, but both Van Dorn and Ben McCulloch are to be looked for.

—◆—

Head Quarters Dept. of New Mexico
Santa Fe N.M. July 19, 1861

Sir:

I am instructed by the Lieut. Colonel Commanding to acknowledge the receipt of your communication of the 16th Inst., and to request that you will immediately communicate by express any new or important information that you may obtain in relation to the movements of the Texans.

He desires that parties of spies may be kept out constantly in the directions suggested, and that you will use your own judgement in the selection of those you send. The Chief Quartermaster has been instructed to employ some Pueblo Indians and send them out to you, if they can be found in this neighborhood. You will not, however, rely upon this, but employ them from the neighborhood of your post if they can be found there.

From information received from the Commanding Officer at Fort Wise, it is apprehended that some of the contractors' trains have taken the Cimarron route. If you have any information upon the subject, will you please communicate it.

Very respectfully Sir,
Your obdt. serv't.
A. L. Anderson
2nd Lieut. 5" Inf.
A.A.A. Genl

To Bvt. Lt. Col. Wm Chapman 2 Inf.
Comdg. Fort Union N.M.

—◆—

(Copy)

Fort Craig New Mexico
July 19, 1861

Colonel

Dear Sir

The old guide of the post has just come down from Lemitar, and makes the following statement.

An Apache Indian came into Lemitar on Monday last and said that there was a large body of Texans at the Rio Bonito, who were going up the Pecos to capture (Las Posas) or Ft. Union; that their encampment and stock covered near three miles of ground, and that they had artillery with them.

If this is true, it is important that you should know it as early as possible. There are two roads coming into Ft. Union. One course is by Chaparito and Mr. Waters' Ranch seven miles south of Union; the other road comes in by the Wagon Mound east of Turkey Mountain and about twelve or fourteen miles above (south) of Union. I believe the guide's statement to be truthful. Hoping this will reach you in time to intercept them,

    I am Sir

                           Very truly your friend

Colonel E. R. S. Canby   (Signed)   R. M. Morris
Comd'g. Dept. of New Mexico   U.S.A.
Santa Fe N.M.

Head Quarters Department of N.M.
Santa Fe N.M. July 21, 1861

Confidential

Colonel:

In view of the early movement of the troops from this Department, the Lieut. Colonel Commanding desires that some of the regular troops now at or soon to arrive at Fort Union may be detached for distinct service. The company of the 2nd Dragoons now in the neighborhood of Hatches Ranch will be relieved at the expiration of its regular time by a company of mounted volunteers, unless in your judgement the services of Capt. [Antonio Maria?] Vigil's [company] will not be needed more urgently in another direction.

Another company of mounted volunteers will be raised for Fort Union as soon as possible, but in consequence of the difficulty of organizing the foot companies, he does not wish to call for it until after the organization of the infantry regiments is completed.

He wishes also that a volunteer command of three or four infantry companies may be held in readiness, to be ordered on the lower road to the Arkansas as far as the crossing of the Cimarron, if from any information you can obtain, this course will be necessary for the protection of the trains crossing by that route. Lieut. Colonel [Christopher] Carson will be assigned to duty with this command.

One or possibly two parties of Pueblo Indians will be sent out to you in two or three days. They are represented to be reliable and well acquainted with the country east and south of your post.

Very respectfully, Sir,
Your obdt. serv't.

To Bvt. Lieut. Col. Wm Chapman   A. L. Anderson
Major 2nd Infantry   2nd Lieut. 5th Inf.
Comdg. Fort Union N.M.   A.A.A. Genl

Camp near Hatches Ranch
July 24th 1861

Colonel:

I enclose you copies of letters rec^d from the H^d Qrs. of the Department today.

The party out with the surveyor joined me on the 21st. The non-com officer in charge reports that they met with no Indians or Texans, and saw no signs of them. They went within thirty or forty miles of the boundary of Texas.

My Indian spies have not yet returned. I sent them out with the Indian women, giving them 15 days rations. They should have been back last night. Should they on their return report any thing of importance, I will inform you at once. No rumors of Indian depredations have reached me of late.

I am Sir

Colonel Wm Chapman   Respy. your obt. servt.
Commanding   E. Gay
Fort Union N.M.   Lt. 2nd Dragoons

[author's draft]
Hd. Qrs. Fort Union N.M.
July 26, 1861

Sir:

I enclose a copy of a letter received this morning from Lt. Gay 2nd Drag^s at Hatch's Ranch.

I have two parties of spies out at present. One, of two or three men in the employ of Mr. [William] Moore, our sutler, left Tecolote on the 24 inst., with instructions to follow down the Pecos River to the mouth of the Bonita and then ascend that stream to Fort Stanton. The other party of five, headed by the old Indian who accompanied Col. [George B.] Crittenden's expedition against the Comanches and Kioway's, has gone east on and to the south of the Cimarron route to the Arkansas.

I believe both of these parties are reliable, and I hope to receive accurate information on their return.

I am Sir
Very Respy, your obt. Servt.

Lt. A. L. Anderson 5" Inf.   Wm Chapman Major 2nd Inf. &
A.A.A. General   Bv. Lt. Col. U.S.A.
Hd. Qrs. Dept. of N.M. Santa Fe   Comg.
P.S. Capt. Duncan arrived at Fort Wise on the 19' Inst. I think my
Express overtook him there.

Yrs. Respy
Wm Chapman Bv. Lt. Col. U.S.A.

Camp near Hatches Ranch
July 28th 1861

Colonel:

The Pueblo scouts sent out with the Indian women got back today. They found a Comanche camp of about twenty lodges near the Canadian, 150 or 200 miles east of this. Nearly all of the Comanches are hunting Buffalo on the Arkansas; a small portion are camped somewhere on the Pecos. They told the Pueblo Indians that they did not wish any more war with Troops or Mexicans and that they would observe the treaty hereafter. They insist that they were invited in here by Mr. [Alexander] Hatch and that they thought it was all right.

As far as can be ascertained, there are no Texans en route for Fort Union. Should any come up the Pecos or cross the Canadian, the Comanche Indians have promised to inform me of it. I shall keep scouts out to the south and east.

I am Colonel

Colonel Wm Chapman   Resply. your Obt. Servt.
Commanding   E. Gay
Fort Union N.M.   Lt. 2nd Dragoons

Fort Union N.M.
July 31st 1861

Colonel.

I have the honor to report that, in obedience to instructions from Dept. Hd. Qrs. of the 30th June & Orders No. 41 dated Fort Union July 4th 1861, I left this post on the 7th Inst. in command of Cos. "D," "E" and "H," R.M.R., and Companies "A" & "B" 1st Regt. of N.M. Volunteers.

Proceeding as rapidly as practicable via "the Raton Route," we reached Fort Wise on the 19th Inst.

Having learned that six supply trains would reach the lower crossing about the 1st prox., I was about starting to meet them, when your letter of the 16th reached me by express on the morning of the 21st, and I immediately retraced my steps, reaching this post late yesterday afternoon.

Nothing unusual was seen or heard on the trip. Only a few Cheyenne & Arapahoe Indians were seen on the Arkansas, the most of the tribes being absent after Buffalo.

I am, Colonel, Very respectfully
Your obdt. servant
(signed)   Thomas Duncan

Col. Wm Chapman Maj. 2 Infty.   Capt. R.M.R.
Bvt. Lt. Col. U.S.A. Comdg. Fort Union   Comdg. Expedition

———————————— ➤•➤ ————————————

My dear Colonel.

A party of Col. Roberts' spies, from the Horse Head Crossing of the Pecos, came in to Fort Stanton on the 17 inst. At that time there were no Texans on the Pecos between the Crossing and the Fort.

Dr. [John M.] Whitlock has passed his examination and starts out this evening to relieve Dr. [O. W.] Blanchard. If Dr. [Sylvester] Rankin has got back, please advise him to come in at the same time. I hope that the Board will be able to get through this week, & it will probably be able to do so if Dr. Blanchard and Dr. Rankin come down by the stage.

We have no special news here.

Very truly
Yours &c.

Col. Wm Chapman   Ed. R. S. Canby
Comg. &c.
Fort Union   Santa Fe July 31, 1861

———————————— ➤•➤ ————————————

Head Qurs. Dept. New Mexico
Santa Fe N.M. July 31, 1861

Colonel:

An express has just been received from Major Lynde, reporting an engagement with the Texans near Fort Fillmore, in which the loss on our side was three privates killed, two officers (Lts. Brooks and McNally) and four privates wounded.

The express also brought a rumor that Major Lynde had abandoned and burned Fort Fillmore and was moving in the direction of Fort Stanton. I do not consider this rumor reliable but it is given for your information.

The company at Hatch's Ranch will come in at the expiration of its term or sooner if you think it necessary, and will not be replaced at present.

Very respectfully, Sir,
Your obdt. servt.

Col. Chapman   Ed. R. S. Canby
  Comdg. &c   Maj. 10 Infy. & C.
    Fort Union N.M.

———————— ◆ ————————

"A John Brown Song" (con't)
(*Quincy Daily Whig and Republican*, March 5, 1862)

John Brown was John the Baptist for the Christ we are to see,
Christ, who of the bondsman shall the Liberator be;
And soon throughout the sunny South the slaves shall all be free,
For his soul is marching on.
Chorus: Glory, Glory, Hallelujah! Glory, Glory, Glory, Hallelujah!
Glory, Glory, Hallelujah! His soul is marching on.

The conflict that he heralded he looks from Heaven to view,
On the army of the Union, with its flag red, white and blue;
And Heaven shall ring with anthems o're the deeds they mean to do,
For his soul is marching on.
Chorus: Glory, Glory, Hallelujah! &c.

Ye soldiers of Freedom, then strike while strike you may,
The death blow of oppression in a better time and way;
For the dawn of Old John Brown has brightened into day,
And his soul is marching on.
Chorus: Glory, Glory, Hallelujah! &c.

CHAPTER FOUR
Headquarters and Fort Union
Correspondence, August 1861
UNION CORRESPONDENCE

[author's draft]

Hd. Qrs. Fort Union Aug. 2' 1861

Sir

I have the honor to acknowledge the receipt of Col. Canby's communication of July 31' informing me of the engagement near Fort Fillmore between U.S. troops and Texans.

Col. Carson returned from Taos today and heard on the road a report as coming from Indian Traders among the Comanches, that a large force of white men were coming up the Canadian or Pecos Rivers in this direction. ~~The report says the force was about three miles long~~. I presume it is the same report that reached Capt. [Robert M.] Morris at Fort Craig. I have a party of spies ~~out~~ on ~~the Cimarron route~~ and to the South of ~~it~~ the Cimarron route, and tomorrow morning a party of six men from Capt. Vigil's Company will leave to examine the country along the Canadian. Col. Carson will give them instructions.

The order for Capt. Vigil to relieve Lt. Gay 2nd Drag^s at Hatch's Ranch was issued this morning but countermanded on the receipt of Col. Canby's letter. Lt. Gay had been directed to break up his Camp and return to this post. The detachment of "K" Co. R.M.R. which returned with Capt. Duncan leaves in the morning for Fort Stanton with a wagon containing ammunition for that post. An escort on foot to return with the wagon will accompany it. Col. Carson thinks if the Texans are coming he can collect in a few days Mexicans and Ute Indians sufficient to steal all their animals before they reach here. ~~I think it advisable to employ him for that purpose if time will permit~~.

I find the allowance of stationery insufficient for the use of this post. The stationery for the present quarter is nearly all expended & I ask for authority to draw a larger supply or such quantity as may be necessary for public purposes.

I understand from Col. Carson that a company of mounted volunteers will arrive here tomorrow from Taos under the expectation of being mustered into service for three years. I have no authority for mustering

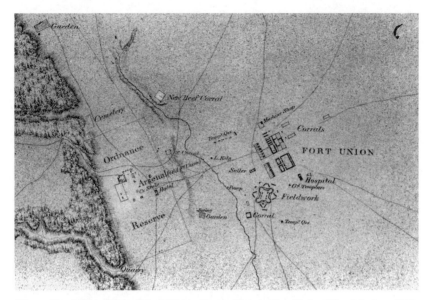

Fig. 4. Detail from Map of the Military Reservation at Fort Union, New Mexico, 1866. Courtesy of Museum of New Mexico, negative no. 180967.

them into service at all unless properly presented, which I am informed they will not be.

> I am Sir, most Respy, your obt. Servt.
> Wᵐ Chapman Major 2 Inf. &c.
> Comg.¹

> Head Quarters Dept. of New Mexico
> Santa Fe N.M. Aug. 2, 1861

Colonel:

The Lieut. Colonel Commanding directs me to inform you that an express just in from Fort Craig reports that Major Lynde has surrendered his whole command to 300 Texas troops. The Texans are said to be marching on Fort Stanton and Fort Craig. The report seems incredible but you will enroll and arm as many of the citizens in the neighborhood of your post as can be relied on. The volunteers will be employed in the position in which they can be most useful in the defense of the post, preferably in houses or behind walls. Keep the regular troops well in hand for emergencies.

Col. Canby desires you to advise him what measures you have taken and what additional measures you consider necessary for the security of your post which must be held at all hazards.

Very respectfully, Sir,
Your ob't. serv't.

To Col. Wm Chapman   A. L. Anderson
2nd Infantry   2nd Lieut. 5th Inf.
Comdg. Fort Union N.M.   A.A.A. Genl

———————————— ◆•◆ ————————————

[author's draft]
Hd. Qrs. Fort Union New Mexico
4½ P.M. Aug. 2, 1861

Sir:

I have just received yours of Aug. 2, 1861, informing me of Major Lynde's surrender of his whole command to 300 Texas troops. I will endeavor to enroll and arm all the reliable citizens in the neighborhood. I have taken no steps towards fortifying this post as I found upon examining the ground on the bluff in the rear of it, that I could not spare a sufficient force to defend any work I might erect there for its defense ~~of the post~~ that would not be commanded by higher ground in the rear and on both flanks. An enemy once in possession of the bluff in rear, would render this post untenable and in attempting to defend it, I should lose all the ordnance stores and provisions. I have determined to cross to the East Side of the creek out of range of field pieces & small arms & construct an entrenched camp with a bomb-proof magazine and store houses sufficient to contain all the stores. It will be necessary in case of an attack by a superior force to burn this post lest the enemy should get possession of it. Capt. [Cuvier] Grover will have charge of the working party on the entrenched camp and it will be pushed forward day and night to completion. I will defend it at all hazards ~~and as long as I have a man to pull a trigger~~. The men off duty have been drilling at Artillery for several days and are progressing very well. These drills will be continued daily. Lt. [Herbert M.] Enos sends tonight to Las Vegas for additional shovels to expedite our work. It will be necessary to have more tents as all the troops will have to encamp in the work.

These Mexican volunteers are more afraid of the Texans than they are of death, and in case of an attack by the latter, I cannot rely upon them. If I can use them in constructing the proper defenses and ~~get them in~~ station them behind entrenchments they may render good service.

Company "H" R.M.R. will leave for Albuquerque tomorrow morning pursuant to instructions from Dept. Hd. Qrs. of Aug. 2, 1861 and will use the transportation brought by "C" Co. 5' Inf. which arrived today, under command of Lt. [William] Nicodemus 5' Inf.

9 P.M. Dr. Bartholow arrived tonight with a message to Capt. [William] Shoemaker in relation to the ammunition for Fort Stanton which left here yesterday with an escort of fifteen men. An express leaves immediately to turn them back to Tecolote where they will meet Lt. Claflin's command and then proceed with him to Albuquerque.

I am Sir &c.

Lt. A. L. Anderson 5' Inf.   Wm Chapman Major 2' Inf. &c.
A.A.A. Genl.
Santa Fe

--------◆--------

Hd. Qs. Fort Union N.M.
August 3rd 1861

Sir.

Upon receipt of this you will immediately break up your camp at Hatch's Ranch and proceed to this Post with your command.

You will send your Pueblo Indian Spies and Guides in the direction of the Canadian Fork and direct them to report to the Commanding Officer of this Post on their return.

By order of B^vt Lt. Col. Chapman
Jno. R. Ritter

To 1st Lieut. E. Gay, 2nd Dragoons   2nd Lt. 5th Inf.
Hatch's Ranch, New Mexico.   Post Adjutant

--------◆--------

[author's draft]

Hd. Qrs. Fort Union N.M.
Aug. 5' 1861

Sir:

Since the Express left for Santa Fe this morning I learned from Col. Carson that a man of Capt. [Charles] Deus' Comp. encamped four miles from this post, saw two white men yesterday afternoon mounted on American horses which appeared to have been ridden hard, about one & a half or two miles northwest of the post with spy glasses examining the post and grounds in this vicinity. They remained about one hour and a half then galloped off. They questioned the man as to the No. of Companies &c. at this post.

Capt. Vigil and ~~his~~ Lieut. [Henry Clay] Pike went out with the man this morning to the point where the white men stood, discovered their tracks and picked up several pieces of ~~dried Buffalo meat~~ jerked beef. The Capt. returned and reported and the Lieut. followed their trail for seven miles he says. I have no doubt they were Texan Spies and sent in by some force not far distant. Col. Carson also thinks they are near at hand. I have heard nothing from my spies on the Cimarron route or Canadian. If we have time to entrench ~~ourselves~~ the command we can defend ourselves against a much superior force. I would prefer having a larger regular force.

In haste, I am Sir, Very Respy.

Lt. A. L. Anderson 5' Inf.   Your ob^t Servt.

A.A.A.G. Santa Fe   Wm Chapman Major 2' Inf. &

P.S. Lt. Claflin left this morning.

Head Quarters Dept. of New Mexico
Santa Fe N.M. Aug. 5, 1861

Sir:

I am instructed by the Colonel Commanding to acknowledge the receipt of your communication of the 2 inst.

The report in relation to the Texans coming up the Canadian or Pecos River is not regarded as probable but every preparation should of course be made to meet it.

Colonel Carson will be authorized to organize as large a party of Mexicans and Ute Indians as he may consider necessary. Please assign him to this duty at once.

The mounted volunteers that may be presented to you under Genl Orders (Dept.) No. 26 will be mustered into the service for six months. Should cavalry for 3 years be authorized hereafter this term can be extended.

The company you report as being on the way from Taos can be mustered in for six months.

The allowance of stationery will be increased to what is necessary for the use of your post.

Very respectfully, Sir
Your obdt. Servt.

Col. Wm Chapman 2 Inf.   A. L. Anderson

Comdg. Fort Union N.M.   2 Lt. 5 Inf. A.A.A. Genl

Hd. Qrs. Fort Union, New Mex°
Aug. 6' 1861

Colonel:

Pursuant to instructions from the Head Quarters Dept. of New Mexico of the 5' Instant, you and Capt. A. H. Pfeiffer of the 1' Regt. N. Mex. Foot Volunteers will proceed to Taos and Abiquiu respectively, and organize at those places as many Ute Indians and Mexicans as you may deem necessary for scouting, herding, &c. at this Post.

I am Colonel,
Very Respectfully
Your ob^t Servt,

Lieut. Colonel C. Carson   Wm Chapman Major 2' Inf. &
1' Regt. N.M. Foot Vol.   Bv. Lt. Col. U.S. Army
Present.   Comg. Fort Union

Head Quarters Dept. of New Mexico
Santa Fe N.M. Aug. 6, 1861

Sir:

I am instructed by the Col. Commanding to acknowledge the receipt of your communications of the 4th & 5th Insts. and to say that the means adopted & prepared by you are fully approved.

There are no tents in the Department that can be furnished but it is believed that very good temporary shelters can be made from the remains of the old fort.

If Albuquerque or Fort Craig should not be immediately threatened the Rifle company will be sent back to you. A train will be kept in readiness to send an infantry company from this place in wagons if the report with regard to the Texans be true.

An influential Mexican has been sent out this morning to stimulate the population between this and Fort Union and send you volunteers to fill up the companies at your post to their maximum. Should men present themselves organize them into companies for one or two months. Let them elect their officers subject to the approval of the Governor.

Instructions have been given to furnish fresh beef to the families of the Ute Indians that may be engaged by Col. Carson.

Very respectfully Sir
Your obdt. servt.

To Col. Wm Chapman 2 Inf.   A. L Anderson
Comdg. Fort Union N.M.   2nd Lt. 5 Inf. A.A.A. Genl

Dear Colonel:

Col. Roberts has instructions to abandon Fort Stanton as soon as he considers it expedient. Please send an express after the wagon with the ammunition to advise them of this fact. Send some intelligent Mexicans of Vigil's company who can go in advance and ascertain the state of affairs at Stanton. Col. Roberts may need the ammunition if the post has not been abandoned. If it has been, the party should make the best of its way back to Fort Union.

Do not spare any expense to any arrangements that you consider necessary for defense or obtaining information. Advise me constantly of any thing that way[?] and of the state of your preparations.

In haste

Col Wm Chapman	Very truly
2nd Infantry	Yours &
Comg. Fort Union N.M.	Ed. R. S. Canby
[Jacket] Rec^d 12½ P.M. Aug. 7, 1861	

Head Quarters Dept. of New Mexico
Santa Fe N.M. Aug. 6, 1861

Colonel:

An express was received this morning from Col. Roberts advising me that he had abandoned Fort Stanton and was marching for Albuquerque, expecting to arrive there tomorrow or the next day. This movement renders the march of Lieut. Claflin unnecessary and instructions have accordingly been sent to him to return to Fort Union.

If you should be threatened by any force before your entrenchments or storehouses are completed, the trains that may arrive should not be unloaded, as the wagons will not only serve for storage but may be of service to you for defense purposes.

Urge the organization of the Utes as rapidly as possible and if any of them are in the immediate neighborhood of your post ask Col. Carson to send them out as spies and to annoy and cripple the Texans by driving off their animals. The mounted volunteers may be usefully employed for this purpose.

I am surprised to learn that additional public trains are coming in. No information has been received of any but those that you have reported. Invoices of the Quartermaster's supplies were received by the last mail but they had then only been started (from) Leavenworth and it is understood with a strong escort.

No further news from the South.

Very respectfully, Sir
Your obdt. servt.

Col. Wm Chapman 2nd Inftry.	Ed. R. S. Canby
Comg. Fort Union	Col. 19. Infy. Comg.

[author's draft]

Hd. Qrs. Fort Union N.M.

Aug. 7, 1861

Sir:

I received at 12 1/2 last night yours of Aug. 5, 1861, and a note from Col. Canby (no date) relative to instructions to Col. Roberts to abandon Ft. Stanton &c.

Col. Carson and Capt. Pfeiffer leave to day, for Taos and Abiquiu respectfully to collect some Ute Indians. Col. Carson thinks 100 will be sufficient for his purposes and will go out with them in person. He informs me the only terms upon which he can engage them will be to feed their families in their absence as they will not go to Ft. Garland. I have authorized him to purchase flour and beef for them at Taos at as cheap rates as possible. I request the Commander of the Dept. to address an order to that effect to Col. Carson at Taos where he will receive it after collecting his Indians.

A party of Capt. Vigil's Company under Lt. Pike will leave this morning to approach cautiously as near as they can do with safety for Fort Stanton to examine the country in that direction and ascertain whether it had been abandoned; and if not, by whom occupied. I have mounted pickets out five or six miles from the post on the North, East and South, occupying prominent points for their lookouts, from which they have extensive can see a large extent of country.

We are working about 200 men every four hours day and night on the entrenchments. They are progressing very well, and in (a) day or two more it will be sufficiently advanced for defense. Capt. Grover and Lt. Nicodemus alternate in directing the work. I have heard nothing from the Spies on the Cimarron and Canadian routes.

I am Sir, very Respectfully

Your ob^t Servt.

Lt. A. L. Anderson   Wm Chapman Bv. Lt. Col. Comg.

Head Quarters Dept. of New Mexico

Santa Fe N.M. Aug. 7, 1861

Sir:

I am instructed by the Colonel Commanding to acknowledge the receipt of your communication of the 4th inst. and to say in reply that there is at present no legal authority to issue clothing to the volunteers, but as they probably have not the means of purchasing, he has directed the Chief Quartermaster to purchase and send to Fort Union immediately a supply that will be sufficient for their present wants.

This clothing issued to the volunteers will be charged to them on the Muster Rolls of their companies under instructions that will be given by the Chief Quartermaster.

Col. Canby is much gratified with the favorable account given of the progress of the volunteers and he hopes that they will soon be in such an effective condition as to be able to give a good account of any enemy whatever.

Very respectfully, Sir,
Your obdt. servt.
A. L. Anderson
2nd Lieut. 5 Inf.
A.A.A. Genl

To Lt. Col. C. Carson
1st Regt. N.M. Vols.
Fort Union N.M.   Thro' C.O. Ft. Union

Head Quarters Dept. of New Mexico.
Santa Fé, August 8, 1861.

Circular.

The writ of Habeas Corpus has been suspended in order to enable every Commander to guard against the treasonable designs of persons disloyal to the Government of the United States, particularly Agents and Spies, persons engaged in furnishing information to, or in other treasonable correspondence with the Enemy, or in inciting insurrection or rebellion.

Care will be taken to guard against any abuse of this power by unauthorized Arrests, or by Annoyances to peaceable and well disposed Citizens, and except in the Case of Overt Acts, Arrests will only be made by the Superior Commander of every District, Post, or body of Troops in the service of the United States, and only upon probable cause of Suspicion of being dangerous to the public safety.

When Arrests are made the person Arrested will immediately be examined, and if there be no grounds for Suspicion will be released. If otherwise, held in confinement until his Case is disposed of by the proper Authorities. If there be evidence of treason or misprision of treason, he will be turned over to the Civil Courts for trial.

In the execution of these duties the troops will at all times unite with, and assist the Civil Authorities in maintaining order throughout the Country.

By order of Colonel E. R. S. Canby,
A. L. Anderson
2nd Lieut. 5th. Infantry.
A.A.A. General

Fort Union

Head Quarters Dept. of New Mexico
Santa Fe N.M. Aug. 9, 1861

Sir:

The Colonel Commanding directs me to acknowledge the receipt of your communication of the 7th inst. and informs you that orders have been given to issue provisions to the families of the Ute Indians in the service of the United States, and that further orders will soon be given for effecting this object.

Very respectfully, Sir
Your obdt. servt.
A. L. Anderson
2nd Lieut. 5th Inf.
A.A.A. Gen[l]

To Col W[m] Chapman 2nd Inf.
Comdg. Fort Union N.M

———————— ➤✦◄ ————————

[author's draft]
Head Qrs. Fort Union N.M. 11 AM. Aug. 10, 1861

Colonel:

I have just received an express from Col. Canby urging the organization of the Utes, to be sent immediately to annoy and follow the movements of the Texans, and if possible drive off their animals.

Col. Roberts has abandoned Fort Stanton and moved to Albuquerque agreeably to his orders. Collect and come on with your Ute Indians as soon as possible, and send word to Capt. Pfeiffer to do the same. No other news.

Yours very truly
W[m] Chapman Major 2nd Inf & Bv.
Lt. Col. U.S. Army

Col. C. Carson 1' Regt. N.M. Vols.
Taos N. Mexico

["A true Copy"]

Ute Village Sunday evening

Col:

I have the honor to acknowledge the receipt of your note of the 10' Inst. and in reply beg to state that I am using every exertion. I will leave here in the morning with all that can be spared from the village, say about 30. I have not time to call at the other villages or probably I might get more. Capt. Pfeiffer I know nothing about, and cannot therefore send to him. Having to call at Maxwell's to purchase some provisions for the families of those who accompany me, I shall not be able to reach the post sooner than Tuesday forenoon.

You must excuse the necessity which obliged me to send back your own letter, as I have no paper with me.

I am Colonel Very Respectfully
C. Carson

To Bv. Lt. Col. Wm Chapman Major 2' Inf.   Lt. Col. N.M.V.
Comg. Fort Union N.M.

A true Copy
Wm Chapman Bv. Lt. Col. U.S.A.

Head Quarters Dept. of New Mexico
Santa Fe N.M. Aug. 10, 1861

Sir:

A Mexican trading with the Comanches reports having seen a body of Texans on the Red River below the mouth of Utah Creek, about 60 or 70 miles south east of Hatches Ranch. The rumor is not considered reliable but the Colonel Commanding directs me to communicate it for your information.

A party of Pueblo Indians will be sent out this morning to examine the country in that direction. If they should discover any thing important they will be instructed to communicate it to you as well as to these Head Quarters.

Very respectfully Sir
Your obdt. servt.
A. L. Anderson

To Col. Wm Chapman   2nd Lieut. 5 Inf.
Comdg. Fort Union N.M.   A.A.A. Genl

Indian Superintendency
Santa Fé N. Mex. August 11th 1861

Sir,

Before this reaches you, most likely, you will have heard of the abandonment of Fort Fillmore and the surrender of the entire command of some six hundred federal troops under Col. [*sic*] Lynde, to a force of three hundred and twenty Texas Volunteers. The particulars of this treacherous and cowardly transaction reached us yesterday, and leaves no longer a doubt of its truth. The officers and men we understand have been released on parole and are now en route for this place.

In consequence of this surrender, Fort Stanton has also been abandoned, thus closing all chance for our agents to continue their management of the southern Apaches. This will make but little difference except as regards the Mescaleros. The most of that band were friendly and receiving rations, but in consequence of the removal of the troops from Stanton we may be unable to continue an agent at that Post. Indeed I have already heard that the Indians had left the neighborhood of the Agency, and it was thought with the intention of joining the discontented part of the band.

The Indians on the Gila are all hostile and as the troops have been withdrawn from that part of the territory there will be but little restraint upon them. The Indians near Tucson, the Pimas, Maricopas and Papagos, must remain without an agent until the troops can again be stationed in that quarter.

Previous to this difficulty, I had sent to the Mesilla a lot [of] farming implements for the last mentioned Indians. These implements were still in the Mesilla, no opportunity having offered to forward them on to Tucson. They will doubtless fall into the hands of the Texans as property belonging to the United States. This will be the case also with some other property belonging to the Agency of Doctor Michael Steck.

It is my intention to send Agent Labadi to the Stanton Agency if I find he can remain there with safety. The Indians of that Agency are in a position to do much mischief if left without some control, either by the troops or the Agent.

I still entertain the hope that it is not the intention of the Government to surrender, without a further struggle, the southern part of this Territory. It should be recovered and held at whatever cost. For this it will be necessary to send out more troops, at least four or five Regiments. With that force, with what we have now here, we could not only retake Forts Fillmore and Bliss, but we could aid in retaking Texas when the Gov⁺ forces move in that direction.

Very respectfully
Your obt. servt.

Hon. Wm. P. Dole   J. L. Collins
Commissioner of Indian Affairs   Sup. Ind. Affs.
Washington City   N. Mex.²

———————————•◆•———————————

Head Quarters Dept. of New Mexico
Santa Fe N.M. Aug. 13, 1861

Sir:

 I am instructed to inform you that the Governor has appointed José

Guadalupe Gallegos of San Miguel, Colonel, José Maria Chaves of Abiquiu Lieut. Colonel, Manuel Baca of Socorro and Joseph Cumming of Santa Fe, Majors of the regiment of New Mexican Mounted Volunteers.

It is expected that four of these companies will be presented at Fort Union and the others at Albuquerque and this place. The time of service of the regiment will be six months. One of the majors (Cumming) will be mustered into the service as soon as one squadron is organized, the Lieut. Colonel as soon as two squadrons are organized, and the Colonel and second major when the organization of the regiment is completed. The mounted companies that have already been mustered in will be incorporated in the regiment if the men consent to extend their term of service. Major Baca will probably be mustered in at Albuquerque and notice will be given you when the Colonel will be mustered in.

It is the intention of the Colonel Commanding that two of these companies under the command of a field officer should be employed in the country east of Hatches Ranch with their depot in the neighborhood of that place, that it should draw its supplies from Fort Union in the manner that has heretofore obtained with the detachments operating in that neighborhood.

As soon as you can spare a volunteer force for that purpose you will reestablish the system that has just been suspended, instructing the Commanding Officer to keep his scouts constantly in the field and to extend their operations to the Canadian and Red River on the East and down the Pecos far enough to give timely warning of the approach of troops from either quarter. Instruct him also to endeavor to establish friendly relations with the Comanches and induce them to bring in information of any movements on the plains.

The scouts and spies from Fort Union should be kept constantly in the field watching every route by which the Territory can be invaded, or your post threatened.

I enclose communications for the Commanding Officer at Forts Wise and Larned which the Colonel Commanding desires may be forwarded by express to Fort Wise.

> Very respectfully, Sir,
> Your obdt. serv't,
> A. L. Anderson

To Col. Wm Chapman 2nd Inf.   2nd Lieut. 5 Inf.
Comdg. Fort Union N.M.   A.A.A. Genl

[author's draft]

Fort Union N.M. Aug 16, 1861

Col:

A reliable man of Mr Moore's who was sent as a spy to Ft. Stanton returned in the night and reported to me at 3 1/2 this morning that the Texans to the number of about 400 men were in possession of Ft. Stanton without artillery, and that about 25 of them with pack mules were on their way in this direction. I wish you would send the Ute Indians to watch and annoy this party. If Col. Carson will give them instructions & a reliable man in whom they have confidence can be found to accompany them, I doubt not the expedition will result favorably.

I have to request that this may be kept as quiet as possible. It is advisable that the whole of the volunteer force should be kept close in hand and none of the men permitted to leave camp except for necessary purposes. The work of course on the entrenchments will go on as usual.

I am Col. very Respect^y

Col. C. St. Vrain   Your ob^t Servt.

Comg. Reg^t N.M. Vols.   Wm Chapman Bv. Lt. Col. U.S.A.

Present   Comg.

[author's draft]

Hd. Qrs. Fort Union N.M.

6½ AM. Aug. 16' 1861

Sir:

A reliable man of Mr Moore's sent as a spy to Fort Stanton returned at 3 ½ this morning and reports that Post in possession of about 400 Texans without artillery and that about 25 of them with pack mules are coming up this way. I have requested Col. St. Vrain to send out the Utes to watch and annoy this party, under some reliable men in whom they have confidence.

The Commander of the Dept. I presume is aware that Colonel St. Vrain and Lt. Col^o. Carson are both present and are my seniors in rank. I have ceased to issue orders to the volunteers under their command and transact all my business with them by requests which have been promptly complied with thus far. They continue to send the morning report of the Regt. to me and it is consolidated with that of the regular Command. I do not anticipate any difficulty with these gentlemen on account of rank, but something might occur to require the presence of a Superior.

Col. St. Vrain informed Lt. Enos that quarters can be had at Mora for the accommodation of the women and children if it is necessary to remove them.

The man left Stanton early Wednesday night.

I am Sir very Respectfully
Your ob^t Servt.

Lt. A. L. Anderson 5' Inf.   Wm Chapman Major 2' Inf. &
A.A.A. Genl. Santa Fe   Bv. Lt. Col. U.S.A. Comg.

[author's draft]

Hd. Qrs. Fort Union N.M.
August 16, 1861

Sir:

You will escort with "D" Co. R.M.R. as far as Bernal Springs or San José if necessary a wagon which leaves this post today for Santa Fe. Should you meet a company of the 5' Inf. before reaching Bernal Springs and they report the road clear, let the wagon proceed to Santa Fe with the escort of three men on foot who go with it from this post. You will then turn off with your mounted command with pack mules in the direction of Fort Stanton with the view of cutting off a scouting party of Texans known to be en route from Fort Stanton in the direction of this post. The Qr. Master will send with the troops four pack saddles to be used with your team mules after leaving your wagon in some safe place.

Capt. Pfeiffer leaves to day with the Utes in the direction of Fort Stanton with the same (verbal) instructions. I mention this to place you on your guard in case you should meet that party in your route.

It is advisable not to follow the road after leaving your wagon, but to travel in sight of it so that no party on it can escape your observation. When you camp at night keep a constant watch upon the road.

Your command will take ten days rations.

I am sir very Respectfully
Your ob^t Servt.

Lieut. Jos. G. Tilford   Wm Chapman Major 2' Inf. &
Comg. "D" Co. R.M.R. Present   Bv. Lt. Col. U.S. Army Comg.

Hd. Qrs. Fort Union New Mex°
August 17, 1861

Sir:

After the express left yesterday with my letter in relation to the occupation of Fort Stanton by Texans, I detached Lt. J. G. Tilford in command of "D" Co. R.M.R. to escort the ammunition wagon for Santa Fe as far as

Bernal Springs or San José if necessary, then to turn off in the direction of Fort Stanton & endeavor to intercept the Texan scouting party known to be coming in the direction of this post. Lt. Tilford took ten days rations with him, but I think will not be absent beyond seven or eight days.

A supply train of 26 wagons loaded principally with bacon arrived at 6 ½ this morning. There is another train about fifteen miles behind which I expect in to day. This last I am informed is loaded with whiskey, molasses &c. The wagon master already arrived reports several other trains loading when he left.

I have to acknowledge the receipt of S.O. N° 118 and Col° Canby's letter dated Hd. Qrs. Dept. N. Mex° Santa Fe Aug. 14, 1861.

We have not been able as yet to erect store houses. The work on those laid out adjoining the old ones was suspended as soon as it was found necessary to employ the whole force of the Command in the defenses of the post.

The Field Work now under construction when completed would be well suited for an Ordnance Depot and if this post is to be continued it would be advisable to rebuild it near the Field Work, where temporary store houses might be commenced at once.

I am Sir very Respectfully
Your ob^t Servt.

Lt. A. L. Anderson 5' Inf.   Wm Chapman Major 2' Inf. &
A.A.A. Genl.   Bv. Lt. Col° U.S. Army Comg.

Head Quarters Dept. of New Mexico
Santa Fe N.M. Aug. 17, 1861.

Sir:

I am instructed by the Colonel Commanding to enclose for your information a copy of a report from the Commanding Officer at Fort Union.

In addition to this the Colonel Commanding has no doubt that an invasion of the Territory will be attempted from the Arkansas frontier or the Indian nation if the Confederate troops are not so fully employed at home as to prevent it. They are now threatening our trains on the Arkansas, as he has no doubt is a part of their general plan. It is for this reason that he wishes the regular troops to be kept well in hand in order that they may be concentrated as rapidly as possible.

Fort Craig will eventually be held by volunteer troops if they can be raised, but his doubts on this point are so strong that he does not wish to accumulate supplies at that post beyond the immediate wants of the troops to be stationed there. He has already expressed the wish that the troops under your command should be encumbered with as little baggage as possible, in order that they may be moved as rapidly as possible to any point that may be threatened.

The garrison of Fort Craig will eventually be 6 companies of foot and four of mounted volunteers and as fast as they can be raised he wishes the regular companies withdrawn and placed in reserve near Albuquerque or sent to Fort Union as they can be spared.

If an invasion from the East is attempted it is his intention to concentrate all the regular troops for the purpose of resisting that invasion, and leave the defense of the lower portion of the country to the volunteers and National Guard.

Fort Union is now entrenched and will be able to resist attack by a very superior force but it will be necessary to weaken its garrison in order to protect the trains en route to that post and he desires that you will put as many of your companies in march for that post as can be spared or have been replaced by volunteers.

Is there any hope that the Mexican population in your district will organize for defense or take any steps to resist an invasion of their country?

Very respectfully Sir
Your obdt. servt.

To Lt. Col. B. S. Roberts   A. L. Anderson
Comdg. Sout^n Mil. Dist.   2nd Lieut. 5 Inf.
Fort Craig N.M.[3]   A.A.A. Genl

Head Quarters Dept. of New Mexico
Santa Fe N.M. Aug. 17, 1861

Colonel:

Your communications of the 15th and 16th have been received, and I am instructed by the Colonel Commanding to say that it is presumed that all the regular troops that arrive at Fort Union will be provided with tents. It is known that supplies of camp equipage are on the way out but on what part of the road has not yet been ascertained. Until they arrive it will be necessary for the troops to bivouac under such temporary shelter as can be provided. All the surplus clothing and camp equipage on hand in the Department has been ordered to Fort Union.

The command of Fort Union will not be changed by the organization of the volunteer regiments as the officers will not be on duty with that intention. Of course if the whole command is engaged in any combined operations the senior must command. The officers of the regular army will be assigned to duty according to their brevet rank which will remove to some extent the difficulties in the way of command.

It is believed that the party of Texans coming up the country from Fort Stanton will endeavor to intercept some of the trains. It is known from Mr. Perrin that at least three of the trains have taken the route by the Cimarron. The Colonel Commanding wishes that every exertion should be made to protect these trains, but without reducing your command below what is necessary to place the defense of Fort Union upon a sure footing. The Utes and Spies and Guides should be kept out in all directions and every means used to harass and retard their approach.

The Colonel Commanding desires that he may be advised daily or oftener of every thing of interest in your neighborhood.

Very respectfully, Sir
Your obd't. serv't.
A. L. Anderson

To Lt. Col. Wm Chapman 2 Inf.   2nd Lieut. 5 Inf.
Comdg. Fort Union N.M.   A.A.A. Genl

Head Quarters Dept. of New Mexico
Santa Fe N.M. Aug. 19, 1861

Colonel:

Your note of the [blank] has just been received. I wish you would take some occasion to say to Col. St. Vrain that all communications addressed to a common superior in relation to military affairs should be sent through his immediate commander. The matters of his communications have long since been full[y] represented to the Head Quarters by reports and by an officer (Capt. [R. A.] Wainwright) sent expressly for that purpose. With the exception of the paroled troops I do not propose to send the regular troops out of the country while it is threatened with invasion or until the best possible arrangements for its defense have been made. I have not much faith in the disposition of the Mexicans to second us in this matter but will do whatever I can to rouse them and put the Territory in the best possible position for defense.

I am now sending Commissioners to every part of the Territory in the hope of filling up the regiments and companies that have been called for, and completing the organization of the Home Guard and Militia.

Please send me as soon as you can a plan of your entrenchment with a statement of its capacity and the strength of the garrison that will be required to place its security beyond question. This exclusive of four or five companies that will be kept at the post for service on the plains.

Very respectfully &

Col. Wm Chapman   Ed. R. S. Canby
19 [sic] Infantry Cmg. Fort Union   Cmdg.

[author's draft]
Hd. Qrs. Fort Union N.M. Aug. 20, 1861

Sir:

A party of Mnt^d Volunteers sent down, and beyond the Pecos, returned today. They say they went to the Sierra Gallina ninety some miles from Anton Chico, and sixty five from Fort Stanton. They saw no Texans, nor trails of them or any body of men, and every thing was quiet on their route.

As the Mnt^d Volunteers are now held for service on the plains, I shall be compelled to employ as Spies &c. such Mexicans as can be hired in this neighborhood, and who can come recommended by some reliable persons known to the officers of this Post. As soon as Capt. Pfeiffer returns with the Indians they will be divided into several parties to scour the country in all directions and watch the movements of any force that may approach the post.

There appears to be a regular system of expresses between Santa Fe and the volunteer camp here, and I frequently hear news from the volunteer officers some hours, or even a day before it is communicated through the official channels.

Major [J. Francisco] Chaves received the news by mail of the capture of his train between his ranch near the gold mines in the vicinity of Stanton and Albuquerque, and of a company of militia (unarmed) by the Texans. I presume by "company of militia unarmed" his informer meant his employees and others who accompanied his train on their way to Albuquerque.

I am Sir, very Respectfully, your ob^t Servt.
Wm Chapman, Major 2' Inf. &
Bv. Lt. Col. U.S. Army Comdg.

Lt. A. L. Anderson 5. Inf.
A.A.A. Genl. Santa Fe

[author's draft]
Hd. Qrs. Fort Union N. Mex° Aug. 20, 1861

Sir

Can you furnish me with a form of the Muster Roll for Field and Staff of a volunteer Reg^t and if not, please inform me whether the ages of the officers and the valuation of their horses and equipments should be stated on the Rolls. I wish the form of the Certificate for the Mustering Officer.

A man named Thompson from Anton Chico informed Lt. Pike Mnt^d Vols. yesterday, that about 1000 Texans were seen on the Pecos by some Mexican shepherds eighty miles below Anton Chico. I had no opportunity of gaining any further information from Thompson as he had left the Post before the report was made to me.

A train of 7 wagons from Albuquerque and Anton Chico arrived this morning. The wagon master reports another of the wagons behind on the same road.

I have to acknowledge the receipt of Sp. Orders No. 122 Hd. Qrs. Dept. N.M. Aug. 18, 1861.

Capt. Duncan's Command left at 9½ A.M. for Fort Wise.

I am Sir very Respectfully your ob^t Servt.
Wm Chapman Major 2' Inf. &
Bv. Lt. Col. U.S.A. Comg.

———◄►———

Head Quarters Dept. of New Mexico,
Santa Fe August 20, 1861

Circular

The Commissioners sent into the different parts of the Territory are authorized to enroll and send to the most convenient Military Station the Volunteer recruits that are required to fill up the Companies of the several regiments that have been called into the service of the United States. The Mustering Officers at Fort Union, Fort Marcy, Albuquerque, Fort Craig and Fort Garland will accordingly muster into the service in the manner prescribed by Dept. General Orders No. 21 of July 17, 1861, any volunteer recruits that may be presented to them for the Infantry or Cavalry Companies. If the Volunteers for the 1st and 2nd Infantry Regiments are not enrolled for particular Companies they will be assigned by the Regimental Commander, or by the Post Commanders where detached Companies are serving, to the weakest Companies of their respective Commands.

Mounted Companies that may be presented at Fort Union, Fort Marcy, Albuquerque or Fort Craig will at once be mustered into the Service and organized into Squadrons and Regiments. The Field Officers will be designated and mustered in as the organization of the Regiment progresses, and in the manner directed by General Orders No. 15, of May 4, 1861.

The term of the Mounted Companies will be for six months and as soon as mustered in they will be armed and equipped for immediate service.

By order of Colonel E. R. S. Canby,
A. L. Anderson
2nd Lieut. 5th Infantry
A.A.A. General

Fort Union

Head Quarters Dept. of New Mexico
Santa Fe N.M. Aug. 21, 1861

Colonel:

The man Thompson referred to in your letter of yesterday is understood to be a Secessionist and is probably a spy. While it is desirable to secure information from all sources it is believed that many reports are put in circulation for sinister purposes, and with a view to retard the organization of the volunteer companies and discourage the Mexicans from attempting to organize for the defense of their country. All persons engaged in opposing either directly or indirectly any of the measures of the government should be regarded as dangerous and arrested or removed.

It is believed that Thompson, Giddings and Stewart have been engaged in the circulation of these reports and in opposing the organization of the volunteers, either for selfish purposes of their own or for the purpose of opposing the Government. In either case they should be looked after and quieted by arrest or removed from the Country.

Very respectfully Sir
Your obdt. Servt.

Col. W[m] Chapman
Comg. &c & Fort Union

Ed. R. S. Canby
Col. 19 Inf. Comg.

[author's draft]
Hd. Qrs. Fort Union New Mex°
Aug. 22 1861

Sir:

Captain A. H. Pfeiffer and the Ute Indians returned yesterday. They took the direction of Hatch's Ranch, made a thorough examination of the country to the south and east of that point & crossed all the trails leading from there to Fort Union, Anton Chico and Santa Fe, in the hope of discovering the trail of the scouting party of Texans reported to be coming in the direction of this post, but saw no signs whatever of them.

Capt. Pfeiffer reports numerous herds of cattle and sheep grazing to the east and south of Hatch's Ranch, which have been drawn in from the Red River and other distant grazing grounds.

The Utes will be sent out again, to examine the country below the road from Anton Chico to Albuquerque, much traveled of late by the trains coming to that post.

Capt. Grover is preparing a plan of the Field Work laid out and constructed under his superintendence, which will be forwarded when completed. The tents of "A" Co. 5' Inf. were destroyed at Fort Stanton. They are now occupying those of "G" Co. 2' Drags.

The transportation of Capt. Duncan's Command and that called for by the four companies of volunteers now ready for service on the plains will necessarily retard our work to a considerable extent. We have mules and harness, but not enough wagons.

I am Sir very Respy, your ob^t Servt.
Wm Chapman Major 2' Inf. &

Lt. A. L. Anderson A.A.A. Genl.   Lt. Col. Comg.

P.S. 11 A.M. Aug. 22, 1861. Col. Carson has just informed me that the Ute Indians have all gone home. He says nothing would induce them to stay. Sickness in the chief's family is the cause assigned for their departure. Upon seeing a party of Indians moving up the valley from the volunteers camp, I called upon Col. Carson to know if his Indians had left the camp, and for what purpose, when he gave me the above information.

I am Sir very Respectfully
Your ob^t Servt.
Wm Chapman Bv. Lt. Col. U.S.A.
Comg.

Head Quarters Dept. of New Mexico
Santa Fe N.M. Aug. 22, 1861

Sir;

The Department Commander directs me to inform you that you are authorized to employ spies for the purpose indicated in one of your communications of the 20" inst.

Your respectfully Sir
Your obdt. serv't
A. L. Anderson
2nd Lieut. 5 Inf.

To Lt. Col. Wm Chapman
Comdg. Fort Union N.M.   A.A.A. Genl

Santa Fe August 23ʳᵈ 1861
Col. Chapman
Fort Union
Sir.

Will you please inform me as early as possible, at what time the Government train that left Fort Leavenworth July 22ⁿᵈ will probably reach Union.

That train contains some seventy boxes of clothing &c. for the Volunteers, and I desire them to stop at that post.

If any thing should prevent my arrival at Ft. Union before the trains, I desire that you should stop that portion of it.

You can perhaps ascertain from the train that preceded it a few days, when the other will arrive, and I will meet it accordingly.

By addressing me here when you obtain information in regard to the train of which I speak, you will confer a favor upon

> Your Obt. Svt.
> E. O. Perrin
> Special Agt. U.S.
> for New Mexico.

[author's draft]
> Hd. Qrs. Fort Union N. Mexico
> Aug. 23,' 1861

Sir:

By the express which arrived this morning between 5 & 6 o'clock I received your letters (2) of the 22' and Col. Canby's communication of the 21' inst. I am hourly expecting some Mexicans from Mora and vicinity to be employed for the purpose indicated in my letter of the 20' Inst.

From conversations with some of the volunteer officers I find I can organize a permanent party of twenty or twenty-five Mounted Men, from the 1. Regt. N.M. Vols. to be employed as Spies &c., who will furnish their own horses for the allowance granted to mounted men for their use. A party thus organized would be less expensive, quite as reliable as any Mexicans I can engage for such purposes, and would be more under my control.

> I am Sir very Respectfully,
> Your obᵗ Servt.

Lieut. A. L. Anderson 5 Inf.   Wᵐ Chapman Major 2' Inf. &
A.A.A. Genl. Santa Fe N.M.   Bv. Lt. Col. U.S.A. Comg.

[author's draft]

Hd. Qrs. Fort Union New Mex°

Aug. 24, 1861

Sir:

I have to report the departure this morning of four companies (3 foot, [Francisco] Abreu's, [Antonio?] Sena's & ~~Deus~~'s Pfeiffer's; Vigil's mounted) under the command of Lt. Col. C. Carson 1' Reg^t N.M. Vols. for the protection of the Government trains on the Cimarron route.

Captain Vigil's Company of Mounted Volunteers have declined to extend their time to six months. The Captain says he can raise a company of six months men at the expiration of his present term of service. His men have become dissatisfied from a report made by one Manuel Garcia of Santa Fe to the effect that they are not to be paid by the U.S. Govt. from the funds of the Territory.

Three parties of Mexicans left before daylight this morning for the Red & Pecos Rivers and the country to the south of the road from Anton Chico to Albuquerque.

The men and horses of the Mounted Companies at this post are unequally distributed, some companies having more men than horses and others the reverse. As there seems to be a doubt whether recruits will arrive this season to fill up the companies, a transfer of horses from one company to another, would increase the efficiency of the mounted force of this Command.

Corpl. Clark and six privates for Capt. Abreu's Co. 1' Regt. N.M. Vols. arrived this morning from Santa Fe.

I am Sir very Respectfully

Your obt. Servt.

Lieut. A. L. Anderson 5' Inf.   Wm Chapman Major 2 Inf. &

A.A.A. Genl. Santa Fe N.M.   Bv. Lt. Col. U.S. Army Comg.

Head Quarters Dept. of New Mexico

Santa Fe N.M. Aug. 24, 1861

Sir:

I am instructed by the Department Commander to enclose to you the accompanying copy of a communication from Col. Roberts and to inform you that a party of spies and guides who are represented to be well acquainted with the country east and south of Fort Union will be sent to you to replace the Utes.

Colonel Canby desires to know whether a mixed company of Mexicans and Ute or Pueblo Indians with Pfeiffer at the head can be organized.

> Very respectfully, Sir
> Your obdt. servt.
> A. L. Anderson

To Lt. Col. Wm Chapman 2 Inf.   2nd Lieut. 5 Inf.
Comdg. Fort Union N.M.   A.A.A. Genl

> Hd. Qrs. Dept. of New Mexico
> Santa Fe N.M. Aug. 24, 1861

Captain Phillips with his party of Spies and Guides will proceed without delay to Fort Union N.M. and report for duty to the Commanding Officer at that post.

> [Signed]   E. R. S. Canby Col° 19. Inf.
> Comg. Dept.

(A true copy)
Wm Chapman Bv. Lt. Colo. U.S.A.

> Capt. Philips
> Comg. Spy Company

> [author's draft]
> Hd. Qrs. Fort Union N.M. Aug. 25' 1861

Sir:

I have to acknowledge the receipt of the following communications viz: (Extract) Sp. orders No. 127 and Sp. orders No. 125 Hd. Qrs. Dept. N.M. Santa Fe Aug 24, 1861.

Letter   Hd. Qrs. Dept. N.M. Santa Fe Aug. 23, 1861.

do (with a copy of Col. Roberts' communication of Aug. 20) Dept. N.M. Santa Fe Aug. 24, 1861.

Lieut. A. B. Carey 7' Inf. and Mr. Bill [sp?] his clerk arrived yesterday. Lieut. Carey will immediately relieve Lt. Enos in the duties of A.C. Subsistence at this post.

In reporting the departure of Col. Carson's Command yesterday I mentioned Capt. Deus' as one of the Foot Companies. It should have been Pfeiffer's. I was not aware that a change had been made until after the express left for Santa Fe.

A sergeant and eight mounted volunteers returned from the Red River yesterday. They were gone ten days and reached a point on that river called Jacinta which is represented to be only about sixty-five or seventy miles from here. They saw nothing of course.

I hope the Spies and Guides to arrive from Santa Fe will be more reliable men ~~and worthy of the confidence~~ who will follow my instructions more closely.

I will inquire what prospect there is of organizing a mixed company of spies and guides from Mexicans and Indians.

Lt. Tilford with "D" Co. R.M.R. returned from his scout in the direction of Fort Stanton. I will forward his report by express tomorrow.

~~I feel greatly the want of a correct map of this Territory. The one I have~~

Please inform me if Sergt. Cordua's application for discharge was received at your office.

[Lt. Col. Wm Chapman?]

Head Quarters Dept. of New Mexico
Santa Fe N.M. Aug. 25, 1861

Sir:

I have the honor to acknowledge the receipt of your communication of the 24th inst.

I am instructed by the Colonel Commanding to say that the Volunteer troops in New Mexico have been called into the service of the United States and will be paid by the United States.

The Chief Quartermaster will be instructed to direct the proper distribution of the cavalry horses at Fort Union.

Very respectfully, Sir
Your obdt. servt.
A. L. Anderson

To Lt. Col. Wm Chapman 2nd Inf.　　　2nd Lieut. 5 Inf.
Comdg. Fort Union N.M.　　　　　A.A.A. Genl

Statement of Prisoners (as interpreted by Lieut. Colonel Chaves) confined at Fort Union N.M. for trading with the different Indian tribes of New Mexico.

Pedro Urioste. "There are five of us, our names are Phillipe Madrid, Antonio Aban Gallegos, Juan de Dios Tapia, & Manuel Urioste. They [*sic*] are a great many from nearly all parts of the territory, going and coming, I do not know them as they are not of my company." I went among the Indians to purchase animals, dressed skins, buffalo robes, and things of this kind. The goods we took in exchange for these articles, consisted of biscocho, corn, shirts, blue drilling, vermillion & knives. We took no arms, or ammunition of any kind. I purchased all these things of Don Miguel Sena y Quintana." Phillipe Madrid says the same thing as Pedro Urioste, and adds that his object "was to get two burros from the Indians, the property of Miguel Garcia. I took no powder or ammunition of any kind. My men were poorly armed. I purchased my trading articles of Antonio José Gallegos."

Tapia says "I purchased my goods of Lorenzo Lopes, merchant of Las Vegas."

Manuel Urioste makes about the same statement as his brother Pedro & adds that he purchased no arms or ammunition of any kind, but traded & got from the Indians two small rifles. I bought my goods of Maxwell at Vegas. Pedro Urioste & his brother live at La Puebla, and the other three prisoners at La Cuesta.

A Correct Translation
H. B. Bristol
1st Lt. 5 Inf. Post Adjt.

Asst. Q^r M^r. Office
Santa Fe Aug. 25th 1861

Colonel:

In reply to your suggestion in reference to the apportionment of the horses amongst the several mounted companies at Fort Union the Department Commander directs me to say, that you will have them distributed so as to mount the men of the several companies, excluding the company of paroled men, and if there is any surplus after such distribution, it will be turned over to the Quartermaster's Department for distribution to the other mounted companies in the Department.

Respy. I am
Yr. Ob^d Svt.
J. L. Donaldson
Q^r M^r

Lt. Col. W. Chapman
Comg. Fort Union

Fort Union N.M.
August 26, 1861

Sir:

I have the honor to report that agreeably to instructions from the Post Commander I left the post on the 16th of August with Co. D, R.M.R. and escorted a government wagon as far as San José, where I ascertained that the road was clear of Texans. I then left the road, proceeding in the direction of Fort Stanton as far as "Agua Venada" where I arrived on the 5th day. I could learn nothing of any party of Texans in that direction.

I arrived at this post on the 24th.

I am Sir
Respectfully your obdt. servant
(Signed)   J. G. Tilford

1st Lieut. J. F. Ritter   1st Lieut. R.M.R.
15th Infantry   Comdg. Co. 'D' R.M.R.
Post Adjutant

Head Quarters Dept. of New Mexico
Santa Fe N.M. Aug. 26, 1861

Sir:

The Colonel Commanding directs me to inform you that the Commissioners sent into San Miguel and Mora Counties report that two companies of mounted volunteers and one of foot (for Col. [Miguel E.] Pino's regiment) will be raised and sent to Fort Union in the early part of this week. As soon as they are equipped the Colonel Commanding desires that the mounted companies may be sent to the neighborhood of Hatches Ranch, drawing their supplies monthly from Fort Union. They will be charged with the duty of guarding and watching that portion of the frontier, keeping their spies and scouting parties constantly in the field east and south of that place, and reporting everything of interest.

The company of Pino's regiment will be sent as soon as it is organized to Albuquerque.

Major Cummings has resigned, and I have not learned yet who will be appointed in his place. As soon as I do I will advise you. Please show this to Major [Gabriel R.] Paul who will muster these troops into service.

Sergt. Cordua's application for discharge will not be acted on for the present. Should his company be needed out of the Department he will be discharged.

Very respectfully Sir,
Your obdt. serv't.
A. L. Anderson

To Lt. Col. Wᵐ Chapman 2 Inf.   2ⁿᵈ Lieut. 5 Inf.
Comdg. Fort Union N.M.   A.A.A. Genˡ

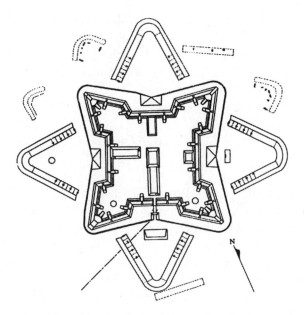

Fig. 5. National Park Service representation of the second (earthwork) Fort Union based upon archaeological evidence, aerial photographs, and written descriptions. Captain Grover's plan from August 1861 has not been found.

Hd. Qrs. Fort Union N. Mex°

Aug. 26, 1861

Colonel:

I send by the express a plan of the Field Work neatly executed by Capt. Grover 10' Inf. It is not as capacious as it might have been under other circumstances, but considering the time at which it was commenced, the necessity for its rapid completion and the force to be employed upon it, we have accomplished more than I expected, and I believe with a garrison of 600 good and reliable troops it can be defended against any force likely to be brought against it.

The alacrity with which the work was undertaken and laid out by Capt. Grover, and the zeal, energy and perseverance displayed by him and 1' Lieut. Nicodemus 10' Inf. (late of the 5') in superintending and prosecuting it to completion, have placed me under many obligations to those officers for their able assistance, and I commend them to you as worthy of your confidence and perfectly reliable for any duty which you may be pleased to assign them.

The work is now ready for occupation, but some parts of it require dressing off.

I am Colonel very Respectfully
Your ob[t] Servant

Colonel E. R. S. Canby 19' Inf. W[m] Chapman, Major 2' Inf. &
Comg. Dept. N. Mex[o]   Bv. Lt. Col. U.S. Army Comg.
Santa Fe

------------------◆------------------

Confidential

Head Quarters Dept. of New Mexico
Santa Fe N.M. Aug. 27, 1861

Colonel.

Messers David Stuart and J. R. Giddings have been reported to these Head Quarters as having opposed the Government and prevented the organization of volunteer companies and National Guards in the neighborhood of Anton Chico, and the Colonel Commanding directs that you detach a sufficient party and cause them to be arrested & taken to Fort Union to be held as prisoners until their cases are properly disposed of.

He also directs that a man named Vallet formerly a soldier of the 8th Infantry, but now a reputed agent of Texas & who has gone to Fort Union as a spy, be arrested. This man has lived for some time in Albuquerque and is known by Lt. [Asa B.] Carey or can probably be pointed out by some of the men of I company M[td] Rifles now with Capt. Gibbs. He will probably stay at Moro Crossing (about four miles from Fort Union).

Very respectfully, Sir,
Your obdt. servt
A. L. Anderson

To Lt. Col. W[m] Chapman 2 Inf. 2nd Lieut. 5 Inf.
Comdg. Fort Union N.M.   A.A.A. Gen[l]

------------------◆------------------

[author's draft]

Hd. Qrs. Fort Union New Mex[o]
Aug. 28' 1861

Sir:

I have this day rec[d] G.O. N[o] 30 & S.O. N[o] 130 Hd. Qrs. Dept. N.M. Aug. 26 and letter of Aug. 27, 1861.

Major Lynde 7 Inf. Lt. McNally R.M.R. and Dr. McKee U.S.A. Capt. Phillips and ten spies and guides arrived at this post yesterday.

Upon information received from Albuquerque I caused P. A. Vallet and B. F. Hartley to be arrested yesterday at Loma Parda on suspicion of being spies. After an examination I was satisfied they were not spies but came here especially the former, for the purpose of gambling with the men. I released them after administering an oath not to aid or abet the enemies of, nor take up arms against the United States upon condition that they would immediately leave the vicinity of this post.

I will organize a party of mounted men under an officer to carry out your instructions of yesterday.

11½ A.M. Capt. Gibbs and command have just arrived. They will encamp about a mile above the post.

I am Sir very Respectfully
Your ob^t Servt.

To A. L. Anderson 5' Inf.　　　Your ob^t Servt.

A.A.A. Genl.　　　　　　　Wm Chapman Major 2 Inf.

Santa Fe N.M.　　　　　　Bv. Lt. Col. U.S.A. Comg.

Aug. 29/61

Dear Colonel.

By some oversight the form for the Muster Roll of the Field and Staff was not sent you at the time. I send it this morning.

We have rumors coming from Duval [*sic*; Alexander Duvall] of a large force of Texans at Stanton, and of a force advancing upon Fort Craig. I do not place much reliance on these but it will be well to look out, and get your property in the entrenchments as soon as possible.

Very truly

Col. Chapman　　　　　　Yours &c.

Comg. &c. &　　　　　　　Ed. R. S. Canby

[author's draft]

Hd. Qrs. Fort Union New Mexico

Aug. 29' 1861

Sir:

Pursuant to instructions from the Hd. Qrs. Dept. of New Mexico of Aug. 27, 1861 you will proceed with twenty-five mounted men and pack mules to Anton Chico and arrest David Stuart and J. R. Giddings of that place and bring them to this post.

You will avoid the traveled roads as much as possible in order that your party may not be discovered and its approach announced before your arrival. It is advisable to take the trail leading towards Hatch's Ranch, taking care to avoid all settlements, and approach the town from the south, and endeavor to arrive early in the day that you may make the arrest and immediately commence your return march to this post, placing as great a distance as possible without injury to your animals, between your command and Anton Chico during the first twenty four hours after leaving that place.

It is possible that you may meet with parties of Texans scouting in the vicinity of Anton Chico, and you should take every precaution to guard against surprise by sending reliable men in advance to warn you of the approach of any forces in time for you to make your arrangements to receive them or to make good your retreat, should the force be too strong for your party.

Run no unnecessary risks as your only object will be to arrest the above named persons, and it should be effected as quietly and expeditiously as possible. You will take six days rations. ~~The Qr. master will furnish you with a guide.~~ Two men of Capt. Phillips' Company will accompany you as guides.

I am Sir,
Very Respectfully
Your ob^t Servt.
Wm Chapman Major 2' Inf. &
Bv. Lt. Col. U.S. Army Comg.

Lt. E. Gay 2' Drag^s

[author's draft]

Hd. Qrs. Fort Union New Mex°
August 30, 1861

Sir:

I have this day rec^d Genl Orders No. 32 and Letter Hd. Qrs. Dept. N.M. Aug. 28, 1861 also Col. Canby's note of the 29' Inst. with a form of Field & Staff Muster Roll and a copy of instructions to Col. St. Vrain for mustering them in, the Field and Staff of his Regt.

Mr. [Oliver P.] Hovey arrived yesterday and is now here. Capt. Manuel Ortiz arrived this morning with his Company of Mtd. Vols. (48 Aggregate) from Las Vegas which Major Paul is now mustering into service. Mr. Hovey thinks another company of about 30 men will be here this afternoon.

A party of eight spies and guides employed by Mr. Wm B. Russell under the authority of Mr. Hovey and the other commissioners arrived from Las Vegas. Mr. Russell expected to have command of these men and now asks authority to raise a Spy Company. The men will be mustered in Capt. Phillips' Company.

I am Sir
Very Respectfully
Your ob^t Servt.
Wm Chapman Major 2' Inf. &
Bv. Lt. Col. U.S. Army Comg.

Lt. A. L. Anderson 5' Inf.
A.A.A.G. Santa Fe N.M.

[author's draft]

Hd. Qrs. Fort Union N. Mex°

August 30, 1861

Colonel:

I enclose herewith the papers connected with the case of Robert Speakman who was arrested at Tecolote at the suggestion of the commissioners and brought to the post for examination.

Francisco Yara who made the complaint against Speakman states that he had heard him at various times acknowledge that he was a spy for the Texans, that he had gone for the Texans to come up to Stanton after it was abandoned, and returned with them, and that his business at Tecolote when arrested, was to gain information and communicate it to the Texans at Fort Stanton.

In the course of Yara's examination he charged Mr. Duvall with being associated with the Texans, whom he accompanied from Fort Fillmore and preceded to Fort Stanton where he informed the people who were for the North that they had better submit at once to Texan authority or leave the Country.

Several persons necessarily present who heard Yara's statements were struck with his vindictiveness of manner and pronounced them false or highly colored with prejudice. Messrs. Moore and Duvall who are well known to the people of New Mexico give Speakman a good character and believe the accusation false.

Speakman is here and will remain until his case is disposed of by you.

I am Colonel very Respectfully

Your ob^t Servt.

Wm Chapman Major 2' Inf. &

Col. E. R. S. Canby 19' Inf.   Bv. Lt. Col. U.S. Army Comg.

Comg. Dept. New Mex^{o4}

[Wm Chapman's notes]

Mem^a. for Aug. 31, 1861.

Lossburg I Co. discharged 31' Aug. time expires 12' Sept.

Train N° 8 arrived and unloaded. Another is expected on Sunday or Monday. Heard of Nos. 9, 10, 11 & 12. N° 13 not heard from, all coming by the Raton.

Report Robert Speakman's case. Messrs. Moore and Duvall give him a good character and don't believe he is a spy. He was employed by the citizens at Fort Stanton after it was abandoned to go express and request Col.

Baylor to send troops to protect them. (Neff and Kelly of "A" Co. Rifles to go to Albuquerque tomorrow with a train, 7 days rations to include 6 September) He was sent by [H. M.] Beckwith, [Silas] Hare, King & White, the latter went with him. They paid $15. each. The Alcalde gave a horse for the express. Francisco Yara says Mr. Duvall came up from Fillmore with Texans and preceded them to Stanton and told the people all who were for the North had better knuckle down or leave the country. Speakman took a pistol from H. Trujillo and said he had made that much anyhow. He also heard Speakman say at various times he was a spy for the Texans. White, deserter from "A" Co. Rifles, and Teodosio Aragón were also spies for Texans. He says the Capt. of the Texans (Walker) offered Aragón a horse to go with Speakman & White as a spy after Indians or wherever he might wish them to go. They did not go. He understood from Aragón that Speakman was to come to Tecolote and return in 10 days. Lt. Gay and 25 of his Company left for the south yesterday.

I, Alexander Duvall, being called upon to give a statement in regard to the circumstances of the arrest of Robt. Speigman [*sic*] as a spy from the Texans Command report the following as all the information within my knowledge, viz: That said Speigman took an express from the citizens of the Rio Bonito to Fort Fillmore to solicit aid to the citizens of the Rio Bonito Valley in protecting themselves from the Indians and Mexicans which were then threatening them.

As for the charges against him for being a Spy I regard them as wholly unfounded; and further, that he came to Tecolote (where he was arrested) at my request and in my employ a portion of the way as teamster. I believe the charges have been made with malicious intentions and without the slightest cause.

Alex^r Duvall

Fort Union
August 30th 1861.

P.S. A portion of my goods which were stolen from me at Stanton after the evacuation of the Post by the U.S. Troops I found in the house occupied by the Mexican who informed upon Mr. Speigman (the name of the Mexican is Francisco Yara).

Alex^r Duvall[5]

Fort Union N.M.
Aug[t] 30 1861

D Sir

By request of Mr. Rob[t] Speakman I address you on his behalf.

He has been in my employ for the last five or six years past, and during that time, have, under all circumstances found him a good and trusty man.

With regard to the report of the Mexican about Mr. Speakman I truly believe that he is telling a positive falsehood, for the reason, that a number of articles stolen by the Mexicans & Indians were found in possession of the Mexican by Mr. Duvall & Mr. Speakman after the store had been sacked. Hoping you will release Mr. Speakman from custody,

I remain

Col. Canby   Your obt. servt.
Santa Fe[6]   W. H. Moore

Hd. Qrs. Fort Union N.M. August 31, 1861

Sir:

Train No. 8 with bacon arrived yesterday by the Raton route and unloaded at the Field Work. Another is expected on Sunday or Monday. Trains Nos. 9, 10, 11 & 12 are coming by the same route but the wagon master of No. 8 with the above exception could give no information as to the times of their arrival here. No. 13 was not heard from.

Lieut. Gay with 25 men of "G" Co. 2' Dragoons left yesterday pursuant to instructions from Dept. Hd. Qrs. of Aug. 27, 1861.

I have reliable information that six days since there were only 100 Texans at Fort Stanton and 100 expected. They were firing [*sic*] the guns left by Col. Roberts as useless.

I have this day discharged ~~from the service~~ Private Henry Lossing of "I" Co. 5' Inf. under par. 1 G.O. No. 24 War Dept. Nov. 30, 1859, to return to the States by a train leaving today. His time would have expired on the 12 Sept. 1861.

I acknowledge the receipt of Circular of 29' and Sp. Orders No. 131 of Aug. 30, 1861 Hd. Qrs. Dept. N. Mex°.

I am Sir very Respectfully
Your ob[t] Servt.

Lt. A. L. Anderson 5' Inf.   W[m] Chapman Major 2' Inf. &
A.A.A. Genl. Santa Fe   Bv. Lt. Col. U.S.A. Comg.

"Battle Hymn of the Republic"
(Julia Ward Howe, 1861)

Mine eyes have seen the glory of the coming of the Lord;
He is trampling out the vintage where the grapes of wrath are stored;
He hath loosed the fateful lightning of His terrible swift sword;
His truth is marching on.
Chorus: Glory, glory, Hallelujah! Glory, glory, Hallelujah!
Glory, glory, Hallelujah! His truth is marching on.

I have seen Him in the watch-fires of a hundred circling camps,
They have builded Him an altar in the evening dews and damps;
I have read His righteous sentence by the dim and flaring lamps;
His day is marching on.
Chorus: Glory, glory, Hallelujah! &c.

I have read a fiery gospel, writ in burnished rows of steel;
"As ye deal with my contemners, so with you my grace shall deal;
Let the Hero, born of woman, crush the serpent with his heel,
Since God is marching on."
Chorus: Glory, glory, Hallelujah! &c.

CHAPTER FIVE
The Retreat from Arizona
July–August 1861
UNION CORRESPONDENCE

(copy)

Fort Craig, New Mexico.
September 1ˢᵗ, 1861.

Sir:

I have the honor to report that being in command at Fort Breckinridge, New Mexico, I received the order for its abandonment and the movement of its garrison to Fort Buchanan, N.M., on the 3ʳᵈ of July.

Mr. [William S.] Grant's train of twelve wagons, the only transportation to be had in that part of New Mexico, was then at Fort Breckinridge; it was hired, and, with the train belonging to the post, sent to Tucson with as much of the property as could be carried. At the same time, an express was sent to Fort Buchanan for the train there, and the trains of both posts with Mr. Grant's arrived at Fort Breckinridge on the 9ᵗʰ of July. Everything worth transportation was at once loaded up and the post abandoned and burned, with the property not worth transportation, on the 10ᵗʰ of July.

By sending twenty loads in the first place, to be stored at Mr. Grant's mill in Tucson, one week was saved in time, as after relieving the companies of the 7ᵗʰ Infantry at Fort Buchanan, I could send at any time for the property left in store at Tucson.

At the Cañon del Oro, twenty-five miles from Fort Breckinridge, I received by express a letter from Captain [Gurden] Chapin, commanding Fort Buchanan, informing me that that post was also to be abandoned. Taking an escort, I repaired at once to Fort Buchanan and, on learning the urgency of the case, sent the enclosed order to Lieutenant [Richard S. C.] Lord in command of the troops en route from Fort Breckinridge—his report in the case I forward.

It may be as well to state here that the American population of that part of New Mexico, being mostly outlaws having everything to gain and nothing to lose, in case of any disturbance of the peace and quiet of the country, were early sympathizers with the secessionists, and for some time previous were prevented interfering with my supplies only by being made aware of the fact that I would use, on provocation, the force under my command.

There were two men of Lieutenant Lord's command left in Tucson;

they with their horses and arms were reported to me as prisoners. I immediately sent and demanded that the men and property be restored to me, which was complied with, but in this case there was a distinct disavowal that they were held as prisoners, and an explanation given that they were drunk and that some of their arms had been stolen.

In abandoning Tucson, Lieut. Lord, at Mr. Grant's request, burned a mill owned by Mr. Grant, and erected by him at an expense of several thousand dollars, on the faith of his contract for furnishing supplies to the posts in that part of New Mexico. This being the only mill in the country, the supply of flour to Confederate troops who might enter with the design of operating from that point was entirely cut off. I am perfectly satisfied that Mr. Grant could not, without periling his life, have remained in the country after the troops left, even had he not have burned his mill, his loyalty being so conspicuous as to render him odious to the outlaws of Tucson.

Whilst individualizing it may be as well to state that I had such conclusive proof of the double policy pursued by Sylvester Mowry, formerly delegate from Arizona, that I refused to sell him supplies above what was necessary for his ordinary use, supposing that he would use them for the supply of any troops entering the territory from the Confederate states.

To resume the report, I found that Captain Chapin, commanding Fort Buchanan, had advertised an auction sale of commissary and quartermasters' stores, which accordingly took place, but netted very little to the government. The stores in the commissary department were placed, as a minimum, at the New York and St. Louis prices, without freight, but found no buyers. Quartermasters' stores were almost unsalable at any price; this being the case I closed the sale, and these being all the stores in Western Arizona, in order to carry out completely the policy of depriving the country of supplies, after supplying some purchasers from Sonora, and giving a portion of the commissary stores and some spades and hoes &c. to the Papago and Pimo [sic] Indians, reserving all the ammunition, arms, clothing, and camp and garrison equipage, I prepared to burn everything else which could not be transported to the Rio Grande.

Being ordered to hire transportation if possible, I tried to do so, but failed. There was but little transportation to be had in any way, in addition to the wagons of Mr. Grant, and he objected to taking his train into Fort Fillmore in the uncertain state of the country. Knowing that my arms, ammunition, clothing, tents &c. would be very much needed if a large volunteer force was called into the field, I finally arranged with Mr. Grant to freight his train to Fort Fillmore at the lowest rate and in case his train was lost to buy it from him as if purchased at Fort Buchanan, adding to the price

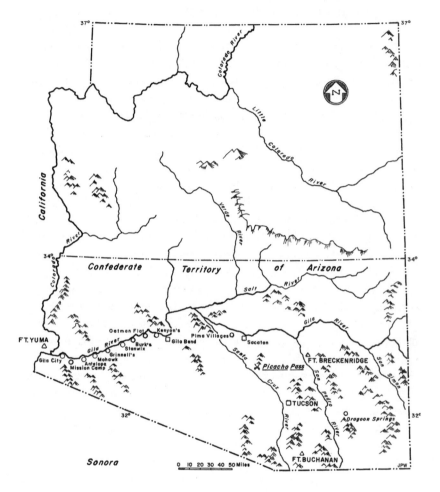

Map 2. Arizona in 1861–1862.

of the train only the expenses of his teamsters. By this arrangement and the purchase of two wagons and teams already engaged by the A.A.Q.M. at the post, my train consisted of upwards of thirty serviceable wagons.

Some few horses were bought to mount the Dragoons and in some cases, where the vendors were from Sonora, were paid for in Sugar and Coffee.

The artillery of the post, consisting of two six-pound guns with caissons, was put under the command of Captain Chapin; his infantry cannoneers were armed with large sized Colt's revolvers, each piece and caisson drawn by four large American mules, with two Dragoon drivers. In two or three days, by a zealous devotion to his duty, he had formed a very efficient battery, on which, under his charge, I would have placed much dependence.

Having repaired the wagons and selected and loaded up the stores, I finally abandoned and burned Fort Buchanan the 23d of July.

The sutler at Fort Buchanan—Mr. White—was so situated that he could neither find transportation for all his goods, nor stay behind, there being a lawless band of desperadoes who had publicly stated that on the departure of the troops they would take his goods. In this dilemma he finally freighted with his most valuable goods a train of six wagons which happened to arrive from Sonora. I offered to him to make the statement made above, if instead of leaving any goods in his store he would burn what he could not transport. He seemed to have decided to do so, but after having stated such intention, at the last moment he thought that his claim could be made stronger, could he induce the troops, in the general burning, to fire his store. Sentinels were put over his store to prevent his rascality being successful. His store was partially burned, but it was done by his employees, soldiers being attracted to the spot by liquor which was plentifully distributed by his connivance. Should any claim be presented for remuneration in his case, the officers of Forts Breckinridge and Buchanan could make such statements as effectually to prevent his recovering.

During my stay at Fort Buchanan, A. S. Johnston, formerly of the Regular Army, passed through Tucson with several other resigned officers and thirty or forty armed but unorganized citizens of California. Hearing that these persons were going to their homes in the South, I sent an express to Major Lynde—the officer commanding the Southern District of New Mexico—in order that, should he see fit, he could detain them. Understanding that they had awaited in California the acceptance of their resignations, had been permitted to leave the Department of California unquestioned, and knowing that, at our latest dates from the Rio Grande, a resigned officer, Lieutenant Garland, my senior, was in command of Fort Fillmore (the post to which we were ordered) to be shortly relieved by Major Lynde, who had openly stated to Lieut. [Andrew Wallace] Evans that he would not fight the South, and whose Acting Assistant Adjutant General was a resigned officer—Lieut. Brooks—who has since been dropped for disloyalty, even then apparent. Knowing these facts, whatever might have been my action under other circumstances, founded on the fact that these citizens had been officers, I could take no other action in the case.

After leaving Fort Buchanan, the extreme scarcity of water compelled us to make long and hard marches, and in consequence of this and the heat, when we arrived at the San Simon there were sixty men on the sick report, generally with intermittent fever. Not being able to haul so many, a halt of three days was made and the sick, by rest and proper treatment, were reduced to twenty.

On arriving at Ojo la Vaca, we discovered a party of about twenty men in a valley near the spring. Chase was made but they could not be overtaken. They afterwards proved to be Copewood's [*sic;* Coopwood's] spies.

At Cook's Peak, the trails of scouting parties on the Mesilla road were numerous and fresh, and not having heard from Major Lynde, I sent at dark a party of four soldiers with a spy hired for the occasion, to find out and report what was doing on the river. They returned in about an hour, having fallen in with the express from Fort Craig.

By this express we received the information that the ten companies under Major Lynde at Fort Fillmore, after a fight in which he was beaten, had abandoned their fortified position and a large amount of stores, retreating in the direction of Fort Stanton, and on pursuit had laid down their arms without firing a shot; and that the commanding officer of Fort Craig was preparing to resist an expected attack.

The letters by the express also stated that a party of 322 men had determined to attack my column, but on further questioning, the number seemed to have been written without any definite knowledge, and the only point certainly established was that our party was the one to the capture of which the enemy would next direct its efforts.

The above information having been received, it was to be decided whether to risk returning to California, in which case my stores might have been saved if we were not pursued by a large force, or to take, if possible, the effective force at my disposal, and by concentrating with the first forces met with going north, to assist in making a stand against what was then thought a large force. The latter appeared to be the proper course to pursue, and having known the country for a number of years, I felt confident of being able to march with a column free from encumbrances even to Fort Union.

I immediately directed that the property, with the exception of the necessary arms, ammunition and clothing, and ten days' provisions, be destroyed in the quartermaster's and commissary departments and in the companies; that the trains of Mr. Grant and the Government be burned, and that Captain Chapin, with all the sick, about six or seven, under charge of Assistant Surgeon K. Ryand [sic; Ryland], and the laundresses, sixteen, with an escort of twenty-five men and the wagons he might require, proceed by the river route to Fort Craig. Whilst with the other troops under my command, I would make my way into Fort Craig through such country as would enable me to resist almost any attack which could reasonably be expected, even from a large force.

In carrying out these orders the men were working nearly all night, and in the darkness and confusion many articles were destroyed, the loss of which will be severely felt in the companies. The officers and men destroyed nearly all their private property with great willingness, and the general destruction was complete, nothing being left but articles which would not burn, and some of Mr. Grant's mules which, frightened by the fires and explosions of ammunition, stampeded to the mountains.

The pieces of artillery were bent at the trunnions, spiked, and muzzles battered in, their carriages being burned and the ammunition and harness destroyed.

Nothing was sent by Captain Chapin's wagons, as it was supposed that his party would only be permitted to pass up the river because the enemy would not care to capture the impediments of my column.

Captain Chapin's report has already been forwarded; he deserves all credit for his zeal and efficiency.

I would also desire to make especial mention of Dr. Irvin [B. J. D. Irwin] and Lieutenants Lord and [Charles H.] Ingraham, who during the march on every occasion, did all in their power to promote the discipline and efficiency of the column.

I arrived without further accident at Fort Craig, New Mexico, on the 11th of August.

Major [Augustus H.] Seward, Paymaster U.S.A., with his escort, was with the column under my command, and continued with me until our arrival at Fort Craig. To him as a senior officer, I am indebted for his approval of my action in the affairs at Buchanan and Cooks Peak.

At Fort Craig, New Mexico, I gave Lieut. Ingraham orders to purchase of Mr. Grant such articles as he had lost on the road from his train; the mules saved were not purchased.

It may here be proper to state that had we had good information of the force of the Texans, no officer or soldier in the command would have been willing to destroy a particle of property—it was not possible to conceive of such a disgraceful surrender as made at San Augustine Spring.

Very respectfully
Your obedient Servant
(Signed)   I. N. Moore
Captain 3rd Cavalry
Comd'g. squadron 1st cavalry,
& Co^s. "C" & "H" 7th Infy.

The foregoing is a true copy.
Adjt. Genl's. Office,
Washington, D.C.
June 23, 1863.

E. D. Townsend,
Asst. Adjt. Genl.[1]

Fort Craig, New Mexico.
11th August 1861.

General,

I have the honor to report myself at this Post, under orders from Capt. Morris, Comdg, to proceed to Albuquerque, New Mexico, and await further instructions.

I was in command of Companies G & H, 7th Infantry, at Fort Buchanan N.M. until relieved on the 16th July by Captain I. N. Moore, 1st Dragoons, and formed a part of his Column, commanding a section of Artillery, until the night of the 5th August, when Captain Moore learning of Major Lynde's surrender of his Command near Fort Fillmore on the 27th July, determined to make his way to Fort Craig. He accordingly left Cook's Springs before day on the morning of the 6th, leaving me five wagons and twenty-four mules, with directions to conduct the women & children of the Command to Fort Craig, under protection of twenty-five Infantry soldiers.

I burned and destroyed all the property not needed, public and private, including a large quantity of ammunition overlooked by Capt. Moore in the darkness of the previous night, and started at 6 o'clock on the 6th in constant expectation of attack from the enemy, who, I afterwards learned, was in camp with masked Artillery at Picacho. On this day I marched thirty-six miles, having no rest the night previous, and making a detour through the mountains, encamped in a concealed position on the Rio Grande.

I continued the march constantly, the animals worn down and weak from labor and starvation, turning them out to graze at convenient points, where they would be concealed. In this way I had proceeded to a point on the river near Alamosa and within thirty-five miles of Fort Craig. There I expected rest for my command. It was after dark when I made camp. In a few moments I ascertained from a reliable source that a large party of the enemy were below on the river, in pursuit. I took a saddle mule from one of the teams and rode all night to Fort Craig, where I arrived next morning at 7 o'clock. I procured thirty-two fresh mules from Capt. Morris and an escort of Captain Hubbell's company of Mounted Volunteers, and immediately rode back to my command. As soon as I arrived in its camp, I hitched up the fresh mules and started for [Fort] Craig. This was late in the evening and night coming on with rain. I proceeded ahead in the road carrying a lighted candle, and marched in this way for several miles. I then turned out, and waiting for day, proceeded to Fort Craig, where the whole party arrived safely on the 10th. I thus saved to the Government the twenty-five men with their arms, ammunition &c., five wagons and teams, & brought in twenty women & ten children to this Post.

I am very much exhausted from want of sleep and constant labor, and I managed to carry all of my escort in the wagons to save it from breaking down.

I beg leave to mention my indebtedness to much of the success of the march to Sergeant Patrick Murry of Co. G., 7 Infantry, who was useful and energetic in all that I called upon him to do.

I am now here as the representative to the Government of Company I, 7th Infantry, which Major Lynde surrendered near [Fort] Fillmore, and I respectfully offer my services, having no company, to the U. States in any capacity in which they may be required.

I am, General,

Very Respectfully

Yr. Obt. Ser.

G. Chapin

Capt. 7. Inf.

To: Col. L. Thomas
Adj. Gen. Bvt. Br. Gen. U.S.A.
Washington City, D.C.
Address: Care of Dept. Commander
      Santa Fe, N.M.²

"There Was An Old Soldier"

Oh, there was an old soldier and he had a wooden leg,
He had no tobacco but tobacco he could beg.
Another old soldier, as sly as a fox,
He always had tobacco in his old tobacco box.

Said the one old soldier, "Won't you give me a chew?"
Said the other old soldier, "I'll be hanged if I do,
Save up your pennies and put away your rocks,
And you'll always have tobacco in your old tobacco box."

There was an old hen and she had a wooden foot,
And she made her nest by a mulberry root,
She laid more eggs than any hen on the farm,
Another wooden foot wouldn't do her any harm.

CHAPTER SIX
Headquarters and Southern District
Correspondence, August–December 1861
UNION CORRESPONDENCE

Albuquerque N.M.
August 1 1861

Colonel,

I this morning mustered Lt. Col. M. [Manuel] Chavez into the U.S. Service, as Lt. Col. 2nd Regt. N.M. foot volunteers. I had no form for the Muster Roll, but made it as thought would be right. I do not exactly understand how I am to leave this roll open if I do not muster in all the Field & Staff. Of course, whoever may complete the Muster will (I suppose) have to make their own Muster Roll. It seems to me that Col. [Miguel E.] Pino ought to sign this roll, but I suppose he is not considered in service until mustered in. Col. Chavez may be obliged to wait here a few days before he can get transportation to [Fort] Fauntleroy. There is none available just now. In case the rumor is true that Maj. Lynde has surrendered his command and the Texans come this way, shall I, if asked to do so by the citizens of Albuquerque, issue them arms & ammunition? I shall look anxiously for instructions. This place (the people I mean) are a good deal scared.

(Entre nous) Do you know Capt. [John H.] Mink? He asked me this morning if I would not send his company to Judge [Spruce M.] Baird's place. That he could look out for the enemy and get better grass for his horses. Judge Baird is said to be a secessionist & someone, I do not recollect who, said that Capt. Mink had been touched with the same complaint. I told Capt. Mink I could not send his company there at present. He then wished to send his horses. I told him I might want them any moment. If we only knew whom we could trust, but it seems as if the Devil had possession of so many that it makes me suspicious, and I am by nature just the contrary.

Respectfully
Your obt. sevt.
N. B. Rossell
Bvt. Maj. Capt. 5

To Col. E. R. S. Canby
Santa Fe N.M.[1]

Fort Craig N.M.
August 1" 1861

Colonel—

Sir. This morning 1st Sergt. Sunday, Co. B. RMR, came in nearly starved. He makes the following statement. Capt. Gibbs on getting beyond the Point [of] Rocks a short distance, turned off over the sand hills. The Capt. moved forward with the main body of the Company, with instructions for him to follow on his trail with the beef cattle and wagons. He did so for some distance. Capt. G. sent word back to him [to] close up, as the Texans were in sight. He moved forward as rapidly as his tired mules would permit. When reaching the mouth of a cañon, he was surrounded by about one hundred & twenty Texans, and was captured by them, they seizing all the property, their two hows. [howitzers], arms &c.

He was then marched towards Las Cruces, and slipped away just on the edge of the town and hid himself until night near the road. While there, he saw Major Lynde and another officer driven into Cruces in an ambulance. He also saw Infantry muskets being hauled in. At dark [he] pursued his way to this Post. Whilst being on the road to 'Cruces, he was told by a Captain that Capt. Gibbs had, with the Rifles, taken the direction of Stanton. There is no indication of their coming this way so far as known. I have a Picket guard out as far as the Laguna on the Jornada, one above towards Stapleton's Ranch, and Capt. [Santiago L.] Hubbell's Company in the Bosque a mile above the Fort, at the ford. Capt. [Juan de Dios?] Baca's Company I have in garrison. The Post is tolerably well fortified with sand bags.

Very Respectfully
Yr. Obt. Sevt.

Colonel E. R. Canby   R. M. Morris
10" Inf.[2]   Capt. RMR

———————————— ⬥ ————————————

Head Quarters, Southern District of New Mexico,
Fort Craig, Aug. 16, 1861.

Sir,

From information which he has received, the Lieut. Col. commanding the District is satisfied that Judge Baird and a Judge Wells, of Albuquerque, are in treasonable correspondence with the enemy.

You will, therefore, cause their immediate arrest, and hold them in close confinement for trial, if, on examination and search, you should find sufficient evidence for their committal and probable conviction by the Federal Court.

Mr. Claude Jones, from El Paso, is reported to be at Judge Baird's and is known to be a rebel. His business must be mischievous and his arrest, and close confinement, would be justifiable.

You will also cause the Prefect of the county, resident in Albuquerque, to be closely watched and to be confined unless he can justify to you his course of conduct, which has been such as to create in the public mind a general impression that he is disloyal to the Government. It is essential to the public safety that all civil officers should be above suspicion.

You will send immediately to this post the pieces of artillery brought by Capt. [Henry R.] Selden to Albuquerque, and all of the ammunition pertaining to them.

You will direct the Depôt Commissary to send to this place the subsistence stores prepared for transportation to Fort Buchanan.

The train of wagons which was used for the transportation of the troops just arrived here from Albuquerque, will be sent back, very soon, to the Depôt.

I am, Sir, very respectfully,
Your obedient servant,

To The Commanding Officer,   A. McRae, Lt. Mtd. Rifles,
Albuquerque, N.M.³   A.A.A.G.

Head Quarters Southern Mil. District,
Dept. N.M., 16 Aug. 1861.

Colonel,

I have the honor to report that I arrived at this Post [Fort Craig] yesterday at 12 M. Capt. Selden, with his command of two companies of the 7th and two of foot volunteers, and Lieut. [George W.] Howland with companies "C" and "K," Mounted Riflemen, arrived soon after.

The command now consists of Companies "F," "C" and "H," of the 7th Infantry, and "D" and "F," 5th Infantry; "C," "G" and "K," Mounted Riflemen, "D" & "G," 1st Dragoons; Captain [James "Santiago"] Hubbell's company of mounted volunteers, and the foot companies of Captains [Gregorio?] Otero, [Ethan W.] Eaton, and [Roman A.] Baca; making a total present of 850 rank and file. Of this number, 675 are Regular troops, in effective condition, and all loyal and true men.

I have found this Post almost entirely destitute of ordnance, and tomorrow I send my requisitions direct to Fort Union for such as I consider necessary for the defense of the Post and for operating against the Texans in the Mesilla and at Fort Bliss, should operations in that direction be deemed expedient. The two pieces of ordnance and ammunition for small arms sent into Albuquerque by Captain Selden, I have ordered to be forwarded here without delay. I have also directed Capt. Shoemaker to supply another 12 pounder howitzer, and one more 6 pounder piece, with their proper appointments. Your order to the acting Qr. Master at Fort Union to furnish transportation to Albuquerque may be necessary to hasten on this necessary ordnance.

The requisitions to refit and remount the companies of this command will go by this express. Not half of the command have canteens, and it is understood that none are in the Department, unless some came by the last supply train from the States. Permit me to suggest that you order canteens and horse-shoe nails to be sent to Albuquerque without any delay, if these essential supplies have reached Fort Union. None are in the Department unless they are in store there.

I shall take immediate steps to place this post in a state of defense; but little, however, can be done until I receive entrenching tools from Albuquerque. The place is quite defensible, however, as in all directions there is full range for musketry and all the enclosures can be looped in the next 3 days. There are no commanding points where artillery can be brought to bear, that would defile batteries from the longer range of our muskets, rifles & carbines. No force from below with artillery and wagons can pass this place without my knowledge, and I shall permit no such passage. No force can approach by the Pecos, except by Fort Fillmore or Albuquerque.

I have reliable information that there are not at this time 600 Texan troops in the Mesilla Valley and at Fort Bliss. One Company of 63 men have [*sic*] been sent to occupy Fort Stanton and protect the Rebels on the Bonito. This force is reported to be very much disorganized, is without clothing or pay, and are seizing the property of citizens as they need it, without remuneration or even promises of pay. It is believed that the masses of Mexicans on both sides of the river would join any force sent down to repossess the Forts and to drive the Rebels from the Country.

I am Very Respectfully
Your Ob^t Servt,

Col. E. R. S. Canby	(Signed) B. S. Roberts
19th Infantry	Lieut. Col. U.S.A.
Comdg. Dept. N.M.⁴	Comdg. S. Mil. District

———————— ◆ ————————

Head Quarters Southern Military District
Fort Craig N.M.
August 17th 1861

Colonel

I have the honor to report that the pickets of Captain Hubbell's

Company brought into this post last evening a deserter from "D" Co., Mounted Riflemen, who was drummed out of the Army at this place by the sentence of a Genl. Court Martial last fall. His name is John Anderson. He states substantially that he attempted to escape with those coming from the service of the Confederate Army, tired of the experiment. He has been serving in Capt. McAllister's Co. of foot. That there are now in Arizona the force as follows: Capt. Hardeman's Co. of Mounted Riflemen, 100 strong. Capt. Stafford's, same strength. Capt. Teel's Artillery Co., 100 strong. Capt. Walker's, 90 (gone to occupy Fort Stanton); Capt. Pyron's Co., 44 strong, arrived since Major Lynde surrendered. Capt. Frazer's Co. Mt^d., 40 strong at Fort Fillmore. Cookwood's [sic; Coopwood's] Spy Co. of Pino Alto miners, 40 strong. Capt. McAllister's foot, 40 strong, and a force of 40 Mesilla gamblers raised by Capt. Mastin to capture Capt. Moore's Command. Five men of Cap$^{t.}$ Pyron's Co. were left to guard Camp Lancaster and five men of Capt. Walker's to garrison Fort Davis. Fort Quitman has been abandoned.

This information corroborates that already rec^d. relating to the strength of the Confederate forces, and I believe it to be substantially correct. This deserter was mounted on one of the "A" Co. horses stolen at Fort Fillmore. He is now before a Military Commission on trial as a spy and Rebel. He knows nothing of any expected reinforcements of their forces, but says they are informed that a paymaster is en route to pay the troops at present in Arizona. He also says they are well rationed at present, but that many are discontented. The people of the country are tired of them.

He had heard there that a force from the Choctaw nation was en route to take Fort Union, but says their camps are filled daily with groundless rumors.

I take the liberty of detaining Capt. Chapin a few days, as he is making drawings for the defense of the post and on special duty drilling and instructing volunteer officers.

I am Very Respectfully
Your ob^t Servt.
(Signed)   B. S. Roberts
Lt. Col. U.S. Army
Comdg. S.M. District of N.M.

To Colonel E. R. S. Canby
19th Infantry
Comdg. Dept. of New Mexico[5]

Albuquerque New Mexico
August 18th 1861

Dear Colonel.

Your communications of the 17th inst. were received this morning. There is no doubt that the Texans have occupied Fort Stanton. I have received the information from several different sources. Last night I received a visit from Bonifacio Chaves, a stepson of Dr. [Henry] Connelly, and Mr. Lorenzo Labadie, Indian agent. They said they were in the hands of the Texans and escaped on the 13th inst., but I imagine they allowed them to escape, as Mr. Chaves had a pass from the Texan commander. These gentlemen told me, and it agrees with the information I have received from other sources, that the Texans at Stanton are only about sixty or one hundred strong. I have the promise of information from Manzano in case there is any approach to this place, and I now have a small party out in that direction and have employed two men, who say they know the country, and I shall keep them busy. I have already sent Col. Roberts the same information I sent you about Stanton. I refer to that received from Dr. Connelly. I have already written you that I forwarded to [Fort] Craig this morning the artillery that Selden brought from [Fort] Fauntleroy.

In case of necessity I could turn out today, by arming the Band, Musicians, and extra & daily duty men, & men casually at the Post, about one hundred & twenty five Regulars and about eighty N.M. Volunteers Mounted & Foot. The people here say they will fight in case of actual invasion; that remains to be seen. I do not, as I once before stated to you, consider Albuquerque a defensible position. It can be approached in almost any direction. We are all, however, ready to do the best we can, and I feel all the regular troops and no doubt many of the volunteers can be relied on. I shall not close this until afternoon, as I hope by that time to find out what the people of the neighborhood will do.

Capt. Chapin has been detained at Fort Craig. I hope, however, that on the receipt of the order to relieve me as ordnance officer, he will come up, as it will be a great relief to me to get it off my hands.

I had an interview with Dr. Connelly just before dinner. He has been in conversation with several of the rich & influential men here and in the neighborhood, and they say that at present all the loose men are enrolled in the volunteers; that every one now has their own business; which it is impossible for them to leave to be enrolled. But that they are all loyal, and in case this valley is invaded will assist the troops, bringing out what arms they have, & ask for more. The townspeople here say about the same thing; that they are willing to fight if the town or neighborhood is invaded, but they do

Fig. 6. "House in Alberkerque," apparently the Armijo place (La Placita). Sketch by A. B. Peticolas in his diary on Apr. 11, 1862. Courtesy of Arizona Historical Society, Tucson, negative no. 60286.

not like to enroll themselves. I have now done all I can in this matter. If the Texans come, some of the people will probably help us, many will stand neutral, and a few may perhaps take sides against us. In conversation with Dr. Connelly, he stated repeatedly that there would be no invasion of this valley unless the Regular troops were withdrawn, and the Texans were invited into the valley. I said he seemed very positive & I asked him why he thought so. He replied that it was against Jefferson Davis' orders to invade the Territory, and it was against the interest of the Texans themselves, and that all Texas cared for at present was that part of the country around Mesilla & [Fort] Stanton.

The Mexicans are a peculiar people, and the sooner I get east of the Mississippi, the better I shall like it. I do not exactly know what to make of them. I do not doubt many of them feel brave enough now, but how it will be in case of actual invasion, time only can determine.

                                    Very truly yours
To Colonel E. R. S. Canby   N. B. Rossell
U.S. Army
Santa Fe N.M.

I mentioned to Dr. Connelly, & told him he might tell those other gentlemen, that I had information that I believed was reliable, that McCulloch was on the Pecos & his force. I thought it best to do this. I did not tell him how this information was obtained.

                         N. B. R.[6]

<u>Copy</u>

Head Quarters 7th Infantry
Albuquerque N.M. Augt. 20, 1861.

Sir;

I have the honor to transmit herewith Field Return of Battalion, 7th Infantry, for the month of July, 1861, also lists of property turned over to the C.S. forces, pertaining to the non-commissioned Staff and Band and Companies "A," "B," "D," "E," "G," "I," and "K," 7th Infantry, and Rolls of same with lists of those declining to accept parole and those who joined the Texas forces.

The small number of men shown by the lists enclosed as having joined the enemy will, I trust, prove a satisfactory refutation of the slanderous reports as to their demoralization. We have no reason to believe that the men who refused to accept the parole intended to join the enemy; some of those stated as a reason, that they understood the President had refused to acknowledge the validity of the oath, and under the circumstances preferred remaining as prisoners of war; others, that they feared an immediate discharge from the service, and having no other profession than that of arms, would be entirely without means of support. I believe these men were conscientious, and the reasons assigned for their action true ones.

Having an officer to a company, I shall not be compelled to break up any of them.

I am, Sir, very respectfully,
Your obdt. Servt.

To   (Signed)   J. H. Potter
The Actg. Asst. Adjt. General   Captain 7th Infty.
Hd. Qrs. Dept. of N. Mexico.   Comd'g. 7th Infty.
Santa Fe, N.M.

Hd. Qrs. Dept. of New Mex.
Santa Fe, Octr. 6, 1861.

A true copy
A. L. Anderson
2nd. Lieut. 5th. Infantry
A.A.A. General[7]

———————— ◆ ————————

Head Quarters Southern Military Dis.
Fort Craig N.M. Aug. 20th 1861

Colonel

I have the honor to acknowledge the receipt of your instructions of 17th inst. and the enclosed from Colonel Chapman.

My impression is that the report of Mr. Moore's spy that 400 troops are at Fort Stanton is an exaggeration. A deserter from the Confederate army came in yesterday and delivered himself up at this Post. His account confirms previous information that the force at Fort Stanton, Fillmore, Bliss, and in the Mesilla Valley does not exceed 600 men. He gives the names of all the captains, the strength of their companies, and their posts. He says,

Captain	Hardemans	Mounted Rifles	is at Fort Bliss	100	strong
"	Stafford	"	"	" "	100	"
"	Teels	Artillery	Fort Fillmore	100	"
"	Walkers	Mounted Rifles	" Stanton	90	"
Captain	Ryen [Pyron]	Mounted Rifles	just arrived	44	strong
"	Frazers	"	"	Fort Fillmore	40	"
"	Cookewoods	Spy Compy	" "	40	"
"	McAllisters	(foot)	is at " "	40	"

Besides, a gambler, Marsten [Mastin] has raised a company of some 40 men and has gone to Pino Alto. I shall soon know with certainty the exact condition of things, and keep you advised of any important movement.

The people in the towns along the river are disposed to defend their own homes, but they seem indisposed to leave them to join in the defense of our posts. They don't see the necessity of organization. Volunteers are coming in here daily in small numbers. This is the busy season, when the Mexicans are mainly securing their crops. I am of the opinion that after the crops are secured, the Regiments of Volunteers will be filled up as well as the National Guards.

I am sir
Very respectfully
Your obdt. servt.

Colonel E. R. S. Canby
19th Infantry
Comdg. Dept. N.M.
Official Copy for Col. Chapman[8]

B. S. Roberts
Lieut. Col. U.S.A.
Comdg. S. Mil. Dist.

Head Quarters Southern Military District
Fort Craig N.M. Aug. 21st, 1861.

Sir

I have the honor to enclose for the Colonel Commanding the Department the copy of a letter from Mr. W. Pelham, now as I understand in arrest at Santa Fe, charged with treasonable correspondence with the enemy. The letter was brought in yesterday by some Mexicans scouting from Captain Hubbell's Co. and [was] picked up with some other packages on the Hornado [sic], where the Indians attacked the Texans returning from here with the arms that had been loaned by Col. Baylor to the paroled men of Major Lynde's Command. If evidence was wanting before to convict him of conspiracy against this Territory & correspondence with the Rebels, it will no longer be wanting. The original letter I will send by a safer means than by express. It is a genuine letter. It clearly implicates Mr. Clever and one Diego Archuleta, who is in Commission, as I am informed, as Captain of a Co. of volunteers. It is believed by Capt. Hubbell that Gov. Rencher, Hon. M. Otero, Col. Collins & Mr. Hovey are in this conspiracy.

Yesterday the scouts brought in two more of the men of "A" Co., Mounted Rifles, who deserted at Fort Fillmore. They report of course that they have deserted from the Confederate forces, and came here to deliver themselves up. As they confess that they took up arms against the government and actually served in Capt. McAllister's Co., they had better be tried before the Civil Court for treason. I fear that a court martial would not convict them of desertion in time of war, and examples certainly should be made of some of these cases.

The stories of all these men go to render my conviction stronger that the force of the Texans in the Mesilla Valley & at Stanton does not much exceed five hundred men.

The letter that was brought here by a Mexican in Capt. Moore's employ, purporting to date on the Rio Pecos and to be written by a Col. H. E. McCulloch, is doubtless a forgery and intended to intimidate this region. The Mexican who brought it was not known by the Texans to be in our interest, and they requested him to stop at this post and to drop the letter where it would be picked up. In your letter [to] me, nothing is said of its history, and I presumed you infer that it is a genuine correspondence. I get no information from any quarter touching reinforcements of Texans, or the expectation of any.

I am Very Respectfully
Your obt. Servt.
(Signed) B. S. Roberts

Lieut. A. L. Anderson   Lieut. Col. U.S.A.
A.A.A. Genl. Santa Fe N.M.[9]   Comdg. S.M. District

Head Qrs. Southern Military District
Fort Craig N.M. Aug. 24th 1861.

Sir

I have the honor to report that on Tuesday morning I detached twenty picked men from the Dragoons & Mounted Riflemen to accompany

Captain Hubbell of the Mounted Volunteers on a scout toward Roblero [sic], where the Texans keep their advanced pickets. About 2 A.M. Friday morning he came upon their advance, about 100 strong, in camp on the Jornado 30 miles from this post. Having been fired upon by their sentinel, he opened a spirited fire on their Camp, and seizing a good position, he skirmished with their entire force until day light, when they abandoned their Camp and returned toward the Laguna.

Captain Hubbell having expressed to me his position, I detached two columns of Dragoons & Mounted Riflemen, each eighty strong, to his re-lief—Capt. Moore & Lieut. Howland to reach him directly on the Jornado, and Capt. Lane & Lieut. Lord to pass down the river & cut off any retreat the Texans may attempt by taking a pass through the mountains toward Ft. Thorn.

I hope before night to hear of the defeat & capture of the advance of Rebels & outlaws.

When I last heard from Capt. Moore, he was within 20 miles of the Texans and they were not aware that he had reinforced Capt. Hubbell and was pursuing them.

I am Sir Very Respectfully

To Lieut. A. L. Anderson   Your obt. servt.
A.A.A. General   (Signed) B. S. Roberts
Dept. of N.M.   Lieut. Colonel U.S.A.
Santa Fe N.M.[10]   Comdg. S.M. Dist.

Subsistence Office
Santa Fe N.M. Aug. 25th 1861.

General,

Knowing that there was a large amount of Subsistence funds in the hands of Lieuts. [Charles B.] Stivers and [Augustus H.] Plummer, 7" Infty, at the date of Major Lynde's surrender, I addressed each of them a note on the 10" inst: requesting them to furnish a description of any drafts that might have gotten into the hands of the rebels.

Receiving no reply from Lieut. Plummer, but hearing incidentally that the money in his possession had been lost and found by the Texans, I applied to the Department Commander and obtained from him an order for Lieut. Plummer to furnish immediately a description of the checks. The order was issued on the 20th inst.

The return express brought Lt. P.'s reply, in which he states that the checks amounting to about ten thousand dollars Subsistence funds and six thousand dollars Qr. master's funds, were lost at Fort Fillmore, found by the Texans, and that the Commanding Officer [i.e., John R. Baylor] gave him a receipt for thirteen thousand five hundred dollars, the amount represented to have been found.

He can give no description of the checks except that they were endorsed in blank by Major G. R. Paul and Lieut. W. B. Lane. Those endorsed by Lieut. Lane were most probably drawn by Colonel Grayson and are the Subsistence funds. I have written to the Asst. Treasurer, New York, on the subject. A copy of my letter I include with this.

Major [James L.] Donaldson, Chief Quartermaster, and myself will together bring charges against Lieut. Plummer, for criminal carelessness in allowing checks endorsed in blank to fall into the hands of the enemy.

Very Resp. Yr. obdt. Svt.
Jno. P. Hatch
Capt. R.M.R.
Act'g C.S.

Maj. Genl. Geo. Gibson
Comy. Genl. of Subs.[11]

(Copy)

Subsistence Office
Santa Fe N.M. Aug. 25, 1861

Sir,

There fell into the hands of the Texas rebels at Fort Fillmore about ten thousand dollars Subsistence funds. I can get no description of the checks from Lieut. A. H. Plummer, 7th Infy., a.a.c.s.[*sic*] who was the holder of the checks, except that they were endorsed in blank by Lieut. W. B. Lane, R.M.R.

I presume they were drawn by Colonel Jno. B. Grayson, and would recommend the careful scrutiny of every draft bearing Lieut. Lane's endorsement before payment.

Drafts drawn by Colonel Jno. B. Grayson in favor of Lieut. W. B. Lane, endorsed by him to Lieut. C. B. Stivers, since transferred to Lieut. Saml. Archer, are now in the hands of the last named gentleman, and will be paid out by him in business transactions.

Very Respectfully
Your obdt. Svt.
Jno. P. Hatch
Capt. R.M.R.
Act'g C.S.

Asst. Treasurer U.S.
New York[12]

Head Quarters Southern Military Dist.
Fort Craig N.M. Aug. 26, "61.
Sir

I have the honor to report for the information of the commanding of-
ficer of the Department, that the two columns of Dragoons and Mounted
Riflemen detached from this post to the support of Capt. Hubbell of the
New Mexico Mounted Volunteers, returned yesterday.

They pursued the retreating Texans to the "Point of Rock" on the
Jornado. There was no probability of overtaking the fugitives in their rapid
retreat, and further pursuit was abandoned. The Texans were well mounted
and had extra horses.

I am Sir very Respectfully
Your obt. servt.
(Signed) B. S. Roberts
To Lieut. A. L. Anderson   Lt. Col. U.S.A.
A.A.A. General   Comdg. Southern Mil. Dist.
Dept. of N.M.
Santa Fe N.M.[13]

Fort Craig N.M. 4th Sept. 1861
Dear Colonel:

I send the moving command from this Post, taking the <u>Abo</u> pass by
Punta de l'Agua for Fort Union. This cuts off some 70 or more miles, is a
better road, better watered & better grass. I send from here all the tents,
horse equipments &c. that may be needed at Union, to put the columns
that march from there in condition to cross the plains. No stores will be left
here not needed for the volunteers. It takes all the small ordnance at the
Post to supply the regulars with 100 rounds each for the march. The columns march with 12 days rations, and they exhaust the commissary stores
of the Post; but the train en route from Albuquerque will supply the volunteers to include the middle of October.

Captain Moore, with the command he marched here from Breckinridge
and Buchanan, starts tomorrow morning. Capt. Selden, with the remainder
of the regulars, will leave on Monday the 9th, following Capt. Moore by the
Abo pass. I shall take [the road by way of?] Albuquerque and see to the final
arrangement of moving the regulars remaining there, and go on to Fort
Union at such time as may seem best, when I know the condition of things
at that Post.

The Gen[l] Court has adjourned without doing anything. I understand it so construed the Gen¹ Order from Washington of 3ʳᵈ July, constituting the Department of the West, and assigning Gen¹ Fremont to its command, as to deprive you of the legal right to order a General Court. I take it for granted the proceedings will advise you fully of what was done.

It is said there was no captious disposition manifested questioning your ample military powers to command the Department, but the question relating to the legal constitution of the Court was a matter of doubt and they did not proceed.

Nothing new from below.

Very truly Colonel
I remain Yours

Col. E. R. S. Canby   B. S. Roberts
U.S. Army   Lt. Col. U.S.A.

N.B. By moving across by Manzano, I avoid all the river towns, where the small pox is making its ravages. There is not a case in the command, although it is all round the Post. There is no serious sickness at the Post, and yet the malaria of Forts Buchanan & Breckinridge keeps some 60 on the sick list. It is thought crossing the country will do more than the entire pharmacopeia to remove this malaria.

B. S. R.[14]

Fort Craig Sept. 7, 1861

Dear Sir:

Since writing an hour ago, I have recᵈ the enclosed from the Padre of Las Cruces, sent by a Mexican. It was sewed up in [the] bottom lining of his pantaloons. The German it mentions is the man you gave a letter, asking to pass him below. He agreed to send me, without delay, reliable information in this way, and I believe it is reliable. This Padre (Chavis) is reported as loyal & true to the U.S. Government.

The bearer of the note came with a party of Mr. [Pinckney R.] Tully, a former sutler at Fort Fillmore, and had a pass from Col. Baylor, asking Col. McCulloch to permit him to cross the Jornada.

Yours truly,

Col. E. R. S. Canby   B. S. Roberts
U.S. Army   Lt. Col. U.S.A.
Santa Fe, N.M.[15]

<u>Copy</u>

Fort Fauntleroy N. Mexico
September 13, 1861.

Hon. Sir,

It is with deepest grief that I have to report that about the hour of four o'clock, a large meeting of the Navajo Indians having assembled for the purpose of running their horses, they were within two hundred yards of the Fort, in front of the Guard house. At first they appeared to be very peaceable, but after their race was over, they all approached and stood within a hundred yards of the Guard house, when one of them attacked a sentinel, trying to take his arms from him and cocking his pistol on the sentinel's breast.

At the same time an [Indian?] of the name Miguelito, belonging to the peaceable portion of the Navajo tribe, seeing that the other Indians had entered into difficulties with the sentinel, and were making every preparation of war that they possibly could. He then shot and killed an Indian of a party called Chay's Ladrons, who had come for the purpose of attacking the post. After this happening, the Indians of Chay's—numbering about two hundred, well armed and mounted, advanced towards the Guard, shooting at the men that were on guard, but immediately the Officer of the Guard charged upon the Indians and immediately the companies protected the Guard and fired into them, when they put off in different directions, leaving twelve dead bodies and forty prisoners or captives.

At the same time that they attacked the Fort, another party of Indians attacked the escort that was with the citizens engaged as herders herding Government animals. First Lt. José Ma. Sanchez of Capt. José D. Sena's company was immediately sent with twelve mounted and thirty-two Infty. to protect the Govt. property, who overtook the Indians and recovered all the property that they were trying to drive off, without losing a man, and having only one wounded (a citizen engaged as a herder), taking with them only five horses belonging to the companies and one mule and two oxen belonging to the Gov't. But at the same time we have in our possession seven horses that were taken away from them.

I hope that you will send me the companies that have to fill the garrison of this Fort as soon as you think it proper, as our circumstances require it.

Very respectfully Yours
(Signed)   Manuel Chavez

Col. E. R. S. Canby   Ten'te Corl. 2nd R.N.M.V[l].
Comd'g. Dept. of N. Mex.[16]   Comandante del Fuerte

Fig. 7. Manuel Chavez y Garcia de Noriega, Lieutenant Colonel, Second Regiment, New Mexico Volunteers. Courtesy of Museum of New Mexico, negative no. 9833.

Head Quarters Southern Military District of N.M.
Fort Craig N.M. Sept. 17th 1861.

(Confidential)

Colonel

I have the honor to submit to you my plan for the general disposition of the forces in this Military District. I propose to hold all the regulars at this post and at Albuquerque, the greater portion of both mounted and foot being kept well in hand here. Colonel Pino's Regiment of 2nd foot volunteers, I shall post in the main towns along the river, from Albuquerque down to Socorro, say one company at Los Lunas or Peralta, two at or near Sabinal, and two at or near Limitar. The other three Companies of this Regiment garrison Fort Fauntleroy, and this arrangement disposes of the eight Companies at present organized. When the other two Companies that complete the organization of this Regiment are mustered in, they can be profitably stationed at intermediate points, or in the town of Cañada Lamosa below here.

By this disposition, these forces can furnish all the details for the escort of trains, and no escort will be obliged to make more than a two-days march, by a system of relief from post to post. The towns will moreover be protected from Indian depredations, and the people, under the sense of security of arms, will more willingly rally to repel invasion, should one be made. The habit of Mexican soldiers to have their wives follow the Camp, can in this way be somewhat indulged, as their families can be housed with them, and their general poverty will find relief in sharing the rations of the men. I doubt not many more volunteers will enter the ranks, encouraged by this plan, and by the presence and efforts of officers in their midst.

There will be no difficulty, as I conceive, in arranging with the Prefects of these towns a plan to rent convenient buildings to accommodate the troops.

This arrangement would, in my judgement, be most profitable and expedient. It will enable me to hold all the regulars at this post & at Albuquerque, ready for emergencies; and save the constant waste of mounted forces by calls for escort duty. The Mounted Volunteers should be held here to operate with the regulars. They serve exceedingly well for scouting and picket duty.

I am cutting 7000 *terrones* per day, compelled to resort to that expedient to finish the defenses, as the continued rains destroyed all the adobes. I shall continue the cutting and drying of *terrones* until enough are made to add to the Quarters, Stables & Corrals, so as to accommodate at least 6 mounted companies and to quarter a thousand or more troops. It appears to me a necessity to enlarge this post, as well as to strengthen it. Additional store houses must also be built. This is decidedly the strongest point on the river, and the key for military operations. By the employment of spies at Manzano, and by occupying the Abo pass with one or two mounted volunteer Co's, all attempts of Texan forces to pass round this fort, or to reach Albuquerque by Chililí, will be known to me and frustrated.

The defenses that were well in progress and washed away by the recent floods are going rapidly forward and will be completed at the earliest day. Lack of timber, entrenching tools and other force, has made the work more an uphill business than I had expected. But the post will be very strong when the works are completed.

Captain Selden concurs with me fully in presenting this plan.

I am Colonel very Respectfully
Your obt. servt.

Colonel E. R. S. Canby   (Signed) B. S. Roberts
U.S. Army,   Lieut. Col. U.S. Army
Comdg. Dept. N.M.[17]   Comdg. Sou[th] District

———◆———

Head Quarters Southern Mil. Dist. of N.M.
Sabinal Sept. 27th 1861.

Sir

The Lieut. Col. comdg. the District, having learned that another company of Mt[d]. Volunteers has arrived at Albuquerque, directs that the two companies now there be sent to relieve Capt. Moore's command near Manzano, with instructions to observe the country south & east of that position, and give timely notice if possible to the commanders of Albuquerque & Fort Craig, of the approach of the enemy towards Abo pass.

These companies of volunteers will, without further instructions from these H[d] Q[rs], be kept supplied by the Depôt Commissary with one month's provisions.

On the arrival of these troops at the point designated, Capt. Moore's command will probably be found absent, having been ordered to Fort Craig. The commander of the Squadron of Volunteers will, however, proceed to establish a camp at some point suitable for the purpose indicated, and immediately thereafter will report, by express, to Dist. H[d]. Q[rs]. at Fort Craig.

I am, Sir, very Respectfully
Your obt. Servt.

To   Signed A. McRae
The Commanding Officer   Capt. 3rd Cav.
Albuquerque N.M.[18]   A.A.A.G.

———◆———

Fort Craig 5th Oct. 1861.

(unofficial)

My Dear Col:

I could not well send Dr. [Joseph H.] Bill to Santa Fe, as urgently requested in the enclosed letter, but thought it better to send the communication directly to you and leave at your discretion such action as it demands.
It is some 3 weeks since Dr. Bill, by my direction, made out his requisitions
covering the instruments he asks and the medicines &c. as much needed,
but as you have informed me that Hospital supplies, medicines &c. have
been ordered, I infer that they will reach this Post at as early a day, without
Dr. Bill's presence, as is possible.

Capt. Moore's squadron reached this Post last evening. He brings in a
soldier charged with the murder of a Mexican woman in Manzano, under
circumstances of great atrocity, and I learn unofficially that you had ordered him to send the murderer into Albuquerque. As your order was not
rec^d until after Capt. Moore was directed by me to report at this Post, he
brought him with his command, and by this express I send to your Adjutant
General the charges & ask a Court or a Military Commission for his trial. It
appears to me that examples must be made of soldiers guilty of these atrocities. I have two deserters here who deserted from [Fort] Fillmore in April
and joined the Confederate Rebels. They ought to be hanged without trial,
on their own confession. I think a Military Commission would best dispose
of such cases.

I am merciless enough to charge all our misfortunes in this Territory to
drunkness [*sic*] of officers. In my estimation, it is the cause of the great
demoralization throughout the ranks. If officers daily debauch themselves
with whiskey, what can be expected of [the] men? Lynde's surrender was, as
I believe, consequential upon whiskey! The tampering with the loyalty of
the men by the officers who have joined the Rebels, helped to effect the
mass [*sic*], but the principal "leven" was whiskey. I am resolved to abate this
nuisance in this region, and am destroying all the whiskey about me and
seizing the property of all persons who bring it about the Post or sell or give
it to soldiers.

The territorial laws prohibit selling or giving whiskey to any soldier
under any circumstances, under severe penalties—those laws I am execut-
ing and hope to find good results.

Nothing is new from below. I fix Capt. Moore in camp 10 miles below,
with his squadron & Mink's Co. I have attached Capt. [James "Paddy"]
Graydon to that Co. for temporary duty. I have broken up four Companies
of my Regiment, transferred the men to the other Cos. and attached non

com^d officers temporarily, and yet after Capt. Hatch's Co. is filled up to 76, these 5 Cos. will not average 50 as an aggregate. By this arrangement, & having Capt. Claflin for duty, there will be one spare Co. officer to act as my Adjutant General &c. &c.

I am preparing instructions for Capt. Archer & shall fix the Camp at Sabinal, the moment Camp & Garrison equipage arrives.

I will send you a copy of my orders tomorrow.

> Very truly yours
> B. S. Roberts
> Lt. Col. U.S.A.

Col. E. R. S. Canby U.S.A.
Santa Fe, N.M.
"<u>Leaven</u>" (Webster) but he is wrong.

N.B. My spies are just in from Fort Thorne and report that the Texans have all fallen back from that place to the Mesilla.[19]

> Head Quarters Albuquerque New Mexico
> October 18, 1861.

Sir,

I have the honor to report the arrival at this Post, from Fort Union, of Companies "I" & "K," 1st Regt. New Mexican Foot Volunteers, with the following Officers,—1st Lieut. E. Everett, Rgtl. Adjt.; 1st Lieut. L. G. Murphy, R. Qr. Mr.; Captain R. Chacon, 1st Lieuts. A. P. Damours and B. Machowicz; and 2nd Lieuts. J. Soliz [Saiz?], A. A. Gallegos, and J. Murphy, same Regiment—the latter unattached. The oaths of allegiance, which were administered to the above named Officers to-day, will be forwarded by tomorrow's express.

> I am, Sir
> very respectfully
> Your obedient Servant,
> Saml. Archer
> Capt. 5" If.

Lieut. A. L. Anderson   Comdg. Post
A.A.A.G.
Hd. Qrs. Dept. New Mexico
Santa Fe, N.M.[20]

Head Quarters Southern Military District
Dept. of N.M. Fort Craig 21ˢᵗ Oct. 1861.

Sir

I have the honor to report for the information of the Commanding Colonel of the Department, the completion of the defenses of this Post. Embarrassments not anticipated when I received the order "to put Fort Craig in condition for permanent defense" have delayed the work, but the command has been diligent at its labors and the defenses are strong and of permanent character.

The Post is laid on a parallelogram, the long sides being three hundred yards long, the shorter two. The rear of the Quarters, Store houses, Stables and Corrals are on the lines of these sides and connected with adobe walls eight feet high & musket proof. Wall and buildings are looped for musketry at every three & a half feet, giving an effective fire for the longest range over a level plain on all sides.

The sides are flanked by two regular bastions on the diagonal corners, one with a capacity for two guns & two Mountain Howitzers, the other for two guns or two howitzers. The longest conveniently covers two hundred & fifty men, and has an effective fire for two hundred muskets down two sides of the Post. The smaller protects the other two sides by the fires of two Mountain Howitzers and one hundred & fifty muskets. Besides, there are five outworks with open gorges towards the Post, crowning commanding points on the river bluffs, sustaining each other, covering the rear to water and preventing approaches by the river bottom.

Captain [Peter] Plympton of the 7ᵗʰ Infantry has had the immediate charge of building the permanent portion of the defenses and I cannot withhold the expression of my perfect satisfaction with his industry, labour and success. Two mortars would now enable this Post to withstand quite a siege by a regularly appointed army. If any are in the Department, I would respectfully recommend their being sent to this Post.

I have the honor to be very
Respectfully Your obt. Servt.
(Signed) B. S. Roberts

To The Asst. Adjt. Genl. U.S.A.   Lieut. Col. U.S.A.
Santa Fe N. M.²¹   Comdg.

Hᵈ. Qʳˢ Southern Miliary District of N.M.
Fort Craig Oct. 30ᵗʰ 1861

Sir

I am directed to report for the information of the Department Commander, that it is understood that Colonel Miguel Pino has absented himself without leave from the District in which he was assigned to duty, and is spending his time in Santa Fe.

This information was derived through an officer who was sent for the purpose of bringing in the recruits who were supposed to have been enlisted. He reports that no enlistments have been made. That this want of success is due to a lack of exertion on the part of the officers detailed for this duty is plain from the fact that Captain Graydon of the independent Mounted Volunteers, who has just returned here, after an absence of less than eight days, has succeeded in raising sixty men.

The District Commander therefore recommends that the effort to fill up Colonel Pino's Reg^t. on its present Company organization be abandoned, and that the existing Companies be consolidated into a number having the maximum strength according to merit, and the services of the superfluous may be dispensed with.

The aggregate of the four volunteer companies at Fort Craig is 254. After forming two companies, the third could probably be filled up.

I am Sir Very Respectfully

Your ob^t Servt.

To.   (Signed) A. McRae

The Act. Asst. Adjt. Genl   Capt. 3rd Cav.

Dept. of N.M   A.A.A.G.

Santa Fe N.M.

Head Quarters, S. Mil. District, N.M.

Fort Craig, N.M. Nov. 2' 1861.

Captain

If the people of Paraje have corn for sale, they must supply your camp, and if they refuse to do so or ask more than three dollars a fanega, you are directed to take the corn, giving receipts for the amounts.

Whenever you are convinced that families have no more corn than they need for their own use, you will not of course deprive them of that, but if they are reserving corn for higher prices, you will take it.

I am, Capt., very respectfully

Your obdt. Servant

Capt. I. N. Moore,   Sig. B. S. Roberts

1st Cavalry

Commanding at Paraje

Hd. Qrs. Southern Mil. District Dept. N.M.
Fort Craig N.M. Nov. 10, 1861.

Sir

In reply to your letter of today, I am directed to inform you that seven days' rations will be sent to you at the Cañada Alamosa, where you will remain for the present.

To avoid a misfortune similar to that which occurred to Captain Mink's Company, it will be necessary for you to observe the utmost vigilance, and to watch well not only the movements of the Texan Scouts, but those of the people at the Cañada.

With confidence that you will use these precautions to prevent a surprise, your suggestion has been adopted.

I am Respectfully
Your obt. Servant

Capt. J. Graydon   (sgd.)   A. McRae
Independent Vols.   Capt. 3rd Cavalry
Camp at Cañada Alamosa   A.A.A.G.

Head Quarters Southern Military District Dept. of N.M.
Fort Craig N.M. November 10th, 1861.

My Dear Colonel:

Captain Graydon's Spy Pickets fell upon a party of 13 Texans scouting some 30 miles from this Post on Friday; killed one of them and took one officer and two [men?] prisoners. They are now in confinement here. I get nothing new from them, as by examining them separately and keeping them confined apart, their stories are contradictory, and many of them I think false.

It is quite probable that Genl. Sibley is on his way from San Antonio to reinforce Col. Baylor with about one thousand men; and that the troops are now throwing up entrenchments at Doña Ana. But there seems to me doubts as to the possibility of the Texans subsisting that force in the Mesilla. They have no money and certainly Texans cannot furnish supplies for the large forces reported to be in the field.

I do not recognize Lieut. [William] Simmons, the officer made prisoner by Capt. Graydon, as entitled to the treatment of a prisoner of war. He acknowledges that he has no commission from the Southern Confederate States, and pretends only to be in office by appointment from Col. Baylor. He is the Lieut. of Capt. Frazer's Company, and that company was raised from the outlaws in and around Fort Bliss, Franklin &c., and bore arms against the Government of the United States voluntarily as an organization of bandits & thieves. I have therefore told him that I confine him and hold him as a rebel and not as a prisoner of war.

I am Colonel Very Respectfully
Your obt. Servant.
(Sig^d) B. S. Roberts

To Col. E. R. S. Canby   Lieut. Col. U.S.A.

U.S.A. Comdg.   Comdg.

Hd. Qrs. So. Mil. Dist. of N.M.,
Fort Craig, Nov. 13, 1861.

Sir,

The Commanding Officer of the District having endeavored to ascertain the character of the officers of Col. Pino's Regiment, in order to point out those who deserve advancement, those who are capable of instruction, and those who may be dropped with benefit to the service, directs me to make the following report.

Captains Roman Baca and Gregorio Otero have been on recruiting service some six weeks, without securing a recruit, and, it is believed on good authority, without making an effort to do so.

2nd Lieut. Mexicano, of Capt. Otero's Company (D), has been, for some time, absent without leave.

2nd Lieut. Sisnero [Diego Sisneros], of Capt. [Juan] Labadi's Company (H), is considered incapable of instruction.

It is recommended that these officers be dropped.

1st Lieut. William Brady, Adjutant, and 1st Lt. C. E. Cooley, R.Q.M., are considered officers of merit, and are recommended for promotion.

To

The A.A.A.G.

Dept. of N.M.,

Santa Fe, N.M.

Hd. Qrs. Southern Military District of N.M.
Fort Craig N.M. Nov. 30th 1861

Sir,

In reference to the order requiring the Companies of yours to place themselves in huts, I am directed to say that while Col. Roberts supposed that they might use to advantage the vacant houses of the Bosque Bonito, and authorized you to transfer your camp to that place, he intended to leave the matter to your discretion.

If you decide not to occupy these houses, it will be necessary for you to commence immediately the construction of huts.

I am, Sir, Very Respectfully

Your obt. Servt.

(Sigd) A. McRae

Commanding Officer   Capt. 3rd Cav.

Camp San Cristoval N.M.   A.A.A.G.

Hd. Qrs. Southern Mil. District of N.M.

Fort Craig N.M. December 5th 1861

Captain:

You will proceed with your Company and Captain [Edward] Treacy's of the 3rd Cavalry to Cañada Alamosa and take temporary post at or near that town, taking rations with you to include the 20th inst.

The object of posting you at this point is to watch the movements of the Texans, and that you may not be surprised by them I place with you on picket duty three Companies. Should you find yourself threatened at any time by any considerable force of the enemy, you will express notice of the fact to the forces nearest to you and to myself without delay; and repel or hold in check such attempts as will not endanger your command, but make no general engagement or advance on the Mesilla, unless you are assured of decided advantage.

You will forage your horses & mules as far as possible on grass and corn the inhabitants of the town must supply, and you will require their services for this purpose, but take no corn or wheat to an extent that will exhaust their domestic supply.

The Quarter Master of the Post will give you such transportation as will enable you to carry these instructions into effect.

I am Captain Very Respectfully

Your obt. Servant

Captain R. M. Morris   sig. B. S. Roberts

3rd Cavalry   Lt. Col. U.S.A.

Fort Craig   Comdg.

Head Quarters Southern Mil. Dist. of N.M.

Fort Craig N.M. Dec. 5th 1861.

Sir.

I am directed by the Commanding Officer of the Southern Military District to inform you that you are especially charged with guarding the crossing of the river at your camp. You will cause all *carretas* to be inspected and persons passing with stores of any kind, and seize the property of any one found carrying intoxicating liquors to Paraje, into your camp, or into the military reservation of Fort Craig. No soldiers will be permitted to go below your camp on your side of the river without a pass from the Commanding Officer of Fort Craig or myself. During the day you will send them back to the Commands to which they belong, and if any attempts are made to pass you in the night without my own written authority, you will confine the persons making such attempts. The communication on this side of the river to Captain Moore's command is not subject to your supervision, and you will not interfere with this side of the river, unless you have reason to believe suspicious persons are trying to evade the crossing at your camp to reach Paraje or the Jornado.

The town of Paraje is under the directions of Captain Moore of the 1st Cavalry, and you will take no observance of that place, without his consent and directions.

I wish you to keep a picket on the bluff on your side of the river and permit no one to pass up or down the road on that mesa. Arrest all persons attempting to pass you by that way.

Captain Moore of the 1st Cavalry is authorized to call for your services in any emergency, and you will obey his orders accordingly.

Citizens known to you to be living in Paraje and to be loyal, you can pass to this post, and see that they report to you on their return. If you find public arms or public property in their possession, you will seize it and make them prisoners. They must, however, pass and return between sunrise and sunset. None can pass in the night. If you have occasion to go on to the Jornado in pursuit of deserters or otherwise, you must report that fact to Captain Moore in order that his pickets may know how to treat your men.

I am Sir, Very Respectfully
Your obedient Servant

To Captain Juan Barrientos   sig^d   A. McRae
Independent Volunteers   Capt. 3rd Cav.
Comdg. Camp near Fort Craig N.M.   A.A.A.G.

Hd. Qrs. Southern Mil. Dist. of N.M.
Fort Craig N.M. Dec. 13th 1861

Sir,

The Commanding Officer of the District directs that on your arrival at Captain Moore's camp at the Bosque Bonito, you will place your company in camp there, forming a part of that command, and that you will report in person at these Head Quarters.

I am, Sir, Very Respectfully
Your obt. Servant

To Capt. R. M. Morris   (sig^d.)   A. McRae
3rd Cavalry   Capt. 3rd Cav.
En route to Fort Craig   A.A.A.G.

Head Qrs. S.M. District, N.M.
Fort Craig, Dec. 16" 1861.

Sir.

I have the honor to report to the Commanding Officer of the Department the arrest of Captain R. M. Morris of the 3rd Rgmt. of Cavalry, U.S. Army, and the facts that have led me up to this necessity.

On the 5th inst., I assigned this Officer to the command of Cañon Lamosa, the advanced picket of this District, with instructions as per copy herewith enclosed marked No. 1. About midnight of the 11th, Captain Moore of the First Cavalry, stationed 8 miles below this post, received the enclosed marked No. 2. Captain Moore declined to obey this order and expressed it to me with a note asking instructions, and sent me by same express the enclosed from Captain Morris marked No. 3.

I replied to Capt. Moore that he would not obey the order, and forthwith ordered Lieut. Lord of the 1st Cavalry to proceed with his Company to Cañon Lamosa and relieve Captain Morris, with orders to the latter officer to report to me in person at the Head Quarters. My instructions to Capt. Morris are very explicit, and his attempt to draw in this manner any part of these forces to his aid, and to make an independent movement against the Texans, is one of those high breaches of discipline that I cannot overlook.

No Command is safe, when orders of superiors are held in this disregard, and responsibility of this grave character assumed by Juniors. Capt. Morris is now in arrest at this post and his case is referred to the Col. Commanding the Department for his orders thereon.

I am, Sir, very respectfully
Your obedt. Servant,

A. Asst. Adjt. Genl.   Signed B. S. Roberts
Dpt. N.M.   Lt. Col. U.S. Army
Santa Fe   Comd'g

Hd. Qrs. So. Mil. Dist. Dept. N. Mex°.

Fort Craig 23ᵈ Decʳ 1861.

Captain.

I have directed Lieut. Mishler of Co. I, 5 Infantry, to report to you for duty in conformity with your request for additional forces. It is not my intention to garrison troops at the Cañon Lamosa, but to keep such force as will make picket and scouting duty as easy as may be, and secure you and the troops above from any surprise and loss of stock.

It is my policy to hold Cañon Lamosa against such enterprises as the Texans have heretofore made in this direction, that seemed to have been intended for the purpose of plunder and information. But not to attempt to engage any large force at that point, that can be drawn nearer to this Post to accomplish their capture and total defeat. You will therefore be governed accordingly.

I am sir very Respt.

Your ob. sert.

Sgd. B. S. Roberts

Capt. R. S. C. Lord   Col. Vols. Comdg.

1ˢᵗ Cavly.

Hd. Qrs. So. Mil. Dist. Dept. N.M.

Fort Craig N. Mex°.

[no date; ca. Dec. 23, 1861]

Captain:

I have directed Captain Lord with all or such portion of his command as may in his judgement seem best, to report to you; and I have ordered Capt. Barrientos, with his company of Independent Mounted Vols. to proceed to the "Cañada Lamosa" and relieve Captain Graydon's from picket duty there, should the latter officer be left there on that service.

You will communicate daily with that picket, and keep me advised of the state of things in that direction and on the Jornada.

Capt. Graydon is ordered to report to you, on being relieved by Captain Barrientos, and the latter officer is instructed to fall in upon you, if seriously threatened by the Texans.

I rely wholly on the vigilance of your command to convert the enterprises of the Texans upon our stock to our own advantage, by stampeding and seizing their caballo yards [*sic*] whenever such opportunity is offered.

You are sensible, Captain, that unusual diligence must be brought against the volunteers and irregular habits of such an enemy as the Texans, and your experience and intelligence will suggest expedients to defeat their purpose and to make them an easy enemy to demoralize and to conquer.

I am Capt. very Respectfully
Your obt. Servant

To Capt. I. N. Moore, 1ˢᵗ Cavalry   Sgd. B. S. Roberts
Comdg. at Bosque Bonito N.M.   Col. Vols. Comdg.

Canad A La Mosa
December 25" 1861

Dear Col.

Graydon has just arrived from El Paso. He left there on the night of the 23ʳᵈ. He says he counted on the 22ⁿᵈ pass Harts Mill 900 hundred Mt. Men just from San Antonio. 11 Companies, 3 of Lancers, and two of Negros. 600 men had left for [Fort] Fillmore the day before, which he did not see. There are at Ft. Bliss also 500 men, and the original number at Ft. Fillmore. Sibley is on the Pecos, on his road to Ft. Stanton with 2000 men. They have in all 4000 men, 32 pieces of artillery. Graydon has all his information from the Priest and it is reliable.

I am Your Obᵈᵗ Serᵛᵗ
R. S. C. Lord
1 Lieut. Cavly Comdg.

9 O'clock A.M.
P.S. The Priest says they will march for Ft. Craig in a few days.

Lt. Lord

Head Quarters Southern M" Dist: Fort Craig N.M.
25 Dec" 1861.

Colonel:

I send you this report expressed to me in haste from Cañon La Mosa. There appears to be no doubt about the truth of this news. I shall forthwith make preparations here, and the supplies should be hurried on.

There is a rumor here in the garrison this morning that 650 Texans have already reached ~~Cañon La Mosa~~ Fort Thorne.

Very truly yours
B. S. Roberts
Lt. Col. U.S.A.
Comdg.[22]

Sabinal Dec. 26, 1861.

D. Major

If the information contained in the enclosed letter be correct, the plan of the Texans will, in my judgement, be to threaten Fort Craig with a portion of their force, and act with the main body upon Fort Union or Albuquerque. The news by the next express will probably develop this and if it should, it is my intention to garrison Fort Craig strongly and move the main body of the Command now there in the direction of Manzano, strengthening it by the available forces from other points. I have ordered six companies of volunteers to be concentrated at Albuquerque as soon as possible, and can add two or three more if the news by the express should indicate its necessity.

If Fort Union is the point aimed at, we can reinforce it before it can be reached by the Texans. Paul needs an efficient second there and additional regular troops. To unite both objects, I have ordered Capt. [William H.] Lewis from Santa Fe. A Company of Colorado Volunteers is ordered from Fort Garland to Santa Fe. The resources of your department will be taxed to provide for the operations that will be necessary, if this news be true.

Of course, all Indian operations will be subordinate to those against the Texans, and the volunteer companies at or ordered to points in the District for protection against the Indians will be called in, if you think it necessary, and sent where they are more needed.

Please communicate this information to Maj. Paul as soon as possible, and send an express to Fort Garland with the orders for the company from that place.

In haste
Very Truly
Yours &-
Ed. R. S. Canby
Col. 19. Infy.

Maj. Donaldson
Santa Fe N.M.[23]

———————— ◆ ————————

Head Quarters Dept. of N.M.
Sabinal N.M. Dec. 26" 1861.

Special Orders No. 228.

    I Company "G" 5 Infantry will proceed without delay to Fort Union and report for duty to the Commanding Officer of that post.

    II The Company of Colorado Volunteers now at Fort Garland will be sent with as little delay as possible to Santa Fe to report for duty at that place.

III Major J. L. Donaldson, already assigned to duty according to his brevet rank, is assigned to the command of the District of Santa Fe.

By order of Col. E. R. S. Canby
W^m. J. L. Nicodemus

For Major J. L. Donaldson   1 Lt. 11 Infantry
Comdg. Mil. Dist. of Santa Fe   A.A.A. General
Santa Fe N.M.²⁴

Hd. Qrs. Southern Mil. District of N.M.
Fort Craig N.M. Dec. 30th 1861.

Captain:

I received your note by Graydon. The spies will all be paid. As they are all to be here or pass by here very soon, I will pay them here. I have ordered Paraje to be abandoned & all the stock to be driven above. You will bring everybody from Cañada Alamosa and cause all the stock to be driven above this Post. Barrientos' Company or part of it, as you think best, will remain as spies, and Captain Moore will communicate daily with him.

I have resolved that none but my own troops shall be between me and the Texans, and then we can know what we are about. I send you the last paper.

I am Captain Very Respectfully
Your obt. servant,
(Sig^d) B. S. Roberts

Capt. R. S. C. Lord 1st Cav.   Colonel Volunteers
Comdg. Cañada Alamosa N.M.²⁵   Commdg.

Head Quarters Dept. of New Mex.
Fort Craig Dec. 31, 1861.

Major:

The information from the Mesilla is still indefinite, and the number of troops there does not correspond with the number known to have been raised in San Antonio for New Mexico. Sibley is believed to be at El Paso, but the matter was kept so close that some trick is apprehended. Three regiments (Riley's, Green's & Steele's) were raised for Sibley's Brigade. Riley and Steele are in the Mesilla. Nothing is known of Green except that he marched from San Antonio on the 9th of Novr. I have some doubts of the movement up the Pecos, although with their whole force, it would undoubtedly be their true policy. I expect to get certain information in a day or two.

I wish you would say to Governor Connelly that the feelings of the people in the lower country is not so favorable, I think, as it should be, and that in my judgment he can do a great deal of good by coming down and visiting the river towns personally, and setting the people right.

The people and stock below Fort Craig will be moved up above this place, so that the Texans that come in this direction will find no means of support on this side of the Jornada.

In haste,
Very truly Yours &-
Ed. R. S. Canby

Maj. Donaldson
Cmg. &c. &c. Santa Fe N.M.[26]

"Battle Hymn of the Republic" (con't.)
(Julia Ward Howe, 1861)

He has sounded forth the trumpet that shall never call retreat;
He is sifting out the hearts of men before His judgment-seat;
Oh, be swift, my soul, to answer Him, be jubilant, my feet!
Our God is marching on.

Chorus: Glory, glory, Hallelujah! Glory, glory, Hallelujah!
Glory, glory, Hallelujah! Our God is marching on.

In the beauty of the lilies Christ was born across the sea,
With a glory in His bosom that transfigures you and me;
As he died to make men holy, let us die to make men free,
While God is marching on.
Chorus: Glory, glory, Hallelujah! &c.

He is coming like the glory of the morning on the wave,
He is wisdom to the mighty, he is honor to the brave;
So the world shall be his footstool, and the soul of wrong his slave,
Our God is marching on!
Chorus: Glory, glory, Hallelujah! &c

CHAPTER SEVEN
Confederate Correspondence,
July–December 1861

Adjt. and Inspr. Generals Office
Richmond V^a July 9th 1861

General

General H. H. Sibley under instructions from the President is to proceed to Texas, there to carry out, in concert with yourself, certain measures, of which he will advise you upon his arrival at San Antonio. It is desired that you will extend every facility to General Sibley in successfully carrying out his instructions, supplying as far as possible, the material for the armament & equipment of his command, and such needful supplies as he may require from the different departments under your control.

I am Sir Resply
Yr. Obdt. Ser't
S. Cooper
A. & I. G.

To Brig. Genl. Earl Van Dorn
Comd'g San Antonio Texas[1]

————————◆——————————

Head Quarters Ft. Bliss
July 17th 1861

Gen. Earl Van Dorn
Sir

Enclosed I send you a letter written by one of the most reliable men in New Mexico. It will give you some items of importance. I have supposed that a concentration of the U.S. forces would be followed by an attack on this place, for the reason that they would have a superiority of numbers, and I could see no reason for concentrating at [Fort] Fillmore all the forces in New Mexico and Arizona. I shall make all the necessary preparation for resisting an attack.

I learn from Capt. Garland that the enemy are sending 12 pound cannon to Fillmore. Capt. Jones has escaped from Ft. Fillmore and will be here tomorrow. I took the man [W. W.] Mills (mentioned in the letter I send) a

Fig. 8. Lieutenant Colonel John R. Baylor, CSA. Courtesy of Colorado Historical Society, negative no. F-24389.

prisoner and have him confined in the guard house. I will iron him and send him to San Antonio.

Very Respectfully
Jno. R. Baylor
Lt. Col. Comdg.
2nd Regt. T.M.R.[2]

———————— ◄►◄► ————————

Santa Fe July 7th 1861

Judge Crosby

　　D. Sir. The object of this letter must be my excuse for writing to you, and the principal part of that object is the safety of friends in your neighborhood.

The return of Judge Watts to this place from Wash. City has inaugurated a new state of affairs in New Mexico. He brought out with him commissions for the officers of two Regiments of Troops to be raised here for three years, immediately, and another as soon as those two were completed, this last to be Cavalry. That the 5th & 7th U.S. Infantry was to go to the States with the greatest dispatch, the two Mexican Regiments to relieve and take the place of those leaving—at the same time, the information leaked out that there was six hundred recruits on the road from Fort Leavenworth to fill up the vacancies in those two returning Regiments.

These two accounts created in my mind a doubt of the correctness of one of them, and I commenced a very cautious examination of all sources of information and became convinced, that there is no recall of troops from New Mexico, & that the information was circulated to throw your part of the country off their guard. That the two Mexican regiments would partly take the place of the U.S. Troops, which latter would concentrate at Forts Fillmore, Stanton & Craig & make a descent on Texas, down the Rio Grande. That there will be over one thousand Troops at Fort Fillmore before the first of August, and that many of our friends will be treated as traitors, according to the part they have taken in our present difficulties, is predetermined on.

Yesterday a young Lieut. arrived here from Fort Union, and during the evening, over a social glass (at my expense), he told me that the officers are fortifying Fort Union, & that all the troops are concentrating there from the upper posts in the Territory & that Major, Colonel, or General Earl Van Dorn was on the march from Texas to intercept & capture the six hundred recruits before mentioned, together with two hundred & fifty thousand dollars in transitu for New Mexico, & after which capture, Van Dorn would turn this course & attack Fort Union.

But, said the Lt., the Texans can't come it. The recruits & money turned north & are coming in by way of Denver City & Fort Garland, & will be in Sa fe [Santa Fe] by the first of August. I give you this for what it is worth, as young Lts. are not apt to know a commander's views, nor very correct over Juleps & Coblers. I wish you to advise our friends (as far as you can without compromising me, for this letter would hang me here, to the flag staff) of danger, particularly Judge Hart, McGoffin [sic], P. T. Herbert, Dowell & such as you can trust, but particularly Judge Hart, who will fare badly if taken. Please consider this confidential, & if you acknowledge this, I will if possible write you more anon.

Gen. [Claude] Jones & Mr. Mills arrived here yesterday p- mail. The General has become convinced there is ropes here if there is no cotton wood & is consequently silent. Mr. Mills appears to be "at Home" with Judge Watts & Col. Canby, present commander of this Department. Why do you let this man Mills stay among you? The next mail we will receive a new commanding officer, in the person of Gen. Stanton of Kansas notoriety, who is made a Gen[l] officer expressly to regulate & command New Mexico & Arizonia [*sic*].

If you write, your letter must be mailed at Fort Fillmore. No letters can leave here p- mail for Texas, & I send this privately. Wishing yourself and all friends clear of all difficulties, with this————present difficulties of our Country, I remain,

                    your friend [name torn out]

Judge Jos. F. Crosby
El paso Texas[3]

----•◆•----

That interesting little paper, the *Mesilla Times*, is at hand, with a week's later news, and that highly important. . . . The *Times* of the 3d August publishes the following: . . .

The U.S. troops have abandoned Western Arizona, destroying Fort Breckinridge and Fort Buchanan, with all the stores, etc., valued at $500,000. Col. Baylor captured at Fort Fillmore the following commissary stores:[4]

54 head beef cattle, 46,308 lbs. flour,[5] 663 lbs. rice, 6068 lbs. Rio coffee,[6] 588 gallons vinegar,[7] 325 lbs. tea, 2246 lbs. soap,[8] 18,847 lbs. hay,[9] 9000 lbs. bacon,[10] 56 bu. [bushels] beans,[11] 1273 [lbs.] preserved vegetables,[12] 7857 lbs. sugar, 1834 lbs. star candles,[13] 355 lbs. sperm candles,[14] 270 boxes soap.[15] [In addition to this, there is] an immense amount of corn and barley. 270 head of cattle sent from Fort Craig arrived just in time to be included in the surrender.

----•◆•----

                    Head Quarters Dept. of New Mexico
                    Santa Fe N.M. Aug. 17, 1861

Sir:

I have the honor to transmit for your information the enclosed copy of a letter from Col. McCulloch to Lt. Col. Baylor C.S.A.

                    Very respectfully Sir
                    Your obdt. servt.
                    A. L. Anderson

To Lt. Col. Chapman   2nd Lieut. 5 Inf.
Comdg. Fort Union N.M.   A.A.A. Gen[l].

----•◆•----

Rio Pecos July 21st 1861

Col. J. R Baylor
Sir:

You will make no attempt to take Fort Fillmore until I can effect a junction with you. I have besides my own regiment five hundred men with two batteries of artillery, Capt. Eagers and Capt. Michling's. I had a few animals stolen at Chadbourne, but recovered them with the loss, I am sorry to say, of Capt. Davidson and one private.

Do nothing to alarm the U.S. Troops, as my object is to surprise them while they are noticing you. Don't send any more expresses with less than ten men; it is not safe. Send copies of your dispatches by each of the men, so as to ensure my getting them. I will write you soon.

	Yours in haste
Official Copy for C.O. Fort Union	H. E. McCulloch
A. L. Anderson	Col. Comdg. 1st Reg't Rifles
2nd Lieut. 5 Inf.	C.S.A.
A.A.A. Genl.[16]	

--------------◆--------------

Head Quarters Ft. Bliss Aug. 12th 1861

Genl. Van Dorn
Sir.

I would respectfully ask that I may be allowed to go to Virginia to defend the graves of my Ancestors, and I ask for leave of absence for two months. My horses are broken down and will not be sufficiently recruited in less time for service, and, as there is nothing to do here, I would like to go where I can render some service to our country. I ask that some competent man may be sent to relieve me and that you will grant my request. I intend resigning at the expiration of my leave as I desire active service.

very respectfully
Jno. R. Baylor
Lt. Col. cmdg.
2nd Regmt. Mtd. Rifles
C.S.A.[17]

--------------◆--------------

Head Quarters Doña Ana
Capt. T. A. Washington   Sept. 26, 1861
A.A. Genl. C.S. Army
San Antonio

Sir: Enclosed herewith I send you a copy of Muster Roll of Company "A," U.S. Army, who were made Prisoners of War by the surrender of Maj. I. Lynde 7 Infty. U.S. Army, on the 26 of August [sic] last, not given in my

Return of Sept. 21 inst., supposing this Muster Roll to have been amongst those that I have mentioned as lost.

Also find a list of ordinance and ord. stores which I permitted Major I. Lynde to take with him to protect his command, conditioned that he would send them back on his arrival at Fort Craig, protected by an escort. He failed to send the promised guard, consequently the whole outfit was captured by the Indians.

You will please make this part of my report of the 21st inst.

(Sig^d) Jno. R. Baylor
Lt. Col. Comdg.
2nd Reg^t Mtd. Rifles[18]

Head Quarters, Doña Ana
Sept. 28th 1861

Sir:

I have the honor to acknowledge the receipt of your letter requiring me to furnish a list of the companies here and their respective positions & numbers. I have long since informed the Genl. Comd'g the Department that I had raised three companies of mounted troops, which I include in the forces under my command. The following companies comprise my command.

Captains	Co.	Station	Av.	Total	Remarks
P. Hardeman	"A"	Ft. Bliss	101		
C. L. Pyron	"B"	C. Roblero	89		A detachment of 26 men at Camp Stockton.
W. C. Adams	"C"	Ft. Davis	87		A detachment of 20 men @ Fort Lancaster.
Jas. Walker	"D"	Cmp. Roblero	85		A detachment of 20 men @ Ft. Davis.
I. C. Stafford	"E"	do.	95		
S. J. Richardson	"F"	Camp Wood	100		A detachment of 25 men @ Ft. Clark
H. A. Hammer	"H"	En Rte Ft. Bliss	100		
B. Coopwood		C'mp. Roblero	45		
G. F. Frazer		do. do.	40		
T. J. Mastin		Pino Alto	40		
T. T. Teel	"B"	Ft. Fillmore	90		Artillery
Jas. Davis		do. do.	50	922.	Infantry

By the next mail I shall be able to send a regular return of my command.

I have concentrated all the force I could muster about 9 miles above these Head Quarters, fearing an attack from Fort Craig, and I am daily [expecting] a strong force from that point to move against me. I regret that Capt. Hammer was not allowed to come here, as it would have been much easier to get reinforcements from San Antonio than [from] any other point. I would respectfully ask, that if I am expected to hold fifteen hundred regular troops and four regiments of New Mexican volunteers in check, with less than five hundred men, that some other force be sent to operate against the Indians.

Capt. Coopwood with one hundred and eighteen men was ordered up to Fort Craig to reconnoitre, and had an engagement with the enemy, 180 strong, above Fort Thorn, losing two men killed and several wounded, he killing ten or twelve of the enemy. I am now on my way to meet them and therefore need every man I have. [I will?] send by next mail the full particulars; in the mean time until reinforcements arrive, I beg that my strength here may not be diminished, for obvious reasons. New Mexico is literally opposed to us, and will have to be coerced.

Yours Respectfully
Jno. R. Baylor
Lt. Col. Comd'g
Texas Mts. Rifles

D. C. Stith
Capt T. A. Washington
A.A. Genl. C.S. Army
San Antonio
Texas[19]

— ⋅ —

Attack on Pino Alto by the Indians

The Mesilla Times, of the 3rd inst. [October 3, 1861], has the following account of an attack on Pino Alto by the Indians, and the partial destruction of the town:

By an express from Pino Alto and the Rio Membris, bringing urgent appeals for assistance from the citizens, we have startling intelligence from that quarter. The Apaches seem to have united, and their tribes have gathered in hosts and commenced a war of extermination against the whites, in earnest. In such formidable numbers they have never assembled before on the war scout, and never before have they, in all time, evinced such boldness and daring as to attack a town of two or three hundred houses in open daylight.

Nineteen-twentieths of the Territory of Arizona is under their undisputed control. We have Indians all around us. The slightest journey must be performed in numbers, and with armed bodies of men. The highways of a continent are impassable, but to armies. Every day brings from the east, west, north and south, appalling additions to our black list of Indian murders. Homes deserted, friends fallen victims to the savage foe. Added to this the scourge of war, and our situation is most piteous and most unfortunate. In our very midst is a multitude of friends, willing and ready to render assistance, but prevented by the presence of another foe.

On the morning of the 27th, the Apaches, 250 or 300 strong, attacked the town of Pino Alto. Capt. [Thomas J.] Mastin, and fifteen of the Aza. Guards, having opportunely arrived the night before, a desperate fight was kept up with the Indians for several hours, from the houses and corrals. The Indians were finally compelled to raise the siege with the loss of many of their braves. Private [J. B.] Corwin, of the Guards, was killed in the fight, and three citizens; two men were severely wounded, and several others slightly, and several missing. Many houses were burned. Capt. Mastin, of the Arizona Guards, is severely wounded; his arm being fractured. His conduct and that of his men is most enthusiastically spoken of by the citizens of Pino Alto.

Flornoy's train, en route for Sonora, with which were two American families, and some emigrants, was attacked one day out of Palo Pinto Mines, by about 150 Indians. They threw up a breastwork and defended themselves fourteen hours against the Apaches, losing two men. They would all have been inevitably massacred but for the arrival of Lieut. Swilling, with a detachment of the Arizona Guards, who escorted them safely to the Membris river. A Mexican train from Mesilla is corralled by the Indians at White Water.[20]

Head Quarters
Mesilla Aza. Ty.
Nov. 10th 1861

Col. H. E. McCulloch
Comdg. Dep't. of Texas
San Antonio.
Sir:

I have the honor to report that my picket guards caught a Lieutenant and three soldiers, mounted on U.S. horses and with government arms. I have them in the guard house and will keep them until further orders.

They report that they deserted as they had not been paid, and did not want to engage in the war. I think them spies. I will send you a report of their statement as soon as I can get them to relate anything of any importance.

Respectfully Your
Obt. Servt.
Jno. R. Baylor
Lieut. Col. Comdg troops
in Arizona Ty.[21]

Head Quarters,
La Mesilla Aza. Ty.
Nov. 10" 1861.

Sir:

I have moved my Head Qrs. from Doña Ana to this place for the following reasons: 1st I have a great deal of business to attend to as Governor of the Territory and it is essential that I should have troops here to enforce my authority, and maintain order. 2nd The small pox made its appearance at Doña Ana and I was forced to scatter the troops to prevent a contagion. I have rented suitable buildings for one company and have them now here. I trust this will meet your approval.

Respectfully Your Obt. Servt.
Jno. R. Baylor
Lieut. Col. Commanding
Troops Arizona[22]

El Paso Hd Qrs. Army
of New Mexico. Dec. 16, 1861.

Dear Genl.

It affords me pleasure to inform you, the representative of Texas at Richmond, that our "Texas Army," for the invasion & conquest of New Mexico, are almost all in the field. I will give you for the Texas Delegation a detailed statement of our forces, intentions, &c., satisfied that you will do all in your power for our Army, exclusively formed from your own gallant state, & whose mission we hope will be productive of such good results, perhaps glorious ones, for the future. You will remember that you advised me, as a Father & mentor, to accept the appointment Gen. Sibley had so kindly tendered me on his Staff. Well, so that you can whenever called upon state our condition, position, &c., I commence.

In the first place, Gen. Sibley was authorized by the President to take what force he thought proper to conquer New Mexico, Arizonia [sic] &c.—

drive every Federal soldier from its boundaries. Gen. Sibley chose Texas troops for this purpose. He left immediately for San Antonio. On account of the hardships &c. incident to a western campaign across our plains, mountains &c., it was very difficult to raise the men, the youth & chivalry preferring the grander fields of the Old Dominion, Missouri & Kentucky.

After immense labor & without <u>one cent of money</u> Gen. Sibley raised, almost entirely armed (<u>sometimes on his own private account</u>), clothed & drilled <u>three thousand of the finest Cavalry</u> in the C.S. Army. You know his men; they are truly "Texas Rangers," a large majority of them being "Cow Boys" & old Indian hunters from the extreme Western portions—without yet having received a <u>cent in money</u> (although he had twice dispatched me to Richmond for that purpose)—he <u>moved</u> his Army, with a train of <u>several hundred</u> wagons, toward New Mexico, all his immense supplies, beef, corn & flour <u>principally</u>, having plenty of transportation.

We left San Antonio on the 18th & on the way have passed Reily's Reg^t (1st), Tom Green's Regt. (2nd), & on the 2nd ult. Steele's (3rd) left San Antonio to join us. Reily's Regt. has already arrived here. Green's Regt. will be here in five days, Steele's in fourteen days. This force with Baylor's gallant Reg^t will make out little Army "<u>four thousand</u>" <u>strong</u>, with three companies of artillery (12 & 6 pounders). We have also <u>five hundred lanceros</u> (the lances were made in San Antonio by order of Gen. Sibley).

Gen. Sibley is very much pleased with the course of Lt. Col. Baylor in this department, & by virtue of his authority has appointed him Colonel, authorizing him to muster in "<u>for the</u> war" the 12 month troops now in his Regt. (2nd Texas Mt. Rifles), besides Arizonia & California volunteers to make the complement. Gen. Sibley hopes that the Texas Delegation, who so well know the gallantry & high worth of Col. Baylor, will see that his action in the matter will be confirmed.

Gen. Sibley, since his arrival here, has seen fit to declare "Martial Law." His action was heartily concurred in by Judge Crosby, the chief civil officer in this section, as by Magoffin, Hart, White & others of the chief inhabitants of the county. Gen. Sibley found this country perfectly overrun with desperadoes, gamblers, &c., who set at utter defiance every rule & system of organized society, who incited innocent citizens of the valley to rebel against the proper authorities, & only a few days ago compelled Col. Baylor, commanding the department, to shove one of them down in the <u>streets</u> of Mesilla in the protection of his life. When it arrived at this stage, when an officer high in command in the Confederate Army has to defend himself against the attack of every ruffian in the country, it was high time that a new state of affairs was inaugurated. Gen. Sibley called a council composed of his staff, all the leading respectable citizens (both Mexican & American) of the valley, who unhesitatingly concurred with him in his declaration of Martial Law.

Our Head Quarters are at present at Ft. Bliss. Our scouts are out & within ten miles of Ft. Craig. They report 2800 or 3000 men there intrenched; also Col. Canby, comdg. the Dep^t., by information of our spies at Santa Fe. We rec^d information also that Gen. Sumner was at Guaymas, Sonora, with several thousand more coming down on us. In two months we will drive every one of them from the country.

Providence seems to have cast its benefits broadcast upon us so far, giving us the best weather I have ever seen, no rain or cold although in Nov. & Dec. The grass for our march from San Antonio over <u>seven</u> <u>hundred</u> <u>miles</u> is the best ever known on the route, although the Indians are worse than ever before known. We had no stampede or any losses of any kind. If we are only blessed for 8 weeks more of such weather, we will certainly lay New Mexico at the feet of the first Confederate Congress.

Gen. Sibley will look to You & Father to attend to our interests. If you can spare me the time, please let me know the reception of this letter. Present me sincerely to Mr. Wigfall & the girls & Holsy & believe me

Truly Yrs

Tom P. Ochiltree

Aid D. C. to Gen. Sibley[23]

———————— ◆ ————————

Houston, Tx., Dec. 31st 1862

Major

I have the honor to enclose:

My Report in reply to an order from the President, calling for an explanation of an Order issued by me, in Arizona, last Spring against certain Indians.

Accompanying it, an Indian warrior's shield with a white woman's scalp attached, which I particularly desire forwarded to the President with the Report.

Also two reports of my military operations in Arizona, which I respectfully request you to have forwarded to Adj. Gen. Cooper—my original reports having been lost on the way.

Very respfly

Yr. obdt. servt.

Maj. Dickinson   Jno. R. Baylor

A.A.A. Houston, Texas.[24]   Gov. Arz.

———————— ◆ ————————

"The Yellow Rose of Texas"
(1858 version)

There's a Yellow Rose in Texas, that I am going to see,
No other darkey knows her, no darkey only me,
She cried so when I left her, it like to broke my heart,
And if I ever find her, we never more will part.

She's the sweetest rose of color this darkey ever knew,
Her eyes are bright as diamonds, they sparkle like the dew,
You may talk about your dearest May, and sing of Rosa Lee,
But the Yellow Rose of Texas beats the belles of Tennessee.

Where the Rio Grande is flowing, and the starry skies
    are bright,
She walks along the river in the quiet summer night;
She thinks if I remember, when we parted long ago,
I promised to come back again and not to leave her so.

CHAPTER EIGHT
Rio Bonito and Manzano Theater, August 1861–January 1862
UNION AND CONFEDERATE CORRESPONDENCE

Head Quarters, 2nd Regt. N.M. Vols.
Albuquerque, N.M. Aug[t] 26/61

Sir:

I have the honor of enclosing herewith by direction of the Colonel Commanding for the information of Department Head Quarters a letter from H. M. Beckwith to Major J. Francisco Chaves, regarding the contemplated movement of Texan Troops at Fort Stanton into the Territory, also another from Fort Stanton anonymously written but the writer is well known to Col. M. E. Pino and Capt[n] Labadi as a gentleman of truth and veracity, but does not deem himself justifiable from the peculiar position of affairs at Fort Stanton (where he is a resident) in giving publicity to his name.

I am Sir
Very Respy

Lieut. A. L. Anderson   Your obdt. Servt.
5th Regt. U.S. Infty.   W. Brady
A.A. Adjt. Genl.   1st Lt. & Adjutant
Dept. Head Qrs. N.M.   2nd N.M. Vols.
Santa Fe N.M.

———◆———

Peralta Aug. 24, 1861

Dear Frank

Here within this I enclose a letter from H. M. Beckwith who is now at Fort Stanton and playing gull in general with every body. Charles Beach is prisoner. Gregorio Herrera has been brutally murdered.

I am now starting for Manzano to organize a home guard and place myself at the head of it.

I [am in] a hurry. I remain as ever

You's
J. F. Chaves

———◆———

Fort Stanton, Arizona Territory
August 18th 1861.

Major J. Francisco Chaves.
        Manzano
My dear Sir,
    Being actually in need of a few mules I have taken the liberty, (owing to
the intimacy which has always existed between us, and the public service
needing it, and feeling assured of your loyalty and patriotism in behalf of
the Confederate States of America,) to detain four (4) of your mules. Expecting to have the pleasure of seeing you at this post very shortly, I will
hold myself responsible and accountable for the same. I presume that you
are aware of the arrival of Capt. Walker & his company of Texas Rangers
at this post. His command is now very busily engaged in putting matters to
rights, as he is expecting the arrival of Capt[n] Hardeman's & Adam's companies here, and wishes to have suitable accommodations for them. As soon
after their arrival as practicable, that is to say, as soon as their horses are
rested, it is the intention of Captain Walker to proceed with his whole
command towards Albuquerque and Santa Fe, where they expect to meet
Col. Baylor and Gen[l] McCulloch's commands. Now, if we will not have
protection for life and property, if the Indians will not be exterminated,
and if we are not secured in every way from the encroachments of savages
or enemies of any kind, you may rest assured that it is out of the power and
possibility of humans to protect us. But I have no fears for the future, for I
consider this section of the country more secure than it has been since the
establishment of this Fort.
        Hoping soon to see you,
                            I remain You'rs Very Truly
                            H. M. Beckwith

                    Rec[d] Dept. N. Mex[o] Augt. 27, 1861

––––––––––––—◆◆◆––––––––––––

Río B. Agosto 15 de 1861
S.D.L.L.
Donde se halle
Amigo mio:
    Estas circunstancias me proporcionan de hacerle a usted una terminante
declaración, respecto de la presente política del territorio. Juro a usted
ante Dios y sobre los Santos Evangelios, ser un fiel servidor del gobierno,
quiero salir de aquí y reunirme con usted para deliberar sobre nuestros

planes de guerra, esto es, si contamos con elementos de gente.

El desgraciado 12 que usted salió de aquí como a las tres horas enarbolaron los tejanos en estas placitas, su sucio pabellón, y fue victoriosamente por varios mejicanos, in capite por Alderete nuestro amigo, el cual juró adhesión y defender los principios sureños hasta con la ultima gota de su sangre. Omito por ahora decir a usted quienes y como se han portado los amigos de usted y míos, lo haré sin duda en nuestra vista, que será muy pronto.

El día 13 me nombró el pueblo para que a su nombre pidiera guarantías sobre sus vidas, intereses y familias, las cuales concedió de pico, porque en la misma noche todas sus satélites andaban forzando puertas, violando mugeres y niñas, y lo menos que nos han hecho es saquearnos hasta lo que no teníamos, con el pretexto de ser todo propiedad del antiguo gobierno.

En el mismo día en que usted y mi amigo Don B. fueron tomados en el camino, salió sobre ustedes por influjo de Beckwith una sección de 15 hombres sobre el placer y las fuerzas que allí había las cuales si tomaron o no, eso no lo sé, pero si sé que Don Juanito Olona y otros amigos están presos.

Hoy mismo salí para el Fort, a hablar a estos amigos y antes de llegar supe que traían al amigo Don J^to de guía sobre los placeres en compañia del Sr. Walker nuestro reconquistador.

De las cosas nuestras y del gobierno están plenty estos hermanos por algún tiempo, y según se están resueltos a defenderse aquí en este Fort, y salir por el Manzano y el interior.

Mi situación en este río es lamentable, tanto por ser más o el único descontento, cuanto por que he hablado mucho acerca del asesinato de Gregorio Herrera, de cuyo hombre ya su cuerpo está bajo una piedra. Yo me he visto por tres veces con las pistolas en el pecho, de suerte amigo mío puede usted asegurar a sus amigos que yo tengo dos brazos los cuales consagro en favor de las leyes que dan guarantías, y no por la causa tan cochina de estos 70 vagamundos que no nos traen hasta ahora más que desolación y lagrimas. No sé decir a usted nada de Don Jun^to ni tampoco de mi paradero, quizá en ocho dias ¿quién sabe? estaré junto con usted y no dude que tiene hasta lo último un amigo que nunca ha sabido donde se ha de morir.

Cortina va como de extraordinario, el mismo una idea de mi triste situación, que por no dejar a una mujer en este teatro de peligros, no salí el día 12, ni salgo ahora, pero no dude que nosotros y Dios y el corazón están ya juntos. Salúdeme a Don Boni y dígale que el picarillo desapareció del catálogo, así como sus intereses.

Adiós amigo, muy pronto será su compañero y pasaré la lista de nuestros enemigos capitales, que desde hoy los llamaré mortales &c.[1]

[translation]

Río Bonito
August 15, 1861

Señor Don Lorenzo Labadi,
Wherever he may be

My friend:

The current circumstances allow me an opportunity to make a determinate statement to you, with respect to the present politics of the Territory. I swear to you before God and upon the Holy Gospels, to be a loyal servant of the Government. I want to leave here and join with you in order to go over our campaign plans. That is, if we rely upon good people as the principal elements.

The disgraceful 12th, when you left here, about three o'clock the Texans hoisted their dirty banner in these settlements. It went victoriously among various Mexicans led [*in capite*] by our friend Alderete, he who swore adhesion to and defense of Southern principles to the last drop of his blood. I omit for now telling you just who and how your friends and mine behaved. Without doubt, I will do so during our visit, which will be very soon.

On the 13th, the people appointed me to request, in their name, guaranties of their lives, interests and families. These they [the Texans] granted, in word only, because the same night all of their creatures went around forcing open doors, raping women and girls, and the least they have done to us is to plunder us until we have nothing left, under the pretext of everything being the property of the old government.

On the same day you and my friend Don B. [Boni?] were taken captive on the road, through Beckwith's influence, a detachment of fifteen men left for the placer[s] after you. The forces that they had here, whom they captured or didn't capture, I don't know, but I know for certain that Don Juanito Olona and other friends are prisoners.

I departed for the *Fort* today to speak to these friends. Before arriving there I learned that they [the Texans] were bringing in friend Don Juanito, for a guide over to the placers in the company of Señor Walker, our reconquerer.

With our own things and those of the government, these brothers of ours are *plenty* [i.e., well-fixed] for some time. They seem to be determined to defend themselves here in this *Fort* and to leave for Manzano and the interior.

My situation on this *río* is deplorable, as much from being mostly or singularly discontented, as because I have spoken out about the murder of

Fig. 9. Diego Archuleta, 1883. Courtesy of Museum of New Mexico, negative no. 50322.

Gregorio Herrera, whose body is already under a stone. On three occasions I have seen myself with pistols at my chest, so that, my friend, you can assure your friends that I have two arms, which I consecrate in behalf of laws that offer guarantees, and not for the filthy cause of these seventy vagabonds, who until now bring us nothing more than suffering and tears.

I know nothing to tell you either of Don Juanito or of my whereabouts. Perhaps in a week, who knows, I will be with you. Have no doubt that you have a friend to the end, who has never known where he is to die.

Cortina goes about like some strange person, he himself an example of my gloomy situation, which by not forsaking a woman in this dangerous theater, I didn't leave on the 12th nor am I leaving now. Have no doubt that we, and God, and courage, are all joined together. Give my greetings to Don Boni and tell him that the little rogue [Judge Watts?] dropped from sight, as well as his interests.

Good-by, my friend, very soon I will be your companion and will pass on the list of our mortal enemies; from today I will call them dead men, etc.

[Diego Archuleta]

Albuquerque New Mexico
August 19th 1861

Sir,

I have just received information that I believe to be perfectly reliable, that the Texans (troops) now at Fort Stanton, amount to eighty men. A man named Beckwith and others in the neighborhood of Rio Bonito have joined these troops & increased their numbers to about one hundred & fifty. It is said that they have treated the people badly, all about that part of the country.

	Respectfully Sir
To	Your obt. servt.
Lt. A. L. Anderson	N. B. Rossell
A.A.A.G. U.S.A.	Brevt. Maj. Capt. 5"
Santa Fe N.M.²	<u>CM</u>

Sierra de la Gallina a 24 de Agosto de 1861.
Señor Comandante General de Santa Fe,

A estas horas a que son las dos de la tarde mando a usted las informaciones más exactas que he conseguido por informes muy ciertos, y desengañados por mí misma vista los más.

El capitán que manda esta compañía única que hay en el fuerte del Río Bonito que son de 80 hombres y el capitán de ella se nombra Santiago Guaca, estos han venido a este fuerte el 10 del presente mes, los espías que tienen son Apaches, uno se nombra el Cadete, otro Manuelito, y el otro el Chato, estos son capitansillos y se cree que tendrán algunos indios de espías. A estos tejanos se les han agregado D. Enrique Becore, y es el que está haciendo más picardías, otro americano que se llama Rey, Boes, y Dubol; mexicanos agregados a estos, son uno, Pablo Alderete y el otro Teodosio Aragón.   ·

Según los informes que he recibido por personas de confianza, estos intentan tomar el Manzano pronto.

Por el camino de Tejas no vienen ningunas fuerzas por donde sospechan las gentes del la plaza de Jicarilla que vengan fuerzas, es de La Mesilla.

Según tengo información por los ciudadanos de la plaza de Jicarilla, el armamento que tienen son dos pistolas y rifle cada uno, y una pieza de artillería que montaron de las mismas que estaban abandonadas del fuerte, esta compañía es toda montada en buenos caballos, y han traído estos un carro de provisiones y otro de municiones.

Esta información la tengo por Don Francisco Sánches que estubo prisionero por estos nueve días y este hombre ha tenido la fortuna de salvarse, es hombre que es de bien y dice verdad.

He recibido información que están haciendo muchos daños, diariamente a las familias de las plazas, y estas están saliendo por el Manzano.

Hoy mismo he salido de esta sierra a otra por tener en esta mucho riesgo por los tejanos y los apaches espías, pues solo estos hombres que mando ahora de correo saben donde me pueden encontrar. Espero que a estos mismos me vuelva usted a mandar y aquí quedo observando todo lo posible para avisar a usted inmediatamente.

Su seguro servidor
Saturnino Barrientos[3]

[translation]

Gallinas Mountains
August 24, 1861

Commanding General
Santa Fe
Sir:

At this time, 2 o'clock in the afternoon, I send you the most precise information that I have gathered from very reliable reports, and mostly confirmed by my own observations.

The [Confederate] Captain who commands the sole company at the fort on the Rio Bonito is James Walker. The company has eighty men. They arrived at this fort the 10th of the present month. Their scouts are Apaches, one named Cadete, another Manuelito, and one other, Chato. These are band leaders, and it is believed that they will employ a number of Indians as scouts. Joined with these Texans is Don Enrique Becore [Henry M. Beckwith], and it is he who acts with the greatest malice; other American[s] are named Rey [B. L. Rees?], Boes [Dr. Stephen Boice?] and Dubol [Alexander Duvall?]. Mexicans allied with them are, one, Pablo Alderete, and the other, Teodosio Aragon.

According to reports I have received by trustworthy persons, these parties intend to occupy Manzano at once.

By the road from Texas no forces are coming. From this, the people of the Plaza de Jicarilla suspect that if troops are coming, it is from La Mesilla.

According to information I have from the citizens of the Plaza de Jicarilla, they [the Texans] are each armed with two pistols and a rifle and [with] one piece of artillery, which they mounted from the pieces that were abandoned at the fort. This company is all mounted on good horses and has brought one wagon load of provisions and another of ammunition.

I have this information from Don Francisco Sanches, who was a prisoner of theirs nine days. This man has had the good fortune of escaping. He is a good man who tells the truth.

I have received information that they are causing much harm every day to the families of the plazas, and [the families] are leaving for Manzano.

Today I have left this mountain range for another, because there is a great risk in this one from the Texans and the Apache scouts. Indeed, only the men whom I now send as couriers know where to find me. I hope that you will order them to return to me. I remain here, observing everything possible, in order to notify you at once.

Your Obedient Servant,
[Capt.] Saturnino Barrientos

We have the *Mesilla Times* of the 10th ult., from which we take the following interesting items. . . .

Kiowas Massacre Three Men. We have received from Capt. Walker, particulars of the late massacre of three of his company by the Kiowa Indians. A spy party of 4 men were sent out on the 2nd of Sept. On the 3rd, while at dinner near the fork of the Albuquerque and Fort Union roads, eighty-five miles from Fort Stanton, they were suddenly surrounded by thirty or

forty Indians, supposed to be Kiowas. After four hours hard fighting, three
of the Americans were killed, and the fourth, Sergeant F. A. Sanders, succeeded in making his escape, having a very fast horse.

The names of those killed are, Jos. Emmanacker, Jas. Mosse, and T. G.
Pemberton, all of Lavaca County, Texas. Emmanacker was the last one that
fell, having received many wounds. As soon as he fell, he was surrounded by
Indians, who commenced torturing him with arrows, etc., to which he returned scorn and contempt, and showed them when dying, an undaunted
spirit. His last words heard by his comrade, were taunts to his persecutors.
When his body was found, his tongue and eyes had been cut out, most
probably while still alive. Those who visited the scene for the purpose of
burying the dead, report that at least ten or twelve Indians must have been
killed. Behind every pine tree in the vicinity was blood.4

Barranco Colorado, a 12 de Septiembre 1861
Señor,
Ayer he agarrado dos hombres en el camino del Río Bonito; uno de ellos
es Teodosio Aragón y el otro, Gregorio Montaño. El primero es el mismo
hombre que ha ido comisionado por los del Río Bonito a el fuerte del Bracito,
por traer a los tejanos, y este es el mismo que los ha traido. A este mismo le
he encontrado todas esas cartas que le remito a usted y estos mismos hombres
me aseguran mucho que lo que dice en las cartas es la verdad.
Espero en esto punto las órdenes de usted.

                          Con mucho respeto que
Sr. Coronel Comandante   da su servidor
de los Cuarteles de N.M.5   Capitán Saturnino Barrientos

[translation]

Cañon Colorado [Red Canyon]
September 12, 1861
Sir.
Yesterday I seized two men on the road from the Rio Bonito. One of
them is Teodosio Aragon, and the other, Gregorio Montaño. The first is
the same person who went, commissioned by those of the Rio Bonito, to
the fort at Bracito [Fort Fillmore] to bring the Texans, and he is the one
who brought them. On this same person I found all these letters that I send
on to you, and these same men assure me, many times over, that what is said
in the letters is the truth.

I await your orders at this place.

With much respect,

Sir, Colonel Commanding which your servant offers.
the Districts of New Mexico Captain Saturnino Barrientos

Cerro de la Espia near Manzano
Sep. 19, 1861

Sir

I have the honor to report for the information of the Col. Commanding that by information obtained thru a party of Capt. Barrientos' spies, it appears that Fort Stanton is still occupied by the Texans. The spies found trails of their men thirty miles on this side of the fort and being badly mounted did not go farther. I am about to try again for information.

The Mexican who has formerly carried the mail from Albuquerque to Stanton, and who it appears is now carrying it between Albuquerque and this place, made an effort, by sending his father, to forward some mail matter to Stanton: he was taken by the Texans on this side of the Caresi [Carrizo?] spring, near Stanton, disarmed and sent back. I have him as a prisoner, more for example than otherwise, it being evident that harm was not intended, by the <u>old</u> <u>man</u> at least.

Very Respectfully

Lt. A. L. Anderson Your Obt. Servt.
5th Infty. I. N. Moore
A.A.A.G. Cap. 1st Cavy. cm.
Santa Fé N. Mex^{o6}

Camp near Manzano N. Mex^o
Sep. 20th 1861

Sir

I send this by express to overtake my party going for supplies from Albuquerque.

The letter written last night, to correct the impressions made by a package of letters, taken from a Mexican, and sent to H^d Q^{rs} by two of Senr Barrientos' spies—conveys probably a wrong impression.

The inhabitants of the Fort Stanton country are now arriving, having left there on account of risk from Indians. As they are still some miles off, I send simply what they report to the spies—which agrees with the contents of the letters forwarded several days ago to Dept. H^d. Q^{rs}.

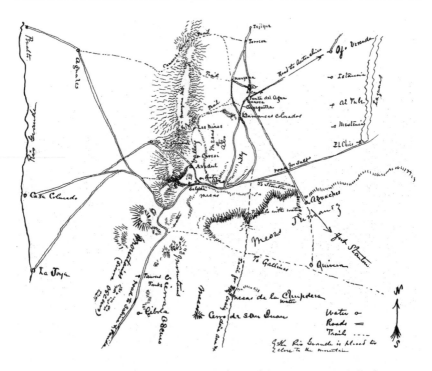

Fig. 10. Captain Isaiah Moore's rough sketch of the country around Abo Pass, dated Sept. 27, 1861 (no scale).

A Mexican, under charges for murdering a soldier some months ago, and who went to the Mesilla for the Texans, and was very active as one of their partisans—by name Pablo Diretti [Alderete]—I will hold as a prisoner subject to decision at H^d Q^{rs}.

I will examine and endeavor to establish the truth or falsity of the report and should there be reason to suppose the Texans still present at Stanton, will send such information by express. Many of the settlers in the country about Fort Stanton took an active part with the Texans. Should there be any of these among those arriving, I will arrest them and await instructions.

The Indians have not been in this neighborhood recently—but may have intercepted the express sent direct to Santa Fe.

	Very Respectfully
To Lieut. A. L. Anderson	Your Obt. Svt.
5th Infty.	I. N. Moore
A.A.A.G. U.S.A.	Cap. 1st Cvy.
Santa Fé[7]	Cmg

Camp near Manzano N. Mex.
Sep. 27th 1861

Sir.

I have the honor to forward a rough sketch of the country about Abo pass.

I have just returned from the Avadûl near the Salada (2½ or 3 miles) and find it to be a good point for a camp or a permanent post. There are some old houses near Salada (marked on the map) with good water near, which would answer the wants of a company.

At the Avadûl there is plenty of water, wood and grass, and a mesa on which there could be placed a four company post. The position overlooks the Salada and nothing could pass without being seen. The Salada is quite a large cienega, which would furnish good grazing, but the water is bad. Abo has water but very little grass, ~~and~~ is too hilly, and is overgrown with cedar and piñon.

Timber for a post would have to be obtained from the cienega, near Manzano, about ~~fifteen~~ eighteen miles from Avadûl. The roads and waters marked on the map are nearly all known to me.

For the protection of the settlements against Indians, probably the Barrancas Coloradas would answer as well as any other point, and would be near timber and forage. There is plenty of water and wood, and good grass at present.

	Very Respectfully
To Capt. G. Chapin 7th Infy.	Your Obt. Sert.
A.A.A. Genl.	I. N. Moore
Dept. N. Mex[o8]	Cap. 1st Cvy.

Camp near Manzano
Sep. 29th 1861

Sir

I have the honor to report that in compliance with the enclosed order I start this morning for Fort Craig, with the squadron now stationed at this point.

As yet the spies have not been sent to Fort Stanton, they being afraid of the Indians at that point, and wishing to go in a larger party than they number at present. It is almost certain that there are no Texans at [Fort] Stanton. Twenty-five men left here the other day to gather their crops in that country.

I send to Albuquerque by Capt. Barrientos the two prisoners ordered there and Pablo Detete [Alderete]. Dr. Ghisilin [James T. Ghiselin] also goes there with a small escort in compliance with [the] same order.

                                   Very Respectfully
                                   Your Obt. Sert.
                                   I. N. Moore
To Capt. G. Chapin 7th Infty.   Cap. 1st Cavy.
A.A.A. Genl.[9]   Cmdg. Squadron

                                   Mansano Octubre 30 de 1861

Haviendo ido a cumplir con la orden de usted de cuyo resultado, informo a usted que me parese todo una niñería.

En ese momento de mi llegada, sin desensillar fue a mi conocimiento habían robado los navajos la mayor parte de la caballada de las compañías situadas en Abó. Inmediatamente salí con 57 soldados, incluso dos ofisiales, de los cuales en alcance llegaron dos soldados, y el abajo firmado, el resto de tropa no llegaron por que seis caballos quedaron cansados. Quitamos 58 caballos haviendo quedado en el campo un indio muerto, un caballo muerto, y otro herido.

Y nosotros perdimos un caballo que fue muerto, otro herido. Además me falta un soldado el cual fue extraviado después del combate y se busca con empeño, si se perdiere sera a su conocimiento. El nombre del soldado es Felipe Garsía.

                                   Saturnino Barrientos
Señor. Coronel Commandante   Capitán de la Compañía de Espías
Don Eduardo Cambí en los   y Guías de N. Mexico
Cuarteles de Santa Fe, Nuevo México[10]

[translation]

                                   Manzano October 30, 1861

Having complied with your order, I inform you of what resulted, which seems to me mere child's play.

Immediately upon my arrival, without unsaddling, it was brought to my attention [that] the Navajos had stolen the greater part of the horse herd from the companies stationed at Abó. I set off at once with fifty-seven soldiers, including two officers. Of those in pursuit, two soldiers and the undersigned caught up. The rest of the troop did not arrive because six worn-out horses stayed behind. We came away with fifty-eight horses, having left in the camp one dead Indian, a dead horse and another injured one.

We lost one horse killed and another wounded. In addition, I am short one soldier, who was missing after the fight. He is being searched for, diligently. If he has become lost, it will be made known to you. The soldier's name is Felipe García.

Saturnino Barrientos

Sir, Captain of the Company

Mr. Edward Canby of Spies and Guides of New Mexico.

Colonel Commanding the

Districts of Santa Fe, N.M.

———————— ◆ ————————

Mansano a 1 de Noviembre 1861

Señor,

El 29 del mes pasado yo mismo he pasado a Abó a observar aquel campo, según usted me ordena; y al mismo momento que yo llegué a aquel campo había tocado la desgracia que los indios navajos habían robado la caballada a las compañias del capitán Gonzáles y capitán Sarracino, y entonces yo como que es mi deber, dar auxilio a todos casos, y más uno como este, inmediatamente, ofrecí mis servicios al capitán comandante de aquel punto, quien me hizo el fabor de ponerme a la cabeza de 58 hombres, y inmediatamente salimos, y como los caballos de estas compañias están bastante fatales, los caballos en el camino se cansaron, pero yo propuesto a alcanzar los indios los seguí, y cuando los alcanzamos, únicamente fuimos siete hombres, pero al tiempo de comenzer a pelear, 2 de los caballos se cansaron del todo, y sólo yo con dos hombres seguimos a los indios. Los indios eran 5, pero de estos, dos arreaban la caballeda, y tres peleaban con nosotros, pero a cosa de media hora, logré que nos revolveríamos nosotros con indios y caballada, y así seguimos peleando como media hora más logrando al mismo tiempo quitarles 58 caballos pertenecientes a las compañías ya dichas y además un caballo de los indios, habiéndoles matado a los indios un indio, un caballo y un caballo herido, y teniendo yo por mi parte un caballo herido, y dos caballos muertos.

Hasta ahora tengo en mi compañía 33 hombres y espero en esta semana concluirla, y inmediatamente saldré a Alburquerque a recibir las órdenes de usted.

Queda de usted su respetuoso

Señor Coronel Comandante Capítan B. de E. y G.

Don Eduardo Cambí de los de Nuevo México

Cuarteles del Territorio

de Nuevo México[11]

[Jacket] From Saturnino Barrientos, Captain, Spies & Guides
    Nov. 1, 1861
                    [translation]

                                    Manzano
                            November 1, 1861
Sir,

The 29th of the past month I went in person to Abó to look over that camp, as you ordered me to do. At the very moment I arrived there, the misfortune befell that the Navajo Indians stole the horses of the companies of Captain Gonzáles and Captain Sarracino. At that time I, as is my duty, gave assistance at all events, the more so at one such as this. I immediately volunteered my services to the captain commanding at that place, who did me the favor of placing me at the head of fifty-eight men.

We started off at once and, as the horses of these companies were in bad shape, the animals became tired on the way; but I, having proposed to catch up with the Indians, followed them. When we caught them we were only seven men. At the time the fight began, two of the horses were entirely worn out, and only I with two men were pursuing the Indians. The Indians were five in number, two of whom were driving the horses, and three fighting with us.

After half an hour, more or less, I caught up [and] we came face to face with the Indians and horse herd. Thus we continued in pursuit, fighting, for another half hour, succeeding at the same time in taking from them fifty-eight horses belonging to the aforesaid companies, besides one of the Indians' horses, having killed one Indian and one horse, and wounded one horse, and on my part having one horse wounded and two killed.

As of now I have thirty-three men in my company and expect to fill it up this week. I will then leave promptly for Albuquerque to receive your orders.
                          Yours respectfully,
Sir,   Captain B. [Barrientos, of the Company]
Colonel Commanding   of Spies and Guides of New Mexico.
Don Edward Canby of the
Districts of the Territory
of New Mexico.

                      Head Quarters Albuquerque N.M.
                            Dec. 6th 1861

Dear Colonel

In reply to your note of inquiry relative to the late massacre reported to have taken place near the Rio Bonito, I have to state that the slip enclosed is the first information that I have received in reference thereto. The whole report is fabulous, and as far as I can learn, arose in this way.

A party of twenty men left the settlements to go to Stanton to see about the crops they had left there. They were gone longer than they expected to be and had a skirmish with the Indians, in which one Indian was killed, and from this report the whole story arose. I am satisfied from the best information that no Texans were killed. A party of them was seen near Fort Stanton, but upon being discovered they decamped and have not since been seen in that country.

I am Colonel Very Respy
Your obt. Servt.
C. Carson

Colonel E. R. S. Canby Colonel 1st N.M. Vols
Comdg. Dept. New Mexico Comdg. Central Dist.
Santa Fe, N.M.[12]

Camp Near Abo Pass, New Mexico
December 20" 1861

Col.
 Sir.

I have the honor to enclose herewith, the Monthly Post Return for Dec. 20th.

Special Orders No. 215 in reference to the transfer of Pvt. Pedro Padilla of Capt. Sarrasino's Co. 6 <u>Month</u> to that of Capt. S. L. Hubbell's Co. 3 <u>Years</u> have been complied with.

I am Sir, Very Respt.
Your obt. Servt.
L. M. Baca

Col. E. R. S. Canby Maj. Comdg. Camp Near
Comdg. Depart. of Abo Pass, N.M.
New Mexico

P.S. Lieut. Francisco Peña has just returned with his party from Río Pecos & vicinity, who reports as having seen nothing worthy of notice. He had a talk with five Comanches at Bosque Redondo, who said that there were many men under arms in San Antonio, Texas, but that they saw none coming towards New Mexico. The Indians being friendly were let pass.[13]

Head Quarters Central Mil. District
Albuquerque December 31' 1861

Major L. M. Baca
  Comdg. Abo Pass
    Major,
    I have received your letter of December 28' and have forwarded it to
Colonel Canby, Commdg. the Department.
    I wish you to keep a vigilant watch for the approach of any hostile force.
By so doing you can certainly know of their coming, and in what force,
some three days before they can reach you. Should you discover that they
intend to attack you, and in such numbers that you cannot withstand them,
you will destroy everything of any value (especially forage, provisions and
ordnance) that you cannot take with you, and march rapidly to this Post
with all your Command, at the same time sending an express to advise me
of your movement.
    Much dependence is placed upon your keeping a good lookout in your
section of country, as it is more than probable a Texan force is marching
north through that section.
    I must enjoin you, that in case you should have to abandon your post,
you will not let anything fall into the hands of the enemy that can aid or
assist them in any manner, and further, that you will not leave your station
upon the strength of any unfounded report. Ascertain fully whether the
reports you may receive are correct and reliable, and act accordingly.
    I have been creditably informed that there is a large amount of corn and
other supplies in and around the valley of the Bonito. In case the Texans are
approaching that valley, I wish you to have everything that will be of use to
them destroyed, without regard to the owners, as, if left there, they will be
converted to the use of the enemy.
                                        I am Major Very Respy
                                          Your obt. Servt.
                              (sd)   C. Carson
                                       Colonel 1st N.M. Vols.
                                       Comdg. Central Dist.

Copy respectfully furnished for the information of the Colonel Commanding the Depart.
                                        Eben Everett
                                          1st Lieut. & Adj. 1st N.M. Vols.[14]

Head Quarters Central Mil. District
Albuquerque Dec. 31st 1861

Captain Wm J. L. Nicodemus
  A.A. Asst. General
    Hd. Qrs. Dept. New Mexico
      Fort Craig N.M.
        Captain,

         I have the honor to enclose herewith for the information of the Dept. Commander a letter received yesterday from the Comdg. Officer at Abo Pass and also a copy of a letter I have this morning written to him, the contents of which I hope the Dept. Commander will approve as I believe them to be best for the interests of the service, and such as he himself would give in this case.

         I intend going out into the mountains some twenty miles east of this post with a view to examine the passes through which an enemy would have to approach this valley, and ascertain how they could best be defended. I shall not be absent more than two days or three at most. Should the Texans attempt to march upon this place, I shall make them fight their way through every mountain pass, and over every inch of ground that I can make tenable for a moment, and the country is well adapted for this kind of fighting.

         Should I be reinforced by Colonel Chaves' command from Fort Union, I will answer that two thousand Texans shall never enter this town. In case of a battle being apprehended, I shall order into service <u>every</u> <u>man</u> in this vicinity that can be armed. I am afraid, however, that we are sadly deficient in ammunition (cartridges) for a long contested battle.

         Even with the present force I have no fear for the result, should we be attacked, as I think I could raise a thousand citizens in the valley, and nearly a thousand more troops under my command, and with the advantage of position I could, I think, make a successful defense.

         Captain Pino with the two companies from Cubero has not yet arrived, but will be here today. Of Lieut. Colonel Chaves and the four companies under his command, I have heard nothing as to where they are or when they will be here.

         I have heard of no Indian news since my last report, except that a party sent as escort to Cubero, were on their return, attacked by the Navajoes on the Puerco. A corporal of Co. "I" 1st N.M. Vols. was severely wounded in the throat, by an ~~bullet~~ arrow, and one Indian was killed. The party returned last night.

I am Captain, Very Respectfully
Your obt. Servt.

C. Carson
Colonel 1st N.M. Vols.
Comdg. Central Dist.

P.S. 11 o'clock A.M.

Captain Pino with his command, aggregate 146, have just arrived.

C. Carson
Colonel 1st N.M. Vols. Comdg.[15]

Fort Craig 6th Jany 1862.

Dear Colonel:

Major Baca reports to me from Abo Pass of date Jany 3^d that his scouts had just come in from the Rio Bonito, and having examined the country about Fort Stanton, report no signs of Texans in that region.

He reports that there are still remaining there a number of families, and that they informed his Lieutenant, that no Texans had been heard of for a long time & no reports of any on the Pecos.

I am Colonel truly yours
B. S. Roberts
Col. Vols.

Col. E. R. S. Canby
  En route for Santa Fe[16]

"Maryland, My Maryland"
(James Ryder Randall, 1861; melody after O Tannenbaum)

The despot's heel is on thy shore, Maryland! My Maryland!
His torch is at thy temple door, Maryland! My Maryland!
Avenge the patriotic gore, that flecked the streets of Baltimore,
And be the Battle Queen of yore, Maryland! My Maryland!

Dear Mother! burst the tyrant's chain, Maryland! My Maryland!
Virginia should not call in vain! Maryland! My Maryland!
She meets her sisters on the plain, "Sic Semper" 'tis the proud refrain,
That baffles minions back amain, Maryland! My Maryland!

Hark to a wandering Son's appeal! Maryland, My Maryland!
My Mother State! to thee I kneel, Maryland! My Maryland!
For life and death, for woe and weal, they peerless chivalry reveal,
And gird thy beauteous limbs with steel, Maryland! My Maryland!

CHAPTER NINE
Southern Arizona
August 1861–August 1862
UNION AND CONFEDERATE CORRESPONDENCE

Head Qrs. Fort Yuma
August 9th 1861

Gentlemen—

Since my arrival here a few days since, I have heard various rumors of the movement of Texans & the people of Tucson, hostile to the United States. You will therefore do me a great favor, if you will inform me by the earliest means of any such intentions, known to you or which you may hear from reliable sources.

If you find that there is any hostile expeditions fitting out against Guaymas or this place please inform me without delay. If the matter should be <u>urgent</u> & <u>important</u>, any reasonable expense incurred by you, thro the means of a special express, will be re-funded at this Post.

My object in writing you, arises from the assurances I have received at Los Angeles & this Post, that I may depend with the utmost confidence upon your Patriotism and intelligence.

I am Gentlemen
Very Respectfully
Yr. ob. Servt.
Messrs. Noyes & White   Geo. Andrews
Merchants   Lt. Col. 6th Inf.
Pimos Villages[1]   Com[dg] Post

———————————◆+◆———————————

Stanwix Ranch
Sept. 8, 1861
A.M. White Esq.
Dear Sir

I left the Colorado River intending to go as far as your place but am obliged to stop here on account of the mules being in bad condition. I would like you to make out the monthly registers of arrivals and departures of Mails at your office since the commencement of service on Route 8076 up to the present time also your bill for care of animals.

I expect the Supt. of the Line will be at Yuma on Saturday and I wish to meet him there as soon as possible. There will be no mail from beyond your place I suppose at present till matters get quiet about Tucson.

Fig. 11. Ammi White's mill and store near Casa Blanca at the Pima Villages, from a sketch by J. Ross Browne. Harper's New Monthly Magazine, *November* 1864.

Please make up the Mail to send to Yuma on Wednesday [Sept. 11]. If you have any news from Tucson please communicate. Report says that 5,000 Govt. Troops are to be marched across from Cal. to Texas. Whether they pass through Arizona or land at Mazatlan and march through Sonora is not known yet. There is nothing new from the States by last Pony.

Yours &c.

Saml [Samuel] A. Ames[2]

Col. J. R. West   Pimo Villages Dec. 14th 1861
Com^{dg} Southern Dist. California
Dr Sir

Short time before your arrival at Fort Yuma I had an interview with Col. [George] Andrews, Com^{dg,} and urged upon him the importance of establishing a small Military Post at this place. Among other reasons I urged the important one of preserving the loyalty of the Pimo and Papago Indians. There are in Arizona about fourteen thousand (say 6,000 Pimos and 8,000 Papagoes) Indians, all speaking the same language, and are one and the same people who live in villages, cultivate the soil and are in all respects a mild and simple people.

They are all friendly to Americans, but think they are neglected or forgotten by our Government because no presents have been sent to them, and no agent comes among them. They are easily operated upon, and you can rely upon it the Agents of the South have not failed to improve every opportunity of filling their minds with promises and lies. Some of the Capitans have letters or papers, signed by one De Witt, K.G.C. written in cypher and characters or symbols. Last week their Gen. [Antonio Azul] returned from a visit to Tucson, perfectly elated with the news that Troops were coming and stages were on the way from the Rio Grande. I had some difficulty to persuade him that it was all a lie.

This point is about two hundred miles easterly from Fort Yuma on the great route from Texas to Cal. and is so situated that no body of men can possibly avoid coming to the Gila for water at Sacaton, when on their way from the east. (At this time after leaving the River no water is found for 64 miles).

Subsistence and Forage can always be had and at less prices than any other part of the Territory at the same time giving a stimulus to the industry of the Indians.

In case you should wish to operate against the Apaches, a few men in conjunction with the Pimos would do more to subdue and exterminate the rascals than six companies could at any Fort. During the past year 1861, the Pimos have killed more than one hundred Apachies, and lost but two men in battle.

Until your Messenger arrived last evening, we had had no news from the United States for more than two months. We were delighted and nearly talked the night out.

I can send an Indian to Tucson at any time I wish, and receive letters from a friend every week. My orders from Col. Andrews were, in case of any movement in this direction, to send news by express to him. This I was prepared to do without delay, keeping animals constantly in the Corral ready at a moment's warning.

Fully appreciating the confidence you have seen fit to repose in me, I beg to assure you that every drop of blood and all else at my disposal are subject to your command. Perhaps it may be well to add a list of what articles can be furnished here.

Blacksmith Tools, Carpenters Tools, complete with exception of Sledge Ham^r. Grain—Flour (Superfine), Frijoles, Beef, about 30 large Hogs, Salt, Corn & Corn Fodder. In Spring, Green Peas & Corn Vegetables with Fish, Game & chickens all the time.

Very Respectfully
Your Obt. Servt.
Ammi M. White[3]

Fort Yuma Jan. 10th 1862

To Col. James H. Carleton
Dear Sir

I arrived at Fort Yuma on the 8th at 10 o'clock P.M. I have just saw [*sic*] Mr. Jager [Jaeger] in regard to the hay to be put at Stations on the Desert. He says that unless Mr. Wild can make the arrangements which I spoke of in my letter previous to this, that it will be impossible to put any hay out there for there is none in the country to be had at any price.

Upon my arrival I found Mr. Grinell [*sic;* Grinnell] here and made arrangements with him to furnish ten tons of hay at Capt. Dyes Ranch, ten tons at Texas Hill, ten tons at Burkes Station ~~ten tons~~ above that. He says he can not go unless he is protected from the Indians. The price of the hay is fifty-five dollars per ton. It is the very lowest that I could get it done for. I can not find out the exact amount paid by the Overland Mail Company for hay at the above named Stations but as near as [I] can learn from Gila City to Texas Hill the price was forty-five dollars per ton. From Texas Hill to Oatman Flat sixty dollars per ton. The men will start tomorrow to cut the hay for Gila City. I shall also start for the Pimos ~~tomorrow~~ at the same time.

I spoke to the Major about the red mule and he said he would send him in by the first teams that go that way.

Very Respectfully Yours &c.

To Col. James H. Carleton   Andrew J. Keen
1st Cala. Vol^s.⁴

Pimo Villages Jany. 16th 1862

Col. James H. Carleton
Com^{dg} Cal. Vols.
Los Angeles
D^r. Sir

Your favor of Jany. 1st at hand and in reply have to say that I am disposed to be governed in regard to prices of <u>all</u> articles raised or produced here, by those paid by the O.M. Co. and by the Contractor for furnishing supplies at Fort "Breckinridge." All the Wheat we have on hand was bought to fill a contract with Mr. Grant to be delivered here at 3¢ per pound.

We have on hand more than one thousand bags of Wheat averaging 100# Ea.

say	100,000#	3 cents pr. lb.
Two hundred sacks Corn	16,000#	3 " "
Twenty do. Beans	2,000"	10¢
Six do. Salt	1,000	8

In regard to Flour, I will commence grinding at once, and think without doubt we can make twenty hundred pounds pr. day. We will use all diligence to furnish all in our power at seven (7) cents pr. lb. the bran and shorts at four cents. We shall kill only some of our largest Hogs for Bacon, reserving all of 150# or less for to use fresh as they may be wanted. Beef we can get from the Pimos as wanted and will furnish at 15¢ pr. lb. I have 200 or more full grown Chickens fifty cents ea.

Hay we will provide a sufficient quantity and we will arrange the price to your satisfaction. As regards Hay for the Stations at Gila Bend and Kenyons I would not undertake to furnish at present. Mr. Woolsey who has taken the contract is the only man who in my opinion could fill it satisfactorily and the price is as low as paid by O.M. Co. at those places.

I will be at Fort Yuma on the 15th of Feby. and come up with your Train and would like to send a small amt. of Ft [sic] also. The crop of the Pimos is not half sold and if you think favorable we can I think keep your Train supplied with Wheat and Flour for a long time. The new crop will come in in May and a very large amt. of land is planted and looks well.

As to Guides. You can rely upon the services of their best men. The "Capitan" of the Coco Maricopas knows every inch of the "Tonto" Range and nothing could give him such pleasure as to know that the Americans were after them. You are wrong in thinking it extra hazardous to send a large Train over this Road. There are not Americans or Indians enough in this part of the Country to injure it and a Force from Mesilla must pass a long distance through Papago & Pimo Country and we get notice by the Indian Telegraph a long time before they could reach here. There is no other Road except via Altar or Sonoyita, in Sonora.

Please inform me which grain you prefer Wheat or Corn. At Ft. Breckinridge Corn was preferred. But the O.M. Co. had more experience and preferred Wheat and my own experience is much in favor of the latter.

Very Respectfully
Your Obt. Servt.
Ammi M. White

Mem° of Wheat Flour &c. At the Pimo Villages
Jany. 16, 1862

1000 Sacks	Wheat		100,000#	3
	Flour	say	30,000	7
	Bran & Shorts		10,000	4
	Salt		1,000	8
	Corn		16,000	3

Beans		2,000	10
Chickens		200	50
Bacon		1,500	
Hogs	Beef	Pumpkins &c.⁵	

Head Quarters Baylors Regt. Mtd. Vols.
La Mesilla Aza. Ty.
February 9ᵗʰ 1862

Capt. S. Hunter
Commanding Co. "A" Baylors Regt. Mtd. Vols.
Sir

I am ordered by the Genl. Comdg. to furnish you with the necessary instructions as to your operations in Western Arizona, and herewith send such as I deem necessary.

You will necessarily be in command of a large district of country which from the population and peculiar circumstances in which you are placed will require all the prudence and forethought you can command. I confidently intrust to you this important Command having the utmost confidence in your patriotism and ability.

You will at all risks maintain law and order both among citizens and soldiers, bearing in mind that all civil matters come under the jurisdiction of the civil authorities and that all criminal offences are to be tried by military commission.

With the citizens of Sonora you will cultivate amicable relations and use all honorable means of gaining their confidence and good will. At the same time whilst you ask for nothing but what is right, submit to nothing but what is that is wrong.

You will as soon as practicable send for the Chiefs and principal men of the Pemo [*sic*] & Papago Indians and make a treaty with them. And rigidly maintain peaceful relations between those Indians and your troops. You will take such steps as in your judgment may be necessary to preserve the sobriety and welfare of those Indians whose friendship is of the utmost importance.

You will at the also at the earliest moment possible take such steps for recruiting Southern Californians as you deem best and will make the necessary arrangements for furnishing supplies to recruits. You will not limit yourself to any number but get all that can be had, and report their numbers to these Head Quarters at the earliest date.

Your present Company you will station at some point near Tucson, having in view a favorable selection for a military encampment in <u>all</u> respects. And keep your men and officers out of <u>towns</u> and <u>villages</u>, <u>as</u> <u>much</u> <u>as</u> <u>possible</u>.

Establish some means of getting reliable information from Ft. Yuma and Southern California and be vigilant in preventing a surprise by the enemy and for that you might use the Pimo Indians. Watch closely the movement of the enemy and forward by express any move on their part that induces you to anticipate an invasion from either Guaymas or Ft. Yuma.

Should a favorable opportunity present itself, you will communicate with some of the Southern men in California, notifying them that all who choose to join our cause may come with the assurance that they will be welcomed and provided for.

You will appoint temporarily a Collector of Customs and use such funds as may be collected in the purchase of supplies necessary for your Command, keeping a strict account of all funds and in what manner expended.

You will when called on by the proper authorities sustain and enforce <u>the</u> <u>Civil</u> <u>law</u>. Should questions arise upon which you have not been instructed, you will act as you deem best calculated to meet the ends of justice and the public service.

Very respectfully
Jno. R. Baylor
Col. Comdg.
Baylors Regt.[6]

[Jacket]   Mesilla Feby 10, 1862 John R. Baylor
             Instructions to Capt. Hunter

[Contents]   Head Quarters Mesilla
                                                           Feb. 10th 1862

Sir

You will without delay move with your Company to Tucson and select some point in the vicinity of that place for a Camp until further orders.

You will escort Col. Jas. Riley [Reily] to the line of Sonora or to some point beyond, where he can get an escort from the Mexican authorities. The detachment of Capt. Helm's Company will return with Col. Riley.

Respectfully
Jno. R. Baylor
Col. Comdg.[7]

Distances from Fort Yuma to Gennels [*sic;* Grinnell's] on the road to the Pimos Villages.

Distance from Fort Yuma to Gila City, good road.	18 miles
From Gila City to Mission Camp, heavy road.	14 miles
From Mission Camp to Antelope (Station) Peak, good road and plenty of grass.	16 miles
From Antelope Peak to Capt. Dyes, or Mohawk Station, heavy sand, water plenty.	12 miles
From Antelope Peak (or Mohawk Station) to Texas Hill, good road, water plenty.	13 miles
From Texas Hill to Stanwix Ranch, good road, plenty water. "This latter place is Gennels."	18 miles

Head Quarters Fort Yuma
March 3rd 1862

Capt.,

You will take six men from your detachment & proceed tomorrow to the Hay Camp, near Mission Camp. It is reported that the Tonto Appaches [*sic*] are roaming near Stanwix Station (Gennels). If on your arrival at Camp finding everything all well there, you can proceed if you wish as far as Gennels, Stanwix Station, observing the condition of the Roads, points easily defended, & such other matters as you may deem of importance to the Commanding Officer at this post. Above is a correct list of distances from Station to Station. On your return you will report in writing the result of your observations.

Edwin S. Rigg

To Capt. Wm. McCleave   Maj. 1 Infy. Cal. Vol.
Commdg. Detach^t Co. A,   Commdg.
1st Cavaly Cal. Vol.[8]

Pima Villages
Mar. 8th 1862

Inventory of goods Seized from A. White

7 prs. Shoes
7 flannel shirts
5 Buck skins
14 prs. Linen Pants

9 Common Wool Hats
2 Boxes Candles
½ Box Pols [?] Soap
1 Doz. Calafornia [*sic*] Bridle Bits
3 Pr. Spurs
1½ Doz. Pistol Scabbards
1 Gross Maches [*sic*]
1 Box Axes
2 Minnie Muskets
2 Citizen [?] Rifle
4 Muskets
3 Cans waggon grease
½ Doz. Brooms
1 Coil Rope
4 lbs. Saleratus
1 Pair Counter Scales
½ Sack Coffee
7 pr. cotton drawers
4 Regatta Shirts
14 packages envelopes
25 lbs. Bacon
2 B. mats
50 lb. Sugar
2 Shot guns[9]

Tucson March 19th 1862

~~Col Jno R. Baylor~~

H. H. Sibley Brig. Gen. Sir

After a march made as speedily as practable [*sic*] from the Rio Grande, attended by some violently stormy weather, but with no accident or misfortune save the loss of one of my men (Benjamin Mays) who died at the San Cimon [*sic*; Simon], I have the honor of reporting to you my arrival at this place on the 28th day of February. My timely arrival with my command was hailed by a majority, I may say by the entire population, of the town of Tucson.

I found rumors here circulating to the effect that the town was about being attacked by a large body of Indians and that military stores of the

Federal Army had been landed at Guaymas to a large amount. That troops from California, consisting of many companies, were on the march up the Gila River for this place, and these rumors were so well accredited that a few of the citizens more ultra in their Southern feelings than the rest, were about rather than fall in the hands of their northern foes to sacrifice all of their interest in this place, risk a trip through the Apache Country and look for safety among their Southern brethren on the Rio Grande.

Immediately after the departure of Col. Riley [*sic*] on the 3ᵈ of March for Sonora, accompanied by an escort of twenty men under Lieut. Tevis, I started with the rest of my command for the Pimo Villages, where after my arrival I negotiated friendly relations with the Indians, arrested A. White who was trading with the Indians. He was also acting as U.S. Contractor. I confiscated his property & now hold him prisoner. A list of the property I have sent to the Gen. Comdg in connection with my report. Among the articles confiscated were 1500 <u>sacks</u> of wheat accumulated by Mr. White & intended for the use of the Federal Army. This I distributed among the Indians, as I had no means of transportation and deemed this a better mode of disposing of it than [to] destroy it or have it for the benefit should it fall in the hands of the enemy.

Whilst delaying near the Villages, awaiting the arrival of a train of 52 wagons accompanied by an escort of Cavalry, which was reported to be en route to the Pimos for the aforesaid wheat, which report however turned out to be untrue, my Picket discovered the approach of a detachment of Cavalry, & which detachment I am happy to report to you we succeeded in capturing without the firing of a gun. The detachment consisted of Capt. McCleave & 9 of his men Co. A 1ˢᵗ Regt. Cala. Cav. Vol. I have them prisoners at this place, but intend sending them to Head Qrs. when Col. Riley returns from Sonora.

I have learned from reliable sources that at every station formerly overland between Fort Yuma & the Pimos, there has been hay provided for the use of the Federal Govt. This however was asserted to be for the use of teams hauling grain from the Pimos to Fort Yuma. I had destroyed at two of the stations thus provided. My actions since I have been necessarily embarrassed owing to the reported number of troops destined to this place from Calafornia [*sic*] and if I have not literally obeyed orders, circumstances by which I have been surrounded must plead my excuse. The success which has thus far rewarded my efforts & the efforts of those I have the honor to command asserts the vigilance which I have & which I will for the future endeavor to keep up.

In conclusion, allow me to say that I have no opinion to offer in relation to all of those rumors that are afloat but give them to you as I received them knowing that your judgment and experience will dictate the proper course to pursue.

Very Respectfully
Your Obed. Servt
S. Hunter
Capt. Com'dg Post
Tucson[10]

Mesilla, Arizona,
April 17, 1862.

E. H. Cushing.—Col. Reily, C.S.A., arrived here yesterday, accompanied by a small mounted escort. This officer was dispatched by Gen. Sibley on a mission to the Governor of Sonora. It is understood he has succeeded beyond all expectation, and under the most discouraging circumstances. His success is of great importance to this Territory and the army of New Mexico.

This is the second formal recognition of the Confederate States, obtained by this officer, and opens to our flag the port of Guaymas. Col. Reily has marched, in 61 days, over 1,400 miles, negotiated a treaty, and is the first officer of the Confederate States army who has carried the Southern flag to the waters of the Pacific ocean. May many others soon follow.

On the night of the 2nd March, Colonel Reily, with a small escort, reached Tucson. On the morning of the 3rd, the balance of his escort came into town, when the Confederate flag was hoisted. The troops saluted it, and Col. Reily made a speech to the soldiers and citizens. On the 7th March, a detachment captured at Pimo Village, a Mr. White, agent for the Federal Government, with 200,000 pounds of wheat, sacked and marked Ft. Yumas. In Mr. White's desk was found a letter addressed to a friend in San Francisco, California, in which he said, speaking of his negotiations with Col. Carleton, "I thank God I have been permitted to do some good for my country, and hope to be able to do more." But the Federals did not get the wheat!

Whilst waiting for fifty Federal wagons that were to come to Pimo village for the wheat, Capt. McCane [McCleave], of company A, 1st regiment California cavalry, from Fort Yumas, came with nine men to visit Mr. White. The Captain and party arrived about 2 o'clock, A.M. Much to the surprise and chagrin of the Captain, he found himself and troopers prisoners to the Tejanos. The correspondence between Col. Carleton, 1st regiment California cavalry, commanding on the line from Los Angelos up the Colorado, and Mr. White, was also found in the house of White. The mill, most of the goods, and the wheat, were turned over to the Pimo Indians. Pimo village is 90 miles from Tucson. This act of liberality has made them our friends.

On the evening of the 17th March, some scouts of Capt. Hunter's company fired upon the picket guard of a cavalry detachment near Fort Yumas, badly wounding one. The pickets never waited to return the fire. Col. Reily left Capt. Hunter's company near Tucson. Before this, they have driven in other pickets, no doubt.

Capt. McLane and Mr. White were turned over this morning to Col. Steele, of 3rd Regiment [of the Sibley Brigade] at Doña Ana.

The scouts sent out on the 17th, burnt immense stacks of hay that had been cut and gathered at various points for the teams that Col. Carleton was to send from Yuma to get the wheat at White's mill. Neither the wheat nor hay can be replaced for a long time, and there is a desert march of 96 miles to make.

Our detachment encountered at the San Ciman [*sic*; Simon] and Apache Pass, two very violent snow storms going, and one at San Pedro returning. From this point to Tucson, 350 miles, the Apaches have made and kept the road a desert. We made the first tracks that have been made on the road for months. At San Ciman, early in the morning, we buried one of our comrades [Private Benjamin Mays] who died the night previous from pleurisy. The storm hung like a huge dark pall over his grave, and but few in the detachment as they turned to look back at the lonely and deserted spot where our comrade was left, that did not feel we were shutting ourselves out from all support, we were advancing to what fate none then knew, still we marched on in despite of rain mud and doubt, and that night encamped near the head of Doubtful Pass, named so from the many terrible Indian massacres that have there occurred. It was here the Indians hung by the feet some of the overland mail passengers about one year since and kindled fires under the heads of their victims. The tree still stands and some of the lariats hang to the limbs, with which the victims were tied, but their charred bones are buried near by, and nothing but a heap of rude stones mark the spot.

We found the climate of Sonora very warm. Near Hermosilla saw oranges and wheat in the same inclosure. On the Yaqui oranges, wheat and sugar are on the same plantation.

Col. Reily was received with great distrust and suspicion by Sonoran authorities. The Black Republican newspapers of California had heralded the march of Sibley's brigade, and proclaimed it as an army of <u>Fillibusteros</u>, coming to revolutionize, rob and plunder Sonora. Then again the Colonel was denounced as the advance of a party marching to avenge the massacre of Col. Crabb and party. Our escort of Confederate troops was halted at the frontier town of Magdalena and a Mexican escort furnished in their place. With them we went to Hermosilla, where we found Governor Pesqueira.

The first news we had from the time of our departure from the Rio Grande, was on the night of the 13th, at Fort McLane. An express came in with a copy of the "Mesilla Times," containing an account of the battle of Valverde.

We leave in the morning for Headquarters, and will have to run gauntlet of the enemy's scouts, and pickets; but Col. Reily is determined to rejoin his regiment, and leave others hereafter to fight diplomatic battles.

One of the Escort.[11]

Arizona Apr. 18th 1862

Col. J. R. Baylor
Sir

On the 16th Inst. at 2 o'clock P.M. my picket, consisting of a sergeant & nine privates, were attacked at El Picacho 40 miles from this place by the advance guard of the enemy. After fighting desperately for one hour & a half, the federals withdrew, leaving a Lieutenant & two men dead on the field and carrying off several wounded. Three of my picket are missing, supposed to have been taken prisoners, having been cut off by the enemy before the fight opened.

As soon as I heard of the skirmish, I dispatched Lieut. Tevis with ten men to the battle ground in search of the missing. As he approached, the enemy, consisting of two hundred cavalry and five wagons, were moving off toward [the] Pimo Villages, distant eighty miles, at which place I have learned from my spies who have just come in, there are three companies of Infantry & two of Cavalry.

I have also heard that 1500 troops were marching up the Gila River. Our position is rather critical, though with a reinforcement of 250 men, we can hold in check all the forces that can be sent from California. I have heard also from a Mexican direct from Los Angeles that Judge D. S. Terry is in Southern California and that there are 1,000 Southern men at Beals Crossing of the Colorado River. I submit the facts to you, hoping that you will be able to send some reinforcement immediately.

I Am Sir
Most Respt Yours
S. Hunter
Capt. Comdg. Co. 'A'
Baylor's Regt.[12]

Fig. 12. J. Ross Browne's sketch of Tucson, Arizona. After commenting on the town's "rare attractions," Browne concluded that "the best view of Tucson is the rear view on the road to Fort Yuma." Harper's New Monthly Magazine, *October 1864.*

Tucson, Az. April 18ᵗʰ 1862

Brigadier H. H. Sibley
Sir

After a march made as speedily as practible [*sic*] from the Rio Grande, attended by some violently stormy weather but with no accident or misfortune save the loss of one of my men (Benjamin Mays) who died at the Samon [*sic*, San Simon], I have the honor of reporting to you my arrival at this place the last day of February.

My timely arrival with my command was hailed with manifest joy by a majority, I may say by the universal population, of the town of Tucson. I found rumors here circulating to the effect that the town was about to being attacked by a large body of Indians, and that military stores of for the Federal Army had been landed at Guaymas to a large amount; that troops in force from California in force were on the march up the Gila for this place. And these rumors were so well founded that a few of the leading citizens were about (rather than fall in the hands of their northern foes) to sacrifice all their Interest, risk a trip through the Apache country, and look for safety among their southern brethren on the Rio Grande.

Immediately after the departure of Col. Riley [*sic*], who left this place on the third day of March for Sonora accompanied by an escort of twenty men under the command of Lieut. Tevis, I started with the rest of men my command for the Pimo villages. On my arrival I negotiated friendly relations with the Pimos, Pagagos [*sic*] & Maricopas. The agent Mr. White I took a prisoner & confiscated his property, a list of which I will furnish you. Among the articles confiscated were fifteen hundred sacks of wheat accumulated by Mr. White and intended for the use of the Northern Army. This I distributed among the Indians, as I had no means of transportation and deemed this a better policy of disposing of it than to destroy it or leave it for the benefit should it fall in the hands of the enemy.

While delaying near the Pimo Villages awaiting the arrival of a train of fifty two wagons accompanied by an escort of Cavalry which was reported to be en route to the villages for the aforesaid wheat, which report however turned out to be untrue, my picket discovered the approach of a detachment of Cavalry, and which detachment I am happy to report to you he succeeded in capturing without the firing of a gun. This detachment consisted of Capt. McCleave and nine of his men of Company A, 1st Dragoons, California Volunteers. I have them as yet prisoners at this place. I have learned from reliable sources, that at any station on the overland route between Fort Yuma and the Pimo Villages, there has been hay provided for the use of the Federal government. This however was asserted to be for the use of teams hauling grain from the Pimos Villages to Fort Yuma. I have destroyed at two of the stations all of the hay thus provided. I would beg to state to you the necessity of having an agent placed over these Indians, and one should be appointed at the earliest possible convenience.

[Incomplete draft][13]

Fort Yuma May 15th 1862

To General Carleton
Sir

Some five or six months ago you ordered me to go from Los Angeles to the Pimo Villages to ascertain what amount of supplies could be obtained for men and animals at that place. You directed me to Mr. White, then a merchant at the Pimos, with instructions to examine his stock of produce, and report to you the amount on hand, and what the price would be for the same in case the government should require them. I told Mr. White that I was not authorized to buy his supplies. My business was to get a memorandum of the amount on hand the prices &c. And report the same to you.

I Remain Very Respectfully &c.

To Brigadier General   Andrew J. Keen
James H. Carleton
Commanding Southern
District Cal.[14]

Pimo Villages, New Mexico, May 25th 1862.

Col. J. H. Carleton,

Dear Sir,

The undersigned hereby respectfully represent that they have, during the past two years, been doing a mercantile business at this place, and in the prosecution of said business have built and occupied certain buildings, to wit a store, flour mill, dwelling house and store house, together with corrals, wells and sheds; that the said premises together with the appurtenances thereunto belonging have been converted to the use and service of the United States and are now occupied by their forces under the name of Fort Barrett.

Being thus prevented from the further prosecution of our business, we respectfully request you to take such action in the premises as will reimburse us for our loss.

Respectfully your obt. servants,

White & Noyes.[15]

Proceedings of a Board of Officers which convened at Fort Barrett, Pimos Villages, Arizona Territory, May 25th, 1862, pursuant to the following order.

Head Quarters Column from
California, Fort Barrett, Pimos
Villages, Arizona. May 25th 1862.

Special Orders No. 1. . . .

A Board of Officers to consist of Surgeon James M. McNulty, 1st Infantry, California Volunteers, Captain Tredwell Moore, A.Q.M., U.S.A., Captain Joseph Smith, 5th Infantry, Cal. Vols., Captain Thomas Cox, 1st Infantry, Cal. Vols., and 1st Lieut. and Adjutant Benjamin C. Cutler, 1st Inf. Cal. Vols. will assemble at this Post, at 2 o'clock P.M. today, to enquire into all the particulars of a claim to certain buildings enclosed within the walls of Fort Barrett, which has been made by White and Noyes in a communication of this date, addressed to Colonel James H. Carleton.

- - - - -

Ignacio Robledo, born in Sonora was then examined. Joseph K. Hooper of Fort Yuma, being duly sworn by the President of the Board, acted as Interpreter.

Robledo has lived at the Pimos Villages for the last 18 months. He was at that point when the Confederate Troops under Capt. Hunter arrived there. When Hunter left for Tucson he took with him about 100 pounds of Bacon,

2,~~500~~ ~~POUNDS OF FLOUR, AND ABOUT~~ 70 Hogs, and 400 Hens and chickens, but previous to his departure he called in the Indians, and gave over to them all that was left at the place, including about 150 tons of Wheat, about 2,000 pounds Bacon, [and] about 2,000 pounds of Flour.

Hunter destroyed the Bolting cloth of the Mill, and took to Tucson the <u>Spindle</u>. With these two exceptions, the Mill was left by Hunter in the same condition as when he came here, as was also the house. Before leaving, Hunter called in the Indians and told them that the mill and everything appertaining to it belonged to them and that they could use it for their own benefit.

When Captain Hunter loaded his wagon for Tucson he took a list of all he put into it. That list fell from his pocket, was picked up by one of the Indians, and is now in the possession of Mr. Noyes the partner of Mr. White.

Some days after Hunter left, the Indians were trying to see how the mill worked. In the attempt, one of their number became entangled in the machinery and broke his leg. This so enraged the Indians that they proceeded at once to destroy the mill. All of the injuries sustained by White and Noyes, in the destruction of their mill, and tearing out the doors and windows of the houses, and the carrying away of the wheat and stores contained on the premises, was occasioned by the Indians after Hunter left, and before Captain [William P.] Calloway arrived at this point. The Indians wished to burn up the buildings but were dissuaded therefrom by Robledo. White occasionally trusted the Indians at his store, and when Hunter arrived, White was their creditor to the amount of several hundred dollars. The Indians wanted Hunter to kill or carry off White, in order that they might be relieved from the necessity of paying him.

Robledo is a citizen of the United States, having been a citizen of California at the time that state was admitted into the Union.[16]

Casa Blanca, Arizona.
August 18th 1862.

Sir

This afternoon in putting together the machinery of the mill, with the expectation of making flour tomorrow morning, Mr. Wise the miller (who arrived by the wagon train from Tucson at noon today) discovered that an important iron called the "driver" was missing, and had been entirely overlooked by the millwright. Mr. Wise says that this is the iron that was "cached" by Mr. Burt of Tucson. If Mr. Burt can be sent here and will show us where he hid the iron, we can be making flour in less than an hour after his arrival.

Very respectfully

Major D. Fergusson	Your Obd^t Serv^ts
1st Cavalry, C.V.	(Signed) White & Lennan
Comd^g Tucson^17	

———————— ◆ ————————

"Dixie"

(lyrics by Albert Pike)

Southrons, hear your country call you!
Up, lest worse than death befall you!
To arms! To arms! To arms, in Dixie!
Lo! all the beacon-fires are lighted,
Let all hearts be now united!
To arms! To arms! To arms, in Dixie!
Chorus: Advance the flag of Dixie, Hurrah! Hurrah!
For Dixie's land we take our stand,
To live or die for Dixie!
To arms! to arms! and conquer peace for Dixie!
To arms! to arms! and conquer peace for Dixie!

How the South's great heart rejoices,
At your cannons' ringing voices!
To arms! To arms! To arms, in Dixie!
For faith betrayed, and pledges broken,
Wrongs inflicted, insults spoken.
To arms! To arms! To arms, in Dixie!
Chorus: Advance the flag of Dixie, &c.

Swear upon your country's altar,
Never to submit or falter;
To arms! To arms! To arms, in Dixie!
Till the spoilers are defeated,
Till the Lord's work is completed!
To arms! To arms! To arms, in Dixie!
Chorus: Advance the flag of Dixie, &c."

CHAPTER TEN
Confederate Correspondence
January–April 1862

La Mesilla Jan. 19th

Capt. Hunter will deliver Marshall to Mr. Phillips comd. party.

Jno. R. Baylor
Col. Comdg.

Also deliver the others to be <u>questioned</u> and <u>sentenced</u>.

Jno. R. Baylor
Col. Comdg.

———————— ◆ ————————

[Jacket]   Invoice of Sundries taken from John Lemons by J. R. Baylor

[Contents] Invoice of Sundries taken from John Lemons by Capt. S. Hunter on Jany. 19th 1862 at Doña Ana by order of Col. J. R. Baylor Commanding.

1 draft in favor of W. S. Grant drawn on Messrs. Peirce & Bacon Boston

	For	"	66.28
	W. R. Ake		350.00
Note on Andrew Childers			140.00
" Sofio Henkle			71.62
Order on Hayward & McGrorty			50
Gold Coin			1741.00
1 Lot Dust			150.00

1 Lot Sharp Shooter and Pistol Cartridges
1 Double Spy Glass
2 D.B. Shot Guns
2 Inft. Muskets
1 Citizen Rifle
1 Miné Rifle
1 Wagon
1 Ambulance
6 Mules
6 Set Harness
1 Horse
1 Wall Pint [?]

1 Saddle
1 Port folio
1 8 Dollar Note
Michigan Bank Deed for 160 Acres Land on Rio Membres
1 Colt Navy Six Shooter
2 Deringers

Sent Jny. 22/62

Recd. From Capt. S. Hunter
  2 Double Barrel Shot Guns
  1 Rifle belong to John Lemons and taken by me.
Doña Ana Jany. 22/62

Samuel G. Bean
C.S. Receiver[1]

El Paso. 8 Feby. 1862

Captain.

Until such time as my general agent Mr. Antonio Perez can return from Chihuahua and proceed to Tucson, Arizona, to attend to furnishing your command permanently with supplies of flour and corn, Maj. Stickney will for the present attend to this matter. I have requested Maj. S. to exhibit to you my letter of instructions of this date. He is to act in consultation and under your direction.

My arrangement with the government is to furnish at the old U.S. prices, so you see the importance of our commencing in Arizona upon a proper basis. I have directed Maj. S. to purchase for you, some 10,000 pounds of flour, at the usual prices, and to get my corn at Santa Cruz should you require it before Mr. Perez arrives at the west.

You will greatly advance the interest of the public service by preventing attempts to impose high prices for supplies of the army. Sonora as you know is a State of great abundance, and as we may have to draw large supplies from there for our army in New Mexico, it behooves both you and I, the one as the first commander of the C.S. to be stationed in Arizona West, and the other as contractor, to inaugurate such steps as will enable us to accomplish all that may be expected from us. Any combinations to extort high prices on the Sonora lardier [*sic*], not put down at the start, would so cripple [word crossed out] all concerned, that an entire failure of supplies might ensue. I trust you will fully consult with Col. Baylor touching these matters, and take his advice and adopt his counsel in these matters.

Fig. 13. Elsberg and Amberg wagon train on the plaza, Santa Fe, New Mexico, October 1861. Courtesy of Museum of New Mexico, negative no. 11254.

The rank and station of Col. Reily might serve the good cause, should he think and feel on this subject as does Col. Baylor, yourself, and myself. I hope you will talk the matter over with Col. Reily as you journey along west. I will thank you to see that Maj. Stickney be furnished with proper official duplicate receipts to be sent to me for flour and corn, as per my instructions to him.

I hope to be able to send funds for all necessary purposes of the service when my general agent Mr. Antonio Perez goes to Tucson, but you must bear in mind yourself that it will be in Southern Confederacy notes and bonds.

I hope to hear from you now and then.

                                                    Very Respectfully Yours
To Capt. S. Hunter C.S.A.   S. Hart
Com'g Expedition to Tucson

I send with this a file of newspapers; all I could get together for you to take west with you.[2]

Santa Fe N.M.
March 12th 1862.

Col. Paul, Comdg. Fort Union N.M.

Sir

As commander of the troops of the Confederate States of America now occupying Santa Fe N.M. I have the honor to inform you that I have taken as prisoners of war Sergeant Wall and privates James Kessler and George Hogg, U.S.A. In conformity to the general custom of the Government of the Confederate States, these prisoners are released on parole. I desire to exchange these prisoners for the same number taken by the U.S. Troops and if it be in conformity to the rules of civilized warfare as contended by the United States Government, I propose to exchange the prisoners taken and released on parole as above specified in the following manner, to wit, Sergeant Wall and privates James Kessler and George Hogg for privates Andrew Long, William Perryman and William Cappers, privates of the C.S.A. released on parole by you. I hereby return the transportation furnished our prisoners. You will please notify me by earliest opportunity when this arrangement can be effected.

Very Respectfully
Your obt. Servt.
John G. Phillips
Capt. C.S.A.[3]

Mesilla, March 17, 1862

Sir:

I herewith tender my resignation as Colonel and Governor of this Territory, which the General Com[dg] did me the honor to confer upon me.

I should be wanting in self respect were I to serve or hold a Commission under an Officer who has shown so palpable a want of confidence in my courage or ability.

I have the honor to be
Very Respectfully &c.

Maj. A. M. Jackson   Jno. R. Baylor
A.A. Gen[l]   Lt. Col. Com[dg]
Army of New Mexico   T.M.R.
Official Copy—
A. M. Jackson A.A.G.[4]

(Copy)

H^d Qrs. Army of New Mexico
Albuquerque April 1st 1862

Captain

You will proceed with all dispatch to Richmond Virginia and deliver to the Adjt. Genl. of the Army the despatches entrusted to you—urge upon the President, but first upon the Governor of the State of Texas, the necessity for Reinforcements—Infantry. We have cavalry & guns enough.

You will rejoin this army as soon as possible.

Very Resply Yr.
obt. svt.
H. H. Sibley
Capt. T. P. Ochiltree   Brig. Genl.
A.A.G.   Comdg.

I certify on honor that the above is a true copy of my orders.

Tom. P. Ochiltree
Capt. & A.A.G. C.S.A.[5]

Mesilla, April 7th 1862

Capt. Acock (*sic;* John T. Aycock)
Present
Sir,

The condition of your Company, it being nearly without arms, and partially dismounted, induces me to authorize you to take advantage of the present opportunity of a train, which will enable you to be on the road to Texas at the expiration of your term of service.

You will turn over revolvers and such other arms as may not be necessary for your protection on the road, to the acting Q.M. at Fort Bliss, to be subject to my order.

The supply of Commissary stores at Fort Bliss being all that can be expected to arrive for some time to come, you will make your calculations to subsist your command, so far as possible, upon the beef you can get at Quitman, Davis, Stockton, Lancaster and Hudson and Clark.

The men of Capt. Stafford's and other companies, will await the action of Genl Sibley in regard to their Companies.

Your Obt. Servt.
Wm Steele
Col.[6]

Hd. Qrs. 7th Regt. T.M.M.

Camp above Doña Ana

April 17th 1862.

Genl.

I have the honor to enclose to you the resignation of Lt. Col. A. P. Bagby of my Regt., also a copy of charges against him. I send this direct on account of the difficulty of communication with Genl. Sibley.

Knowing myself that the first charge is true, I have authorized Lt. Col. Bagby to proceed to his home (Gonzales) in Texas, and await the action of the President.

[Col. Wm. Steele]

Genl. S. Cooper

Adjt. & Inspt. Genl.7

Respectfully referred to the Secretary of State

Rec'd Aug. 12   John H. Reagan

P.M. General

La Mesilla, April 17th 1862

Hon. J. H. Reagan &c &c &c.

Have just returned from mission to Sonora. It has been the most difficult & troublesome mission I ever had charge of. However, I succeeded in establishing friendly relations with the authorities of that State, counteracted the influence of Republicanism that was operating so much against us there, obtained the unlimited & unrestricted right to buy supplies in Sonora, obtained the right of transit from Port of Guaymas through the State, obtained the right to establish a Confederate State Depot at Guaymas, & was informed that transit or international dues would not exceed 10 per cent on the tariff, & goods bought or introduced by our Agent at Guaymas would not ~~exceed~~ be subject to tariff dues if removed within 6 months.

I ascertained quite conclusively that the Federal Commander had negotiated with Governor Pesquiera the right to occupy Guaymas with troops & ~~perhaps~~ to be used against us. This arrangement I broke up.

A steamer came in from Mazatlan with express for Governor Pesquiera bearing programme of treaty between Allied Powers & Mexico:

1st   Provisional Government for 5 years.

2nd   Government to be central & established at city of Mexico.

3.   The Electors to be possessed of an income of $2,000 per year.

4th Income from no[?] Church property to be estimated unless the
      title to such property has been fairly acquired.
5.   The Allied Powers guarantee a loan to Mexico of $125,000,000.
6th The debt of the nation to be consolidated at 3 per cent interest.
7th The interest on the loan of $125,000,000 to be paid semi annually.

This make [sic] a dictator in Mexico. The treaty will be ratified, but in a
year or so it will occasion revolution in Chihuahua, Sonora, Sinaloa,
Durango, & other States.

Genl. Carleton in command of Colorado [California?] line has from
Los Angeles to Stanwick ranch but 1,500 men. A mixed command [of] 5
companies cavalry, 10 of infantry.

The men of my escort went to Pimo villages & captured Capt. McLane
[McCleave] comp'y A, Carleton's Rt. [Regiment] & 9 men, with horses,
guns &c. The Capt. came through with me & is now at Doña Ana. This is
our first victory on the Pacific. Others will follow.

The advance of a respectable force on Ft. Yuma would rouse Southern
California. A majority of the people are with the South.

This is the second recognition I have obtained of [the] Southern Confederacy.

The Governor of this Territory [of] Arizona ought to [be a] military
man and intelligent civilian. We have much to do with Chihuahua & Sonora.

I have lost the chances of being in the battles where my regiment have
been engaged, but hope to make it up lost time. Shall push on to rejoin it at
all hazards. My son Lt. Reily I am proud to learn did his duty with his
Artillery.

As it will be some time before Genl. Sibley can communicate my despatches to the Secretary of War, I give you this hasty synopsis [so] that if
you see fit you can communicate it to the President or Secretary.

Immediate military possession should be taken of Sierra [sic; Cerro]
Colorado or Colt's silver mine. It will be sacrificed to fraud & the government receive no benefit. No real estate should be sold by [the] Receiver in
this territory now, for there is no money here. If military possession is not
taken of mines & machinery & ranches of Northern capitalists in this territory, then claims will be made against them & [the] most valuable property
sacrificed for a mere song. Already the mine, machinery, & ranch worth
many thousand dollars of Sierra Colorado, or Colt's mine, has been levied
on by virtue of judgment in [the] form of Haywood [Hayward] & McGrorty
of this place for $2700 vs. Sonora Mining Company, non residents, & ad-
vertised for sale [the] 3rd Monday in May. This is unjust to the government.

You will have learned before this of the death in battle of Major H. W. Raguet of my regiment. He was a gallant soldier & his loss a great one.

I have negotiated friendly relations with Sonora & marched over 1400 miles in 61 days, nearly all the time around [?] the Apache Indians.

With great respect

Truly Yours

James Reily

Col. 1ˢᵗ Rt. S. Bde

4ᵗʰ Rt. T.M.V.

Hon. John H. Reagan

&c &c &c

Richmond, Va.

P.S. We are to have hard & close fighting this summer & especially in New Mexico. If the President should consider that I could be of service in the diplomatic line & desires to send me to Mexico, Peru, Chile, or any other point where I could serve my country, an express should reach me at Head Quarters of Army of New Mexico. By that time I shall have served my country in the field & will then be willing to go into diplomatic life.

I can make the overland journey either to Mexico via. Chihuahua or Guaymas to Mazatlan. Think of my propositions.[8]

Hd. Qrs. 7ᵗʰ Regt. T.M.M.

Camp above Doña Ana

April 19ᵗʰ 1862.

Genl.

I have the honor to state that Lt. A. Middleton of Company G 7ᵗʰ Regt. Texas Mounted Men, whose resignation was tendered on the 28ᵗʰ of February last on account of ill health, and which was conditionally accepted, died on his way home at Fort Davis, Texas, about the 12ᵗʰ of March 1862.

Respectfully

Your Obt. Servt.

Wᵐ Steele

Col. 7ᵗʰ R., T.M.M.

Genl. S. Cooper

Adjt. & Inspt. Gnl.[9]

"The Homespun Dress"
(Carrie Bell Sinclair; melody after "The Bonnie Blue Flag")

Oh, yes I am a Southern girl and glory in the name,
And boast it with far greater pride than glittering wealth or fame.
We envy not the Northern girl, her robes of beauty rare,
Though diamonds grace her snowy neck, and pearls bedeck her hair.
Chorus: Hurrah! hurrah! for the sunny South so dear,
Three cheers for the homespun dress the Southern ladies wear,

The homespun dress is plain, I know, my hat's palmetto, too;
But then it shows what Southern girls for Southern rights will do.
We've sent the bravest of our land to battle with the foe,
And we will lend a helping hand, we love the South, you know.
Chorus: Hurrah! hurrah! &c.

And now, young man, a word to you, if you would win the fair,
Go to the field where honor calls and win your lady there.
Remember that our brightest smiles are for the true and brave,
And that our tears are all for those who fill a soldiers' grave.
Chorus: Hurrah! hurrah! &c.

CHAPTER ELEVEN
Headquarters and Other Correspondence
January–March 1862
UNION CORRESPONDENCE

Head Quarters Dept. Of New Mex.
Fort Craig N.M. Jany. 1, 1862

Major:

Your communication of the 29 ulto. has just been received. Information from below states that 1200 men with 7 pieces of artillery are on the march to this place. I can learn nothing more with regard to the reputed Pecos expedition.

I am glad that you have countermanded the order with regard to the Cavalry Company at Fort Union, as I should not rely upon it if it should be brought within the reach of its former commander. Use your own judgement with regard to the measures to be undertaken in your command. I have written to the Governor this morning in relation to the militia and some matters connected with [the] present state of affairs.

Please keep me advised of everything of importance and communicate to neighboring commands any information that may affect them. Send duplicates of important papers by special expresses.

I have enclosed a communication for Governor [William] Gilpin [of Colorado]. Please send it by a special express and take the other measures suggested.

In haste

Very respectfully Sir
Your obdt. Servt.
Ed. R. S. Canby
Col. 19. Inf.
Comg.

Maj. J. L. Donaldson
Comg. District &
Santa Fe N.M.[1]

(Duplicate)

                                              Head Qrs. Central Mil. District
Captain Wm. J. L. Nicodemus   Albuquerque N.M. Jan. 2/62
A.A.A. General
Hd. Qrs. Dept. N.M.
Fort Craig N.M.
Captain:

I have the honor to acknowledge the receipt of Dept. Letters of Decr 31st in reference to escorts for trains going to Fort Craig, and also authorizing the calling in of one of the companies from Cubero. In accordance therewith I have deemed it best to send out to-day three wagons with an escort of twenty men, and have ordered the Commanding Officer of Cubero to send in immediately Captain [Ricardo] Branch's Co. 3rd N.M. Vols. In the state of uncertainty now existing as to the Texan forces, I think it proper to concentrate at this point as large a force as possible, so that if attacked we may successfully defend ourselves, and also if the enemy should march to Fort Union, we can cut them off from below and attack them from this direction.

I have this morning received a letter from Major [Luis] Baca, Comdg. Abo Pass. He reports the departure of Agent Labadi for the Bonito with 70 men, and also that Capt. [Juan] Sarracino with 40 men is scouting south of the Bonito on the Pecos, so that it will be impossible for a force to approach that country without being discovered.

                                              I am Captain
                                               Very Respy.
                                            Yr. Obt. Servt.
                                             C. Carson
                                              Colonel 1st N.M. Vols.
                                               Comdg. Cent. Mil. Dist.
Copy sent by express Jany. 2nd 1862[2]

                                              Hd. Qrs. Dept. of New Mexico
                                              Fort Craig, N.M. January 3, 1862

Colonel C. Carson 1st N.M. Vols.
Commg. Central Mil. District
Albuquerque, N.M.
Colonel.

The Dep. Commander approves your course in relation to the concentration of troops at Albuquerque.

Fig. 14. Colonel Christopher "Kit" Carson, St. Louis, Missouri, December 1864. Courtesy of Museum of New Mexico, negative no. 58388.

The Texans about 500 in number entered Alamosa yesterday morning. They no doubt hoped to surprise the outpost at that place and failing in that, appear to have returned as rapidly as they came. Their retreat may be a feint and intended to divert attention from other points, and this I am disposed to think is the case.

No further news from the Pecos.

Very Respectfully, Colonel
Your obedt. servant
Signed   Wᵐ J. L. Nicodemus
Cap. 12 Infy.
A.A.A.G.[3]

Hd. Quarters, Dept. Of New Mexico.
Fort Craig, N.M. January 4, 1862

"Copy."

Colonel.

I am prepared to move with a strong force to assist you if the Texans should attempt to invade the Country from the direction of Fort Stanton. Keep your force in readiness to move in any direction, at any moment.

A train with 10,000 rations in addition to what is required for your own Command (for 10 days) will be kept in readiness.

Very respectfully Sir
Your obedt. servant

"Official."   Signed/   E. R. S. Canby
Wm J. L. Nicodemus   Colonel 19. Infantry
Captain 12 Infantry   Commg. Dept.
A.A.A. General

Copies of the above have been furnished to Colonel Carson, Capt. Enos, & Captain Bascom.[4]

———— ✦ ————

Fort Craig Jany. 4, 61. [*sic;* 1862]

Major:

Yours of the 1st has been received. I am greatly gratified to learn of the spirit that appears to prevail in and about Santa Fe. Every thing now is I think well arranged and the place can be held against any force that can be brought against it. I am prepared to move with a strong force to the upper country if the attack should come from the Pecos or Canadian.

Very sincerely

Maj. J. L. Donaldson   Yours &
Comg. District &c.   Ed. R. S. Canby
Santa Fe N.M.[50]

———— ✦ ————

Head Quarters, Dept. of N. Mexico.
Santa Fe, N.M. 5th Jan. 1862.

Confidential

Major James L. Donaldson, U.S.A.
Comdg. District of Santa Fe,
Sir,

Under existing circumstances, when the Territory has been invaded by a rebellious and ungenerous foe, who doubtless counts upon assistance from the Secession elements of Albuquerque and Santa Fe, I feel it to be my duty to suggest to you the propriety—nay the necessity, of adopting some measures to secure the loyal people of these towns from the influences which those intestine rebels will bring to bear upon them.

It is only necessary to apply the test-oath to all who may be suspected of sympathy with the invaders, and a refusal to be sworn cannot but be evidence of a desire to assist the rebels. Let all such characters be put out of harm's way.

In this connection I respectfully call your attention to the notorious secession proclivity of Judge [Spruce M.] Baird, and Major Weller of Albuquerque; the arrest of these parties strikes me not only as politic, but as absolutely demanded.

> Very Respectfully, Sir
> Your obt. Servant
> Gurden Chapin
> Capt. 7 Inf.
> Act. Inspec. Gen.[6]

Head Quarters Dept. of New Mex.
Camp Connelly Jany. 7, 1862

Dear Major:

Yours of the 4th has just been received. I think from a letter from Col. Collins that the Governor has misapprehended my meaning in asking him to make a visit to this lower country. I did not mean to convey the idea that they were "discontented." On my way down I found the opinions, from observation and report, that they were apathetic & indifferent and were willing that the questions at issue should be decided by others, without any active interference on their part.

The near approach of the Texans has I think made a considerable change, or has brought to the surface some expression of the real feeling. Whether this will bear the test of actual contact with the Texans, quien sabe? I do not think it necessary that the militia should be called out. I asked the Governor to hold them in readiness for the purpose of reinforcing points from which it might be necessary to withdraw other troops. They would be an embarrassment in the field and I think we will have enough without them.

We missed the express last night and your letter has just been received with the mail sent back from Fort Craig. Please tell Col. Collins that his letters have also just been received and that the cases he refers to will be attended to. I have kept the express waiting.

Very truly

Yours &c.

Maj. Donaldson   Ed. R. S. Canby

Comg. District &c.[7]

Head Qrs. Sⁿ. M" Dist. Dept. N.M.

Fort Craig 7th Jany 1862.

Dear Colonel:

Capt. Lord returned at 11. last night from the Cañada Lamosa, and reports no Texans there since the day they attempted to surprise him. The Alcalde and others report to him that Colonel Baylor, one other Colonel and ten captains, were with the Texan troops that entered their town. That Col. Baylor signified to the people there, that he had no idea of fighting at Fort Craig, or going there; but would pass round and come in at Socorro and proceed on to raise the Confederate flag in Santa Fe.

I am convinced that Colonel Baylor has sent letters to secessionists above by a Mexican whose name I cannot learn, but who went by here three or four days ago with José Truxillo of San Antonio, N.M., and I have sent this morning to capture the supposed spy.

The express passed you last night and brought me your mail this morning. I sent it back today.

Very truly yours

B. S. Roberts

Col. Vols.[8]

Major:

I send this for your information. Col. Baylor is not so foolish as to publish his real plans.

I still believe that the invasion, if attempted, will not be by the river, but will be prepared to act in either direction.

Ed. R. S. Canby

Col. &

Jany. 8/61 [*sic;* 1862]

Maj. Donaldson[9]

Head Quarters Dept. of New Mex.
Belen N.M. Jany. 12, 1862

Major:

Your communication of the 11th inst. has been received. Colonel Roberts' estimate rendered according to the number of animals withdrawn from his post will amount to 263,220 pounds (1880 fanegas). In addition to the number of animals already withdrawn, I have ordered all the disposable transportation to be sent up. The corn that you have ordered down will therefore be more than sufficient.

I expect Col. Roberts' report tonight and will send it to you tomorrow in order that you may arrange for the disposition of the transportation. The private trains can probably be dispensed with and a portion of the public transportation kept in [Fort] Union where it can be sustained economically and be available at any moment.

Even if there should be no invasion from the Pecos, I do not intend to move any part of the force below Fort Craig until I can organize a sufficient force to secure the upper country from invasion during the absence of troops that may be sent below. Col. Roberts is securing a great deal of grama grass at Fort Craig and will probably be able to keep himself supplied with hay.

Very respectfully, Sir,
Your obdt. Servt.
Ed. R. S. Canby

Maj. J. L. Donaldson   Col. 19. Inf.
Chief Qur. Mr.   Comg. Dept.
  Santa Fe, N.M.[10]

———————— ◆ ————————

Quartermasters Office
Santa Fe, N.M. Jany. 12, 1862

Dear Colonel,

I send you the *Santa Fe Gazette* with late and interesting telegraphic news—also *Missouri Democrat* of 24th ulto. I have directed Capt. Enos to send forthwith to Belen a ream of letter paper. We have no news since yesterday. Everything is quiet here. I expect definite news from the Pecos by Capt.[Julius] Shaw, as I told him to go as far at least as the Bosque Redondo, ninety miles below Anton Chico, and send his scouts out from there.

If the enemy really is advancing by the Pecos, it is of <u>great</u> importance that Giddings Ranch at Agua Negro, forty miles below Anton Chico, should be destroyed, for it is a fortification full of corn & fodder and would be an excellent stopping place for the Texans to recuperate. In fact, it would be a serious annoyance to us, and with that view I wrote to Col. Paul recommending that a party be placed there to destroy the Ranch in case of the enemy advancing in that direction. I have not yet rec^d a reply from Col. Paul.

Very resp.
Yr. Obd. Svt.
J. L. Donaldson

Col. E. R. S. Canby　　　　Qrmaster Comg. District
Comg. Dept. N. Mex°　　　　Santa Fe.
Belen

P.S. Since writing the above, Capt. Chapin informs me that Giddings Ranch is occupied by Capt. [Pablo?] Martines with twenty six men, pursuant to instructions rec^d from me. I presume Maj. Paul has referred my letter to Col. [José] Gallegos in command at Hatch's Ranch.

J. L. D.¹¹

Head Quarters Dept. of New Mex.
Belen N.M. January 13, 1862

Major:

Your communication of the 12th inst. has been received. I supposed that your communication to Col. Paul in relation to Giddings Ranch covered the case completely. To prevent any mistake, however, instructions have been sent to Col. Gallegos, to remove all the corn to Hatch's Ranch and in the event of the approach of the Texans, to destroy any thing that could be of use to them.

Similar instructions were given by Col. Carson with regard to the forage in the neighborhood of Fort Stanton. The people at Paraje with all their property were removed above Fort Craig and it was intended to pursue the same course with regard to those at Cañon Alamosa, but there was not time to accomplish it.

Very respectfully, Sir,
Your obd. Servt.
Ed. R. S. Canby

Maj. J. L. Donaldson　　　　Col. 19. Infy.
Cmg. District &c.　　　　Comg. Dept.
Santa Fe, N.M.¹²

Albuquerque N.M.
January 14, 1862.

Dear Colonel.

I have this morning seen two or three letters from the States directed to Mr. S. Beuthner, which say that there have been several bridges burnt down in Missouri and that the mails have in consequence been stopped.

Major Martin, the paymaster for the Volunteers, is still at Leavenworth, and there is no money on the road to this country nor will there be any this winter sent here. Major Martin is not coming here this winter and there is no saying when the money will come.

The letters say that Mason & Slidell have been demanded by the British Govt. and have been surrendered to them, and they are now probably either in England or on the way there.

If these reports as to the money are true, it will cause a great deal of dissatisfaction among our Volunteer troops, and I am afraid will produce serious trouble. I hope that these reports are not true, but I give them to you as I got them.

I am Col. Yours Truly
C. Carson
Col. 1st N.M. Vols.

P.S. I would call the Colonel's attention to my official letter of Jany. 5, 1862, in reference to the Citizen Aguilar, confined here by your order. As there is no proof against him, I would like to have him released.

C. C.[13]

Fort Union N.M.
Jany. 14' 1862

Dear Major,

I have received information from all parts of the Eastern District & from the Pecos District, and all my scouts say that there is no appearance of any enemy. Scouts are still out, and no forces of any tolerable size can come here, without a previous knowledge of the fact.

The Cavalry company from Fort Garland has not yet arrived here, altho' it has had ample time to come since it left that Post.

Very truly yours
G. R. Paul

Maj. Donaldson
Act. A.[14]

Camp Connelly Polvadera N.M.
Jany 16th 1862

Sir.

I have the honor to inform you of rather a serious occurrence that took place in the two companies under the command of Capt. [Anastacio?] Garcia on their march to this place, at their camp at the town of Socorro. About 30 of the men revolted. These companies were met by Major [Manuel D.] Pino and directed to return to Fort Craig, in compliance with orders from Hd Qrs Dept., which upon receipt of, they would not obey, stating they had not been paid or clad as they had been promised &c.

Upon the receipt of this intelligence, Col. [Miguel E.] Pino started at once for Socorro. The mutineers (30 in number) fled to the mountains, and the two companies were ordered to march to this Post by Col. Pino and are expected within an hour (it is now 11 o'clock). A detailed account will be sent to you tomorrow.

I am Sir, very Respectfully
Your obt. Servt.

To Capt. Nicodemus   Saml. Archer
12th Inf. U.S.A.   Capt. 5th Inf.
Actg. Asst. Adjt. Genl.   Supt. &c. &c.
Belen N.M.[15]

Head Quarters, S.M. District N.M.
Fort Craig, January 17' 1862

Genl L. Thomas
    Adjutant General
    Washington, D.C.
Asst. Adjutant General,
    Dept. N. Mexico
    Belen N.M.

General.

I regret to report the death of Captain I. N. Moore of the 1st Cav., who in a temporary fit of insanity committed suicide at this post on yesterday.

I am, Sir, very respectfully
Your obdt. Servant
Signed   B. S. Roberts
Col. Vols. Comd'g[16]

Hd. Qrs. S.M. District Dpt. N.M.
Fort Craig, Janry 17' 1862

To the Prefects of San Antonio, Socorro.

I send above all the families of the town of Alamosa. Many of them are families of the Militia, and you and the Prefects of the other towns above must provide them with temporary homes.

Signed   B. S. Roberts
Colonel Vols.
Commanding[17]

Head Quarters Dept. of New Mex.
Belen N.M. Jany. 17, 1862

Major:

Yours of the 16th. has been received. The news in relation to the paymaster has been <u>telegraphed</u> all over the country, and one of the first fruits of it is a mutiny in two of Col. Pino's companies. The refusal of the militia at Fort Union to do guard duty I suppose is another. I have instructed Col. Pino to reduce mutineers to absolute submission by force and to let me know if he requires any assistance to accomplish this. The full particulars are not reported yet, but I shall hear tonight. The men allege that they have not been paid and clothed as they were promised!!

I suppose that England will be told that Mason & Slidell are given up because we are in a straight [*sic*], but that the demand is unjust and unfriendly and will be held in lasting remembrance.

From below I have no news except that a party of 150 Texans left Santa Barbara (Fort Thorn) for, it is supposed, Cañada Alamosa. Roberts has sent a support to his pickets and hopes to catch the party.

The Navajo Country appears to have been abandoned by the Indians. I have written to Mr. [John] Ward to see who are left up there. If it was not in the full of the moon, I should suppose the Texans had something to do with it. No other news.

Very truly Yours
Ed. R. S. Canby

Maj. J. L. Donaldson   Col. 19. Infy.
Cmg. District &c.   Cm.
Santa Fe N.M.[18]

Head Quarters Los Lunas, N. Mex.
Jany 17th 1862.

Capt.

I have the honor to report my arrival at this Post this morning and also herewith to acknowledge the receipt of your communication of today from those Head. Qrs. in reference to some mutineers. I will immediately send out a company of men under the command of Capt. [Julian] Espinosa & Lt. D. Montoya, both of the 1st R.N.M. Vols., and the instructions which I received in your communication will be obeyed to the letter.

I have the honor Sir,
To Remain Very Respectfully

Wm J. L. Nicodemus   Your obt. svt.
Capt. 12th Infty.   J. Fran^{co} Chavez
A.A.A. Genl.   Lt. Col. 1st N.M. Vols.
Belen N.M.[19]   Comdg. Post

<u>19</u>

[January 19, 1862]

Dear Major:

Yours of the 18th and the enclosed papers have been received. Capt. Shaw's report, as all his have been, is clear and satisfactory. The acting Executive of Colorado Territory is as non-committal as Governor Gilpin was.

The instructions to Col. Gallegos were made in detail so as to prevent any misconceptions. I have endorsed the substance on Mr. Giddings letter, which I returned. In addition to this, the officer was instructed if he took or destroyed any property, to do it in the presence of Mr. Giddings or his agent.

The officer sent by Col. Pino to capture the mutineers appears to have mismanaged his business, and they are still at large. Two companies from Polvadera are on their trail. I have sent a cavalry company from this place to intercept them if they attempt to go up the Puerco, & another from Los Lunas to the neighborhood of Cubero if they take that direction. If they keep together, they will be caught.

Lists have been sent to the Commanders of Districts with instructions to secure them. No news from below.

Very truly,
Yours &

Maj. Donaldson
Cmg. &-   Ed. R. S. Canby
Santa Fe N.M.[20]

Albuquerque January 20/62

Commanding officer Col. Canby

Dear Sir:

I never yet had the pleasure of addressing you, but considering of absolute necessity to let you know as a citizen of the U.S. the rumors I have heard. There is a great sensation among the people, caused by the delay of funds from the States to pay expenses of the government, specially the volunteers. I really fear there will be a conspiration among the troops, for malicious persons have being [*sic*] diffusing a spirit of distrust against the government among the soldiers. We know that the militians have revolted at [Fort] Union and they tryed [*sic*] here and other places.

I think it would be better to dismiss them as soon as possible and let them be ready at any given moment. I have written to his Exc. the Governor on the same subject. He says it is all in your hands, and is very glad that it is so. I for my part feel very confident that you will do all you can for New Mexico.

Yours truly

Juan C. Armijo[21]

Belen N.M. Jany. 20, 1861 [*sic;* 1862]

Dear Major:

There is a good deal of excitement in the reputable Mexican population of this part of the country, growing out of the fear of a pronunciamento [*sic*] on the part of the militia and volunteers. I do not apprehend this so long as the regular troops remain above the Jornada; still I have been exceedingly fond several months past to leaven the troops with Americans from the Northern States. I did not and do not expect any thing from the official actions of the Colorado authorities, but something may [be] done by the private action of her citizens.

Will you in conversation with the officers of the Colorado Company now at Santa Fe ascertain the probability of forming Companies in this Territory by coming down individually or in small parties and being organized in New Mexico? They could be enrolled at Fort Garland and provisioned from that place to points below, or mustered into the service at any point at which they might present themselves. The expenses of transportation may [be] paid from the fund for Collocating volunteers &c.

Do you know any one in Taos who could be trusted to raise a company to take the place of Capt. Ford's company at Garland?

We have no news here except of Indian depredations. Many of the statements are false, all of them exaggerated, but industriously circulated by designing and evil disposed persons.

Use the enclosed order if and whenever you think it necessary.

                                Very sincerely
Maj. Donaldson   Your obt. servt.
Comg. &c &c.   Ed. R. S. Canby
Santa Fe N.M.[22]

--------------------◆◆◆--------------------

                              Head Qrs. Sn M[il] Dist. Fort Craig N.M.
                                          21 Jany 1861 [*sic*; 1862]
Dear Colonel:

An Express has been sent me from the Cañada Alamosa by the Alcalde with the information that an hour before daylight yesterday morning, two Companies of Texans came into that place and after remaining about one hour, fell back 8 or 9 miles to their camp. The Mexicans could give me no information about other troops at the camp, but I have no doubt that these 2 companies are the advanced guard of a large force advancing on this Post. The Texans all had on their left arms <u>white</u> <u>scarfs</u>, a sign that they intend to operate in the night

The last 2 spies I have sent down to the Mesilla have not returned, nor has any one come up from there since Capt. Graydon returned a month ago. These facts are significant of a movement, and as nothing is heard from them in any other direction, it is convincing to my mind that they will throw all their forces on me. I have no idea the Post will be besieged, or attempted, except by a night attack.

I have been expecting that tonight, and I shall look for it every night, until I get further information. I need all the forces that can be sent here, and they should move without delay. I have lost confidence in the volunteers since you were here.

                              I am Colonel very truly yours
Col. E. R. S. Canby U.S.A.   B. S. Roberts
Comdg. at Belen[23]   Col. Vols. Comdg.

--------------------◆◆◆--------------------

                                                  Belen, N.M.
<u>Private</u>   Jany. 21, 1862.
Dear Major:

I have learned by this evening's mail that the Legislature is greatly exercised at the Indians depredations & is talking loudly about the sacrifices the people of New Mexico are making to sustain the government of the United States and fight an "imaginary evil" "when the real evil is at their doors" &c. &c.

If the people of New Mexico are satisfied that the threatened invasion of the country by the Texans is an "imaginary evil" and through the Legislature will give an official expression to that opinion, I shall find myself at liberty to use my discretional authority to withdraw the regular troops from New Mexico.

I presume however that this clamor has been instigated by designing persons for the purpose of embarrassing the operations of the government and to produce as much mischief as possible, and that the persons who talk most are simply the tools of others who keep themselves concealed.

Roberts is a good deal concerned about some apprehended trouble with his volunteers, but I do not think it will amount to any thing. If Governor Connelly decides to come down to Albuquerque and there is nothing special to keep you in Santa Fe, I should be very much pleased if you would come down also.

Very sincerely
Yours &c.
Ed. R. S. Canby
Col. 19. Infy.

Maj. J. L. Donaldson
Cmg. District &c.
Santa Fe N.M.

P.S. Of course I have no thought of withdrawing the troops, but it would be well if some demagogues who are doing a great deal to render their people discontented knew that I had the power.[24]

Belen Jany. 22/62

D. Major:

Some time ago, at his suggestion, I authorized Capt. Shoemaker to have some lances made for the purpose of arming a part of the New Mex. Mtd. Vols., but the fabrication was abandoned in consequence of his inability to get suitable timber for the shafts.

Yesterday Capt. Barrientos applied for lances for his Company, and upon my stating the difficulty about timber, he said that he knew two or three persons in Santa Fe who had timber of the right kind & would look for it when he went up. If he finds any that is suitable, will you take measures to secure enough of it for 200 lances and have it sent to Capt. Shoemaker?

I have no additional news from Fort Craig.

Very truly
Yours &c.

Maj. Donaldson[25]   Ed. R. S. Canby

Head Quarters Dept. of N.M.
Belen N.M. Jany. 22, 1862

Major:

Your communications of the 19. & 21. have been received. It will not be safe to rely upon private trains for the movement of the troops in emergencies. It will be better to reserve a sufficient number of wagons from the public trains and rely upon private transportation for the transfer of supplies &c. The amount required will not be large and if not otherwise required, may be usefully employed in collecting the supplies that may be found in the neighborhood of each command.

As soon as the present emergency has passed, I will turn all the available force into the Navajo Country, and in the mean time will do all that I can without disseminating our force to a dangerous extent. I am not hopeful of any important results from a campaign, as the Navajos are so entirely demoralized and broken up that it will be almost impossible to strike an important blow.

Very respectfully, Sir,
Your obdt. servt.

Maj. J. L. Donaldson   Ed. R. S. Canby
Comg. District &c.   Col. 19. Inf.
Santa Fe N.M.[26]   Comg. Dept.

Major:

I think that the information contained in the dispatch sent you may be relied on in great measure. I am not satisfied, however, that Fort Craig will be the main point of attack. I have directed, however, the concentration of all the disposable force at this place, to be in readiness to march there if it should be. If not, it will be available for any other operations that may be necessary.

I wish every man that can be spared without endangering the safety of the city be sent. You can judge from the temper and disposition of the people whether it can be trusted to the militia and citizens alone without danger of revolt.

I think it would be well for the Governor to come down with any other influential Mexicans to give assurance and confidence to the Mexicans.

In haste
Very sincerely
Yours &
Ed. R. S. Canby

Major Donaldson
Santa Fe, N.M.

Belen N.M. Jany. 23/62 11 P.M.[27]

———◆———

<u>Duplicate</u>

Head Quarters Dept. of N.M.
Belen N.M. Jan. 24" 1862

Major J. L. Donaldson
Comdg. &c. Santa Fe N.M.
Major

By direction of the Colonel Commanding, I make for you a copy of what is considered a reliable paper.

"Genl. Sibley and staff arrived at El Paso about a month ago. Staff officers, A. J. Jackson, Col. Robards, T. Ochiltree, Capt. Dwyer, Judge Crosby A.Q.M. and Receiver to property to be sequestered in N.M.

The 1" and 2" Regiments are now between Roblero [*sic*; Robledo] and Santa Barbara and are not fortifying themselves. They have taken only four additional pieces of artillery, besides those belonging to Col. Baylor's Command (2 thirty-two pounders). Genl. S. & staff were to leave Mesilla for Fort Thorn on yesterday the 16." The 3rd Regt. is expected here next week. The troops are badly provisioned and armed—have had about 200 horses stolen since they passed here. Their only hope is to march into N.M. in quick time or else engage into a war with Mexico (at Paso) to procure provisions. They have no money and their paper is only taken by the merchants, but not by the <u>Mexicans</u>. The Mexican population at El Paso are much opposed to them—also at Mesilla and Doña Ana. Yrrisani & Amburgh's [Ellsberg & Amberg's] goods at Mesilla have been confiscated and that is the order of the day.

S. Hart has done more in aiding and assisting them than the balance of the capitalists here, and has gone as far as to give a list of the principal capitalists in N.M. to confiscate their property, and that is their aim July 17/62 [*sic*]. May God help you all."

The Col. Comdg. desires you will place an officer in charge of the office in the absence of Capt. Chapin, whom he has ordered to report in person to these Hd. Qrs. without delay.

> Very respectfully Major
> Your obt. servt.
> Wm. J. L. Nicodemas
> Capt. 12' Infy.
> A.A.A.G.[28]

Hd Qrs Camp Connelly Polvadera
New Mexico. Jany 24th 1862

Sir.

I have the honor to inform you that a Mr. Lujan of Lemitar brought to me this morning a package of letters containing copies of a Proclamation from Sibley C.S. Army (a copy of which I enclose). It was the intention of Lujan to forward these to the Governor and [he] had them enveloped and addressed accordingly. I took possession of them, told him it was not necessary.

He says they were dropped in the town of Lemitar rolled in a cloth and found by some women and brought to him this morning. Some are addressed to our Officers, some to Officers of the Territory &c.; there has been an apparent struggle to disguise the writing. There are thirteen of these letters. I have opened two, addressed to regular officers, and find they contain English copies. These letters are detained for the direction of the Dept. Commander in the matter.

Capt. Wm. J. L. Nicodemus   I am Sir Very Respectfully,
12th Inf. U.S.A.   Your obt. Servt.
A.A.A. Genl.   Saml. Archer
Belen[29]   Capt. 5th Inf.
                                          Comdg. Post

Hd Qrs Camp Connelly Polvadera
New Mexico Jany 25" 1862

Sir

I have the honor to inform you that Lieut. [John] Falvey arrived at one and a half o'clock P.M. and will leave about ½ past 4 o'clock to return. I send package as required. The two letters I opened, were directed to Captains Morris & Howland. It is my opinion that the person employed to distribute these proclamations about the country is a Mexican. However, so far as I have yet been able to learn, it seems it is an American. I shall do my best to detect the person so employed.

A Sergeant of the command at Abo Pass came here this morning on leave of absence. He had in his possession one of these documents given to him by a person at Lemitar; the person is known, and gave it to the Sergt. at his request, as he says he wished to show it to his Capt. I took it from him and think it was a mere matter of curiosity on his part. I have spies out each day and shall endeavor to keep you informed of any occurrence of importance.

I am Sir Very Respectfully
Your obt. Servt.

To Capt. Wm. J. L. Nicodemus   Saml. Archer
12th Inf. U.S.A.   Capt. 5th Inf. Comdg. Post
A.A.A. Genl. Belen N.M.[30]

H^d Q^{rs} Cubero N.M.
Feby 1st 1862.

Act. Asst. Adj^t General
H^d Qrs. Dept. Santa Fe N.M.
Sir

I have the honor to report that I relieved Capt. A. W. Evans 6th Cavalry in command of Cubero & Western Military District on the 27th of January 1862. Capt. Evans started from this Post on the 28th of January 1862. On the 20th of January a detachment of the 1st Reg^t N.M. Mt Vols. arrived here in pursuit of deserters. They left this place the night of the same date for Savolleta [Cebolleta] accompanied by Lieut. [José Maria?] Sanchez & 20 men of Company B 2nd Regt. N.M. Volts. and one piece of artillery & succeeded in arresting three deserters, and returned for Albuquerque on the 25th inst. No Indian depredations have been committed in the vicinity of this Post. Mr. [John G.] Ward, Indian Agent, left this Post for H^d Qrs. of the Dept. on the 23^d inst.

In compliance with instructions from H^d Qrs. Dept. Belen N.M. by S.O. No. 8, Capt. José D. Sena's Company B 2nd Reg^t N.M. Volts. started for Polvadera on the 25th of January 1862 accompanied by First Lieut. Rafael Ortiz y Chaves, 2 Reg^t N.M. Vols.

Very Respectfully
Your Obedt. Servt.
Francisco Aragon
Comdg. Post[31]

Fig. 15. *Town of Cubero, New Mexico, western outpost on the Thirty-fifth Parallel (Perry Coll. No. 74). Photograph by Alexander Gardner, 1867. Missouri Historical Society, St. Louis, negative no. OutSTL 147.*

Head Quarters Cubero N.M.

February 1st 1862.

Sir: Being unable to procure clothing at this Post for the necessary use of my Company, I beg leave to ask of you whether my Company has any right in drawing clothing from the Government? Most of my men are entirely out of shoes and other necessary articles for life.

Should the owner of Private Store Kap [kept] in this place would know the certain as to the pay of my Company as Militia, I have not the least doubt he would credit my Company, as most of the people of this Territory are under the impression that Militia men will not receive any pay for their services under no considerations.

Yours Respectfully &a

Francisco Aragon

Capt. of N.M. Militia

To E. R. S. Canby,   Commanding W.M. District at Cuvero

Commanding Department

of New Mexico[32]

Head Quarters District of Santa Fe
Santa Fe N.M. February 14, 1862.

<u>"Copy"</u>

Commanding Officer
Fort Marcy, N.M.
Sir:

I desire you, from this moment until affairs have assumed a definite shape at Val Verde, to have your command ready to fall in at a moment's warning, with 20 rounds of ammunition on their persons.

You will not permit the officers or men, except under urgent circumstances, to be absent from their quarters, and you will please be on the alert to watch for any appearance of secession in our midst. Any sympathy tending to the spread of unfavorable news in the event of a battle at [Fort] Craig you will at once check, if necessary, by force of arms and by imprisonment in the Guard House.

At night, detail an extra in-lying picket of one-fourth of your whole command; these will be required to sleep on their arms. <u>Besides this,</u> send an increase of 1 non-commissioned officer and 10 privates every evening after dark to your Guard-House. This increment will not be required to walk post, but only to stay at the Guard House during the night. Should you have any information of any rising or plotting among disaffected persons here, you will at once report it to me.

Please give such orders as may put the sentinels on the alert for fires, and direct the "Officer of the Day" to quietly examine the public buildings frequently during the night. The guards at the stables and Medical Store-room you will cause to be visited during the night.

I especially charge you to keep good men / take some of Mr. Hodges' men / quietly on the alert in the streets of Santa Fe and to take every step to thwart any attempt upon the part of certain persons here to display their sentiments in this town. I wish you to direct your time and energies entirely to this matter and leave nothing undone which you think should be done. I desire no half-way business, for in case of a defeat it may be necessary to commence a fight here, and I am determined to let the <u>blood flow,</u> where it should.

Please order an inspection this afternoon at retreat and inspect your command in person; see to it yourself that everything is in proper order. I intended to tell you this in conversation, but for fear you might not understand, I have written.

Be ready, have everything in order, keep a sharp lookout for certain people, and Santa Fe will be quiet. Please let me know that you have received this and send me your assurances of your hearty cooperation.

Very respectfully

Your obed^t servt.

(Signed)   Gurden Chapin

Capt. 7 Infy.

Comdg. Distr.

"Official"

Gurden Chapin, Captain 7. Infy.

A.I. General

Furnished for the information of the Department Commander.[33]

Hatch's Ranch, New Mex°.

Feby. 15, 1862.

Sir:

I have the honor to report that, in obedience to orders received from Col. I. G. Gallegos, "to proceed to the Rincon del Leon, by way of Colonel Miguel S. Yromero's, at "Pueblo," on [the] Pecos, and follow up a band of Navajo Indians reported by Colonel Yromero as having attacked a train at that place," I left this post at 8 o'clock P.M. on 8th inst., with 25 enlisted men of Co^s. 'E' and 'D' 3rd Reg^t N.M. Mtd. Volts. I reached Anton Chico at 11 o'clock, where I stopped one hour in order to rest my horses and employ a guide. How I acted from leaving Anton Chico until my return here today will be shown by the following, which I copy from notes of Scout, now before me:

"Feby. 9th—Left Anton Chico at Midnight—marched all night—extremely cold. Stopped three times and made fires for men to warm themselves by. 8½ o'clock reached Col. Miguel S. Yromero's, at Pueblo, near San Miguel. Distance from Hatch's Ranch to this place 40 miles. Called on Colonel Romero and enquired of him all about attack of Indians. He told me that four days ago [a] report reached him of the train being attacked, that three teamsters were wounded, and some mules killed; number of Indians about 45.

Met Capt. S. Martinez at the Colonel's. The Colonel told me that Capt. Martinez and party of ten Mtd. Volts. were at his place when the Indians were reported, and that he ordered a Lieutenant and about 40 Militia to join Capt. Martinez & party, who reached the scene of action a few hours after the Indians had left. The whole force, however, returned to the Pueblo same evening, reporting that no Indians could be found. (Singular Captain Martinez did not take the trail & pursue the Indians, instead of returning to village).

1 o' C P.M.—About to start with my party to Rincon del Leon, when [an] express from San Miguel to Colonel Yromero reported a party of Indians immediately in rear of that town, running off stock. Accompanied by the son of Colonel Yromero, I immediately started for San Miguel, where on inquiring, I found report of Indians was false. It appears that a boy seeing Mexicans, in a hurried way, driving cattle through the brushwood, took the Mexicans for Indians and hence the report. I told the father of the boy that were it not for his youth (the boy's), I would have him punished severely for having made false report.

3 o' C P.M. Marched 5 miles to a deep gorge in the bluff above San Miguel, where found some water and encamped for night—no grass."

"Feby. 10th—Left camp at daybreak and after nearly two hours' hard climbing made top of mesa. Marched 2½ miles and halted to cook breakfast and let horses graze—much needed. 10 o' C A.M. marched in westerly direction across mesa. Snow here 5 or 6 inches deep on level ground, which has fallen since the Indians attacked the train, which precludes the possibility of trailing them. Marched till sundown and encamped. No water. Grass good but nearly all covered with snow. Timber—fine—the finest I have seen in New Mex°."

"Feby. 11th—Last night extremely cold—hard on both men & horses. Left camp at sunrise and taking across the mesa, at 3 o' C P.M. came to the verge of the mesa, 8 or 9 miles above San José. The view from this point is grand. Marched on the verge of the mesa until over San José, when descended to valley over the roughest, most rocky & steepest track I have traveled for years. Not the least sign of Indians on this tableland. Marched to El Pueblo, 7 miles down Pecos, and stopped for night."

"Feby. 12th—Started at Sunrise, taking the road for the Rincon del Leon. After marching 7 or 8 miles reached that place. Found three dead mules. An arrow found, the guide informs [me], is an Apache arrow. The snow being nearly all gone here, I tried to find the direction the Indians took on leaving, but could not in consequence of the heavy fall of snow and the Indians being all afoot. I took the direction of Galisteo for some miles. Halted and sent two parties on foot to examine some "passes" in the hills on sight, while the horses grazed. Both parties returned without seeing the least sign of Indians.

3 o' C P.M. Down the "Cañon Blanco" and after sundown reached a place known as "Agua del Medio," where encamped for night. Water, not

good—grass, hardly any. Day's march 37 or 40 miles. The guide informs me that at this place, a few weeks ago, the Apaches captured a Mexican boy and took him as guide on their horse-stealing excursion to the Pecos & that during the night, halting to rest, all the Indians fell asleep, when the poor boy made his escape."

"Feby. 14th—Marched in direction of Anton Chico and after marching about 7 miles struck trail of three ponies. Followed the trail for 5 or 6 miles when coming to herds of cattle, I came to the conclusion that the trail was that of the herders' ponies and left it. The guide agreed with me in this. After marching about 18 miles more, reached Anton Chico at sundown."

"Feby. 15th—Left Anton Chico at 8 o' C and reached Hatch's Ranch at noon, the 7 days' rations that I was ordered to take with me for party having been entirely used up."

I would respectfully recommend that while the Indians continue to commit depredations between Anton Chico and San José, on Pecos, instead of sending Scouts out when reports are made—Scouts that do not, nor cannot, effect anything, the Indians having three or four days to get out of the way—a company of mounted men be stationed, or kept moving, between the places above-named, ready to act on the approach of the Indians.

I am, Sir,
Very Respectfully
Your obt. sevt.

Major F. Baca   Wm. McLaughlin
3rd Reg^t Mtd. Volts.   1st Lieut. 3rd Mtd. Volts.
Comd'g. Hatch's Ranch New Mex°.34   Comd'g. Scout

[Translation in file but original document not present]
Hatch's Ranch, Feby 15 / 1862

Commanding Officer
3rd Regt. N.M. Vol's.
Sir:

In pursuance to orders received at this Post, I started to Agua del Corral, and went as far as Jorupa. The following day I started in the direction of the Pueblo de Pecos, where I arrived at 2 o'clock P.M. Here I was informed that the Navajoes were attacking Don Casimiro Romero's train in the Rincon del Chimal. I immediately proceeded to his assistance, and returned escorting the trail to Pueblo de Pecos, where I stayed over night.

Next day I went to Agua del Corral and encamped on the mesa, without water. From this place I came down to Diegos, where I laid over one day, and started the next in the direction of the Middle Cañon del Agua, where

I stopped till next day. From here I went to near Puertocito, and the next day to Lagunitas. I left this place, taking the road over the mesa of the Chapainas, and came as far as Jorupa where I laid over night, starting next day to this post.

I am Sir
Your obdt. servant
Severiano Martinez
Capt. 3rd Reg't. N.M. Vols.[35]

Head Quarters Eastern District
Fort Union N.M. March 4/62

Major,

I have received your several communications of the 1", 2nd & 3rd of March respectively. I have just received information that <u>seven companies of Colorado Volunteers</u>, would be in Taos on the 2nd or 3rd Inst; that they were making forced marches, and would therefore be in Santa Fe at an early day. Under these circumstances, and in order to make a strong diversion in favor of Col. Canby, I think it expedient that you should return to Santa Fe (if you have already left it) and organize a strong column to send below.

This post is too important to leave it entirely defenseless, but as soon as I learn of the arrival at Santa Fe of the Colorado Volunteers, I shall endeavor to send further reinforcements, being certain that we shall be strong enough to defeat the enemy, and to relieve Colonel Canby's command. If it is possible to do so, an express should be sent to communicate with Col. Canby, and to inform him of approaching relief.

I am Sir, very Respectfully
Your obdt. Svt.

Major J. L. Donaldson   G. R. Paul
Com'dg. Santa Fe District   Col. 4' Regt. N.M. Vols.
Santa Fe N.M.[36]   Com'dg. East^n District

Tecolote N.M.
March 9th 11 o'clock P.M.

Col. G. R. Paul
Comdg. Fort Union
Sir

From reliable sources I am satisfied that the main body of the Texans are watching the movements of Col. Canby, and that there is but about 400 between Albuquerque and Algodones. At nine o'clock this morning Mr. Justus tells me that there was not one Texan in Santa Fe. Mr. Justus is a mail agent for the U.S.

I think that the best thing that could be done would be to move a command <u>immediately</u> to a point on the Galisteo Creek, where a small force could hold the pass against double their number, and thus prevent the enemy from entering Santa Fe. This is my honest opinion and I think it entitled to some consideration. 2 pieces of artillery would be a consideration which I think would be right for you to notice.

I am

Very Respectfully

Your Obt. Servt.

G. W. Howland Capt. 3rd Cavy.

[over]

Dear Col. 11-o' ck-P.M.

For Gods sakes send your troops down. You can hold Santa Fe. My opinion is, that you can be a <u>Brig</u>. <u>Genl</u>. The <u>main</u> <u>body</u> of the <u>enemy</u> are near Fort Craig. I am almost <u>certain</u> of it. Do come!

In haste

Yours truly

J. A. Whitall[37]

Tecolote N.M.

March 15th 1862

Capt. G. Chapin

A.A.A.G. Dist. Eastⁿ N.M.

Fort Union.

Sir

No news to send you. I received yours ordering me to Fort Union as soon as relieved.

It is a shame that Santa Fe was allowed to be taken by Eleven Gamblers, as I am sure it was such men as

J Phillips	
" Kirk	
" Foster	and two
" Holmes	
" Madison	
" McPeilin	

" Thatcher and one other—these are the men who galloped through the streets of Santa Fe and formed in front of Johnson's store. The

Gambler Kirk alone rides into Albuquerque and around the Flag Staff and takes possession of the city. This is all corroborated by my friends who have been and were in both places.

> I am
> Very Respectfully
> Your obt. sevt.
> Geo. W. Howland
> Capt. Comdg. Det. 3 Cav.[38]

"The Battle Cry of Freedom"
(George F. Root, 1862)

Yes, we'll rally 'round the flag, boys, we'll rally once again,
Shouting the battle cry of Freedom,
We will rally from the hillside, we'll gather from the plain,
Shouting the battle cry of Freedom!
Chorus: The Union forever, Hurrah boys, hurrah!
Down with the Traitor, up with the Star;
Yes, we'll rally 'round the flag, boys, we'll rally once again,
Shouting the battle cry of Freedom.

We will welcome to our numbers the loyal true and brave,
Shouting the battle cry of Freedom,
And although he may be poor he shall never be a slave,
Shouting the battle cry of Freedom!
Chorus: The Union forever, &c.

So we're springing to the call from the East and from the West,
Shouting the battle cry of Freedom,
And we'll hurl the rebel crew from the land we love the best,
Shouting the battle cry of Freedom!
Chorus: The Union forever, &c.

CHAPTER TWELVE
Baylor's Raid on Corralitos, February 1862

[17 March 1862]

CHIHUAHUA

En comunicaciones dirigidos a la secretaría de mi despacho con fechas 4 y 6 del mes actual da parte el juez de paz de la municipalidad de Corralitos, en el Cantón Galeana, de que una fuerza de doscientos soldados y cien voluntarios, o poco más, a las órdenes del Coronel Comandante Don Juan B. Baylor, del ejército que obedece a usted, invadió dicho lugar a pretexto de perseguir algunos indios apaches que a la vez se hallaban de paz en aquella población, y suponiéndolos ocultos en la casa del mismo juez y de otros vecinos las cateó y allanó todas, cometiendo otros excesos y tropelías impropias de súbditos de una nación civilizada y amiga de la República Mexicana como es la de los Estados Unidos de América, sin excepción de unionistas y confederados, dando muerte al fin a varios de los indios que fueron hallados a inmediaciones del referido lugar y amagando a sus habitantes con una nueva expedición de la propria naturaleza.

Omito con toda intención encarecer lo extraño y vituperable de semejante comportamiento del Coronel Baylor y de toda la fuerza de su mando, por que usted lo podrá calificar, tanto mejor, cuanto que tengo el más alto concepto de su rectitud y de la buena fe que se ha servido manifestarme por medio de en enviado el señor Coronel Don Santiago Reily al hacerme presente la buena inteligencia y amistosas relaciones que deseaba estrechar como Jefe del Ejército de los Estados Confederados del Sur de América con el gobierno de mi cargo; pero no puedo dispensarme de reclamar ese ultraje a la nación mexicana y a sus ciudadanos y autoridades de Corralitos, cuando ni con el pretexto de la persecución de los bárbaros ha podido ni debido violarse el territorio que elegió para teatro de sus operaciones militares el repetido Coronel Baylor, supuesto lo que expuse a usted en mi nota de 11 de enero último, contestación de la suya relativa fecha 16 de diciembre anterior que me presentó de señor Reily, las que constan publicadas en el adjunto número del periódico oficial de este gobierno.

Y como quedaba establecido por mi parte—que no me era posible ni licito permitir la entrada al estado de tropas extranjeras, aún cuando conocía y conozco las ventajas recíprocas que pudieron alcanzarse de la mutuo conexión que usted me proponía obrándose con toda la circunspección y respeto a uno y otro país, que ciertamente no ha empleado el Coronel Baylor;

me veo estrechado a suplicar a usted y lo espero con la mayor confianza, el castigo y represión de aquel y de cuantos jefes y soldados de la Confederación de los Estados del Sur intenten seguir tan pernicioso ejemplo; en la inteligencia de que, en caso contrario, que ni quiero suponer, se pondrá a este gobierno en la dura necesidad de obrar según sus deberes y como lo exigen los derechos y el decoro de la Nación Mexicana, cuya dignidad e intereses legítimos y reconocidos no pueden menos que resentirse vivamente de ataques tan inmotivados e injustos como el de que me quejo en esta vez.

Me será muy grato volver a dirigir a usted mis comunicaciones sobre asuntos diferentes del muy desagradable que hoy me obligó a ocupar su atención; y entre tanto, tengo la honra de renovar a usted mi respetuosa consideración y particular aprecio.

Dios, Libertad y Reforma. Chihuahua, Marzo 17 de 1862.

Luis Terrazas

Señor Brigadier Don H. H. Sibley,
General en Jefe del Ejército de los Estados Confederados de América.

Donde se halle.[1]

[translation]

CHIHUAHUA [Seal]

In communications dated the 4th and 6th of the present month sent to my Secretary of State, the Justice of Peace of the Municipality of Corralitos, in the Canton of Galeana, reports that a force of two hundred soldiers and one hundred volunteers or a few more, at the orders of Colonel John B. [*sic; R.*] Baylor of the Army under your command, invaded that place on the pretext of pursuing some Apache Indians who, at the time, were at peace in that community.

Supposing them hidden in the house of this same Justice and by other citizens, he broke into all the houses and searched them, committing other excesses and outrages that are improper for the subjects of a civilized nation friendly with the Republic of Mexico, as is the United States of America, without exception of Unionists and Confederates. They visited death upon various Indians who were discovered in the immediate vicinity of the place referred to, and threatened its inhabitants with a new raid of the same nature.

I am intentionally failing to expand on the unwelcome and similarly vituperable behavior of Colonel Baylor and all the forces of his command, because you will be able to judge, so much better, all of that. I hold the highest opinion of your rectitude and of the good faith that has been demonstrated to me through your sending Colonel James Reily. He extended to me the sound understanding and friendly relations that the Chief of the Army of the Confederate States of America desires to embrace with the government in my charge.

However, I can't excuse myself from protesting against this insult to the Mexican Nation, and to the citizens and authorities at Corralitos, when neither with the pretext of persecuting the barbarians did he have authority, nor was the aforesaid Colonel Baylor obliged to violate the territory that he chose as the theater of his military operations. I supposed that which I laid before you in my note of last January 11, in answer to yours dated the preceding December 16, presented to me by Señor Reily, is all on record, published in the enclosed number of the official newspaper of this government [not seen].

And as I was establishing a position on my part, that it was not possible nor lawful to permit the entry of foreign troops into the State, even when I was acquainted with and recognize the reciprocal advantages that may follow from the mutual concessions that you were proposing to me to put into effect with all the circumspection and respect between one country and the other; that, certainly, Colonel Baylor has not exercised. I am constrained to appeal to you, and expect with the greatest confidence, the punishment and repression of each and every officer and soldier of the Confederate States of the South, who may intend to follow such a pernicious example, in the knowledge that in the opposite situation, which I conceive of unwillingly, it will leave this government with the inflexible necessity of proceeding according to its obligations and likewise to exercise the rights and decorum of the Mexican Nation, whose dignity and legitimate interests and recognized rights cannot do less than respond vigorously to attacks so without reason and unjust as that which I complain against on this occasion.

It will give me great pleasure to again direct my communications with you to different matters other than that of a very unpleasant nature, that has obliged me today to occupy your attention. Meanwhile I have the honor of reiterating to you my respectful consideration and particular regard.

God, Liberty, and Reform. Chihuahua, March 17, 1862.

Luis Terrazas [Governor of Chihuahua]

Señor Brigadier Don H. H. Sibley,
General in Chief of the Army of the Confederate States of America,
    Wherever he may be.

———————— ◆ ————————

Chihuahua, March 18, 1862.

Col. J. A. Quintero
Monterey
Dear Sir:

Your much esteemed note of the 23rd ultimo only came to hand yesterday, to which I hasten to reply. You inform me of a report having reached you "that the United States are to transport troops and munitions of war across the State of Chihuahua for the purpose of attacking the Confederate States." Such a report was in circulation here some two months ago to the effect that permission had been granted by the Federal Gov^t of Mexico for troops belonging to the United States to pass through the States of Sonora and Chihuahua into Texas and New Mexico. On hearing this report I immediately called upon the Govr of this State, who assured me no such permission had been granted, but on the contrary stringent orders had been received from the General Gov^t to observe the strictest neutrality in the present struggle between the two sections of the once United States. Notwithstanding the above I called on the Govr again last evening in order to reassure myself in the premises, when he again told me there is no more truth in this new report than there was in the previous one.

I am sorry to inform you that Col. Baylor with a force from 200 to 300 men has invaded the State of Chihuahua (having asked permission of the State Gov^t which was refused) on pretext to operate against the Indians. He went to a place called Corralitos (Real de Minas), found in the houses three Indians, one male & two females, which were instantly killed by his men, although the Indians are said to have been domesticated and servants to D. Pedro Prieto, one of the owners of the mines of Corralitos. The Govr did not mention this to me last evening, which makes me think he has written to Mexico for instructions in the matter.

Fort Craig, New Mexico, is said to be so strongly fortified and well garrisoned and supplied that General Sibley has decided not to attack it with his present small force, said to be composed of only 3000 men—badly armed and equipped and worse rationed.

You must read this the best you can as I write it in great pain, owing to a wound I received at the taking of San Luis Potosi in 1858 having burst open again and three pieces of bone have come out and the wound still remains open, which makes me think other pieces of bone have to come forth.

I have not yet finished my business here but hope to do so by the end of this month and return to Monterey. Meanwhile I remain,

> Yours most respectfully,
> Edw. H. Jordan.

Kind regards to Col. Landgstroth & all friends.[2]

Secretaría   37

Habiéndose internado en el Cantón Galeana una fuerza de americanos, de más de trescientos, al mando del Coronel Don Juan R. Baylor, que con pretexto al perseguir a los apaches invadió al mineral de Corralitos el día 27 de febrero pasado, cometiendo los mayores excesos y tropelías contra aquel vecindario, en mengua de los derechos y dignidad de la nación, y estando averiguado que tal fuerza pertenece al ejército de los Estados Confederados del Sur que se halla a las órdenes del General Don H. H. Sibley; me ordena el C. [Ciudadano] Gobernador del Estado que pregunte a usted si tuvo noticia esa jefatura del movimiento referido, como es muy probable, y por qué no lo comunicó con la oportunidad debida, como deberá verificarlo en cualquier otro lanza de la misma naturaleza que llegare a su conocimiento; estando a la mira en lo sucesivo para procurar la aprehención de los agresores que se presentaren en ese distrito, aunque sea con apariencias de paz y tratando de disimular o disculpar sus atentados; en el concepto de que podían ser remitidos a esta capital sino fuero dable conservarlos hay [*sic*; ahí] con la seguridad competente.

Al trasmitir a usted el acuerdo superior que dejo expuesto para los consiguientes efectos, le renuevo las protestas de mi aprecio y consideración.

Dios, Libertad y Reforma. Chihuahua Marzo 26 de 1862

Juan B Méndez

Ciudadano Jefe Político del Distrito de Bravos   Pasó[3]

[translation]

[Stamp]: Secretary [of State] of   37
the State of Chihuahua
Secretary.

A force of more than three hundred Americans commanded by Colonel Don John R. Baylor having penetrated into the Canton Galeana, with the pretext of pursuing some Apaches, attacked the Corralitos mine [mining district] on the 27th of February ultimo, committing the greatest excesses and outrages against that citizenry, disgracing the rights and honor of the nation by this cowardly conduct. It has been determined that that force belongs to the Army of the Confederate States of the South, as it is called, and is under the orders of General Don H. H. Sibley.

The Citizen Governor of the State orders me to inquire if you notified that Office of the disturbance referred to, as is very probable, and why it wasn't made known with the required timeliness. He will be obliged nonetheless to verify it from whatever else out of this same set of affairs comes to his attention, remaining on watch hereafter to try to seize the aggressors who may show themselves in this District, although it may be with the appearance of peace, seeking to hide or excuse their offences. The thinking is that they can be sent to this capital, if it is not practicable to keep them there with adequate security.

Upon transmitting to you the superior resolution that I allowed to be made public for its consequent effects, I repeat to you the protestations of my esteem and consideration.

> God, Liberty and Reform
> Chihuahua, March 26, 1862
> Juan B. Méndez [rubric]

Civil Political Chief
of the District of Bravos   [El] Paso

> Head Quarters, Army of New Mexico.
> Fort Bliss, Texas, May 17, 1862.

To His Excellency
Don Luis Terrazas
Governor of the State of Chihuahua
Sir:

I have the honor to acknowledge the receipt of your communication of date the 17th day of March 1862, informing me of a certain incursion made upon the Territory of your State by a force under Col. John R. Baylor of the Confederate Army, and complaining of injuries, or depredations upon your citizens perpetrated thereby.

I assure you, Sir, that I receive this information with great regret. The policy of the Confederate States which I have been most anxious to effectuate, is to cherish the most amicable relations with all foreign nations and more particularly with the Mexican States, whose geographic position must always render their good will desirable to the Confederacy.

About two months since Col. John R. Baylor resigned his Commission and left this army and country to go, as I am informed, to the seat of the Confederate Government at Richmond, Va. Had I received your complaint before he left, it would have been a duty which I would have promptly discharged, to have held him answerable for the matters of which you inform me. Inasmuch as he has resigned and departed beyond the limits of this army, you will at once perceive that I have it no longer within my immediate power to institute measures upon the subject.

Under these circumstances I shall this day forward your communication to the proper Department of the Confederate Government at Richmond, Va., and I doubt not it will meet prompt action and such as will prove satisfactory to you.

I shall request my Government to inform you in relation thereto, and

Fig. 16. *Brigadier General Henry Hopkins Sibley, CSA.*
Courtesy of Mr. Arthur W. Bergeron, Jr., Chester, Virginia.

shall not fail upon this or any future occasion to give evidences by my action of the desire of my government and of myself to do prompt justice to
your government and people and to cultivate the most friendly relations
with them.

I have &c.,

Official copy   (signed)   H. H. Sibley
Jos. Ed. Dwyer,   Brig. Gen. Com'd'g.
A.D.C. & A.A.A.G.

[Endorsements on the foregoing letter of Gen. Sibley]
Respectfully submitted to the Sec'y of War.

Jasper W. Whiting

A. & I.G.O.   Maj. & A.A.G.
Aug. 15/62
Respectfully submitted to the Pres't for his information.

G. W. Randolph,
Sec. of War.

The Sec'ty of State will prepare a letter for the Govr. of Chihuahua and it
be necessary to act on the case of Govr. Baylor for this offense and his
order in relation to the Indian tribes.

J. D.

This paper was sent back from the Executive Chamber to the War Office
on the 3d of September and has been on file in the A.G.'s office since that
time. It is now sent to the Secretary of State as directed by the President
in the above endorsement.

Burton N. Harrison
Private Secretary

Oct. 18, 1862[4]

———————— ◆ ————————

[Accompanies letter dated January 20, 1863, on unrelated subject, from J.
P. Benjamin, Secretary of State, to J. A. Quintero, Esq., Confidential
Agent, C.S.A., Monterey, Mexico]:

To His Excellency,
Don Luis Terrazas,
Governor of the State of Chihuahua.
Sir:

It has been reported to the President of the Confederate States that
Col. John R. Baylor in command of certain armed forces, made an irrup-
tion into the State of Chihuahua in the month of March last, under pretext

of pursuing Indians; and a duplicate copy of the letter of your Excellency to Brig. Gen. Sibley, dated on the 17th March last [1862] has recently been received by the President, as well as a copy of the letter written to you in reply by Gen. Sibley under date of 17th May last.

Although the President feels confident that your Excellency will have been fully satisfied by the letter of Gen. Sibley, that this Government could not sanction such outrages as Col. Baylor is reported to have committed, the President is not content to remain silent under the circumstances. I am therefore instructed by the President to express in his name to your Excellency the regret which he feels in learning that any subordinate officer of this government should have been guilty of conduct so justly offensive to our friendly neighbors in Mexico; to thank you in his name for the amiable sentiments toward this people expressed in your letter to Gen. Sibley; and to assure your Excellency that the conduct of Col. Baylor is not only disapproved by this government, but that due punishment shall be inflicted on him for the grave offence of thus entering, without your permission and with armed forces, into the State over which you preside.

In communicating to your Excellency these assurances on the part of the President of the Confederate States, I am gratified to have an opportunity of assuring your Excellency that the sentiments of respect and consideration entertained for you by the President, are shared by

Your Obedient Servant,
J. P. Benjamin,
Secretary of State.[5]

Rec^d 20 Aug. '63.
J. P. B.

Hon. J. P. Benjamin,   Monterey, April 30, 1863.
Richmond.
Sir:

Herewith enclosed please find a despatch from Señor Luis Terrazas, Governor of Chihuahua, together with the correspondence I had with him in transmitting a communication from that Department. Exhibits and translations are marked A. & B.

Reliable information has been received here this morning to the effect that sixteen thousand Frenchmen have landed at Vera Cruz, to re-inforce Gen. Forey.

I have &c.,
J. A. Quintero

Translation-B.

Sup. Government of the State of Chihuahua

J. A. Quintero, Esq.,   Chihuahua, April 9, 1863.

Agent of the C.S.A., Monterey

Sir:

I have the honor to accompany an answer to the despatch of His Excellency the Secretary of State of the Confederate States of America,—which you transmitted to me with your letter of the 18th ult[o].

You will please forward said answer. I avail myself of this opportunity to offer you my consideration and regards.

Your obt. svt.

(signed) Luis Terrazas

CHIHUAHUA

Received 20 Aug. '63

J. P. B.

A Su Excelencia J. P. Benjamin, Secretario de Estado de la Confederación del Sur de América.

Señor:

He tenido la honra de recibir una comunicación de usted relativa a los sucesos que tuvieron lugar en el mes de marzo del año anterior en el Cantón Galeana por parte del coronel que invadió aquel territorio Juan B. Baylor y de que hablé al Señor Brigadier Sibley en mi nota de 17 de mayo siguiente; y me apresuro a significar a usted los sentimientos de gratitud con que veo la desaprobación que ha merecido justamente a Su Excelencia el Presidente de los Estados Confederados la conducta del Coronel Baylor, y su propósito de imponerle el condigno castigo.

No podía esperarse otra cosa de un gobierno amigo de México y aseguro a usted que bajo tales auspicios serán cada día más estrechos los vínculos de amistad y buena inteligencia que felizmente existen entre aquellos estados y él que se haga a mi cargo.

Bajo tal inteligencia me es muy grato ofrecer mis respetos y consideración muy distinguida a Su Excelencia el Presidente de los Estados Confederados del Sur de América, y al mismo tiempo suscribirme de usted muy atento y obediente servidor.

Luis Terrazas

Palacio del Govierno del Estado

de Chihuahua, April 9 de 1863.

[translation]

CHIHUAHUA [Seal]

Received 20 August 1863

To His Excellency J. P. Benjamin,   J. P. B. [Judah P. Benjamin]
Secretary of State of the
Southern Confederation of America.
Sir:

I have had the honor of receiving a despatch from you, relative to the
events that took place in the month of March in the preceding year in the
Canton of Galeana, on the part of the Colonel who invaded that District,
John B. [*sic*] Baylor, and of which I spoke to Brigadier Sibley in my note of
May 17 [*sic;* March 17?] following.

I hasten to make known to you the feelings of gratitude with which I
view the censure that the conduct of Colonel Baylor has justly merited, by
His Excellency the President of the Confederate States, and his [Jefferson
Davis's] intention to impose upon him suitable punishment.

I wasn't expecting anything else from a government friendly to Mexico,
and I assure you that under such auspices, every day the ties of friendship
and understanding that fortunately exist between those States and the one
in my charge will become closer.

In light of such understanding it is very gratifying to me to present my
respects and distinguished consideration to His Excellency the President of
the Southern Confederate States of America, and at the same time, to offer
myself as your most attentive and obedient servant.

Luis Terrazas

Palace of Government of the State
of Chihuahua, April 9, 1863.

Translation A.

C. Gov. Luis Terrazas,   Monterey, March 18, 1863.
Chihuahua
Sir:

I yesterday received the enclosed despatch addressed to you by the Secretary of State of the Confederate States of America.

Should it require an answer, please transmit the same to me at this city,
from whence it shall be immediately forwarded to Richmond.

I avail myself of this opportunity to offer you the assurances of my consideration and regard.

(signed)   J. A. Quintero
Agent C.S.A.[6]

"The Southern Wagon"
(melody after R. P. Buckley's "Wait for the Wagon," 1850s)

Come, all ye sons of freedom, and join our Southern band,
We're going to fight the Yankees, and drive them from our land.
Justice is our motto, and Providence our guide,
So jump into the wagon, and we'll all take a ride!
Chorus: So wait for the wagon! the dissolution wagon;
The South is the wagon, and we'll all take a ride!

Secession is our watchword, our rights we will demand;
To defend our homes and firesides, we pledge our hearts and hands.
Jeff Davis is our president, with Stephens by his side,
Brave Beauregard, our gen'ral, will join us in our ride!
Chorus: Wait for the wagon, &c.

Our wagon is the very best, the running gear is good;
Stuffed 'round the sides with cotton, and made of Southern wood.
Carolina is the driver, with Georgia by her side,
Virginia holds the flag up, while we all take a ride!
Chorus: Wait for the wagon, &c.

CHAPTER THIRTEEN
The Battle of Valverde,
February 1862
UNION AND CONFEDERATE CORRESPONDENCE

Fort Craig, New Mexico
Feb. 24" 1862

Capt. H. R. Selden, 5 Inf^y
Commanding 1" Column
Sir:

In compliance with your order, I have the honor to submit the following report of the part taken by the battalion under my command in the action near this post on the morning of the 21" inst., which battalion, composed of Co. "A" 10" Inf. under the command of Capt. W. H. Rossell, 10" Inf.; Co. "H" 10" Inf. under Lt. G. H. Crosman, 10" Inf; Capt. T. H. Dodd's Company of Colorado Volunteers with Lt. J. C. W. Hall; Co. "C" 7 Inf., Capt. G. N. Bascom 16" Inf.; and my Company "F" 7' Inf., under the command of 1" Sergt. James M. Rockwell, formed the left wing of the column under your command.

After crossing the river at the ford, the battalion was thrown out on the left as skirmishers, and immediately engaged the enemy. During this time, the line succeeded in foiling an attempt made by the enemy to break our left by a charge of a company of Lancers, which attempt was promptly met by a body of skirmishers, conspicuous among whom were a number of Capt. Dodd's Company of Colorado Volunteers, who succeeded in repulsing the enemy with a considerable loss on his side, [and] none on our side. The line then retired slowly to the river, promptly meeting any advance of the enemy.

At the river it remained, until the arrival of Col. Canby. The battery, under the command of Capt. A. McRae, 3rd Cav., was then ordered to take a new position on the right of the enemy and in front of 2 of his guns, and my battalion being directed to support it, I posted it in the rear, and on the left of the battery, where it remained under a very severe and concentrated fire of grape and rifle shot, under cover of which the enemy assembled in force and charged the battery, pistol in hand, after the gunners had all been killed or driven from their guns. Here I must make mention of the gallant conduct of all connected with the battery, who manfully stood their ground under a concentrated fire of grape from a partially masked battery, and that

Fig. 17. Lieutenant J. W. Abert's sketch, ruins of some adobe walls at Valverde and the river valley beyond, November 1846. Thirtieth Congress, First Session, Senate Executive Doc. No. 23 (1848).

of the large force which eventually overwhelmed them, but at a cost to the enemy of many lives. I could not, in justice to these brave men, refrain from paying them this just tribute, although not within my province, they not being under my command.

At this time, a body of Volunteers (Mexican) were seized with a panic, and broke from their position immediately in front of a portion of my command, and rushed precipitately into the river, and I regret to say, took with them a portion of the left of my battalion, in spite of my individual efforts to stay their flight. An effort was then made, in a hand to hand conflict, by a part of my battalion including my Co. "F" 7" Inf., led by its 1' Sergt. James M. Rockwell, who was killed, together with seven others of the Co. and twenty wounded, to retake the battery, but without success. This portion of the battalion then retired, and recrossed the river as best it could, under a severe fire.

I regret to add that Capt. G. N. Bascom, 16" Inf., in command of Co. "C" 7' Inf. was killed, as is supposed in the retreat, his body having been found in the river. Capt. W. H. Rossell, 10" Inf. was taken prisoner. The battalion was before the enemy from about 11½ A.M. until about 4½ o'clock P.M., during which time all did their duty. I have the honor to enclose herewith the reports of battalion and company commanders.

I feel it my duty to make mention of the following named men of my Company [who] behaved bravely throughout the day, particularly in the effort to retake the battery.

    1" Sergt. James M. Rockwell (killed)
    Sergt. William James of Co. "G" 7" Inf. attached to Co. (killed).
    Sergt. Michael Smith
    Sergt. William McMahon
    Corpl. Joseph Taylor
    Pvt. Lewis F. Roe
    Pvt. Andrew Seamans (wounded severely)
    " John Crangle (wounded severely)
    " Henry F. Way wounded severely
    " John Brown severely wounded
    " John Miller   "   "
    " Henry Noeff   "   "
    " Charles Brady slightly wounded
    " Edward Bohl very severely wounded
    " Thomas Arnold lost his leg

                  Respectfully Submitted
                  P. W. L. Plympton
                  Capt. 7 Inf.
                  Com^d 2nd batt^n 1" Column[1]

                            Fort Craig N.M.
                 Feb. 26' 1861 [*sic;* 1862]

Lieut. [Charles] Newbold
Actg. 2' Lieut. 3' Cavl. USA.
A.A.A.G. USA
Sir,
    Pursuant to Circular of to-day, I have the honor to report that "McRae's Battery" under the command of Captain Alexander McRae, 3' Reg. Cavl., having been marched from Fort Craig, marched in column of Pieces along the road up the west bank of the Rio Grande until it arrived at a point north of La Mesa de los Contaderos, at the northeast point of which heavy skirmish firing was carried on between our skirmishers and the enemy. After a short halt, the Battery was ordered forward into a position "in battery" immediately upon the west bank of the river, and at a point commanding the wood occupied by the enemy.
    A few minutes of warm firing from our guns dislodged the Texans from the wood, which was not again occupied until an attempt was made by the

enemy to obtain a position upon the mesa, the point of which runs into the bosque, the summit of which would have commanded the Battery. We again opened fire with Spherical Case and Shell, successfully—driving back the main body of the troops and causing a rapid evacuation of the wood.

Fearful, however, that a sufficient quantity of the enemy had reached the summit of the mesa, to worry and destroy our men and horses by rifle shot, we moved by order of Col. B. S. Roberts 5" Regt. N.M.V. to a position 200 yards in the rear of our first position, and coming again into Battery, we discovered the wood again occupied by the enemy and an attempt being made to establish one of their guns there, which fact being reported to Capt. McRae, he ordered the fire of the Battery to be directed upon it, to dismount it, which was effected at the first fire, and the enemy again dislodged. At our first and second position on the west bank of the river, three men were wounded mortally, two horses disabled, and one wheel broken by the round shot of the enemy, from a Battery established near the center of their line.

The Battery being ordered to cross the river, we marched up the west bank about 500 yards and crossed by what is known as the "upper ford" under a fire of "Round Shot" from the enemy's artillery, suffering no damage. Having crossed, we went "into Battery" at a distance of 75 yards from the east bank of the river, opening at intervals upon the enemy as they occasionally appeared. This position (first on the east bank of the river) we occupied for 2 hours and were here joined by the third section of the Battery. Suffered no damage here. The Battery was then ordered forward 200 yards into its second position on the east bank of the river, which having been reached, we opened warmly upon the passing bodies of the enemy and upon a Battery of two guns they (the enemy) had established upon our front and right.

In a short time, their Battery opened with canister and grape upon us, doing large damage to both men and horses; a more complete destruction being prevented by the order of Capt. McRae for all to be upon the ground at the explosion of their gun, and allow the shot to pass over. This firing was rapidly returned by our Battery with Shell in the hope of dismounting their Pieces, which were well protected behind the sand ridge on our front and right.

Their firing continued vigorously until the charge of their assaulting party upon the Battery, when it ceased when our whole fire of "Canister" and "Double Canister" was directed upon the rapidly advancing body of assailants. Our fire was swift and well directed, and the enemy went down before the guns. Still they came down upon us, and notwithstanding the determined resistance of the Gunners and Drivers with their pistols, the Battery was taken and we fell back. Capt. A. McRae 3' Cavl. Comdg. Battery and 1" Lieut. L. Mishler 5 U.S. Inft. attached died, the one upon the extreme right of the Battery, the other upon the left, commanding 1' Section.

We succeeded in crossing after the Battery was captured, one caisson, to the west bank of the river, where it was abandoned in consequence of the dying and disabled condition of the horses. The little ammunition left in its boxes was destroyed. The Battery Wagon and Forge returned to the Post. A previous report will exhibit the full number of killed, wounded and missing of the engagement.

Hoping that this report will fill all of the requirements of the 'Circular,'

I am Sir Very Respectfully,
Your Obt. Servt.

To   Jos. McC. Bell
Actg. 2' Lieut. Newbold 3' Cavl.   1' Lieut. McRae's Light Battery
A.A.A.G. U.S.A.²   Comd'

--------------------------◄══►══--------------------------

Fort Craig N.M.
Feby. 26' 1862

Sir

In accordance with instructions, I have the honor to make the following report of the Battalion under my command, which took part in the action at Valverde N.M. on the 21' inst. My Battalion was composed of Co. "K" 5 Infy., Co. H 7 Infy. (Capt. Ingraham's), and Capt. Martines and Capt. Hubbell's companies N.M. Vols.

The orders received by me from the Col. Command'g. on leaving the Post were to support Capt. McRae's light Battery. On arriving at the scene of action, I was by order of Col. Roberts detached with my company, and ordered to cross the river & deploy my men as skirmishers in support of the skirmishers of the 3d Cavalry, who were already engaged with the enemy. I accordingly crossed the river and took up a position on the right of the Cavalry, and on the extreme right of our line, and opened a fire on the enemy, who were endeavoring to turn our right.

Of the operations of the two Vol. companies during the remainder of the day, I can say nothing, as they did not come under my observation again. As the enemy were driven by the destructive fire of McRae's Battery from their position in front of our right, I advanced my line and occupied it, keeping up a fire whenever an enemy made his appearance. I occupied this position for several hours, until the arrival of a twenty-four pound howitzer under the command of Lieut. Hall 10' Infy., when I moved forward in support of it, in connection with Capt. Morris's, Capt. Howland's, and Capt. Tilford's Co's 3d Cavalry, and Capt. Ingraham's Co. 7' Infy. The fire of this piece was very destructive and caused the left of the enemy's line to fall back precipitably [precipitately]. We continued steadily advancing until the order was given to retreat, when we retired in good order across the river.

Although under a heavy fire at times during the day, the conduct of the men under my command was excellent. It was their misfortune, not their fault, that they were not with their brave comrades when the battle was so closely and gallantly contested; and I am sure, that if occasion offers, they will prove themselves as worthy of the glorious cause for which we are contending, as their gallant comrades who have fallen.

I am Sir
Very Respectfully
Your Obt. Servt.
D. H. Brotherton
Capt. 5' Infy.
Command'g Batt.³

To
Asst. Adjt. Genl.
Southern Mil. District.

Company G, 1st N.M. Vols.
Camp near Fort Craig
February 25th 1862.

Lieut. Eben Everett
Adjt. 1st N.M. Vols.
Fort Craig—
Sir.

In the Battle of Valverde, a man of my Company "G" 1st N.M. Vols. took from the hand of a Texan, a flag of the Confederate States. Before leaving the Battle Field, this flag was obtained by Captain Graydon from the man who took it, and was by Captain Graydon turned in to the Department Commander as having been captured by him or his Company. I have been to the Head Quarters with the man who took the flag and he has identified it as the one that Capt. Graydon took from him.

As an act of justice to the man who captured the flag (Domingo Salazar), to my Company and my Regiment, I respectfully ask the Colonel Comdg. the Regt. to forward this report to Dept. Head Quarters, so that credit may be given where it is due.

I am Sir Very Respy Yr. Obt. Servt.
Louis Felsenthal
Capt. 1" Rgt. N.M. Vols.
Comdg. Co. (G)⁴

Official list of the [Union] killed, wounded and missing at the
Battle of Valverde, Feby. 21st, 1862.

KILLED

Lyman Mishler, 1st Lieut.	Co. "E"	5th Inft.
Nicholas Hays, private	Co. "B"	"
John Pollock,	" "	
John Stewart, Serg't "	"D"	"
Henry Schutter, Corporal	"	"
Patrick Hughes, private	"	"
John Murphy, "	"	"
Simon Rothchilds, Corporal	Co. "F"	"
Jacob Levy, private	" "	
John Ford, "	"I"	"
Thomas Leary, "	"K"	"
James McDonald, private	Co. "C"	7th Inft.
John Leibrich, "	"	"
James L. Rockwell, 1st Sergt.	"F"	"
Thomas Arnold, private	"	"
Thomas Carey, "	"	"
John Douglas, "	"	"
John Ellard, "	"	"
Alexander Gillon, "	"	"
Eugene Gibbons, "	"	"
Emile F. Kahn, "	"	"
James Nolan, "	"	"
John Tehan, "	"	"
Philip Shoemaker, "	"	"
Joseph Falgan, "	"	"
James Reily, "	"	"
William James, Sergt.Co.	"G"7th Inft.	
James O'Brien, private	Co. "G"	"
Peter Collins, "	"A"	10th Inft.
John Hoggart, "	"	"
Samuel Miller, "	"	"
John Riechling, "	"	"
William Schwear, "	"	"
Charles W. Washburn, private	"	"
Thomas H. Crotty, Corporal	"H"	"
Carl Christiansen, "	"	"
John C. Brown, private	"	"
John Schweep, "	"	"
George N. Bascom, Capt.	16th Inft.	

William Monroe, private	Co.	"D"	1st Cav'y
Emil Bride, private	"C"	2d "	
Simon Cooke, "	"	"	"
James Courtney, private	"	"	"
John Driscoll, "	"	"	"
Joseph Eckles, "	"	"	"
Thomas McTague, "	"	"	"
Mathew O'Brien, "	"	"	"
Patrick Murray, "	"	"	"
John Phillips, "	"	"	"
Alexander McRae, Capt.	Co.	"E"	3d Cavy
John J. Knox, 1st Sergt.		"I"	"
Thomas Hughes, Corporal	"	"	"
John Ludwig, private "	"	"	
Patrick Scanlan, "	"	"	"
John Westervitt, "	"	"	"
H. B. Woodward, private	Co.	"A"	Col. Vol.
Nelson A. West, "	"	"	"
Marcellus Baca, "		"C"	1st N.M. Vol.
José Romero, "		"	2d "
Joachim Soazo, "		"B"	3d "
Rafael Sais, "		"G"	" "
José M. Martin, "		"F"	" "
Antonio Vasques, "	Capt. Mortimore's Co. [Co. "A" 3d N.M. Vol.]		
Albino Herrea, "		"	
Juan J. Sanchez, "		"	
Marcilizo Duran, Corporal		"B"	5th N.M. Vol.
Ramon Candelario, private		"	"
Carlos Bensinger "		"	"

WOUNDED

Benjamin Wingate, Capt.	Co.	"D"	5th Inft.
Geo. McDermott, 1st Sergt.	Co.	"B"	"
Luther Sheppard, "	"	"	"
Patrick Ryan, corporal	"	"	"
Frederick Bently, sergt.	"	"D"	"
John F. Salkauld, "	"	"	"
James Broadbent, private	"	"	"
William Harkness "	"	"	"
Andres Kimberger "	"	"	"
Dennis Lipencott, "	"	"	"
Thomas Murray, "	"	"	"
Michael O'Hara "	"	"	"

Edwin Sullivan   "   "   "   "
Joseph Wells   "   "   "   "
John L. Kennedy, corporal   "   "F"   "
Cornelius Cary, private   "   "   "
Patrick Coleman   "   "   "   "
Phalen Cromer   "   "   "   "
Michael Green   "   "   "   "
Joseph Hudson   "   "   "   "
Thomas McDonald   "   "   "   "
James McGuire   "   "   "   "
Thomas Quigley   "   "   "   "
James M. Snyder   "   "   "   "
Dennis Sullivan   "   "   "   "
Joseph Hoag corporal"   "I"   "
Henry Sawton, private   "   "   "
John Cass   "   "   "   "
John Buchanan, corporal   "   "K"   "
Thomas Dalton, private   "   "   "
Thomas Farley   "   "   "   "
John Morris   "   "   "   "
William A. Smith 1st sergeant   "   "C"   7th Inf.
Timothy Sullivan   "   "   "   "
James Cavender, corporal   "   "   "
Robert Simpson, private   "   "   "
Michael Mara   "   "   "   "
Patrick Carroll   "   "   "   "
Thomas Dowary   "   "   "   "
John Fitzgerald   "   Co. "C"   7th Inf.
Daniel Harrington private   "   "   "
William H I Hatten   "   "   "   "
Patrick O'Brien   "   "   "   "
Robert Adair Sergt. Co.   "F"7th Infy.
John P. Rumble, corporal   "   "   "
B. Baker, private   "   "   "
Edward Bohe   "   "   "
Charles Ballinder   "   "   "
Charles Brady   "   "   "
John Brown.   "   "   "
John Conway   "   "   "
John Crangle   "   "   "
Michael Dillon   "   "   "
Julius Dollars   "   "   "
Theodore Falke   "   "   "

John Foley	"	"	"
Joseph Kelley	"	"	"
John Marks	"	"	"
John Murray	"	"	"
Peter McCan	"	"	"
Patrick McKenna	"	"	"
William Rathney	"	"	"
Andrew J. Seamans	"	"	"
William Smith	"	"	"
Michael Smith	"	"	"
Patrick Smith	"	"	"
John Teahan	"	"	"
Louis Ulrichs private	Co.	"F" 7th Infty.	
Henry S. Way	"	" "	"
Charles Williamson	"	" "	"
William Ward	"	Co. "H"	"
Joseph Brant	"	"A" 10th Infty.	
Andrew Fairy	"	" "	"
Mathew Harrison	"	" "	"
Leandro B. Harrison	"	" "	"
Oliver P. Barney	"	" "F"	"
W. H. C. Conway	"	" "	"
James C. Drake	"	" "	"
Lorenzo Gross	"	" "	"
William Haydock	"	" "	"
Thomas Kelly	"	" "	"
August Konsch	"	" "	"
John Laddy private	Co.	"F" 10th Infty.	
John Loughlan	"	" "	"
Joseph S. Sesmore	"	" "	"
Robert Sullivan	"	" "	"
Timothy Flynn	"	" "	"
James Dunn, private	"	"D" 1st Cav.	
Nathan Golliher	"	" "	"
G. W. M. Merriman, corporal		" "G"	"
Peter Alloworm, private		" "	"
William Berny	"	" "	"
Sylvester Bennett	"	" "	"
Frederick Fellman	"	" "	"
James W. Jackson	"	" "	"
Daniel Johnson	"	" "	"
Daniel Riley, Sergeant		Co. "G" 2nd Cav.	
R. A. Sitzsinger, 2nd Corpl.		" "	"

Barney Dungan private	"	"	"
Jacob Eggerstedt "	"	"	"
William Foster "	"	"	"
Richard Morrison "	"	"	"
Samuel Smith, private	Co. "G"	2nd Cav'y	
Rudolph Wolfer, "	"	"	"
Michael Kennedy, serg't	Co. "C"	3rd	"
Jas. McNally, corporal	" "D"	"	"
Frederick Buhler, private	" "G"	"	"
Charles Bowmer, corporal	" "H"	"	"
Otto Mains "	" "I"	"	"
Wm. O. Smith "	" "	"	"
Otto Egganschueller, Brger [bugler] "	"	"	"
James D. Martin, private	" "	"	"
Mathew Meyer "	" "	"	"
John Orr "	" "	"	"
John Sullivan "	" "	"	"
Wm. F. Shallard "	" "	"	"
William Smith "	" "	"	"
Wm. N. Anderson Sergt.	Co. "A"	Col. Vol.	
James H. Custard, corporal	" "	"	"
Hugh Brown private "	" "	"	
John Branch "	" "	"	
F. M. Bridgeman "	" "	"	
George Simpson "	" "	"	
George Sanford "	" "	"	
Garrett Tienan "	" "	"	
Andrew J. Thompson"	" "	"	
John G. Thompson Co.	"A" Col.	Vol.	
Asa Talbot "	" "	"	
S. S. Vaughn "	" "	"	
John M. Weaver "	" "	"	
George Williams "	" "	"	
S. W. T. Young "	" "	"	
Andrew R. Duran "	" "	"	
Patrick H. Duffy "	" "	"	
Francis L. Finch "	" "	"	
William F. Kenton "	" "	"	
Jas. T. Newman "	" "	"	
Franz Pampanch "	" "	"	
Thomas Payne "	" "	"	
Ludlow Pruden "	" "	"	
Edward P. Robinson "	" "	"	

William Cook	Co.	"B"	Colorado Volunteers.
Albon R. Sanburn	"	"	" "
Albino Brito private	Co.	"K"	N.M. Vols.
Rafael Gallegos Corporal		Co. "A"	2d N.M. Vols.
Albon R———(*sic*) private		Co. "D" "	" "
William Mortimore, Capt.		[Co."A"] 3d	" "
Edward Walters Sergt.		[Capt.]	Mortimore's Co.
José A. Crespin private		"	" "
Thomas Gallegher		"	" "
Lorenzo Romero	Co.	"A"	4th N.M. Vols.
Roderic Stone, Capt.		4th [*sic*; 5th U.S.]Infantry	

MISSING[5]

William H. Rossell, Captain	Co. "E" [*sic*; Co. "A" 10th U.S. Inf.]
Charles J. East, private	Co. "E" [*sic*; Co. "C" 7th U.S. Inf.]
Daniel McGany [McGarry]	" " " "
Owen O'Connell	Co. "F" [7th U.S. Inf.]
Geo. A. Putnam	" " " "
John Dillon	[Co. "A" 10th U.S. Inf.]
John Kane [Cain]	" " " "
Charles Murphy	" " " "
Wm. Montgomery	" " " "
D.[Dolphus] S. Skinner	" " " "
Charles W. Taylor	Co. "D" [1st U.S. Cavalry]
Terence Brady	Co. "G" [2d U.S. Cavalry]
John W. Ames corporal	Co. "G" [*sic*; Co. "A" Col. Vol.]
S.[Sydenham] Mills	" " " "
James Martin private	" " " "
Sylvester Gibson	" " " "
William Worthington	" " " "
S. Westfield [Samuel Westerfield]	" " " "
Joachim Burtz [Burz][6]	" " " "

———◆◆◆———

BATTLE OF VALVERDE

The following is a list of the [Confederate] killed, wounded, and casualties in the battle of Valverde, fought on the 21st of February, 1862, between _____ Confederates and 6,300 Federals near Fort Craig, New Mexico.

Col. Thomas Green, 5th Texas M _____ Commanding in the field after 2 o'clock P.M., wounded in the leg, the same shooting his horse under him.

Col. W. L. Robards, volunteer Aide-de-camp to Gen. Sibley, was wounded _____ arm, in the lance charge of Capt. Lang _____ he led.

Capt. Tom. P. Ochiltree, Aide-de-camp to Gen. Sibley, and acting Aide
_____ Green, had his horse shot from under him in the charge upon the
enemy's battery, and _____ horse killed in the act of mounting him.

Capt. T. T. Teel's Company of Texas Light Artillery, privates Atticus H.
Ryman and Joseph Page killed. Sergeant Nicholas Mitchell, wounded, severely; James Logan, John Maloney and Herman Lowenstein, seriously.
Capt. Teel was slightly wounded. 25 horses killed and wounded, 1 6-pounder
gun disabled and 8 sets of harness _____ unserviceable; 300 rounds of 6-
pound _____ and cannister expended.

[SECOND REGIMENT]
[three lines missing]

Co. B. 1 killed._____ Pete Ryman killed in Teel's
battery.

Co. D. 1 killed, and 5 wounded; 1 severely and 4 slightly.

Co. E. Capt. Stafford, 1 wounded and 1 missing.

San Elizario Spy Co. (Coopwood's), 2 killed, 1 wounded; Sgt. Merchant,
severely.

Arizona Rangers, 1 slightly wounded.

FIFTH REGIMENT

Thomas Green, Colonel, slightly wounded. S. A. Lockridge, Major,
killed.

Co. A. Private Josiah E. Smith, killed. D. A. Hubbard, 2nd Lieut.; Geo.
O. Sloneker, 3rd sergeant; R. H. Carter [corporal]; M. C. Knowlton, far-
rier; J. J. Stolts, Sandford Putnam, J. Q. Knowles, A. L. Baker and J. H.
David severely wounded; H. D. Donald, slightly; T. B. Gillespie, A. L. Grow,
A. G. Mitchell, [S.] G. Clapp, severely; J. D. Campbell, F. E. Caldwell, J. D.
Montgomery, Sam. Henderson, J. H. McLeary[?], slightly; Martin Pankey,
severely; W. G. Roberts and Aug. Schubert, slightly.

Co. B. Silas Ivans, F. M. Canty, J. L. Curry, J. R. Daugherty, Isaac Mar-
lin, R. H. Mitchell, J. M. Ferguson, killed; W. L. Lang, Captain, D. M.
Bass, 1st Lieut., J. A. Forbes, sergeant, W. A. Bell, A. J. Davis, H. J. Persons,
J. P. Parker, Geo. Polster, J. A. Sowders and W. H. Coleman, severely
wounded; T. N. Lea, Hilary Pierson and Edmond Shelton, slightly.

Co. C. T. V. Johnson and J. D. Moore, slightly wounded.

Co. D. W. S. Tyson, killed; D. Brown, A. Lorenz and James Ladd,
wounded.

Co. F. Privates W. B. Craig and C. M. Tidwell, killed; Lieut. B. B. Seat,
D. Kothour, W. A. Anderson, F. M. McMinn and G _____ slightly
wounded; C. M. Hensley, _____

Fig. 18. *Graves of Texans killed at the Battle of Valverde, on the battlefield itself. Sketch by A. B. Peticolas in his diary. Courtesy of Arizona Historical Society, Tucson, negative no. 60282.*

Co. G. Allen B. Jones _____ Gro ____ J. P. Byrnes and Hugh Wiester _____ wounded.

Co. H. Harvey McClinton _____ W. J. Good, C. Bird, Lucius W. Smith, _____ H. Walling and Wm. Norman, _____ corporal T. R. Orenbaun, A. _____ G. W. Grooms and S. C. Hager, _____

Co. I. Sergt. J. E. Winburn _____ H. J. Smith, killed; _____ L. Harrison _____ wounded.

Total killed in 5th Reg	20
Severely wounded	38
Slightly wounded	34

About 25 of those wounded in this regiment have since died.

FOURTH REGIMENT
Lieut. Col. Wm. R. Scurry commanding.

Co. B. Thomas Nixon killed.

Co. D. D. D. Gilleland and E. S. Slaughter killed.

Co. F. Lieut. D. R. McCormick killed.

Co. G. Capt. M. V. Heuvel and private H. Gaethe killed.

Co. H. J. K. Walton, Jas. T. Williams killed.

Co. I. Corp. Jerry Odell killed.

Co. K. Sergt. J. M. Vining killed.

Wounded—Major Henry W. Raguet

Co. A. Capt. W. P. Hardeman, slightly. Lts. N. D. Cartwright and J. C. Roberts, Corporal J. Francis, and privates W. A. Ferguson, Henry Maney, R. McCright, D. L. Wiley, G. W. White, J. Lott, J. W. Cook and B. L. Hysaw.

Co. B. Lieut. J. Nix, slightly; privates J. L. Bunton, A. T. Brooks, M. Hendricks, T. Harris and J. Williams.

Co. C. Sergt. A. G. Field, privates L. Berkowitz, J. Crook, S. Schmidt, W. H. Onderdonk and Otto Kleberg.

Co. D. Private A. Huffman.

Co. E. Privates A. J. Long and Y. W. Granthan.

Co. F. Privates J. B. Cook and W. F. Matthews.

Co. G. Privates W. _____ H. Trenckmann, _____ J. Sternenberg, T. S.____ _____ W. Becker, J. Voelkel, R. Schlick, _____

Co. H. Privates M. W. Russell, E. J. Tindall, N. B. Coats, H. N. White, James R. Castles and Thomas T. Pitts.

Co. I. Lieut. J. P. Stephenson, Sergeant R. M. Atmar, privates Zeb Gossett, A. J. Dawson.

[Co. K.] J. Rodes, J. A. Sharp and John Campbell.

    Total killed in 4th regiment   10
    Total wounded   54

SEVENTH REGIMENT

Lieut. Col. J. Schuyler Sutton comdg., killed.

Co. B. Private C. Nitsche killed; 2 Linnartz's [i.e., Peter and P. T.], Harms, McGrew, Gelven and Gordon wounded.

Co. F. Private B. A. Richey killed; 1st Lt. J. W. Gray, 2nd Lt. W. C. Wiggins and jr. Lt. S. D. Montgomery, Sergeant F. M. Elkins, Corporals Prather and Garrison, and privates Kendrick, Pruitt, Bradshaw, Sharp, Jones, Quaid, Dial, Johnson and Crews wounded.

Co. I. Privates Tucker, Vannoy, Holliman, Cone, Jones, Alexander, Barnett, Kennedy and Lyles wounded.

The following deaths have occurred in the Confederate Hospital at Socorro, New Mexico, caused by wounds received in the battle of Valverde.

Capt. W. L. Lang, Lieut. _____ T. J. Leatherman, Lewis Rosenberg, Jo_ _____ Lieut. D. A. Hubbard, Sandford Putnam, _____ W. A. Bell, Thos. Garrison, Henry F. Figley, Samuel Yokum, H. Pierson, Silas Johnson, _____ Zeb Gossett, J. N. Jones, James Harris and A. W. Prather. About 20 more have died since, but no report of their names has been received.

The above is an official account of the casualties at the battle of Valverde.

TOM P. OCHILTREE

Asst. Adjt. Genl. Army of N.M.[7]

"All Quiet Along the Potomac Tonight"
(Ethel Lynn Beers, 1861)

"All quiet along the Potomac tonight,"
Except here and there a stray picket,
Is shot as he walks on his beat to and fro,
By a rifleman hid in the thicket.

'Tis nothing! A private or two now and then,
Will not count in the news of the battle,
Not an officer lost! only one of the men,
Moaning out all alone the death rattle.

"All quiet along the Potomac tonight,"
There's only the sound of the lone sentry's tread,
As he tramps from the rock to the fountain,
And he thinks of the two on the low trundle bed,
Far away in the cot on the mountain.

His musket falls slack—his face, dark and grim,
Grows gentle with memories so tender,
As he mutters a prayer for the children asleep,
And their mother, "May heaven defend her!"

"All quiet along the Potomac tonight,"
Hark! was it the night-wind that rustles the leaves!
Was it the moonlight so wondrously flashing?
It looked like a rifle! "Ah, Mary goodbye!"
And his life-blood is ebbing and plashing.

"All quiet along the Potomac tonight,"
No sound save the rush of the river,
While soft falls the dew on the face of the dead,
"The Picket's" off duty for ever.

CHAPTER FOURTEEN
Apache Pass and Glorieta, March 1862

UNION AND CONFEDERATE CORRESPONDENCE

[Editorial Note accompanying article in *The Pueblo Chieftain*]:

It was in the battle of Apache Cañon, N.M., in 1862, that the Colorado troops met a force of Texas rangers, and while the outcome of the conflict was somewhat sanguinary, it resulted in ridding the southern forces of the idea of invading the northern Rocky Mountain region. So far as is known, this was the only battle in which the Colorado troops met the Confederates. While this battle was not as spectacular as some of the conflicts in the east, where thousands of men were engaged, it was none the less hotly contested.

Among the Colorado troops were a number of Pueblo boys, of whom one was John D. Miller, present city auditor of Pueblo. A few days following the battle, Mr. Miller wrote to his father in New York, giving a graphic description of the conflict. This letter was at the time published in the Ithaca, N.Y. *Chronicle*. It has since not appeared in print, but as it gives an accurate account of the engagement, it is of more than ordinary interest to those people who are concerned about the part taken by the Colorado boys in the great Civil War struggle here in the west. Mr. Miller's letter follows:

———

Fort Union, New Mexico,
April 3, 1862.

Dear Father,

Having just returned to this post with Col. Slough's command, which got in last night, after having passed through two sharp engagements and numerous hairbreadth escapes, I still find myself on my pegs. I take this opportunity to let you know that I am still alive and in good health and spirits. My last letter to you was written on the 21st of March, and the next day the 22nd (my birthday) the command marched from Fort Union for Santa Fe. The command consisted of all the first regiment of Colorado Volunteers, and one company of regulars of infantry and a part of two companies of regular cavalry, consisting of about 120 men, making in all about 1,200 men. The command started in the morning, but I remained behind with the quartermaster, sergeant and captain to help them invoice some stores and turn them in to department.

We did not leave the fort until after dark. The captain was with us, and he wanted to go another road which passed through a Mexican town. Of course we could make no objection. We went a round about course and it made seven miles to the town, where we arrived about 9 o'clock. After we had been there about an hour, one of the men came in and said that Freeman, a private in our company, had been shot through the thigh, accidentally. I mounted my horse, rode back to the fort after the surgeon. I found him and brought him back to town, where he soon extracted the ball. We sent Freeman back to the fort the next morning. He was a sober, steady, industrious fellow, and was standing by as a spectator in a saloon, when a couple of drunken soldiers (regulars) got into a quarrel and one drew his revolver to shoot the other, and accidentally shot one of our best men. He got so much for being in bad company. I staid with him all night and the next morning we started on to overtake the command. We overtook them at Las Vegas, after traveling about twenty miles. I was very tired and hungry, and also my horse, having had nothing to eat, and no sleep, since the morning of the 22nd.

The next morning, the 24th, the cavalry were routed out at 3 o'clock, and after getting a hurried breakfast, we started off in advance. We passed through the town of Tucalote [Tecolote], twelve miles from Las Vegas, and four miles farther on, another town named Brunnell [Bernal] Springs. Ten miles farther we came to the town of San José (San-wo-za), here we encamped. We found here Company E, regulars of the Third Cavalry, who were stationed here to act as a picket guard. We had no grub nor blankets along, and consequently there was some cursing among our men. The command did not catch up with us that night, and we remained at San José until the next evening, the evening of the 25th of March, when ten or twelve mule wagons came along, having in them 150 infantry boys of our regiment.

Boots and saddles were immediately sounded and we started together with the company of cavalry, who were on picket. We started about an hour before sun down and our forces numbered 200 mounted men and 150 infantrymen in wagons, making 350 in all. We traveled about twenty-five miles and at 11 o'clock encamped at a place called Gray's ranch.¹ I was detailed for picket guard, and twenty men of our company under command of our first lieutenant, George Nelson, were sent out on pickets. We roamed around all the rest of the night, and about day break came to Pigeon's ranch, five miles beyond Gray's ranch.

Here we searched the premises, and after old Pigeon found out who we were, after we told him we were Pike's Peakers or Colorado boys, he fairly danced, he was so delighted. He told us that four Texans had been there the night before and had went on toward Gray's. He said if we did not meet them, we could probably find them in the ruins of an old town about one mile from Gray's ranch. We traveled on and after going about one mile made a sudden turn down a hill and came upon four Texans well mounted and armed. They asked us if we came to relieve them (they were the picket guards of the enemy). Our lieutenant told them yes, we came to relieve you of your arms. He turned to us and said, ready! We cocked our rifles and drew them up in our faces. He then told them to throw down their arms and surrender, which they did without further orders. One of them was a captain. We took from the four men nine good Colts revolvers and four splendid Maynard rifles, and marched them into camp.

After we arrived at camp we got some breakfast and put the prisoners into a wagon with a strong guard and sent them, together with the wagons that the infantry came in, back to the main command, who were still thirty-five miles back at Brunnell Springs. We started about 10 o'clock, our detachment, the infantry on foot, with their knapsacks and guns, and under the command of Major [John M.] Chivington. We marched on by Pigeon's ranch, which is five miles from Gray's.

I must state here that the country all of the way from Las Vegas, as far as we went, was very rough and mountainous. The face of the country is very rough and rocky and covered with stunted pines and cedars. What soil there is, is very light and easy washed, and consequently full of deep washed ravines and gullies. About four miles beyond Pigeon's ranch we strike the head of what is called Apache Cañon, a deep gulf or valley in the mountains with high rocky sides. It is famous as having been a stronghold of the Apache Indians. We heard that the enemy were going to get possession of the cañon (pronounced "kanyon") to stop us on the march. It is so situated that a few hundred men can hold it against three or four times their number, if they have artillery. I think the object of sending 350 of us ahead, was to get possession of the cañon and hold it until our forces came up. It was afternoon when we got to the head of the cañon, which is six or eight miles long. We traveled along for three or four miles. When we first strike it, it is open, but it gradually grows deeper and more narrow.

After traveling down it about three miles, we saw our pickets and scouts coming in on the run. They said the enemy were just in advance. We could not tell their number. The cañon here was from four to eight rods wide, with a deep gully from ten to fifteen feet, which had been washed out by the rains. Our boys were all anxious for a fight and you ought to see the infantry throw away their haversacks, and the cavalry their saddlebags and over-coats. The infantry started at a double quick: we soon came in sight of the enemy, who carried a rag on a pole. When within 600 yards of the enemy, and just as we were crossing this gully on a bridge, boom went a cannon and a shell passed over our heads and exploded a few rods in [the] rear of our columns. The infantry divided, one-half taking one side of the cañon and the other half the other side. The regular cavalry, who were just in advance of us, broke ranks and ran, but company F, who was just on the bridge, marched forward in the road.

They threw the shells and grape thick for a while. The infantry de-ployed on the right and left and soon opened fire upon them. In the mean-time, company F had got a little out of the road, and had dismounted to fight on foot. We were then ordered to mount, as the enemy were retreat-ing. The infantry put the lead into them too hot, and they retreated down the cañon out of sight. If we had charged as soon as we had mounted, we could have taken their artillery, but we had no head, no one to go ahead and give orders. The captains and lieutenants stood around like "stoughton bottles." We went on down the cañon half a mile further when, discovering the enemy, we halted.

The infantry took each side of the cañon, as before. The major came up and told us he wanted the cavalry to charge on their battery and take it (two twelve-pounders, mountain howitzers). The other cavalry companies had somewhat recovered from their fright, but not enough to volunteer to make the charge, so Captain [Samuel H.] Cook told the major that Company F would charge on the battery when the major was ready for them. The in-fantry took the sides of the cañon as before, and after waiting half an hour for them to flank the cañon, we were ordered to charge.

The road was narrow and we could only charge four abreast. Captain Cook was at the head of the column. My place was on the left of the first section. I was in the fifth set of four. The first lieutenant was by my side. We did not receive a shot for the first 200 or 400 yards. We were riding at a fast gallop. We received a volley and the man in front of me fell from his horse. After that the balls fell thicker and faster all the time. We then let our horses out and, with our revolvers in our hands, went in, every man for himself. Some horses fell and threw their riders, some were shot down, but my horse ran with the speed of the wind. I kept right by the side of the lieutenant. Before we had gone 200 yards from where the first man fell, we had passed the captain and every man in the section. We rode about 800 yards through an awful fire, the balls whistling by our ears. The cannon was so near that we could feel the hot air from their guns on our faces.

The balls came from in front, rear, on both sides, above and all around. The men were behind rocks, trees, and there was so much smoke and dust I could not often get sight of one. We passed a point of rock and the cañon opened out wider. I saw three men kneel down and take dead aim at the lieutenant and myself. I pointed my revolver at them and I saw one kneel. Seeing that we were way in advance of the rest of the company, and that there was no battery in sight, we thought it would be foolish to go further through such a murderous fire, so we turned to the right and ran up into the hills. I was not afraid. I felt just as if the bullet was not made that was to kill me. I saw men take deliberate aim at me and shoot, but they could not hit me. I just laughed at them. We rode up to five Texans and shot. Three of them threw down their rifles and surrendered. My horse was shot through the hip.

It did not disable him very much, but he bled freely. Captain Cook was shot through the thigh and in the foot. Second Lieutenant W.[William] F. Marshall was killed, Corporal Martin Dutro and Privates [George] Thompson and [Jude W.] Johnson were killed. Captain Cook will get well. Corporals Jesse F. Keel and William F. Hall were wounded; Privates Charles H. Bristol, C. W. Logan, Martin Patterson, Buck Pratt, Benjamin F. Ferris, were also wounded. Our party lost in killed five, in wounded twelve. None of our men were taken prisoners. We took sixty-nine prisoners. I do not know how many of the enemy were killed, but think they lost thirty or forty, some say over sixty. I have learned since the fight that the Texans had 700 men in the engagement. As it was nearly night and there was no water in the cañon, we had to fall back to the Pigeon's ranch. Our second lieutenant was slightly wounded, but not dangerously.[2] He took a rifle from the enemy and, having hold of the muzzle, struck it across a rock to break it when it went off, and sent the whole charge into his bowels. The fight was on the 26th of March. It was of short duration, but hotly contested.

There are battles where thousands meet in deadly combat, but not many hotter fires in this war than the one we passed through on the 26th. We claimed the victory on the 26th, but had to fall back for a camping place. On the 27th we moved back five miles to Gray's ranch. Here we stopped and that evening the balance of the regiment came up with us, and they were accompanied by eight pieces of artillery, which had come from Fort Union,—four mountain howitzers and four large cannons, with two companies of regulars. We then numbered about 1,200 men.

On the morning of the 28th of March, the company moved forward again. The major took about 400 men and went around by another road to attack them in the rear, while Colonel [John P.] Slough with the balance of about 800 men and the battery went the same road that we went before. We went on about half a mile beyond Pigeon's ranch, when our pickets were again driven in by the enemy. The artillery came up double quick, and soon the action became general. Owing to the roughness of the country and the thick timber, it was impossible to do much execution with the artillery. Just as we had begun to drive the enemy, Colonel Slough ordered a retreat. We again made a stand at Pigeon's ranch, which we held for three or four hours. All the cavalry, except a company who acted as body guard to Colonel Slough, dismounted and fought on foot. The enemy were reinforced by General Sibley, so that they had about 2,500 or 3,000 men. We could drive them at any one point, but they had so many more men than ourselves that they could flank us.

About 3 o'clock in the afternoon the enemy, to the number of 700, charged on our battery. The men stood by the cannon and fought for all that was out [*sic*], while the boys that were supporting the battery determined to die right there, rather than give up the battery. Company F were on the left of the battery and they did good execution. Colonel Slough ordered another retreat and of course we had to obey, though it went against the grain. We made another stand, but the enemy had enough of our battery. We retreated to Gray's ranch. Before we had been there ten minutes, the Texans came up with a flag of truce. They wanted a cessation of hostilities for twenty-four hours to bury their dead and attend to their wounded. We gave them twenty-four hours. They retreated out through Apache Cañon the same evening, and next morning our command retreated to San José. The Texans had possession of the field, but we had possession of their grub.

Major Chivington, who went around with 400 men, marched them eighteen miles over the mountains, captured their train of supplies of eighty wagons, shells, etc., and burnt all the wagons. They killed six or eight men, took eleven prisoners, spiked one cannon, but got back to the balance of the regiment without a single man killed or wounded. Burning their provisions and stores hurt them more than killing their men. They had to retreat and we returned to Fort Union.

At the last fight on the 28th, which was called the battle of Pigeon's ranch, our side lost 39 killed, about 60 or 70 wounded, and some 10 or 12 taken prisoners. The loss of the enemy was over 200 killed and as many more wounded. We took seven commissioned officers prisoners. They say most of their men were shot through the head. They think we were awful marksmen. You see, they fought behind rocks and trees, and the only part of them you could see to shoot at was their head. The Texans are brave men, but they are afraid of the d—d Yankees, the Colorado boys.

As I was saying before, we returned to San José. I was detailed with a squad of twelve men and two days' provisions to remain at San José on picket guard, while the command went on to Union. As my horse was not able to ride, I left him in care of the company to have him driven along. He was driven with the Cary yard one day, and the next night was stolen from the company. That was while I was back at San José. I was ordered in and overtook the command night before last at Las Vegas, where I learned that my horse was gone. I was very sorry, because he was a very noble, high spirited animal, gentle as a lamb, sound, swift and showy, and carried me safe through a charge, where it would not be supposed either man or horse could go alive. His wound was only a flesh wound, and would not have injured him in the least. I would not take $150 for him if I had him today. Government may pay me for him and they may not.

At any rate, when I think how the battlefield of Pigeon's ranch looked covered with dead and dying, I am thankful that Providence spared me to write this letter, and as I hope some day to see you all, I must close for the present. Your letter of March 2 came to hand today.

Believe me, your affectionate son.

JOHN³

Camp near Kosloski [*sic*] N.M.
March 29ᵗʰ, 1862.

Dear Captain:

Yesterday morning, the whole Command marched from this point, expecting to encounter the enemy <u>somewhere</u>. Four hundred Infantry, including the two Compys. of [William H.] Lewis & [Asa B.] Carey, took the mesa road to Galisteo; the remainder, the Santa Fe road; the Cavalry first, Infantry second, Artillery third, and the Q.M. trains bringing up the rear. I objected to the Supply & Baggage Train moving forward. The men were ordered to take two days rations in their haversacks.

On reaching Pigeon's Ranch, we found the Cavalry halted. The pickets beyond the Ranch reported that the enemy were not near us. For less than five minutes after the Infantry came up, the Cavalry was put in motion, and had only proceeded about six hundred yards when the enemy's Artillery opened upon them. The Infantry was immediately deployed on the right and left of the road. The Artillery got into position on the second rise of ground beyond Pigeon's ranch, where the road makes a bend to the left; [John F.] Ritter's in the road, and [Ira W.] Claflin's battery immediately to its left. The Cavalry fell back and took a position in a hollow to the left of the road and about ten yards in [the] rear of the batteries.

I went to the left of Claflin's battery and from that point was unable to see the enemy's position. I am of the opinion that our batteries fired more for general results than at any particular object. Some few of the enemy's shot passed over our batteries, but the general direction at this time, of their shots, was obliquely across that of our batteries and aimed at the bluff on our right.

The firing now became very brisk on both sides. The enemy now appeared to be ordered to fall back and take a new position, which they did, the whole force retiring. The batteries again retired, taking positions; Ritter's on the right of the road and near Pigeon's house; Claflin's on the left of the road and in front of the house. These positions were held for some time, when Claflin's battery took up a position on the same side of the road and close to Ritter's, where they remained till about a quarter to 4 P.M.

The Infantry & Cavalry had been skirmishing the entire day, changing positions frequently. The enemy once formed, apparently for the purpose of taking the batteries, but were forced back. The enemy had beaten us from the commencement; they were evidently out-flanking us. The train was now put in motion for a third time, for a retreat. The batteries and whole force retired in good order and took a position about ¾ of a mile this side of the ranch. To check the enemy's advance, a few shots were fired from this last position, when the whole force fell back upon this place.

Major Chivington was more successful; having succeeded in capturing and destroying about fifty of the enemy's wagons, containing supplies of various kinds, and one piece of Artillery, which was spiked and thrown down the mesa. Some prisoners were also taken.

Our loss is not yet known, owing to the systematic way we have of doing business. I went back to the field of battle last night, for the dead & wounded. We only brought in a portion of them. I think the Texan loss, in killed and wounded, is much greater than ours. I am of [the] opinion they have many prisoners.

I do not know what the programme is for the future, but presume it will be something brilliant. I will tell you more, if I ever have an opportunity. [marginal note]: [Lt. Peter] McGrath is shot in the knee.

Yours in haste,
(signed)   H. M. Enos

True Copy
J. C. McFerran
Captain & A.Q.M.[4]

Assistant Quartermaster's Office
Fort Union N.M. April 5th, 1862

Captain

I have the honor to submit the following statement relating to the operations of the Q.M. Dept. during the recent expedition under command of Col. Slough, 1st Colorado Vols.

Under your supervision, every arrangement had been made before leaving Fort Union for providing an abundance of transportation. Great care had been taken that the wagons and harness should be in good repair. None but good mules were taken. The wagon-masters and teamsters were selected—mechanics and material furnished for any repairs that might be necessary on the march—the supply trains, baggage wagons, hospital wagons and ambulances were all in good order—expressmen and animals were also provided.

On Saturday the 22nd ult° the 1st Reg^t of Col. Vols. marched from Fort Union. The next day Capt. Lewis' battalion, Capt. Ritter's and Lieut. Claflin's batteries with the supply trains, which I accompanied. The supply trains were escorted by Capt. Lewis' command till we arrived at Bernal Spring, where we joined Col. Slough and the 1st Col. Vols.

Soon after my arrival at the Camp, I was indirectly informed that fifteen wagons and teams had been ordered to transport one hundred and eighty men who were to advance that afternoon under command of Major Chivington, carrying but three or days rations; these wagons were taken from those turned over to the 1st Reg^t. Colorado Volunteers. Also that four mules had been taken from one of the teams and sent off on Express. I then suggested to the Col. Comm^{dg} that if the transportation was to be used in the manner indicated above, that in case the remainder of the command should be compelled to move before the return of Major Chivington's command, there would be no transportation for it. I was informed that he, the Col. Commdg., was responsible for that, and that no other move was contemplated.

On the following morning, Capt. Carey moved with portions of three companies, taking all the wagons that had been assigned for transporting the entire baggage and rations belonging to the companies, leaving detachments and a large portion of their rations. Capt. Lewis moved shortly after, but took all his baggage and rations. I think, however, that the Volunteer companies of Capt. Lewis' command left a portion of their rations, but took their full allowance of transportation. These movements were ordered without my being notified, or directed to furnish transportation.

On the evening of the same day, a letter written by Lieut. [Francis?]

McCabe at San José was referred to me, in which I learned that 12 of the 15 wagons which transported Major Chivington's command on the previous night and day to Pigeon's ranch—a distance of about 34 miles—had returned to San José, the wagon-master reporting to Lieut. McCabe that on his way back, he had met a Captain who had been directed by Col. Slough to turn the wagons back to join Major Chivington, but that the Captain had found the teams broken down and had in consequence directed the wagon-master to proceed to San José and from there report to Head Quarters at Bernal Springs.

This letter was handed to me by an orderly and I was directed to order the wagons back to join Major Chivington. I again represented to Col. Slough that the command at Bernal Springs would be unable to move for want of transportation, unless these 12 wagons joined the command. After some discussion I was permitted to order the wagons to join the command at Bernal Spring, which order was sent the same night. At about 9 o'clock the following morning, the order to move forward was given. The twelve wagons referred to luckily arrived a few moments after, but did not even then prevent some confusion and of course delay.

On reaching San José I found that nine mules belonging to the teams which had been turned over to the mounted companies had been taken to replace broken down horses of Capt. Cook's Volunteer Company. I remonstrated against using the transportation for such purposes, and suggested the propriety of issuing an order to prevent like occurrences in the future, but was told "a few wagons and teams were of no consideration." I informed the Col. Comm'dg. that nearly all the serviceable transportation in the department was with his command and that if it should be broken up, it would be impossible to replace it, and that in case we were victorious, it would be required to furnish supplies for the troops that would be stationed in different posts in the Territory. His reply was that it could not be helped.

The command reached Kozlowski's ranch about 3 o'clock on the morning of the 28th, making but one halt after leaving Bernal Spring. Between 7 and 8 o'clock of the same morning, I discovered that the entire command was preparing to move. After some inquiry, I found that it was a move forward. I am unable to say what orders were given to company commanders relating to the movement, but from a conversation I had with Col. Slough, [I] was under the impression that each man was to carry two days' rations, and a blanket, upon his person, and did believe they had done so till differently informed two days afterwards by one of their captains. Especially as it was known that the enemy were in the cañon beyond Pigeon's ranch, and suggested to Col. Slough that the entire train excepting the hospital wagons and ambulances and the ammunition wagons remain at Kozlowski's ranch with a sufficient guard for its protection. My suggestion was disregarded and the entire train moved forward in [the] rear of the command.

Believing that a fight would come off, I placed the ammunition wagons for Ritter's and Claflin's batteries in front, followed by the hospital train, baggage wagons and supply train in the order named. About one mile before reaching Pigeon's ranch, I selected a place for the purpose of parking the trains, asking Col. Slough to look at, and if he would consent to have the trains parked upon the ground pointed out. He made no objections to the ground, but thought it was not best to park the train yet, and it moved on. In less than forty minutes from this time, the enemy opened their battery upon our advance, about four or five hundred yards beyond Pigeon's house, the head of the train halting at the house. I went forward with the batteries. They had not been in position over three minutes before the ammunition wagons were called for. I went back and met them coming up.

I was placing them under cover from the enemy's fire, a few yards in rear of and to the left of our batteries, when our batteries fell back from the position they had first taken. I had sent word to have the train turned about and was starting to attend to that movement, when one of my expressmen rode up to me and reported that an ammunition wagon was stalled and there was no support near it. I immediately reported the fact to Col. Slough, stating that we were leaving an ammunition wagon behind us and asking that some men be sent to its relief. I was told that there were no men to send, and let the wagon get out the best it can. I then ordered the expressman with one or two other employees of the Q.M. Dept. to go back and bring it up, or burn it. The wagon was saved.

Our batteries soon took another position. I got the train turned about and asked permission to move it off the ground, but was only allowed to move it a short distance. Our batteries again fell back, and I again got permission to move the train. This time I parked the supply train on the ground previously referred to in this report, leaving the other wagons on the road. There had been no guard ordered for the protection of the train and there was none for it the entire day. The ammunition wagons were not even guarded, and the teamsters of them were obliged to carry ammunition to Lieut. Claflin's battery.

At about 4 P.M. I started the train back to Kozlowski's ranch, believing that the enemy were outflanking us on our left. A few moments after, I received an order to move the trains off the ground. Before all the wagons moved, our forces had retreated and did not make another stand till they had passed the point where the wagons had been parked, leaving the rear wagons entirely without protection. As the last wagons moved off, a few shots were fired upon them from the enemy on our left. The wagons were not halted till they reached Kozlowski's ranch, where they were parked for the night.

Our troops arriving [*sic*] soon after, followed by a flag of truce from the enemy. I had wagons unloaded for the purpose of sending them after the dead and wounded, and called upon the Col. Com^dg for a detail of men to accompany the wagons to the field of battle. The detail was not furnished and had it not been for the few teamsters and wagon-masters that I took with me, no wounded would have been brought in on the night of the battle.

Early next morning, ten wagons and ambulances were sent back to bring in the remainder of the dead and wounded. Before they had returned to Kozlowski's ranch, the command had moved towards San José. The entire train did not get up till 9 o'clock at night.

I was unable to procure long forage for the animals after leaving Bernal Spring, and as the animals were in harness during the day and part of the night time, they had no opportunity to graze. We lay in camp at San José one day and then continued our retreat to Fort Union, where we arrived on the 2nd inst. One teamster was wounded, having deserted his team and joined the support of the batteries.

I have only to add that in no instance on the march did the Q.M. Dep^t. fail to render its full share of duty to the expedition and [to] the general service.

Very respectfully
Your ob^dt Servt.
Signed   H. M. Enos
Capt. & A.Q.M.

Capt. J. C. McFerran   Official
Chief Q.M. Dep^t. N. Mexico   J. C. McFerran
Fort Union[5]   Captain & A.Q.M.

Fort Union N.M.
May 18th 1862.

Sir

In my report of the action in Apache Canyon, I neglected to mention the gallant conduct of Lt. Harding [George H. Hardin], 1" Col. Volunteers, and I have deemed it but justice to him to mention it. After the first charge of the enemy, when I gave the command to cease firing, the batteries were enveloped in so dense a smoke as to render it impossible to see whether the enemy had been entirely repulsed. I called to the supports, and Lt.

Harding with about 40 men charged bayonets through the batteries, himself leading, about 30 yards to the front and took position there. I also neglected to mention Lt. Underhill, 4ᵗʰ N.M. Vols., who behaved with gallantry throughout the action. I also cannot too highly praise the conduct of all the enlisted men.

    I am Sir &c.   Jno. F. Ritter
                Capt. 15ᵗʰ Inf.
Capt. G. Chapin   Comdg. Battery
A.A.A.G.
Dept. Of New Mexico, Santa Fe⁶

             A.A.A. General's Office
            Santa Fe, N.M. May 26" 1862

The A.A. Adjutant General
Head Quarters, Dept. of New Mexico
Santa Fe, N.M.
Sir:

 In compliance with Department instructions, I have the honor to report that the following officers constituted the personal staff of Colonel Slough, and that with him they were present in the engagement with the hostile Texan forces which took place on the 28ᵗʰ of March near Pigeon's ranch, on the Santa Fe and Fort Union road, and about 22 miles from the former place.

    Surgeon E. J. Bailey, U.S.A.
    Asst. Surg. J. T. Gheselin, U.S.A.
    Asst. Surg. J. C. Bailey, U.S.A.
    Capt. H. M. Enos, Asst. Q. Master U.S.A.
    1ˢᵗ Lieut. L. G. Murphy, 1ˢᵗ N.M. Vols, A.A.C.S.
    Lieuts. [Jacob P.] Bonesteel and [Alfred S.] Cobb,
    1ˢᵗ Col. Vols., Aˢ.D.C.
    ~~James L. Collins~~
            }Volunteer Aides de Camp
    J. Howe Watts
    Captain G. Chapin, 7ᵗʰ Infantry, U.S.A.,
      A.A. Adjutant General

Having no separate command upon the field, I can bear cheerful testimony to the gallant conduct and soldierly bearing of the entire force engaged. I would particularize, however, the efficient manner in which Captain Ritter and Lieut. Claflin managed the field batteries, and in this connection pay a tribute of worth to the memory of Lieut. Peter

McGrath, 6th U.S. Cavalry, who while meritoriously serving as an artillery officer received a dangerous wound, from which he has since died.

After the close of the action, having been sent with a returning flag of truce to take measures for the burial of the dead, I became an eyewitness to the faithfulness and energy, the kindness and attention bestowed alike upon our own and the enemy's wounded, by Surgeon Bailey and Asst. Surgeons Gheselin and Bailey, who devoted the whole night both at Pigeon's & Kozlowski's to the care and comfort of their numerous cases.

Captain Enos, U.S.A., having the charge of a large train of wagons and teams, is deserving of praise for the energy he displayed in preventing this and other public property from falling into the hands of the enemy, when its capture had become an especial object with them.

Mr. Watts and Lieuts. Bonesteel and Cobb, Colorado Vols., were active and efficient as aides de camp, and rendered in this way valuable services under close fire.

> I am Sir
> Very respectfully
> Your obed[t] servant
> Gurden Chapin
> Capt. 7 Infy.
> A.A.A.G.[7]

[*Second* postscript, omitted from published report of Major J. M. Chivington to General (E. R. S. Canby) in regard to battle of Pigeon's Ranch (Glorieta), March 28, 1862 (*OR, Series I Vol. 9*, pp. 538–39)]:

P.S. 2nd. Complete List of the killed and wounded of the 1st Col. Vols. on the 28th Mch. 62:

Company A.   <u>Wounded</u>. Private [Simon] Ritter.

C.   <u>Killed</u>. Corp[ls] Frank Billiard & Amos R. Peters. Privates Hopkins M. Boone, Jacob Smith and Andrew Pomps. <u>Wounded</u>. Lt. Clark Chambers. Privates Barton S. Mulkey, Phillip Rail, William Baldwin, Joseph W. Tosh, John Schneider, Willis Wilcox, Richard Yates, John Callorey, and Isaac N. Pierce.

Comp'ny D.   <u>Killed</u>. Sergts. A. Davis, M. E. Boyle. Corpl. C. Fenner. Pvts. C. Anderson, A. J. Denny, John Elliott, Ignatus Slauson, J. G. Seeley. <u>Wounded</u>. Corp'ls [Edwin B.] Griffin, C. Barton and—— Ialer [William Iler?]. Pvts. C. F. Creitz, J. W. Davis, J. D.

Downing, William Elliott, Joseph Flinn, T. O. Foote, John
Fleming, T. J. Hawes, C. D. Hicks, Peter Johnson, Patrick
Regan, Matthew Laughlin, J. J. McMillan, John Newcomer,
George Owens, Adam Schuler, J. E. Shepherd, Matthew
Stone, Charles Wilbur, and Benjamin Baker.

Comp'ny G. <u>Killed</u>. O. C. Seymour, Christian Butler.
            <u>Wounded</u>. Jarett Hutson, Harmon Lovelace, William Ford,
            Edward F. Johnson, William Muxlow, E. W. Osborne,
            William S. Clisbee and James D. Neely.

Comp'ny I. <u>Killed</u>. Lieut. John Baker, Q.M. Sergt. Wm. H. Hurst, Sergt.
            John Garwick, Corp¹ Jasper Hotchkiss, Pvts. Samuel Bird,
            John Reeves, Armand Johnson, Gottlieb Heittig, Ignatz
            Mattuash and John Stewart.
            <u>Wounded</u>. Corp'l G. Austin. Pvts. John Benderly, Henry
            Hirshhausen, Frederick Rufer, Lyman Honeywell, John
            Kreider, Wm. Bowman, Henry Johnson, John Henry, Ole
            Oleson, Frank Brass, Henry Backus, Wm. Cudmore, James
            Doyle, Henry Kimball, Frederick Meggers and B. Shonitz.

Comp'ny K. <u>Killed</u>. Pvts. Henry C. Hanley and Moses Jones.
            <u>Wounded</u>. Corpl. Thos. H. Wales. Owen H. Henry, Angus
            McDonald and W. F. Eichbaum.[8]

❖

El Paso, Texas. May 1st, 1862.

Messrs. Editors:

Believing that a list of the [Confederate] killed and wounded of the battle
of Glorieta will be looked for in the columns of some of our State journals,
I herewith forward it for publication to you.

Respectfully,

J. Robards.

Killed andWounded in the Engagement of Glorieta, 28th March, 1862.
Report of the Fourth Regiment—Killed.

Major Henry W. Raguet.

Co. B. Privates E. C. Foley and Jas. McCord.

Co. C. Privates A. Hanna, J. Henson and Alexander Montgomery.

Co. D. E. R. Slaughter, James Stevens, W. M. Straughn and Burton R. Stone.

Co. E. Captain Charles Buckholts, privates J. G. H. Able, S. L. Cotton
and R. A. Alday.

Co. F. Privates J. R. Martin, Reuben Bentley, Will McCormick and W. T.
Parsons.

Fig. 19. Reburial of thirty Confederate soldiers killed in the 1862 Battle of Glorieta at Santa Fe National Cemetery, Apr. 25, 1993. Members of the Sons of Confederate Veterans, foreground and sides, and the Twenty-third New York Volunteer Infantry, rear, form an honor guard around the coffins. Photograph from the Las Cruces Sun-News, *Apr. 26, 1993.*

Co. G. Privates Christoph Gollmer, F. Schaefer and A. Juhl.

Co. H. Sergt. John H. McKnight.

Co. I. Sergt. T. D. Wilson, blacksmith J. Manus, and private F. J. Hopkins.
Total killed in 4th Regt. 24

Wounded.

Ellsberry R. Lane, Adjt.

Rev. L. H. Jones, Chaplain.

Co. B. James Byars, J. E. Standefer, P. A. Crawford and J. C. Stroud.

Co. C. L. J. Bartlett, B. N. White, S. Brown.

Co. D. Elbert Carter, John Stokes, W. M. Farmer, Jesús Flores and
Corp. S. R. Hill.

Co. E. J. J. Young.

Co. F. Corp. John T. Poe; John Harbison, W. F. Matthews, Ord. Sergt.
E. B. Adams.

Co. G. Sergt. [Otto] Schroeder; A. Amthor, H. Ilse.

Co. H. Ord. Sergt. A. A. Nelson; Jesse Jones, Joseph Rogers.

Co. I. Capt. J. M. Odell, 1st Lieut. W. J. Jones; G. W. Walker, T. A.
Wright, N. B. March, and J. Shivers.

Co. K. Lieut. [Edward Livingston] Robb; T. Williams, W. Teer.
Total wounded.   30

Report of Battalion of the Seventh Regiment—Killed.
Co. B. Sergeant S. Marbach and Private A. Habermann.
Co. H. Privates [William] Booker, [Robert P.] Walker, [G. N.]Taylor
and [Peter] Hail.
Co. I. 2nd Lieut. Charles H. Mills and Corporal William Langston.
Total killed in Seventh Batt.   8

Wounded.
Co. H. Capt. Isaac Adair, and Private [Henry P.] Cobb.
Co. B. Sergt. C. Hasenbeck; Reidel [Private Frank Riedel], [Kasper]
Moos and [Fr.] Penshorn, slightly.
Total wounded.   7

Report of Battalion of the Fifth—Killed.
Major [John Samuel] Shropshire of the 5th Regiment.
Co. B. Corp. B. G. Greely.

Wounded.
Co. A. D. H. Taylor.
Co. B. A. J. Nations.
Co. C. 1st Lieut. J. P. Clough; H. D. Lawless, Perry Sapp, slightly; Bugler
N. Bringle and R. P. Catlett, severely.
Co. D. Private [H. T.] Sherwood.
Total wounded.   8

Report of Lieut. Bennett's Battery—Killed.
Private [Edward T.] Burrowes.
Wounded.
Lieut. [James] Bradford, Corp. [William] Carter, Privates [Adolph]
Hermann, Doued [Pat Dowd], [Timothy Dargan] Nettles, [Arthur W.]
White, [N. B.] Roff, Phillips [Eugene Phillippe Jr.], [?] Nurom, [Frank]
Boone.
Total wounded.   10

Private W. K. [William D.] Kirk, of Capt. Phillips' Brigands, wounded.
Total killed in the engagement.   36[9]

"We Are Coming, Father Abraham"
(James Sloan Gibbons, 1862)

We are coming, Father Abra'am, three hundred thousand more,
From Mississippi's winding stream and from New England's shore;
We leave our plows and workshops, our wives and children dear,
With hearts too full for utterance, with but a silent tear;
We dare not look behind us, but steadfastly before,
We are coming, Father Abra'am, three hundred thousand more!

Chorus:
> We are coming, we are coming, our Union to restore;
> We are coming Father Abra'am, with three hundred thousand more,
> We are coming Father Abra'am, with three hundred thousand more.

If you look across the hill tops that meet the northern sky,
Long moving lines of rising dust your vision may descry;
And now the wind, an instant, tears the cloudy veil aside,
And floats aloft our spangled flag in glory and in pride;
And bayonets in the sunlight gleam, and bands brave music pour,
We are coming, Father Abra'am—three hundred thousand more!
Chorus: We are coming, &c.

If you look all up our valleys, where the growing harvests shine,
You may see our sturdy farmer boys fast forming into line;
And children from their mothers' knees are pulling at the weeds,
And learning how to reap and sow, against their country's needs;
And a farewell group stands weeping at every cottage door,
We are coming Father Abra'am—three hundred thousand more!
Chorus: We are coming, &c.

CHAPTER FIFTEEN
Headquarters and Southern District Correspondence, April–August 1862

UNION CORRESPONDENCE

Belen April 3ʳᵈ, 1862

Col.

   Sir.

This morning after capturing the Los Lunas picket, I retreated towards Belen. The Mexicans here tell me they will join. Now 4 P.M. Phillip Jones comes and tells me that the Texans have all left towards Santa Fe except 100–75 of them are starting down with wagons to bring up the stores of Otero in Peralta and requests of me to go and stop them. I have got only 50 men that I can depend upon. I think it better to try them a clatter on the road tonight near Peralta. I will start at 5 P.M. I send by Sergt. Brown escaped from the Texans with 43 more.

1ˢᵗ Sergt. Jas. Coulter	Coopwood's Compy.
Pvt. [Joseph P.] Tate	Walker's Compy.
" [J. W.] Reed	Coopwood's "
" [J. P.] Hanson	Coopwood's "
" [W. H.] Keller	Coopwood's "

Citizen Trotter, who was in Las Lunas confiscating the citizens' property and escorted by Coulter's party. Also Martin Crossgrave, a man who came with me from Craig and tried to let the prisoners loose after I took them. This is a traitorous man and ought to be sent to Santa Fe. Trotter did formerly belong to our force and I believe was with us in battle of Val Verde. I understand the comdg. officer at Union is after him. I am told Sibley left a train in Hells Cañon, his men are awfully disappointed about their last fight. I understand Alderete with a Mexican compy. is stealing horses on other side of river. We saw his fires last night. I will try and stop him.

I am Sir very Respectfully
Jas. Graydon
Capt. U.S. Vols.

P.S. Capt. [Juan Antonio] Sarracino from Pajarita volunteers to bring the prisoners to you. Lieut. [William] Ewing's party are with me and the looks of the Fed regulars will raise the Mexicans quicker.[1]

Fig. 20. The church in Peralta, New Mexico. Copied by A. B. Peticolas from another soldier's sketch. Courtesy of Arizona Historical Society, Tucson, negative no. 60282.

Head Qrs. 2ⁿᵈ Column, Union Army, New Mex°
Camp near Peralta, N.M. April 16ᵗʰ 1862

Sir:

I have the honor to report that the Union Army of New Mexico arrived near Peralta, N.M. during the night of the 14ᵗʰ inst., and laid under arms until daybreak the next day. There was no indication that our arrival was known to the enemy under Genl. H. H. Sibley until the fires in our camp announced the fact to them. The men of our Command had had nothing to eat since 12 o'clock on the 14ᵗʰ inst., and it was found necessary to make fires to cook something. The 2ⁿᵈ Column under my Command consisted of two field pieces under Capt. Jno. F. Ritter, four mountain howitzers under Lieut. I. W. Claflin, two companies of the 5ᵗʰ Inf'y, the 1ˢᵗ Regt. Colorado Volunteers, under Col. Chivington, and one company 4ᵗʰ Regt. New Mex° Volunteers.

Soon after sunrise, several wagons of the enemy were seen approaching Peralta, when orders were given to Lieut. George Nelson, comd'g Comp'y "F" 1ˢᵗ Col. Volunteers (mounted) to capture them. Two infantry companies of the same regiment under Captain S. J. Anthony were detached to support the attack. Lieut. Nelson however reached the wagons before the infantry came up, attacked the escort, killing six, wounding four, and taking fifteen of the enemy prisoners, the rest fleeing precipitately.

In this affair, one twelve pounder mountain howitzer, seven wagons loaded with ordnance, subsistence and other stores, and fifty-three mules were captured. While the skirmish was going on, I moved my column towards the right a few hundred yards and halted on seeing the success of the officer. By order of Col. Canby, I then marched my column, intending to throw the right on or near the Rio Grande, thus crossing and taking possession of the road from Albuquerque.

The enemy had established a battery in a strong position, in a corral, from which I attempted to dislodge him with my artillery but without success, their battery replying and wounding several of my command. I then marched the column by the right flank about six hundred yards towards the river then filing to the left, marched some twelve hundred yards, halted & formed in line of battle, the enemy firing with a battery on us as we came within range. After awaiting further instructions for some time (the enemy's battery having in the meantime ceased firing) I sent out Major Wynkoop 1st Col. Volunteers with four companies of his Regt. as skirmishers, and although they came within a short distance of the enemy, did not succeed in bringing him out. The enemy however fired several rounds of grape &c. into our skirmishers.

Shortly after withdrawing the skirmishers, Col. Canby arrived on the field, and on completing a reconnaissance, directed the column to move off, which was done immediately. While under fire, all the troops behaved with coolness, and only wanted an opportunity to do some signal service. Our loss in the action was two killed and three wounded. The loss of the enemy could not be ascertained.

The Regular Cavalry under Capt. R. M. Morris, 3rd Cavalry, was attached to my column, and moved with it during the operations of the day.

	I am, Sir,
Captain W. J. L. Nicodemus	Very Respectfully,
12th U.S. Infantry	Your obedt. Servt.
A.A.A. Genl.	G. R. Paul
Head Qrs. Dept. New Mex.	Col. 4th N.M. Vols.
Fort Craig, N.M.	Comdg. 2nd Column

List of Killed & Wounded

Pvt. Martin C. Wilson	Co. C 1" Colorado Regt.	Killed
" Joseph Long	Co. C 1" Colorado Regt.	Killed
" Jas. Grealish	Co. K 1" " "	Wounded
" J. Hawley	Co. F 1" " "	Wounded
" George Thompson	Co. G 4" N. Mex° "	Severely wounded[2]

Hd. Quarters South. Dist. N.M.
Fort Craig, N.M. May 7, 1862

Sir:

I have the honor to state that Captain Lewis, 5th Infy, returned yesterday afternoon, without having been able to ~~effect~~ overtake the Texan force. He arrived at the crossing below Fort Thorn two days after their rear guard had crossed. And the river was so high that he could not cross his party. He therefore returned without effecting the object for which he was detailed.

He reports that the rebels had separated into small parties and come to the river road at different points and crossed at the San Diego Crossing. They did not appear to have many wagons, judging from the trail left. Capt. Graydon is out to find out what the enemy left on the road. There is an insufficiency of beef cattle at this post, and much murmuring among the Colorado Volunteers is the consequence.

I am, Sir, Very respectfully,

A.A.A. Genl.   (Signed)   G. R. Paul
Hd. Qrs. Dept. N.M.[3]   Col. Comdg. D.

Head Quarters, Southern District N.M.
Fort Craig, N.M. May 8th, 1862.

Colonel:

I have been informed from various sources that there are a large number of the enlisted men in your regiment absent without leave, beyond our pickets, committing all kinds of depredations on private property. It has also been reported to me that there is a plan among these marauders to seize the sutler's wagons, three in number, which are on their way to this post.

In order to put an end to these outrages, you will please have the rolls called, and ascertain the names of those who are absent, in order that they may be brought forward for trial. Compy. Off. should see for themselves that all absentees are reported, at retreat, reveille and tattoo.

I am Sir,
Very respectfully
Your obedient servant
(Signed)   G. R. Paul

Colonel J. M. Chivington,   Colonel 4th N.M. Vols.
Comdg. 1st Col. Vols.   Commanding District
Camp Val Verde N.M.[4]

                                              Head Qurs. Southern Dist. N.M.
Comdg. Officer,   Fort Craig N.M. May 8ᵗʰ 1862
Cavalry camp
Near Stapleton's
Sir:

   I have heard from various sources that there is a gang of marauders from the troops, who are committing depredations on private property beyond our pickets & that they are waiting for an opportunity for attacking the post sutler's wagons, three in number, now on their way with goods to this post.

   You will therefore scout over the country towards San Antonio, take up all men absent without leave, and afford protection to the wagons referred to. The sutler will inform you when to expect the wagons.

                                  I am, Sir,
                                  Very Respectfully
                                  Your obᵗ Servᵗ
            (Signed)   G. R. Paul
                                  Col. 4ᵗʰ N.M. Vols. Comdg. Dist.[5]

                                              Head Quarters Southern District N.M.
                                              Fort Craig N.M. May 9ᵗʰ 1862
Sir,

   I have the honor to state that Mr. Milligan, employed by the Q.M. Dept. to gather mules and other public property abandoned by Texans etc., in passing through Polvadera with a lot of mules, was interfered with by <u>Major</u> <u>Arthur</u> <u>Morrison</u>, and the mules taken away from him. The matter would not be of much importance if he would account for the mules, but I have been informed that he gives the mules away to whoever chooses to claim them, as having bought them from Texans. Lt. Brooks writes that several of the best animals have been disposed [of] in that way.

   Mr. Milligan reports also that he is creditably informed that Colonels Pino and Manuel Chavez concealed at a ranch, part of a wagon load of <u>flour</u>, <u>coffee</u>, <u>sugar</u> etc., taken from Texans. This he says he can prove.

                                  I am Sir, very respectfully,
                                  Your obedient servant,
                 (Signed) G. R. Paul
Captain Gurdin Chapin, 7ᵗʰ Infantry   Col. 4ᵗʰ N.M. Vols.
A.A.A. General   Commanding District
Hd. Q. Dept. N.M.[6]

Head Quarters Southern Dist. N.M.
Fort Craig May 10th 1862.

Sir,

I have just received a note dated Camp above Doña Ana, May 5th 1862, signed by Wm. Steele, 7th Texan Vols. and of which you were the bearer, informing me that you were sent to bring down the sick and wounded of his regiment from Socorro &c. I have to inform you that the sick have all been removed to Albuquerque N.M. where they could be better taken care of, that I can not give you leave to pass beyond my District, but that if you will wait on the other side of the river, I will send the letter you brought to the Department Commander and await his orders, which will take five days. The letters you brought for your sick will be forwarded if you send them over. The object of the flag of truce which failed to reach General Sibley was to effect an exchange of prisoners.

I am Sir
Your obt. Sevt.
(Signed)   G. R. Paul
Lieut. _____ Taylor [*sic*]   Colonel 4th N.M. Vols.
Tex. Vols.   Comdg. S. Dist.
Near Fort Craig, N.M.⁷

[Postscript below was omitted from published report of Capt. Jas. Graydon to Colonel [Gabriel R.] Paul, Commanding [Fort Craig, N.M.], dated Polvadera, N. Mex., May 14, 1862, with regard to Confederate destruction of their equipment and supplies during the retreat around Fort Craig (see *OR, Series I Vol.* 9, pp. 671–72)]:

. . . .

P.S. Enclosed I send a copy of [The] Mesilla Times. You see old Sibley & Baylor were quarreling about command.

Obt. Ser. J. G.⁸

Head Quarters Southern Military Dist.
Fort Craig N. Mexico 22 May 1862.

Sir:

I have the honor to make the following report, that on the morning of the 21st inst. about 8 o'clock a verbal message was brought into this post by Mr. Ochoa that Captain Tilford, stationed at Paraje, was attacked by Confederate forces (Texans) and said to be about 300 in number. I at once

ordered five companies of the Fifth Regiment, in command of Captain
Bristol, to proceed and take position as near to Paraje as possible, where
the river was narrowest, in order to cover the retreat of Captain Tilford, if
necessary, as it was impossible to send him support owing to the state of
the river.

I also ordered five companies of Colonel Chivington's Colorado Volunteers to proceed, together with four pieces of Macrae's Battery, to join the
command of Captain Bristol. I went myself with the former force. Finding
at the best crossing between the post and Paraje a canoe that will carry from
6 to 900 pounds, I selected 20 of the best swimmers and sent them to the
left bank of the river, Lieutenant Anderson going at the same time with two
men in the canoe with ammunition for Tilford's command, also with instructions to find out the facts from Tilford himself.

He returned informing me that a force of 89 Texans made their appearance early this morning and demanded a surrender of the place. This being
declined, they opened a fire at a distance of four hundred yards, but soon
retired. When they were last seen, they were about 60 miles distant on the
Jornada. I have reinforced Tilford with 120 cavalry. I consider this force
adequate to hold the position. We will have a small flat boat afloat tomorrow morning, to work by a line that was placed yesterday and is capable of
carrying 20 men.

> I am Sir Very Respectfully yours &c.
> Saml. Archer Capt. 5th Inf.
> Comdg. S.M. District

Capt. Chapin
Ass[t]. Adjt. General
Santa Fe N.M.[9]

> Head Quarters Southern District N.M.
> Fort Craig N.M. May 22, 1862.

Capt. G. W. Howland
Comdg. Cavalry Force
Sir:

The District Commdr. directs that you remain in position, at or near
Paraje. In case of an advance of the enemy, you will notify him immediately,
keeping some mounted men on this side of the river to carry your express
to this post. You will, if necessary, inform Capt. Bristol, 5th Infty, Comdg.
Camp Mishler, who will receive instructions to send you reinforcements,
when you call for them. If you find that you can not hold Paraje, fall back

on some tenable point, from which you can reach the point on the river called the "old crossing." Keep scouts out five or 6 miles on the Jornada.

Very respectfully

Your obedient servt.

(Signed)   N. M. Macrae

1st Lieut. 4 N.M. Vols.

A.A.A. General[10]

Head Quarters Southern District

Fort Craig N.M. May 24, 1862

Col. J. M. Chivington, 1st Col. Vols.
Comdg. Camp Val Verde, N.M.
Sir:

The Col. Comdg. the District directs that you detail a detachment of one Comp. Off. and twenty enlisted men from your command to go and meet a supply train now en route to this post. The detachment will be rationed for eight days. The officer in command will report to these Head Quarters as soon as detailed.

Very respectfully,

Your obedient servant,

(Signed)   N. M. Macrae

1st Lt. 4th N.M. Vols.

A.A.A. General[11]

Office of A.A. Com. Subsistence

Albuquerque New Mexico

May 28th 1862.

Captain.

Enclosed I have the honor to transmit a certificate under oath from Mr. Jno. Hubbell, Qr. Masters Agent at this post, whom I deputed to make the average in pursuance of Par: 1188 "Revised Regulations 1861." The fact that I am very busy in settling up my final accounts with the Government was the cause why I did not superintend the taking of the average myself.

It was not practicable to kill and weigh the steers, but myself and Mr. O. P. Hovey each selected a person and mutually elected a third, and the result of their decision is what was given.

The sheep I have seen and from their size and condition (they being 3, 4, & 5 years old) I do not think the average any too great. The beef I did not see, as immediately after they were received by my agent, they were sent out to the commissary herd some fifteen miles from here and Mr. O. P. Hovey and myself declined being present in order that we might not influence the decisions of either of the parties engaged in making the average.

I am Captain
Very respectfully
Yr. Obd. Servt.
Law^{ce} G. Murphy

Capt. A. F. Garrison   A.A. Com. Subsistence
Chief Com. Sub.
Santa Fe, N.M.[12]

Head Qrs. Southⁿ Mil. Dist. N.M.
Fort Craig June 6th 1862

General:

I have the honor to report to you the following information gained by me this day from two Mexicans, who were on their way from [the] Mesilla Valley to Peralta, N.M. They were arrested and brought to my office by an American named McGuire. Said Mexicans were [the] bearers of two letters, one for the French priest at Secora [Socorro], N.M., the other for Governor Connelly's clerk at Peralta, N.M. After talking with them some time and learning what I could, I then opened the letters to ascertain the contents, which turned out to be in my opinion all right.

In the Secora letter, the writer states that there is twenty five hundred California Troops within one hundred miles of Tucson, Arizona. The Texans are confiscating all Union property. Captain Hunter of [the] Texan forces wants five hundred men to go to Cook's Springs to fortify and wait for [the] California troops. The Texans are in a bad state of discipline. The writer asked for a passport to come up the country, and was refused. He lives in Secoro N.M. when at home. He states that he is afraid to write much.

The contents of the Peralta letter amounts to the same thing. The writer says that if Governor Connelly was in [the] Mesilla Valley, he would be welcomed by at least fifteen hundred men. Union sympathy is very strong. Total now claimed by the Texans in [the] Mesilla Valley [is] three thousand men, but it is believed by the Mexicans that there is not more than two thousand. The Mexicans say the Texans captured one captain and four men of the California troops in Tucson, that they paroled the men, and Captain Hunter with sixty Texans brought the Captain and the <u>miller</u> [i.e., Ammi White] at Tucson prisoners to [the] Mesilla Valley. The day before, they left to come up the country.

They say they saw the California Captain and [the] <u>Tucson</u> <u>Miller</u> themselves. They report the Texans mostly at Fort Bliss, only having about five hundred men up the river at different points. They were about to leave the country, when their paymaster came with money to pay them, having about half enough for that purpose, and was urging the people of the country to raise the other half. They have made application to the Mexican authorities to pass through their country to Sonora if the Northern troops follow them and are too strong for them, but the authorities refused to allow them to pass through their country at all. They then said they would go through by force, and the Mexicans have four hundred men under arms to dispute their passage. The Premo [Pima] Indians say that there are five thousand more troops following those near Tucson and that they have plenty of cannon.

Had we not better send out spies, beyond Cooks Springs, to learn something about the California troops? I have sent Mr. Bailey to El Paso; he is the man who brought you the correct information last winter. Had we not better make an early move down the country?

I am General with much respect
Your obedient Servant
J. M. Chivington
Col. 1st Reg. Col. Vols.
Comdg. Southⁿ M. Dist. N.M.

Brig. Genl E. R. S. Canby
Comd'g. Dept. N.M
Santa Fe N.M.[13]

Executive Department
Santa Fe June 15, 1862

Sir

I received today a letter from Placido Romero, enclosing one to him from his father at Mesilla dated June 1st, in which there is this passage, and only this, in relation to the approach of help from California:

"On the 27 of May there arrived here a company of Texans that had been stationed at Tucson, and they said positively, that there were arriving at that place two thousand five hundred Government troops from California and that they saw that number; but that the Pima Indians had told them, that in the rear of those, there were coming four or five thousand, with many cannon and wagons. The Southern Soldiers here are retiring, and the reason is that they have consumed and destroyed everything, even to the growing crops. The people here are with their eyes open towards

the north, in the hope of being relieved from the devastation of these lo-
custs. More than a thousand men are waiting with open arms to receive the
liberal Government of the north."

What reliance is to be placed in the account given, you will have a better
idea than myself.

Very Respectfully Your obt. Servt.

Genl. E. R. S. Canby   Henry Connelly
Com^d Department[14]

Head Quarters 1st Cav'y. Cal. Vol's.
Camp near Fort Thorn A.T.
July 5th 1862

To Col. J. M. Chivington
Commd'g. Sou. Mil. Dis. N.M.
Fort Craig
Colonel,

I have the honor to report my arrival on the Rio Grande, and went into
camp about three miles above Fort Thorn on yesterday the 4" inst. at 7
o'clock P.M. Immediately thereafter the National Colors were raised, [to]
great enthusiasm in the command. I send this morning to Fort Craig four
others of the party whom you sent to meet me. The remaining three I take
the liberty to keep with me until I hear from you. Two of these I send down
the river today, about fifteen miles, to return to camp tonight. I have with
me eighteen prisoners, all Mexicans but two—who are Germans—these
persons I arrested and kept with me in order to secure the secrecy of my
movements. Unless I receive orders from you to the contrary, I will tomorrow send two men to Mesilla to ascertain the strength of the enemy and his
intentions.

My command are greatly in want of fresh meat. If it is not your intention to immediately occupy Mesilla, would it be possible to obtain a few
days supply from Fort Craig? The prisoners with me report from two hundred to eight hundred of the enemy in and about Mesilla.

I am Colonel, Very Respectfully
Your Obt. Svt.
—signed—   E. E. Eyre
Lt. Col. 1st Cav'y. Cal. Vol's.
Commd'g.

P.S. My prisoners have no provisions at all, and I cannot afford to supply them but for a few days, the command having provisions to the 20" inst. only. I am greatly in want of the two mules furnished Mr. Mulligan [Milligan?] and companion. Please send them to me by the first opportunity.

—signed—   E. E. E.

A True Copy
E. E. Eyre
Lt. Col. 1st Cav. Cal. Vols. Comdg.[15]

H^d Q^{rs} 1st Cav. Cal. Volunteers
Fort Thorn, Arizona Territory
July 10th 1862

To Colonel J. M. Chivington
Comdg. Southern M. District, N.M.
Colonel:

I have the honor to acknowledge the receipt of your communication of the 7th inst. Lyon and one of his companions were wounded by the Indians about twenty miles above this post. The party were met by a party which I had sent to Fort Craig, who were also attacked by Indians. Lyon was put in a wagon and sent here, where he arrived about 3 "A.M." and received immediate medical attention.

The wound is not considered dangerous. He is however unable to proceed to Tucson, and the others of his party know nothing of the road. I do not think it safe for a party of less than twenty-five to attempt the trip with anything like a certainty of getting through. The horses of the California Squadron which I brought through are, I think, sufficiently recruited to select the number required and carry through the express, if you think it advisable to send them. I will put Capt. McCleave in charge of the party and have them ready to start immediately on receipt of your supply and the return of the train with provisions.

Capt. Fritz returned from Fort Fillmore last night, having effected an exchange for Capt. McCleave and the men taken with him, also for Expressman Jones and Mr. John Lemmon of Mesilla, all of which will I trust meet with your approval.

Capt. McCleave sent an express informing me of the attack of his party by the Indians. I at once sent Capt. Howland with forty men to his relief, with orders to proceed as far as Cañon "a la Mosa" [Cañada Alamosa] and if possible procure fifty sheep at that point for my command.

Reliable information has reached me that Col. Steele is in full retreat for Texas, being attacked at every point by the Mexicans and once badly whipped by them. This he acknowledges, and report says he lost his two pieces of artillery. He reached Franklin with his command (not exceeding two hundred, owing to desertions) in a starving condition, with little or no ammunition and his transportation nearly all lost. A party of one hundred & fifty Mexicans left the Mesilla on the morning of the 7th inst. for the purpose of running off the little stock he has left. I have but little doubt they will succeed, as they say he has not an animal but what was stolen from them. The Pueblo Indians at Socorro (below Franklin) also attacked a party of Col. Steele's Command and ran them from a ~~hill~~ village and killed a number of their men. They became incensed by the acts of the Texans while ~~passing~~ at their village. I do not think it is policy to send a large command at this time to the Mesilla Valley.

My Command is now more than sufficient to capture Col. Steele's disorganized troops, should I find him this side of Fort Bliss (which is not at all probable), and quite as many as can be subsisted in that part of the country. From nearly all information which I have received, I feel safe in saying that with thirty days rations to start with, the two hundred and thirty-five men now under my command can be fully supplied from Mesilla and El Paso with the exception of some small stores, and at a much less cost than they can be transported by way of Ft. Craig. I feel assured that no portion of the "Column from California" but the command which I brought through has left Tucson for the "Rio Grande." Lyon and his party lost all of their animals.

I am Colonel Very Respectfully
Your obt. Servt.
(Signed)   E. E. Eyre
Lt. Col. 1st Cav. Cal. Vols.

P.S. Enclosed herewith I send copy of Col. Carleton's proclamation, also letters from Col. Steele.

(Signed)   E. E. E.

A True Copy
F. Van Vleet
2nd Lt. 3rd Cav. & A.A.A. Genl.[16]

Hd. Qtrs. South. M. Dist. N.M.
Fort Craig N.M. July 11" 1862.

Captain,

I have the honor to report that I arrived here yesterday and assumed command of the troops in the District. I found Captain Howland with 100 men of the Third Cavalry had gone to Fort Thorn to reinforce the garrison. Six thousand rations have gone forward to Fort Thorn. I enclose estimate of Lieut. Cook of rations at post. Captain Archer reports that it will require 70 wagons in addition to what is now on hand to move the Command with rations sufficient to subsist troops, till trains can return for an additional supply. The river is quite high, so much so, that from near Lemitar to Socorro and from some miles distant from this, the trains have to pass on the hills, that makes the pass quite difficult.

I learned at Lemitar that two companies of Mexicans were at Polvadera, doing nothing, had been out for Indians, but went one day and returned the next. Allow me to suggest that they be employed under some competent officer to improve the roads. Colonel Chivington has ordered two companies of his Regiment to Union; he is anxious to leave the country with his Regiment for duty in the States. I shall inspect the troops on Sunday and learn their condition as to arms and clothing, etc.

I am Captain, very respectfully
Your obt. Servant
M. S. Howe
Colonel 3rd Cavalry
Commanding

Capt. G. Chapin, 7th Infty.
A.A.A. Genl. Dept. N.M.
Santa Fe N.M.[17]

———— ◆ ————

Hd. Qtrs. South. M. District N.M.
Fort Craig N.M. July 11" 1862.

Captain;

On the 8th inst. the dispatches from Hd. Qtrs. Dept. were forwarded by express to General Carleton. Today I sent forward the duplicates. At 4 P.M. an express from Lieut. Colonel Eyre arrived, bringing the intelligence that the expressmen had been attacked by the Indians some thirty miles this side of Fort Thorn, both wounded but not mortally, animals all gone but papers saved. I enclose copy of 2 letters from Lieut. Col. Eyre, proclamation of General Carleton, 1 letter from William Steele, Colonel T.M.V., and one copy of list of prisoners exchanged by Steele and Fritz, Cal. Vols., that the

General may more fully understand the state of affairs at Mesilla at this time, the prospect of crossing the river, etc.

I shall move towards Doña Ana with a portion of the Command at a time and send back transportation for the balance. Colonel Chivington is resolved to resign, or have his Regiment out of the territory; he does not think that he can control his men after being paid, if there is not some enemy to contend with, but if they can have an opportunity to fight, they will cling to him and together. But being a peculiar class of people, and those of this country a peculiar people also, he is of [the] opinion his men will run wild.

I enclose package of letters from the Armijos at Mesilla to friends at Albuquerque for the perusal and disposition of by the General. I have a man in the guard house who took letters from persons at Albuquerque to Rafael Armijo.

Lieut. Charles Newbold 3rd Cavalry and Lieut. Francis H. Wilson 5" Infty. have mutually applied for a transfer. I send their application through Head Quarters. They are anxious to be assigned to the Regiments they have applied for. Till the decision of the Secretary of War shall be made known, will the General direct the exchange? Colonel Chivington has applied for seven days leave to visit the General, will leave on Monday and says he can be back in the term.

I am Captain, Very respectfully
Your obt. Servant
M. S. Howe
Colonel 3rd Cavalry
Captain G. Chapin 7" Infty.   Commanding
A.A.A. Genl. Dept. N.M.
Santa Fe N.M.[18]

Head Qrs. So. Mil. Dist.
Fort Craig N. Mex. July 15, 1862

Capt. G. Chapin
A.A.A. Genl.
Dept. N. Mex.
Captain,

A communication by express this morning of date July 9th 1862 directs that 700 Infantry, 200 Cavalry, and McRae's battery [be] put in march to report to General Carleton at Santa Barbara. The aggregate of the 8 companies 5th Infantry is this morning reported at 446.

The 9 companies 1st Colorado Infy. is 454 (the 2 companies designated for Fort Union not yet marched). Captain Howland took with him all the horses that were fit to march, to Fort Thorn. The remainder are now under charge of Capt. [Edward] Treacy, who I had ordered to encamp in vicinity of Stapleton's Ranch for grass. The animals [are] so poor that they are scarcely able to go to graze and return to garrison [the] same day.

I inspected 5th Infantry on Sunday and found (with the exception of 2 bayonets wanting) all well armed, arms in good order, and most of them in fine order, some in superior order. Clothing, especially pants, shoes and stockings, much needed.

The 1st Col. I inspected yesterday. Found a fine body of men, capable of any endurance, all well armed save some screw-drivers and wipers—but most of them most miserably clad, many of them bare footed and those who apparently had shoes on their feet such as only would be thrown away if others could be purchased.

Two men appeared on parade garbed in shirt and drawers only, all they had. Some I was informed were not so well off; had to remain in tents. I need say no more to have clothing sent forward to clothe men this destitute. Some of the shoes had been purchased at Santa Fe (so says Maj. Winecup [Wynkoop]) and with only the march at review the sole of the shoes came off.

A small party of the 1st Col's went to the mountains on Friday last. Indians attacked them and caused them to return to camp. The expressman this morning reports that the Indians killed a man near Socorro last night. All the available mounted force is now absent at Fort Thorn. I shall put in motion as soon as paid the Battery, 5th Infantry, and a sufficient number of the 1st Col. to make up the 700. If I can raise that number without marching them barefoot and if I do not receive different orders, I shall accompany the Command, since the last instruction did not indicate the contrary.

A Priest from Doña Ana (gone to Santa Fe) reports that the Texan troops attacked a small settlement at Mesilla and 3 Mex[s] were killed, 8 Texans; and some 10 miles from Mesilla made the 2nd attack; 1 Mex. & 18 Texans killed. And it was reported to him the Texans had taken all the flatboats at the Mesilla crossing down the river. The Mex[s] turned out, killed most of the Texans, and recovered the boats. That the Isleta Indians and Mex[s] together had taken all the animals from Steele's command and captured 3 pieces of artillery.

Had the General not ordered that the Command should report at Santa Barbara, I intended if possible to cross the river at this place and thence over the "Jornada." I have men on the road now examining if there is water in the different water holes. They will return this evening or tomorrow.

I am Capt. Very Respectfully,
Your Obt. Servant
M. S. Howe
Col. 3rd Cavalry Comdg.[19]

[pp. 342–43]
[In margin: July 26 No. 524]

Hd. Qrs. Dept. of N.M.
Santa Fe, N. Mex. July 26/62

General, The Adjt. of the Army
Washington, D.C.
Sir:

I have the honor to transmit a copy of a communication addressed to your office on the 6th of January last. In inviting your attention to this subject again, it is proper to refer particularly to some points in the service in this Department, which have hitherto been only referred to incidentally.

In the early part of last year, a large proportion of the officers serving in New Mexico abandoned their position & trusts & by resignations or desertions passed over to the enemy. With many of these with whatever of official or personal influence they possessed was actively employed to induce their men to desert. At that time there were large arrearages of pay due the troops; there has been no complete payment since, & at this time some of the companies have ten, twelve and fourteen months pay due. The service in this country was laborious & unpleasant & there was no prospect of improvement.

Every argument that it was thought could be effective was used. Judicial opinions absolving the soldiers from their allegiance to the United States; tempting offers of advancement & pay; the inability of the Government to pay its debts to them; the promised settlement of all arrearages & a liberal compensation for all public property brought over.

During the past year I knew of but one deserter to the enemy, & that one was committed to avoid the consequences of a serious crime. I have always attributed this result in a good measure to the conduct & example of the non-commissioned officers to whom generally these temptations were addressed.

These assignments were made under peculiar circumstances. The sergeants assigned to these duties had all been previously recommended for appointments and since assignments they have in many instances I believe by conduct in active or special ~~service~~ duty or in ordinary service proved themselves competent and deserving.

I trust that I am not asking too much in again bespeaking for them a favorable consideration of their cases.

Very Respectfully
Your Obt. Svt.
[Ed. R. S. Canby]
Col. 19 Infty. & Brig. Genl.
Comdg. Dept.[20]

———— ❖ ————

Head Quarters 1ˢᵗ Cav. Cal. Vols.
Las Cruces, Arizona Territory
August 1ˢᵗ 1862

Lieutenant.

I have the honor to acknowledge the receipt of the communication of the Colonel commanding of the 26ᵗʰ ultimo.

It reached me on the 30ᵗʰ ultimo when I at once commenced preparation for crossing the supplies spoken of. Men were put to work making a boat twenty feet long and seven feet wide, which was sent this morning by Black's train to the crossing. I sent out an express to meet Mr. Ochoa with orders to come to this town to unload his train. He will be here tomorrow, and will be immediately unloaded and returned to the crossing to load with supplies sought by Captain Updegraff. Black has 13 wagons in his train, and Ochoa 16 in his.

I have been unable as yet to obtain carts to assist in hauling the supplies. Lieut. Baldwin, A.A.Q.M., is now in Doña Ana for that purpose, where I learned this morning a few could be engaged. The boat I had made at Fort Thorn, in which my command was crossed at San Diego, is still at the latter place. Captain Updegraff will therefore have two boats in which to cross his command and the supplies.

I have not ordered Captain Updegraff to report to me at this place, fearing it might conflict with your orders "to report to Senior Officer at Doña Ana, if present, if not, to await orders," but presume on hearing of me being at Las Cruces, [he] will continue his march here and report.

There are no Confederate prisoners (sick or well) at Doña Ana. The two paroled prisoners brought down by Captain Howland are still here.

Their names are James A. Kennedy and John Saxon.

I have no means of ascertaining with any degree of accuracy the number who have died—or their names—since the Texans left the country. Their sick at Doña Ana, Las Cruces, Mesilla, and Fort Fillmore were all sent by Colonel Steele, C.S.A., to Franklin, where I am informed a large number of them died. I am informed about twenty-five or thirty are still at Franklin, in charge of a C.S.A. surgeon. There are a number of deserters from the Texans now in Las Cruces and Mesilla, to all of whom I have administered the oath of allegiance to the United States.

I have not heard from General Carleton since I left Tucson; therefore [I] cannot say when he will arrive. [I] look for an express from him any day. The packages for General Carleton which arrived here on the 22nd ultimo from Fort Craig, I forwarded on the 25th ultimo, agreeing to pay the bearer thereof five hundred dollars to carry them to Tucson, and return there again with an express from the General. It is exceedingly difficult to find reliable persons who will, at any price, consent to attempt the trip to Tucson.

The package for General Carleton which reached me on the 30th ultimo, I will forward as soon as it is possible to find reliable persons to carry it. Lieut. Baldwin has just returned from Doña Ana. He succeeded in engaging ten carts, which will be at the crossing tomorrow evening.

I am Lieutenant,
Very respectfully
Your obd't. Sv't.
E. E. Eyre
Lieut. Col. 1st Cav. Cal. Vols.
Comdg.

Lieutenant F. Van Vliet
3rd Cavalry
A.A.A. General
S. Mil. District N.M.
Fort Craig[21]

"Hard Crackers Come Again No More"
(melody after "Hard Times Come Again No More")

Let us close our game of poker, take our tin cups in our hands,
While we gather 'round the cook tent's door,
Where dry mummies of hard crackers are given to each man;
Oh! hard crackers, come again no more!
Chorus: 'Tis the song, the sigh of the hungry,
Hard crackers, hard crackers, come again no more!
Many days have you lingered, upon our stomachs sore,
Oh! hard crackers, come again no more!

There's a hungry, thirsty soldier, who wears his life away,
With torn clothes, whose better days are o'er;
He is sighing now for whiskey, and with throat as dry as hay,
Sings, Hard crackers, come again no more!
Chorus: 'Tis the song, the sigh, &c.

'Tis the song that is uttered, in camp by night and day;
'Tis the wail that is mingled with each snore;
'Tis the sighing of the soul for spring chickens far away,
Oh, hard crackers, come again no more!
Chorus: 'Tis the song, the sigh, &c.

CHAPTER SIXTEEN
Confederate Correspondence
May–August 1862

(Extract)

Head Quarters 7th T.M. Vol.
Camp above Doña Ana A.T.

General Order   May, 1862
Number __

The pay funds in the hands of the acting Regimental Quartermaster being insufficient for the complete pay of this Command to the 1st of January 1862 and the notes not less than the denomination of twenty dollars, rendering it impossible to make up uneven amounts, the Col. Commanding orders

I. That the Non-Commissioned officers and Privates of Companies A, B, C, D, F, G, H and I be paid by Acting Asst. Quartermaster Capt. A. Kerr Lee, the sum of sixty dollars each, to be noted on the pay rolls as being in part of pay due and accounted for hereafter as a stoppage.

II. xxxxxxxxxxxxxxxxxxxxxxxxxxxxxxxxxxxxxxxxxxxxxxxxxxxxxxxxxxxxxxxxxx

(Signed)   Wm Steele
A True Copy   Col. Commanding
Capt. A.C.S. 7th T.M. Vol. & A.A. Qr. Mr.[1]

Hd. Qrs. 7th Regt. T.M.M.
Camp above Doña Ana
May 11th 1862.

Captain.

In consequence of orders received from Brigade Head Quarters, your company is detailed to take post at the copper mines, for the protection of parties and persons working the same.

Your company will afford protection to Mr. [J. B.] Lacost[e], one of the proprietors of the mines, on his way to them.

These orders are given in consequence of the solicitude expressed by the Confederate Government for the successful working of these mines, of the product of which the Government stands greatly in need.

Thos. C. Howard
Adjt.

Capt. W. H. Cleaver[2]

Jefferson Texas May 13, 1862.

Genl.

I had the pleasure of meeting Mr. Robt. Josseylin, Secretary for the Territory of Arizonia [*sic*] en route to Mesilla, while on my way to this place. I would respectfully suggest that you communicate with him in regard to the movements contemplated in that direction, as he will until the return of Col. Baylor be the actg. Governor of the Territory.

Gov. Josseylin could have an express sent to Gen. Sibley giving the information in regard to the reinforcements, & all other matters relating thereto. If he has passed Houston, he could be addressed through Hon. Jno. A. Wilcox, M.C., San Antonio, who will forward it to him at La Mesilla if he has already proceeded there from San Antonio.

If I remember, I gave you the names of Judge J. F. Crosby, A.A.Q.M., & Judge S. Hart at El Paso, Texas. Either of these gentlemen will exert themselves to have ready supplies for the troops on their arrival at El Paso, also fresh transportation to Ft. Stanton.

I trust you will find the above suggestions worthy of consideration.

I have honor Genl. to be
Respty. &c.
Tom. P. Ochiltree

Gen. P. O. Hébert   A.A.G. Army of N. Mex.
Comdg. Dept. Texas
Houston, Texas[3]

Proceedings of a Council of Officers of the 2d
Regiment, Sibley's Brigade.

——

History of the Campaign in New Mexico

——

At a council of the commissioned officers of the 5th Regiment, T.M.V., held at the hotel of John G. Ward, in the town of Las Cruces, Arizona, on May the 12th, 1862, to take into consideration the removal of said Regiment to Texas.

On motion, Capt. J. B. McCown was called to the chair, and Capt. J. H. Beck appointed Secretary.

The objects of the Council were briefly stated by Capt. [Hugh A.] McPhaill thus:

That the assembling of the officers of the 5th Regiment was to determine upon some course of action in regard to their future movements; that it would appear to some to be rebellious, but such was not the fact, the only object was to determine whether we should quietly see this fine army of ours remain idle, waste away by disease and sloth, and worse than all, with gradual starvation. We wished to hear reports from the A.C.S. of the Regiment, to ascertain the amount of transportation the Regiment had, the chances of procuring more, also the amount of clothing, &c.

I. On motion <u>Resolved</u>, That the A.C.S. and A.Q.M. of the Regiment be requested to report to the next meeting in accordance with the suggestions of Capt. McPhaill.

II. On motion <u>Resolved</u>, That the Surgeons of the Regiment be requested to report at the next meeting the generality of the provisions now used by the Regiment and whether or not the same is unwholesome.

III. On motion of Capt. McPhaill, a committee was appointed, consisting of Capt. [Benton Beck] Seat, Lieut. [William W.] Apperson, and Lieut. [J. P. "Phil"] Clough, to make a brief report of the campaign in New Mexico, and to lay the same before the next meeting.

IV. On motion, <u>Resolved</u>, That the 5th Regiment T.M.V. appreciate the kindness shown to the sick, wounded and prisoners of this regiment by Gen. Canby, commanding the Federal forces in New Mexico.

V. On motion, <u>Resolved</u>, That Col. [Thomas] Green, commanding the 5th Regiment T.M.V. be requested to use speedy means in the removal from New Mexico of the sick and wounded of this regiment.

VI. On motion, it was <u>Resolved</u>, That the commissary stores taken from the enemy in New Mexico should not be charged to the officers using the same, for the reason that whilst they were in New Mexico they were at a heavy expense, and that as they assisted in capturing these supplies, they should not be required to pay for the small portion consumed by them; and that Congress be memorialized upon the subject.

VII. <u>Resolved</u>, That the General commanding this Brigade be requested to move this regiment to some other scene of action, where their services could be more useful to their country.

VIII. On motion, this Council adjourned to meet again on Tuesday, the 16th inst.[4]

Tuesday [*sic*], May 15, 1862.

The Council met pursuant to adjournment, attended largely by the commissioned officers of the regiment—the same officers presiding.

Capt. Seat, chairman of the Committee on Campaign, read his report, which was accompanied by the reports of the A.C.S. and A.Q.M., and the Surgeons of the regiment; and, upon motion, all of which were adopted and ordered to accompany these proceedings.

On motion, <u>Resolved</u>, That one copy of these proceedings, with the accompanying reports, be forwarded to the Hon. Secretary of War at Richmond, one to the Governor of the State of Texas, and one to the *Houston Telegraph* for publication.

On motion, the Council adjourned.

J. B. McCOWN, Chairman.

J. H. Beck, Secretary.

REPORT OF CAPT. J. H. BECK, A.C.S. 5th REGIMENT T.M.V., ARMY OF NEW MEXICO.

Amount of breadstuffs on hand May 12th, 1862, ninety-three days' rations for 600 men. This comprises the whole amount which the A.C.S. will be able to procure in the Territory of Arizona. This is now being deposited in the Commissary at Las Cruces and at Fort Fillmore. The wheat and corn turned over to Capt. Beck by Lt. [Frank H.] Bushick, is now being ground at the mills in Mesilla.

The beef in possession of the Commissary is only about fifteen days' rations, is very poor, and almost unfit for use. Under ordinary circumstances it would be condemned as unwholesome food for troops. There is very little beef to be procured in the Territory, and that of a very inferior quality.

There is neither pork nor bacon in the Commissary, and none can be procured at any price in the Territory, as there is none to be found. Neither is there any lard or tallow in the country. There can be a few beans found, but on account of they being almost exclusively in the hands of the Mexicans, it is very difficult to procure them. There is neither sugar nor coffee in the Territory. No rice can be found—not even enough for the hospital. A tolerable supply of vinegar has been obtained. Salt is abundant, but can only be procured at an exorbitant price. No soap or candles can be found in quantities sufficient for the use of a regiment.

Respectfully,
Capt. J. H. BECK,
A.C.S. 5th Regt., T.M.V.

STATEMENT OF THE QUARTERMASTER.

Report of Capt. T. G. Wright, A.Q.M., 5th Tex. M.V., in regard to transportation and supplies pertaining to his regiment.

First, Transportation.—Twelve wagons with harness; three wagons without harness; one hundred and seventy mules in a bad condition.

Second, Clothing.—None on hand, and none to be found adequate to the necessities of the regiment.

Third, Forage.—On hand, fifty fanegas corn. Hay of an inferior quality is being furnished per contract, upon which alone we have to rely, all the corn having been purchased that can be found in the country.

T. G. WRIGHT,

A.Q.M., 5th Regt. T.M.V.

STATEMENT OF THE ASSISTANT SURGEON.

Las Cruces, Arizona, May 12th, 1862.

To the Commissioned Officers of the 5th Regiment, T.M. Volunteers:

Gentlemen—I have no hesitation in stating that the rations now issued to the troops are of an unwholesome character. Flour without lard or the alkalies necessary to make the bread light and digestible, and miserably poor beef, are now only issued. I am officially informed that there is now flour for the command for ninety days only, this together with beef for twelve days, and some six sacks of coffee, now constitute the commissariat, and should a division occur between the regiments of the brigade, the 5th will have breadstuffs for thirty days only. You will readily understand from so unwholesome a diet, that indigestion, diarrhea, dysentery, &c., must necessarily prevail in the regiment. I regret to say that I have now under treatment a number of such cases.

In this connection I will state that many of the men are now almost in a state of nudity, and that from the organization of the regiment to the present time, it has had an inadequacy of clothing and blankets. Much of the mortality of the past winter was attributable to these causes. I now state in writing, what I have often said in conversation, that at no time has it been properly clad for even a summer campaign. In the retrograde march from Albuquerque, everything in the shape of clothing, with the exception of the suits worn, was cast away—hence much suffering has been the consequence.

I have been with my regiment from its organization, and for months its only medical officer, and I can bear testimony to the fortitude of the men even under treatment the most adverse.

I am, gentlemen, very respectfully.

JOHN M. BRONAUGH, M.D.

Assistant Surgeon, 5th T.M. Volunteers.

I have carefully read the statement of Dr. Bronaugh, and endorse every word therein stated.

J. R. McPHAILL, Ass't Surgeon,
5th Regiment, T.M. Volunteers.

ADDRESS TO THE WAR DEPARTMENT.
To the Hon. G. W. Randolph, Secretary of War
of the Confederate States of America:

We, the commissioned officers of the 5th Regiment Texas Mounted Volunteers respectfully ask leave to submit the following statement of facts: That since we were mustered into the service of the Confederate States of America at San Antonio, Texas, we have endeavored to discharge our duty as good soldiers, fighting for Southern independence and laboring together with our compatriots in arms, to establish a government that will receive the respect and admiration of the world.

That we left Camp Manassas, near San Antonio, on the 1st of November, 1861, and took up our line of march for this territory, not because we desired to come to this remote and far off wilderness, for many had been led to believe that we were going to bleeding and suffering Missouri, that was at the time, with extended hands and bleeding wounds, imploring aid, but as good and willing soldiers, we obeyed the orders of our commander, Gen. [Henry Hopkins] Sibley.

That, prompted by patriotic motives, and an honest desire to save our country, and if necessary, for that country to die, made a tedious march of eleven hundred miles, enduring many privations (but willingly), when on the 4th day of January last, we arrived at Fort Bliss, wearied and exhausted by the fatigue and exposure incident to our long march, but still eager to move on if service to our country could be rendered.

That after halting but about four days in the vicinity of El Paso, we were ordered to resume the march to Fort Thorn. On the 10th of January, we left our camp near Fort Bliss for Fort Thorn, and arrived at the latter place about the 16th of that month. Here it was thought necessary to rest the command a short time. Our marches were necessarily short and slow on account of the fatigue and poverty stricken condition of our horses and mules. Commissary supplies had now become scarce, and the men being on short rations, it became apparent and necessary, that an attack upon Fort Craig should be made.

From information received, we had learned that Fort Craig was garrisoned by near three thousand men, and it was the design of our commander in chief to storm the fort if necessary. When we had approached within the vicinity of the fort, the entire command was halted some two or three days about four miles below, at a point which was regarded as a strong position in case of an attack, and where grass could be obtained for our stock. During this time, reconnoitering parties had been sent out every day from our camp, and some skirmishing had occurred between our pickets and the Federals. As above intimated, it had been supposed that the fort was garrisoned by a force of only three thousand men, and that the citizens of the Territory would be favorably disposed towards us, and if necessary take up arms in our favor.

But reliable intelligence was received that not less than eight thousand troops were in possession of the fort, and that the citizens were either neutral or enlisted on the side of the enemy. A council of war was held, and as we are informed, after some deliberation it was deemed advisable not to storm the fort as had been originally contemplated, but to cross over to the east bank of the river and move above the fort. The object of this movement was to stop all communication between the fort and the country above, and if possible to seize upon certain supply trains which were reported to be daily going into the fort from the interior and from Fort Union.

In pursuance of this projected plan, the Brigade crossed the river on the morning of the 19th February and moved up about four miles, where we camped in full view of the fort—it being situated in the valley below, and the line of our march being across the range of hills on the east bank of the river. Col. Green commanded the entire Brigade, the command having been relinquished to him in consequence of the illness of Gen. Sibley. A strong picket was placed out that night to preclude the possibility of a surprise.

On the morning of the 20th, the command resumed its march and moved on slowly until about 4 o'clock in the evening, when it was discovered that the enemy were pouring out of the fort in large numbers, apparently moving up the valley as if to attack our advance. A line of battle was at once formed on the brow of the hills overlooking the entire forces of the enemy, three pieces of artillery were planted upon the right wing of the army and two upon the left. These opened a brisk fire upon the enemy's columns as they moved up the valley. They responded to our fire by a discharge from their long range guns.

The firing continued until night closed upon the scene, when a large portion of the enemy's force retired into the fort, the balance camping under the brow of the hill between our lines and the fort. Our army camped again on the hills. But little damage was done on either side. During the night of the 20th, about 130 mules belonging to the transportation train of Lieut. Col. [William Read] Scurry (who was in command of the 4th regiment) had strayed off beyond our guard lines and were captured by the enemy. This misfortune, of course, retarded the movements of our army next morning—it having become necessary to divide the transportation of the other regiments in order to enable the 4th regiment to move.

Major [Charles Lynn] Pyron was ordered to move on immediately with his detachment to the nearest point on the river where water could be accessible. Lieut. Col. Scurry and command followed. Col. Green and regiment (the 5th) was ordered to resume the position we held the evening before, in order to watch the movements of the enemy at the fort, while Lt. Col. [John Schuyler] Sutton, with his part of the 7th regiment, was ordered to guard the rear and trains.

The enemy, however, having anticipated our purpose, had already sent up a strong force from the fort and planted their batteries upon the opposite bank of the river and engaged Maj. Pyron's detachment immediately upon his arrival near the river. He sustained the fight against vast odds for a period of about one hour, when Lieut. Col. Scurry with his command went into action, having brought with him three pieces of artillery. Col. Green, in the meantime, had been despatched to hasten to the scene of action as fast as possible, with the force that could be spared from the train and rear. He reached the field about 10 o'clock with his regiment, minus two companies which had been left behind under Lieut. Col. Sutton to guard the trains and prevent an attack upon our rear.

The fight now became general, extending along the river which separates the two armies. In consequence of indisposition, the command was relinquished to Col. Green as soon as he arrived upon the field, and who had command of the entire forces during the balance of the day. Lieut. Col. Sutton arrived upon the field with one company of the 3rd [*sic;* 5th] Regiment and four of the 7th Regiment about 2 o'clock P.M. Our entire available force having been now brought into action, the struggle became terrific, and continued without intermission until near night, when the enemy's lines gave way and a complete rout ensued.

The battle of "Valverde" was fought on the 21st of February, 1862, adding another victory and shedding additional lustre upon our arms, which we believe will occupy a place in history and live in the memories of future generations, "when gorgeous palaces, and cloud capped towers, and solemn temples, shall dissolve and leave not a wreck behind." A report of said battle has, ere this, reached your department. After the victory of "Valverde," by which we obtained an accession of six pieces of artillery and two hundred and fifty stand of arms (improved style), it was made known that there were only six days supplies for the command in our Commissary Department.

A council of war was held the evening after our victory. In consequence of the want of supplies, it was deemed advisable to move on directly into the interior, where supplies could be obtained, and not undertake to lay siege to Fort Craig until sufficient supplies had been taken to justify us in undertaking so heavy a task. Accordingly, on the morning of the 23rd, every active man in our camps was busily engaged making all preparation to move on with the greatest possible despatch to Albuquerque.

This movement was necessary, as we have indicated, in order to reach supplies at the earliest date, and an expeditious march was made that we might get in possession of supplies before the enemy could be able to apprehend our movements. It was deemed advisable to destroy our tents, besides all surplus baggage, in order that our teams, which at that time were in a very dilapidated and broken down condition, might be able to haul our sick and wounded, of whom there were of our Regiment, sixty-seven wounded on the 21st on the battle-field of Valverde.

A detachment of three companies of the 5th Regiment under command of Lieut. Col. [Henry C.] McNeill was sent in advance of the army to procure or seize upon supplies that might be discovered along the line of our march. On the night of the 24th of February, this detachment came upon Socorro, about thirty-five miles above Fort Craig, surprised and took one regiment of Mexicans, commanded by Col. [Nicolás] Pino, prisoners, besides about two hundred and thirty-five stand of arms and one hundred and seventy-five mules. The mules we afterwards learned were returned, or the most of them, as very small quantities of supplies were found at Socorro.

Gen. Sibley, on the morning of the 22nd February, again assumed command of the Brigade. Our march up the valley of the Rio Grande was continued with all the expedition that the worn-out and broken down condition of our teams would admit of until we reached Socorro. Here a hospital was established at once, at which place all the sick and wounded of the command were left. The command moved on as fast as possible until we arrived at Albuquerque, one hundred and ten miles above Fort Craig, on or about the 5th of March.

It had been supposed anterior to that time that sufficient supplies could be collected at this place to subsist our army for several months, but contrary to our expectations, almost everything which could contribute to the support and comfort of an army had been destroyed by the enemy some time previous to our approach. Everything, however, which could be seized upon, was taken charge of by the officers of our subsistence department, for the use of the command.

It had been erroneously supposed also that the citizens of New Mexico would greet us as benefactors and flock to our standard upon our approach. On the contrary, however, we found that there was not a friend to our cause in the territory, with a very few honorable exceptions. Everything needed for the consumption of our command had been destroyed by the enemy, or concealed by the citizens. The troops of the command were sent out some twenty miles from Albuquerque to a bleak, sterile cañon in the mountains, where the most part remained nearly three weeks under orders from head-quarters at Albuquerque.

It was not known at that time what the intentions of our Commander-in-chief were. During the period of our encampment at this place, we were destitute of tents and almost entirely without clothing or blankets, and but little of anything to eat, that could be regarded as wholesome. In consequence of this destitute situation, connected with the rigor of the climate to which we were exposed all the time (heavy snows falling every day), many of our command were taken sick and died.

After having been at this place some ten days, a small portion of the command under Major Pyron was ordered to take possession of Santa Fe. Some two days subsequent, four companies of the 5th Regiment, under Major [John Samuel] Shropshire, were ordered on to support Major Pyron. Major Shropshire had succeeded Major [Samuel A.] Lockridge, who fell in the battle at Valverde. Lieut. Col. Scurry, with a portion of the 4th and 7th Regiments, was ordered to move directly across the mountains in the direction of Fort Union. Six companies of the 5th Regiment, two companies of the 4th, and one company of Maj. Pyron's detachment having been left back under Col. Green, to protect Albuquerque and the supplies which had been taken possession of at that place.

Santa Fe had been taken by Major Pyron without resistance, and the Confederate flag floated from the capitol of New Mexico. When Major Shropshire had arrived with his detachment, he moved on towards Fort Union and continued his march until he had gone fifteen miles above Santa Fe, where he camped. Three pieces of artillery, under command of Lt. [Joseph H.] McGuinness of Col. [John R.] Baylor's command, had gone on two miles in advance of Major Shropshire. Not more than one hour had elapsed after Major Shropshire's detachment had camped, when the firing of cannon was heard in the cañon above. Major Shropshire hastened to the scene of action, and when he reached the field, discovered that he had fallen into an ambuscade, the enemy having decoyed our forces up the cañon until their concealed columns of infantry had flanked them on both sides.

There were at this time not more than 175 men under command of Major Shropshire. This small party encountered over 1,000 of the enemy on the evening of the 26th March, and after a desperate struggle of about one hour, were scattered and cut to pieces by the overpowering numbers of the enemy. The artillery, however, fell back as soon as Maj. Shropshire arrived upon the field, and thus it was saved from falling into the hands of the enemy. Lt. Col. Scurry was dispatched for, and arrived with reinforcements at 4 o'clock A.M. the 27th, having under his command about six hundred men. With this force the enemy were pursued some six miles, where they were met, and where the battle of Glorieta was fought on the 28th.

Having encountered about 1,800 or 2,000 of the enemy, the struggle was terrific. The Texans prevailed, however, killing some 250 Federals, and capturing some 25 or 30 prisoners. A report of this battle has doubtless reached the War Department long since. Although a brilliant victory, and meriting a prominent place in the future history of this war, it was attended with serious disaster to our army. During the engagement the enemy had sent out a detachment to our supply train, which had been left unprotected, and burnt and destroyed the entire subsistence of Lt. Col. Scurry's command.

In consequence of this, our entire force was compelled to fall back to Santa Fe. Col. Green was despatched to come up with his command, and the supplies which had been left for our forces at Santa Fe. He reached Santa Fe about the 1st of April. It had been ascertained that there were no supplies at Santa Fe—that everything fit for the consumption of an army had been destroyed by the enemy or concealed by the citizens upon our approach. It was patent that there was no reliance for the subsistence of our command except that which had been brought up by Col. Green and collected together at Albuquerque.

In view of our destitute situation, and the hopeless prospect of getting supplies in the country, it was deemed advisable to commence at once a retrograde movement towards Mesilla, where we would have a better prospect for subsistence and be again in communication with Texas. Accordingly, about the 4th of April, our whole command took up the line of march down the valley of the Rio Grande. Albuquerque had been threatened in the meantime by the enemy, and some skirmishing between the small force which had been left there under Capt. [James] Walker and the Federals had occurred; also while on our march down the river and also at "Peralta," full reports of which you have doubtless received ere this.

At this time there were but a few days' supplies left and it was evident that the enemy intended to delay us as long as possible—apprehending that if we could be retarded in our movements until our entire subsistence was exhausted, that we might be forced from hunger to do that which they could not effect by force of arms, viz: surrender. In view of this, it was thought advisable to destroy all the baggage and relieve the command of everything which could not be transported on mules across the mountains.

Accordingly, everything was destroyed except seven days' rations and the clothing which could be conveniently carried on mules. We were eight days in the mountains before we reached the river below the enemy. We managed to drag our artillery over the mountains, by hand, where our exhausted animals were unable to draw them. We have arrived at this place with nothing but the artillery and between eighteen hundred and two thousand stand of arms which we took from the enemy. This is chiefly what has been achieved by our expedition into New Mexico. In every contest with the enemy we have vanquished them, and always contending against vast odds. We have achieved several victories, either of which would have immortalized us in any other field of action; but we have necessarily sacrificed many brave Texians [*sic*] to secure them.

We are here almost destitute of everything which could contribute to the comfort or support of an army. The 5th Regiment now only numbering about four hundred and twenty out of nine hundred and twelve mustered into the service at San Antonio, and started from that place with us—but little prospect of future active service, and destitute of the means of subsistence, except as exhibited in the reports herewith appended. In view, therefore, of the foregoing statement of facts, and the circumstances which encompass us as a command, and the imperious necessity for relief, we would respectfully ask that this report receive your favorable consideration, and that we be transferred to some other field of operation, where our services may be rendered more efficient, and our efforts in the great struggle for independence may result more profitably to the cause, than they have in this remote region, where there is nothing to stimulate the heart of the patriot or to nerve the arm of the soldier.

Signed by the Committee,

B. B. SEAT
Capt. Co. "F," 5th Reg. T.M.V.
W. W. APPERSON,
1st Lieut. Co. "H," 5th Reg. T.M.V.
J. PHIL CLOUGH,
1st Lieut. Comd'g. Com. "C," 5th Reg. T.M.V.

Adopted at Las Cruces, Arizona Territory, May 15, 1862.[5]

Head Quarters, Army of New Mexico
Fort Bliss, Texas, June 4, 1862.

General.

I have the honor to report that the following resignations have been tendered, and, subject to the approval of his Excellency the President, have been accepted by me.

For sake of greater convenience I have caused them to be put in tabular form, showing the date at which the provisional acceptances were made. In former communications I have briefly explained the necessity which, however, is sufficiently obvious, for such acceptance in order to maintain the organization of a force so far removed from the seat of government. No resignations have been thus acted on except with reference alone to the interest of the service in this Army.

List.

NAMES.	REGT.	COMP^Y	DATE OF ACCEPTANCE.
1st Lieut. W. B. Key	7th Regt. T. M. Vols.	"I"	Feby. 18, 1862.
Capt. D. A. Nunn	4th " " "	" "I"	Feby. 27, 1862.
" I. C. Stafford	2. " " "	Rifles "E"	" " "
" G. W. Campbell	5. " " "	Vols. "F"	March 8, 1862.
Asst. Surgeon J. F. Matchett	4. " " "	"	" 11, "
Chaplain R. W. Peirce	5. " " "	"	" " "
Asst. Surg. I. W. Cunningham	7. " " "	"	" " "
Capt. J. M. Noble, A.C.S.	4. " " "	"	" 12, "
1st Lieut. W. A. Shannon	5th " " "	" "C"	" 13, "
2nd " F. M. Brown6	4. " " "	" "F"	" 16, "
1st " W. G. Wilkins	5. " " "	" "E"	" 20, "
Capt. M. B. Wyatt, A.Q.M.	5. " " "	"	" 21, "
1st Lieut. J. G. Marshall	5. " " "	" "D"	May 16, "
" " A. L. Hudiburgh	7. " " "	"	Apr. 20, "
1st Lieut. G. W. Eaton	7th Regt. T. M. Vols.		Apr. 20, 1862.
Capt. A. J. Scarborough	4. " " "	" "B"	May 16, "
1st Lieut. J. B. Holland	4. " " "	"	17, "
2nd " R. J. Robinson	5. " " "	" "I"	" 20, "
2nd " B. W. Loveland	2. " " "	"Rifles "E"	" 26, "

I also enclose for your information and any official action deemed expedient, an official copy of a letter of resignation received by me from Lieut. Col. John R. Baylor (provisionally appointed Colonel by me as you were advised on the 16 of December last) 2nd Regt. T. Mt^d. Rifles. I am at a

Fig. 21. "El Paso [present-day Ciudad Juárez] as you approach from the River Crossing."
Sketch by A. B. Peticolas in his diary. Courtesy of Arizona Historical Society,
Tucson, negative no. 60289.

loss to know to what officer allusion is made in the second paragraph of this letter—certainly not, at the date of the letter or previous, with any justice to me.

Many of these resignations would have been reported earlier but for the want of communication from New Mexico. In a separate communication, I advise you of the various provisional appointments made by me during the active operations in New Mexico and since, all of which I respectfully ask the confirmation of his Excellency the President.

I am Sir very Respectfully
Your obd. Sert.
H. H. Sibley
Brig. Genl. Comdg.[7]

Hd. Qrs. 7th Regt. T.M.V.
Fort Fillmore. June 20, 1862

Commanding Officer
Mesilla A.T.
Sir,

Col. [William] Steele desires you to send to him a report of the strength of your command.

He also wishes you to send out Scouts to the north and in the direction of

Tucson, of which reports must be made to him. The Scouts in the direction of [Fort] Craig to go to the vicinity of Alamosa, and the others as far as Cook's Springs.

Very Respectfully
Thos. C. Howard

Lt. Col. [Philemon T.] Herbert[8]   Adjt.

———◆———

Hd. Qrs. 7th Regt. T.M.V.
Fort Fillmore June 27th 1862

Captain

I have ordered a detail of twenty-five men to report to you, which will make your force about fifty. At Mesilla you will be joined by the available force there. Whether there will be an officer senior to yourself or not, I am unable to say.

The object of this expedition is to proceed rapidly to near the Mexican line, and collect from that precinct to Mesilla all the beef cattle and work oxen you may find. Also any other supplies such as mules, horses & c. You will also take from the Mexicans any rifle, musket, or other guns suitable for military purposes.

(Signed) W[m] Steele
Col. Comding

Capt. W[m] H. Cleaver

You will take such supplies as your men may require and give a receipt for the same.

W[m]. S.

Note. Capt. Cleaver was killed when on the above service.[9]

———◆———

Fort Fillmore June 28th 1862

Lt. [John W.] Swilling

If you have interfered with an order given to Alderete's Company to press animals in Picatchie [sic; Picacho], you will immediately turn over to the Lt. in charge the animals taken, and report at these Head Quarters to explain your conduct in this matter.

(Signed) W[m] Steele
Col. Comding

Lt. S. deserted instead of reporting.[10]

———◆———

Fort Fillmore
June 30ᵗʰ 1862

Captain

The Col. approves of your idea of going to Picatchie [Picacho] for the purpose of pressing such property as may be of use to the troops on their way to San Antonio, and you are authorized to proceed in this expedition as soon as you think proper.

Thos. C. Howard
Adjt.

Capt. [Sherod] Hunter
Mesilla¹¹

Fort Bliss, Texas, July 8, 1862.

Ed. Telegraph: One company of Steele's Regiment is now at this post; the rest are on their way from Fort Fillmore. Company E, Capt. Kirksey, will leave this evening for San Antonio. Col. Steele, with the rest of his command, will start in a few days.

Since I first wrote you from Doña Ana, things have assumed quite a different aspect in Arizona. Col. Steele has been forced to abandon the Territory on account of scarcity of provisions. We have been living on <u>dry bread</u> alone for three months, and how the men have managed to live under this diet is a wonder to me. We start to San Antonio with nothing to eat but bread. There is nothing else to be had here, at any rate. We have no transportation of any kind, and are forced to leave nearly everything we possess behind—Sibley having taken all the wagons and mules off with him.

Instead of fighting the Yankees since Sibley left, we have to fight the Mexicans, both in Arizona and near this post. They refused to let us have transportation, and we went to press them into service, thereby creating a civil war with them. They refused to take our paper, which you know is all the current funds now in circulation in Texas. A fight ensued near Mesilla, on the 2ⁿᵈ inst., between one company of Steele's command and some of Baylor's men and the Mexicans, in which we lost 7 men, the enemy losing some 40. It was a desperate fight. A Lieutenant of Col. Baylor's killed 3 Mexicans with his bowie-knife. Capt. Oliver,¹² of Angelina County, and 4 of his men, were killed in the fight. No more damage was done to our side. The Mexicans then caved in.

On the 15ᵗʰ inst. [*sic;* probably should be June 15th], our company, commanded by the gallant Capt. W. L. Kirksey, had quite a lively fight with them, upon the same condition, at Socorro, 15 miles below here, in which we killed 20 and wounded a great many, besides destroying their church and otherwise damaging the town. Two 6-pounder field pieces, belonging to Captain Teel's battery, were engaged in the fight. Not one of our men were either killed or wounded, but we had two horses wounded. On the 3rd inst. a detail of 15 men out of our company went down to Socorro for the purpose of pressing articles we needed into service, when we were surrounded and charged upon by 50 Mexicans, who killed one of our men and took all the rest but five prisoners, myself being among those who escaped. But the death of our comrade has been avenged.

Capt. Kirksey fought bravely, always ahead of his men, where danger was the greatest, and distinguished himself signally on the occasion. This was the first fight our company has been in, and every man fought like heroes, reflecting great credit upon themselves and their gallant leader.

A few words more, and I must close for the present. It is not likely we will have any more trouble before we leave the Rio Grande valley. Most all the sick of Col. Steele's regiment have been sent on to San Antonio. There are some 150 or 200 sick in the hospital here, and what disposition are to be made of them, I am not able to say. Our company enjoys pretty good health, though a few have the scurvy. I will write you from different points on the route to San Antonio.

Yours, J. A. K.[13]

The splendid battery captured from the Lincolnites at Valverde arrived in town last Monday. It consists of six brass pieces; two twelve pound field pieces, three six pound guns, and one twelve pound howitzer, all in fine condition. It was at the taking of this battery that the brave and lamented [Major Samuel A.] Lockridge fell. The battery came in charge of Capt. J. D. Sayers, of Bastrop, a youth under twenty-one years of age, who distinguished himself at the battle of Valverde, as well as in every fight in which he was engaged during the expedition.[14]

Fort Bliss
July 11th 1862

Gentlemen;

Your letter of yesterday's date has been duly received and its contents noted considered.

It appears to me that you are reasoning upon false premises, looking upon the question in the same light as if there had been an invasion of Mexican Territory. Such bases of reasoning cannot be entertained and in fact if such were the case, it would be a question for our respective governments to adjust.

The facts of the case are simply these. It had become necessary to take cattle for the use of the troops under my command. Some fourteen [?] were taken, four or five miles from the line of Mexican Territory. At the time these cattle were being brought over, three men made their appearance from the direction of El Paso and, calling across the river, threatened that they with others would come over and take back the cattle. Some persons did come over at the same place and steal cattle the following night. That the cattle were taken by these persons is evident from the fact that they were seen crossing the river with them, that the tracks were of men without shoes, as of persons who had stripped to swim, and though a heavy rain had prepared the ground to give evidence, no tracks were discovered coming from above, and the cattle on that side of the camp were not molested.

Under these circumstances I believe the cattle to have been taken as a reparation for those taken for the use of the troops.

As to the right of neutrals, it is a question that cannot [enter] into this discussion, the question being as to the right to take for public use, the property of Aliens within our own Territory; which I believe has been admitted and practiced by all Govts, the owners of course having a claim for payment.

The good feeling and friendship of the authorities of El Paso, I have never had reason to doubt; although I have had public and private animals stolen from me and taken to the Territory of Chihuahua, which fact is only mentioned to show that the authorities, however friendly, are not able to restrain some of their people from trying to get whatever they can from us by any means, as I believe to have been the case with the owners of the cattle referred to, who having already reclaimed by stealth an equivalent for their cattle, seek to recover their stock from the Government.

Very Respectfully
Your Obt. Servt.
(Signed)   Wm Steele

José M. Urango and others   Col. Comding
Gefa Polit° El Paso.[15]

News from El Paso

The following intelligence was received by the last El Paso Mail:

Capt. [Gustav] Hoffmann, in passing through a small town some ten or 15 miles this side of El Paso, made a requisition of that place for a certain number of beeves. The population, either acting in bad faith or not being able to fulfill the contract at the stipulated time, delivered but a few beeves. Capt. Hoffman, not satisfied, refused to pay for them, or gave them a receipt for the amount delivered. The inhabitants rallied their fighting men, from 2 to 300 strong, pursued our men, killed some 15 or 20, mostly stragglers, and captured about 15. Major [Trevanion T.] Teel, hearing of these proceedings, came to the rescue, killed 30 Mexicans and liberated the prisoners.[16]

———————— ◆ ————————

San Antonio. Aug. 19th 1862

Genl. Hébert.

Sir

Before leaving Arizona I raised by authority of the Secretary of War one Company for a Regiment of Rangers. They were mustered in for the war. I would ask that Capt. S. Hunter cmdg. that Company be ordered to report to me for duty, as I need the services of his Company for immediate use.

I have the honor to be

respectfully

Jno. R. Baylor

Gov. Arizona

Cmdg. C.S.P.R.[17]

———————— ◆ ————————

"Goober Peas"

Sittin' by the roadside, on a summer's day,
Chatting with my messmates, passing time away,
Lyin' in the shadow, underneath the trees,
Goodness how delicious, eating goober peas!
Chorus: Peas, peas, peas, peas, eating goober peas!
Goodness how delicious, eating goober peas!

When a horseman passes, the soldiers have a rule,
To cry out at their loudest, "Mister, here's your mule!"
But another pleasure, enchantinger than these,
Is wearin' out your grinders, eating goober peas!
Chorus: Peas, peas, peas, peas, &c.

Just before the battle, the General hear a row,
He says "The Yanks are comin,' I hear their rifles now."
He turns around in wonder, and what do you think he sees?
The Georgia Militia, eating goober peas!
Chorus: Peas, peas, peas, peas, &c.

Notes

Introduction

1. Kenneth W. Munden and Henry Putney Beers, *Guide to Federal Archives Relating to the Civil War* (Washington, D.C.: U.S. Government Printing Office, 1962), 379; Jerry Thompson, "'Gloom over Our Fair Land': Socorro County during the Civil War," *New Mexico Historical Review* 73(2): 99–119 (1998), 99.

2. Alvin M. Josephy, Jr., *The Civil War in the American West* (New York: Alfred A. Knopf; 1991), 37–42; *The War of the Rebellion: A Compilation of the Official Records of the Union and Confederate Armies* (hereafter cited as *OR*), Series 1 Vol. 4 (Washington, D.C.: U.S. Government Printing Office, 1882), 35–36, 41–44; Ray C. Colton, *The Civil War in the Western Territories* (Norman: University of Oklahoma Press; 1959), 13–21.

3. Josephy, *Civil War*, 43–50. *OR, Series I Vol. 4*, 2–20; John P. Wilson, "Whiskey at Fort Fillmore: A Story of the Civil War," *New Mexico Historical Review* 68(2): 109–32 (1993).

4. L. Boyd Finch, *Confederate Pathway to the Pacific: Major Sherod Hunter and Arizona Territory, C.S.A.* (Tucson: The Arizona Historical Society, 1996), 87–88, 100, 103; *OR, Series I Vol. 4*, 20–21; John P. Wilson, "Retreat to the Rio Grande: The Report of Captain Isaiah N. Moore," *Rio Grande History* 2(3&4): 4–8 (1975); John P. Wilson, "The Civil War at the Pima Villages," chapter 10 in "Peoples of the Middle Gila: A Documentary History of the Pimas and Maricopas" (unpublished MS, 1999).

5. *OR, Series I Vol. 4*, 24–25; John P. Wilson, *Merchants, Guns, and Money: The Story of Lincoln County and Its Wars* (Santa Fe: Museum of New Mexico Press, 1987), 14–16.

6. Josephy, *Civil War*, 50–51; Finch, *Confederate Pathway to the Pacific*, 82–85; Jerry D. Thompson, *Colonel John Robert Baylor: Texas Indian Fighter and Confederate Soldier*, Hill Junior College Monograph in Texas and Confederate History, No. 5 (Hillsboro, Tex.: Hill Junior College, 1971).

7. Finch, *Confederate Pathway to the Pacific*, 108–9; Martin Hardwick Hall, "The Baylor-Kelley Fight: A Civil War Incident in Old Mesilla," *Password* 5(3): 83–90 (1960a); W. W. Mills, *Forty Years at El Paso, 1858–1898* (El Paso: Carl Hertzog, 1962).

8. *OR, Series I Vol. 4*, 44–87; Colton, *Civil War*, 21–25; Thompson, "'Gloom over Our Fair Land,'" 100–102; Martin Hardwick Hall, *Sibley's New Mexico Campaign* (Austin, Tex.: University of Texas Press, 1960b), 59–74.

9. Hall, *Sibley's New Mexico Campaign*, 32–46.

10. Ibid., 75–109; Josephy, *Civil War*, 59–73; John Taylor, *Bloody Valverde: A Civil War Battle on the Rio Grande, February 21, 1862* (Albuquerque: University of New Mexico Press, 1995).

11. Hall, *Sibley's New Mexico Campaign*, 110–60; Josephy, *Civil War*, 75–85; William Clarke Whitford, *Colorado Volunteers in the Civil War: The New Mexico Campaign in 1862* (1906; repr., Boulder, Colo: Pruett Press, 1963); Douglas W. Owsley,

Bioarchaeology on a Battlefield: The Abortive Confederate Campaign in New Mexico, Museum of New Mexico Office of Archaeological Studies Archaeology Notes 142 (Santa Fe: Museum of New Mexico, 1994).

12. *OR, Series I Vol. 15*, 914–19, repr. in Thompson, *Colonel John Robert Baylor*, 99–103; W. Hubert Curry, *Sun Rising on the West, The Saga of Henry Clay and Elizabeth Smith* (Crosbyton, Tex.: Crosby County Pioneer Memorial, 1979), 94–97.

13. Josephy, *Civil War*, 89–90; Finch, *Confederate Pathway to the Pacific*.

14. Hall, *Sibley's New Mexico Campaign*, 203–14; Finch, *Confederate Pathway to the Pacific*, 165–66; Martin H. Hall, "Native Mexican Relations in Confederate Arizona, 1861–1862," *The Journal of Arizona History* 8(3): 171–78 (1967).

15. *The Tri-Weekly Telegraph* (Houston, Tex.), May 28, 1862, 3 col. 3, and June 6, 1862, 3 col. 1 (repr. from the *Victoria Advocate*, n.d.).

16. Hall, *Sibley's New Mexico Campaign*, 202–3; Josephy, *Civil War*, 91.

17. *The War of the Rebellion: A Compilation of the Official Records of the Union and Confederate Armies, General Index and Additions and Corrections* (hereafter cited as *OR, General Index*) (Washington, D.C.: U.S. Government Printing Office, 1901), iv–v.

18. Peggy and Harold Samuels, *Remembering the Maine* (Washington, D.C.: Smithsonian Institution Press, 1995), 30–31.

19. *OR, General Index*, iii–xxi. See also *OR, Series 1 Vol. 1* (1880), iii–iv; and *OR, Series IV Vol. 3* (1900), iii–v.

20. *OR, General Index*, vi, viii–ix.

21. *OR, Series 1 Vol. 1*, iii.

22. *OR, Series IV Vol. 1*, v.

23. *OR, General Index*, viii–xviii.

24. "War Records. How Old Soldiers Get to Lying About Them." *St. Louis Post-Dispatch*, Mar. 21, 1887, 6.

25. *OR, General Index*, xiv. Munden and Beers, *Guide*, 379.

26. Dust jacket flap to *The American Heritage Picture History of The Civil War* (New York: American Heritage Publishing Co., 1960) estimated an average of perhaps a book a day.

27. Henry Putney Beers, *Guide to the Archives of the Government of the Confederate States of America* (Washington, D.C.: U.S. Government Printing Office, 1968), esp. 413–21. See also Lucille H. Pendell and Elizabeth Bethel, *Preliminary Inventory of the Records of the Adjutant General's Office*, Preliminary Inventory No. 17 (Washington, D.C.: National Archives and Records Service, 1949), 134.

28. Elizabeth Bethel, *Preliminary Inventory of the War Department Collection of Confederate Records (Record Group 109)* (Washington, D.C.: National Archives and Records Service, 1957).

29. Beers, *Guide*.

30. Ibid., 77–81. Library of Congress, Manuscript Division, undated finding aid to the Records of the Confederate States of America ("Pickett Papers"), 24 (Washington, D.C.: Library of Congress, n.d.).

31. Pendell and Bethel, *Preliminary Inventory;* Elaine Everly, et al., *Preliminary Inventory of the Records of United States Army Continental Commands, 1821–1920 (Record Group 393)*, Vols. 1–4 (Washington, D.C.: National Archives and Records Service, 1973).

32. Pendell and Bethel, *Preliminary Inventory*, 132–38.

33. Wilson, "Whiskey at Fort Fillmore."

34. Boyd Finch, "Sherod Hunter and the Confederates in Arizona," *The Journal of Arizona History* 10(3): 137–206 (1969).

35. Hall, "Native Mexican Relations"; Wilson, "Whiskey at Fort Fillmore" and "Civil War"; *OR, Series 1 Vol. 15*, 914–19.

36. Hall, *Sibley's New Mexico Campaign*, 14–16.

37. *OR, Series 1 Vol. 9* (1883), 511.

38. Jerry D. Thompson, *Desert Tiger: Captain Paddy Graydon and the Civil War in the Far Southwest* (El Paso: Texas Western Press, 1992), 76; Martin Hardwick Hall, *The Confederate Army of New Mexico* (Austin, Tex.: Presidial Press, 1978), 373–76; Taylor, *Bloody Valverde*, 105, 164.

39. John P. Wilson, "The End of Sibley's New Mexico Campaign," *La Crónica de Nuevo México*, Issue No. 28, 2–4 (April 1989); also Wilson, "Retreat to the Rio Grande."

40. See n. 34.

41. The original letterbook is in Record Group (hereafter cited as RG) 109 (Bethel, *Preliminary Inventory*, 188).

42. Mills, *Forty Years at El Paso*, 73; Finch, *Confederate Pathway to the Pacific*, 108–9; Hattie M. Anderson, ed., "With the Confederates in New Mexico during the Civil War—Memoirs of Hank Smith," *Panhandle-Plains Historical Review* 2: 65–97 (1929), 89–90.

43. For example, William O. Brown, Jr., and Richard C. K. Burdekin, "Turning Points in the U.S. Civil War: A British Perspective," *The Journal of Economic History* 60(1): 216–31 (2000); Marc D. Weidenmier, "The Market for Confederate Cotton Bonds," *Explorations in Economic History* 37(1): 76–91 (2000). See the list of references with both articles.

44. Jerry D. Thompson, "'Gloom over Our Fair Land.'"

45. *Quincy Daily Whig and Republican*, Mar. 5, 1862.

Chapter 1
1. The Library of Congress, Manuscript Division, Microfilm Edition of the Records of the Confederate States of America, Vol. 24 (Reel No. 14). The reference to Pike's Peakers is to the San Juan gold rush of 1860; see Robert J. Torrez, "The San Juan Gold Rush of 1860 and Its Effect on the Development of Northern New Mexico," *New Mexico Historical Review* 63(3): 257–72 (1988). Texas ratified its ordinance of secession on Feb. 23, 1861, less than a week after Jackson's letter was written.

Chapter 2
1. National Archives, RG 92, Records of the Office of the Quartermaster General, Consolidated File, Fort Fillmore, New Mexico.

2. National Archives, RG 393, Headquarters, Department of New Mexico, Unregistered Letters Received, 1854–61, Microfilm Publication M1120 Roll 28, frames 0885–0886.

3. National Archives, RG 75, Letters Received by the Office of Indian Affairs, New Mexico Superintendency, 1860–1861, Microfilm Publication M234 Roll 550, File No, C-1244-61N.M. (with enclosures).

4. National Archives, RG 393, Headquarters, Department of New Mexico, Unregistered Letters Received, 1854–61, Microfilm Publication M1120 Roll 28, frame 0888.

5. Ibid., frames 0890–0891.

6. National Archives, RG 153, Records of the Office of the Judge Advocate General, File No. 107, Case of Major Isaac P. Lynde, 1861–62.

7. National Archives, RG 393, Headquarters, Department of New Mexico, Unregistered Letters Received, 1854–61, Microfilm Publication M1120 Roll 28, frames 0905–0907.

8. Ibid., frames 0909–0911.

9. National Archives, RG 153, File No. 107, Case of Major Isaac P. Lynde, 1861–62.

10. Ibid.

11. National Archives, RG 75, Letters Received by the Office of Indian Affairs, New Mexico Superintendency, 1860–1861, Microfilm Publication M234 Roll 550, File No. C1286-61N.M.

12. National Archives, RG 393, Headquarters, Department of New Mexico, Unregistered Letters Received, 1854–61, Microfilm Publication M1120 Roll 28, frame 0928. Morris, a captain in the Regiment of Mounted Riflemen, commanded Fort Craig at this time.

13. National Archives, RG 153, File No. 107, Case of Major Isaac P. Lynde, 1861–62.

14. Ibid.

15. National Archives, RG 92, Records of the Office of the Quartermaster General, Consolidated File, Fort Fillmore, New Mexico.

16. National Archives, RG 153, File No. 107, Case of Major Isaac P. Lynde, 1861–62. According to Dr. James Cooper McKee, Lieutenant McNally received a serious chest wound, which he survived, while Lieutenant Brooks had only "a slight scratch from a bullet on one of his forearms." Sergeant James Callaghan's wound was not mortal because he was paroled at Las Cruces on July 31, 1861, along with sixty-three other members of his Company F, Regiment of Mounted Riflemen (National Archives, Records of the Commissary General of Prisoners, RG 249, Miscellaneous List No. 436, Federal Prisoners, 1861–65 [E107]).

17. National Archives, RG 92, Records of the Office of the Quartermaster General, Consolidated File, Fort Fillmore, New Mexico.

18. National Archives, RG 393, Headquarters, Department of New Mexico, Unregistered Letters Received, 1854–61, Microfilm Publication M1120 Roll 28, frame 0953.

19. National Archives, RG 94, Records of the Adjutant General's Office, Letters Received, Microfilm Publication M619 Roll 42, File No. N-189 Encl. 10.

20. National Archives, RG 153, File No. 107, Case of Major Isaac P. Lynde, 1861–62.

21. *Daily Conservative* (Leavenworth, Kans.), Oct. 19, 1861, 2.

22. National Archives, RG 153, File No. 107, Case of Major Isaac P. Lynde, 1861–62.

Chapter 3

1. National Archives, RG 393, Headquarters Records of Fort Union, New Mexico, Letters Received, June 1861. All documents in this chapter are from this same source.

Chapter 4

1. National Archives, RG 393, Headquarters Records of Fort Union, New Mexico, Letters Received, August 1861. Unless otherwise noted, all letters in this chapter are from this same file.

2. National Archives, RG 75, Letters Received by the Office of Indian Affairs, New Mexico Superintendency, 1860–1861, Microfilm Publication M234 Roll 550, File No. C-1316-61N.M.

3. National Archives, RG 393, Entry 111, District of Fort Craig, New Mexico, Letters Received, 1861.

4. National Archives, RG 393, Headquarters Records of Fort Union, New Mexico, Letters Received, August 1861, File No. C-134 of 1861.

5. National Archives, RG 393, Headquarters Records of Fort Union, New Mexico, Letters Received, August 1861, File No. C-134.3 of 1861.

6. National Archives, RG 393, Headquarters Records of Fort Union, New Mexico, Letters Received, August 1861, File No. C-134.4 of 1861.

Chapter 5

1. National Archives, RG 123, United States Court of Claims General Jurisdiction Case No. 1883, *William S. Grant v. The United States,* folder unnumbered.

2. National Archives, RG 94, Records of the Adjutant General's Office, Letters Received, 1861, Report No. 613C 1861, F/W 591P 1861, folder 2.

Chapter 6

1. National Archives, RG 393, Headquarters, Department of New Mexico, Unregistered Letters Received, 1854–61, Microfilm Publication M1120 Roll 28, frames 0968–0969.

2. Ibid., frames 0964–0965.

3. National Archives, RG 393, Entry 733, Southern District of New Mexico, Letters Sent, August 1861–May 1862. McRae's reference to Judge Wells, first name unknown, was probably to the same person as Captain Chapin's Major Weller (chapter 11, sixth document).

4. Ibid.

5. Ibid.

6. National Archives, RG 393, Headquarters, Department of New Mexico, Unregistered Letters Received, 1854–61, Microfilm Publication M1120 Roll 28, frames 1001–1004.

7. National Archives, RG 153, File No. 107, Case of Major Isaac P. Lynde, 1861–62.

8. National Archives, RG 393, Headquarters Records of Fort Union, New Mexico, Letters Received, August 1861.

9. National Archives, RG 393, Entry 733, Southern District of New Mexico, Letters Sent, August 1861–May 1862. The Pelham enclosure is no longer present. For an official copy of McCulloch's letter, see chapter 7.

10. Ibid.

11. National Archives, RG 92, Records of the Office of the Quartermaster General, Consolidated File, Fort Fillmore, New Mexico.

12. Ibid.

13. National Archives, RG 393, Entry 733, Southern District of New Mexico, Letters Sent, August 1861–May 1862.

14. National Archives, RG 393, Headquarters, Department of New Mexico, Unregistered Letters Received, 1854–61, Microfilm Publication M1120 Roll 28, frames 1018–1020.

15. National Archives, RG 393, Headquarters, Department of New Mexico, Unregistered Letters Received, 1854–61, Microfilm Publication M1120 Roll 28, frame 1026. The enclosure is no longer present.

16. National Archives, RG 393, Headquarters, Department of New Mexico, Unregistered Letters Received, 1854–1861, Microfilm Publication M1120 Roll 28. The letter on the microfilm is a copy of the original and Chavez's name here is spelled with a "z." Lt. Col. Chavez's letter was not available when Dr. Marc Simmons wrote about this episode in his article, "Horse Race at Fort Fauntleroy: An Incident of the Navajo Wars," *La Gaceta* 5(1): 3–13 (1970).

17. National Archives, RG 393, Entry 733, Southern District of New Mexico, Letters Sent, August 1861–May 1862. *Terrones* are cut blocks of sod held together by plant roots, air-dried and laid up like adobes. Roberts obviously was having these cut on the bottom lands adjoining the Rio Grande.

18. Ibid.

19. National Archives, RG 393, Headquarters, Department of New Mexico, Unregistered Letters Received, 1854–61, Microfilm Publication M1120 Roll 28, frames 1063–1065. The enclosure is no longer present.

20. National Archives, RG 393, Headquarters, Department of New Mexico, Letters Received, Microfilm Publication M1120 Roll 13, File No. A-39 of 1861.

21. This and the following twelve letters are from the National Archives, RG 393, Entry 733, Southern District of New Mexico, Letters Sent, August 1861–May 1862.

22. National Archives, RG 393, Headquarters, Department of New Mexico, Unregistered Letters Received, 1854–61, Microfilm Publication M1120 Roll 28, frames 1142–1143.

23. National Archives, RG 393, Entry 674, District of Santa Fe, New Mexico, Letters Received, December 1861–March 1865. The enclosure is not present.

24. Ibid.

25. National Archives, RG 393, Entry 733, Southern District of New Mexico, Letters Sent, August 1861–May 1862.

26. National Archives, RG 393, Headquarters, Department of New Mexico, Unregistered Letters Received, 1854–61, Microfilm Publication M1120 Roll 28, frames 1150–1151.

Chapter 7

1. 1. National Archives, RG 109, War Department Collection of Confederate Records, Compiled Military Service Records, Col. John R. Baylor, Second Regiment Texas Cavalry.

2. Ibid.

3. Ibid. The author of this letter was probably Spruce M. Baird or William Pelham.

4. *Galveston News* (Galveston, Tex.), Aug. 20, 1861. There is no known surviving copy of the Aug. 3, 1861, *Mesilla Times*. Reprints of this particular paragraph are also found in the *Dallas Herald*, Aug. 28, 1861, 1; and the New Orleans *Daily Picayune*, Aug. 27, 1861, but typographic errors are evident in all of the reprinted

articles. The figures of 663 lbs. rice, 325 lbs. tea, and 7,857 lbs. sugar are consistent in all three reprint articles and can be accepted as correct. For the other commodities there is no way to decide which totals are the correct ones, barring discovery of the original records. Where the statistics in the three papers differ, the alternative figures are given here as nn. 5 through 15.

5. *Dallas Herald*, August 28, says 43,408 lbs. flour. *Daily Picayune*, August 27, says 4,308 lbs. flour.

6. *Daily Picayune*, August 27, says 6,160 pounds Rio coffee.

7. *Dallas Herald*, August 28, says 288 gallons vinegar.

8. *Dallas Herald*—2,240 lbs. soap. *Daily Picayune*—2,346 pounds soap.

9. *Daily Picayune*—18,047 pounds hay.

10. *Dallas Herald*—5,888 lbs. bacon. *Daily Picayune*—900 pounds bacon.

11. *Daily Picayune*—156 barrels beans.

12. *Dallas Herald*—1,173 [lbs.] preserved vegetables.

13. *Daily Picayune*—1,234 lbs. star candles.

14. *Daily Picayune*—305 lbs. sperm candles.

15. *Daily Picayune*—275 boxes soap.

16. National Archives, RG 393, Headquarters Records of Fort Union, New Mexico, Letters Received, August 1861.

17. National Archives, RG 109, War Department Collection of Confederate Records, Compiled Military Service Records, Col. John R. Baylor, Second Regiment Texas Cavalry.

18. National Archives, RG 249, Commissary General of Prisoners, Miscellaneous List No. 436, Federal Prisoners, 1861–65 [E107] (9W2/19/17/B Box No. 5).

19. National Archives, RG 109, War Department Collection of Confederate Records, Compiled Military Service Records, Col. John R. Baylor, Second Regiment Texas Cavalry.

20. *The Daily Picayune* (New Orleans), Nov. 1, 1861, 1, col. 7. The community of Pinos Altos, just north of Silver City, N.M., was known as Pino Alto until after the Civil War. Captain Mastin died of his wounds and is buried in the cemetery there. Lucien File's *Directory of Mines of New Mexico* (1965) does not list the Palo Pinto Mines.

21. National Archives, RG 109, War Department Collection of Confederate Records, Compiled Military Service Records, Col. John R. Baylor, Second Regiment Texas Cavalry.

22. Ibid.

23. National Archives, RG 109, War Department Collection of Confederate Records, Compiled Military Service Records, Confederate Staff Files, Thomas P. Ochiltree.

24. National Archives, RG 109, War Department Collection of Confederate Records, Compiled Military Service Records, Col. John R. Baylor, Second Regiment Texas Cavalry. The first enclosure was Baylor's report to Magruder dated Dec. 29, 1862, printed in *OR, Series I Vol. 15*, 914–18. The other enclosures have not been found.

Chapter 8

1. National Archives, RG 393, Headquarters, Department of New Mexico, Letters Received, Microfilm Publication M1120 Roll 13, File No. B-17 (and enclosures) of 1861. The unsigned author of the August 15 letter was Diego Archuleta, who

indeed had wide recognition among New Mexicans. I made this identification by comparisons with signed, autograph letters in Archuleta's fine script. Aside from his caustic comments, his concern was not with the Confederate invasion or even the occupation of the Rio Bonito country. Instead, he was on a campaign swing through the settlements near Fort Stanton, for election as the territorial delegate to Congress, and his election prospects were the principal anxiety at the moment. The Confederates arrived and caught him, and undoubtedly would have shot him had they known that he was a captain of militia at the time of the McLeod invasion in 1841.

In the election on Sept. 2, 1861, Archuleta lost heavily; Judge John Watts received more than 63 percent of the total vote and Archuleta carried only three counties (*Santa-Fe Gazette*, Sept. 28, 1861, 2). Soon afterward, Governor Connelly appointed him a brigadier general of militia for Rio Arriba County (*Santa-Fe Gazette*, Sept. 14, 1861, 2). This position apparently carried no command responsibilities. See also Stella M. Drumm, ed., *Down the Santa Fe Trail and into Mexico: The Diary of Susan Shelby Magoffin, 1846–1847* (New Haven: Yale University Press, 1926), 184–86. The Don Boni mentioned in this letter was probably Bonifacio Chaves, who escaped with Lorenzo Labadie; see letter of August 18 from Captain N. B. Rossell in chapter 6. The Spanish transcriptions in this chapter and elsewhere use modernized spellings and provide words in place of abbreviations.

2. National Archives, RG 393, Headquarters, Department of New Mexico, Unregistered Letters Received, 1854–61, Microfilm Publication M1120 Roll 28, frame 1006.

3. National Archives, RG 393, Headquarters, Department of New Mexico, Letters Received, Microfilm Publication M1120 Roll 13, File No. B16 of 1861. The discovery of gold placers at Jicarilla, thirty miles north of Fort Stanton, led to a minor gold rush beginning in June 1861.

4. *The Tri-Weekly Telegraph* (Houston, Tex.), Nov. 1, 1861, 3(?), citing *The Mesilla Times* of Oct. 10, 1861. Captain James Walker commanded Co. D, Second Regiment, Texas Mounted Rifles (Baylor's command). Spellings have been corrected and names are spelled as shown in Martin H. Hall's *The Confederate Army of New Mexico* (Austin: Presidial Press, 1978).

5. National Archives, RG 393, Headquarters, Department of New Mexico, Unregistered Letters Received, 1854–61, Microfilm Publication M1120 Roll 28, frame 1031.

6. National Archives, RG 393, Headquarters, Department of New Mexico, Letters Received, Microfilm Publication M1120 Roll 14, File No. M-74 of 1861.

7. National Archives, RG 393, Headquarters, Department of New Mexico, Letters Received, Microfilm Publication M1120 Roll 14, File No. M-75 of 1861.

8. National Archives, RG 393, Headquarters, Department of New Mexico, Letters Received, Microfilm Publication M1120 Roll 14, File No. M-82 of 1861.

9. National Archives, RG 393, Headquarters, Department of New Mexico, Letters Received, Microfilm Publication M1120 Roll 14, File No. M-83 of 1861.

10. National Archives, RG 393, Headquarters, Department of New Mexico, Letters Received, Microfilm Publication M1120 Roll 13, File No. B-41 of 1861.

11. National Archives, RG 393, Headquarters, Department of New Mexico, Letters Received, Microfilm Publication M1120 Roll 13, File No. B-42 of 1861.

12. National Archives, RG 393, Headquarters, Department of New Mexico, Letters Received, Microfilm Publication M1120 Roll 13, File No. C-292 of 1861.

13. National Archives, RG 393, Headquarters, Department of New Mexico, Unregistered Letters Received, 1854–61, Microfilm Publication M1120 Roll 28, frame 1127.

14. National Archives, RG 393, Headquarters, Department of New Mexico, Letters Received, 1862, Microfilm Publication M1120 Roll 15, File No. C-5.

15. National Archives, RG 393, Headquarters, Department of New Mexico, Letters Received, 1862, Microfilm Publication M1120 Roll 15, File No. C-6.

16. National Archives, RG 393, Headquarters, Department of New Mexico. Unregistered Letters Received, 1862–63, Microfilm Publication M1120 Roll 29, frame 0040.

Chapter 9

1. National Archives, RG 109, War Department Collection of Confederate Records, Microcopy 323, Compiled Service Records of Confederate Soldiers Who Served in Organizations from the State of Texas. Roll 182, Baylor's Cavalry (Second Regiment, Arizona Brigade), A-L. Sherod Hunter jacket.

2. Ibid.

3. National Archives, RG 393, U.S. Army Continental Commands 1821–1920, Entry 3662—Miscellaneous Records of the Column from California, Claim of Messrs. White and Noyes, Pima Villages, 1862. The abbreviation *K.G.C.* stands for Knights of the Golden Circle, a secret society active at the time. The blacksmith's and carpenter's tools, unusual for a trader's store, were obviously obtained from the Pima [Indian] Agency operated by Special Agent Silas St. John from 1859 to 1860 but then abandoned. Ammi White apparently used the former agency buildings for his store and mill.

4. Ibid.

5. Ibid. The Mr. Woolsey was probably King Woolsey. Mr. Grant was William Grant, the government contractor who had been supplying Forts Buchanan and Breckinridge. Grant left Arizona at the end of July 1861, with Captain Moore and the federal troops who withdrew at that time. Ammi White obviously anticipated a profitable war and he did well, but there were some hitches along the way; see John P. Wilson, chapters 10 and 11 in "Peoples of the Middle Gila: A Documentary History of the Pimas and Maricopas" (unpublished MS, 1999).

6. National Archives, RG 109, War Department Collection of Confederate Records, Microcopy 323, Compiled Service Records of Confederate Soldiers Who Served in Organizations from the State of Texas, Roll 182, Baylor's Cavalry (Second Regiment, Arizona Brigade), A-L, Sherod Hunter jacket.

7. Ibid.

8. Ibid. The Table of Distances for the Overland Mail Co. showed the distance from Fort Yuma to Stanwix Station as seventy-seven miles.

9. Ibid. This is Captain Sherod Hunter's inventory of the goods confiscated from Ammi White.

10. National Archives, RG 109, War Department Collection of Confederate Records, Microcopy 323, Compiled Service Records of Confederate Soldiers Who Served in Organizations from the State of Texas, Roll 182, Baylor's Cavalry (Second Regiment, Arizona Brigade), A-L, Sherod Hunter jacket.

11. *The Tri-Weekly Telegraph* (Houston, Tex.), May 12, 1862, 3, cols. 1, 2.

12. National Archives, RG 109, War Department Collection of Confederate

Records, Microcopy 323, Compiled Service Records of Confederate Soldiers Who Served in Organizations from the State of Texas, Roll 182, Baylor's Cavalry (Second Regiment, Arizona Brigade), A-L, Sherod Hunter jacket.

13. Ibid.

14. National Archives, RG 393, U.S. Army Continental Commands 1821–1920, Entry 3662—Miscellaneous Records of the Column from California, Claim of Messrs. White and Noyes, Pima Villages, 1862.

15. Ibid.

16. Ibid.

17. Ibid.

Chapter 10

1. National Archives, RG 109, War Department Collection of Confederate Records. Microcopy 323, Compiled Service Records of Confederate Soldiers Who Served in Organizations from the State of Texas, Roll 182, Baylor's Cavalry (Second Regiment, Arizona Brigade), A-L, Sherod Hunter jacket. General Sibley in a letter of May 9, 1862, ordered that Lemon be released and his property be restored (in Sibley letterbook being edited by John P. Wilson and Jerry Thompson for publication as "The Civil War in West Texas and New Mexico: The Lost Letterbook of Brigadier General Henry Hopkins Sibley" [El Paso: Texas Western Press]).

2. Ibid. Stickney was not a military officer; his title was an assumed one.

3. National Archives, RG 393, Entry 115, Eastern District of New Mexico, Letters Received, March 1862.

4. National Archives, RG 109, War Department Collection of Confederate Records, Compiled Military Service Records, Col. John R. Baylor, Second Regiment Texas Cavalry.

5. National Archives, RG 109, War Department Collection of Confederate Records, Compiled Military Service Records, Confederate Staff Files, Thomas P. Ochiltree.

6. National Archives, RG 109, War Department Collection of Confederate Records, Chapter II, Vol. 270, Letters Sent, General William Steele's Command.

7. Ibid.

8. The Library of Congress, Manuscript Division, Microfilm Edition of the Records of the Confederate States of America, Vol. 24 (Reel 14).

9. National Archives, RG 109, War Department Collection of Confederate Records, Chapter II, Vol. 270, Letters Sent, General William Steele's Command.

Chapter 11

1. National Archives, RG 393, Entry 674, District of Santa Fe, New Mexico, Letters Received, December 1861–March 1865.

2. National Archives, RG 393, Headquarters, Department of New Mexico, Unregistered Letters Received, 1862–63, Microfilm Publication M1120 Roll 29.

3. National Archives, RG 393, Entry 89, Central District of New Mexico, Letters Received, 1862.

4. Ibid.

5. National Archives, RG 393, Entry 674, District of Santa Fe, New Mexico, Letters Received, December 1861–March 1865.

6. Ibid. Weller is unidentified but his title would have been an assumed one.

7. Ibid.

8. National Archives, RG 393, Headquarters, Department of New Mexico, Unregistered Letters Received, 1862–63, Microfilm Publication M1120 Roll 29.

9. Ibid.

10. National Archives, RG 393, Entry 674, District of Santa Fe, New Mexico, Letters Received, December 1861–March 1865.

11. National Archives, RG 393, Headquarters, Department of New Mexico, Letters Received, 1862, Microfilm Publication M1120 Roll 15, File No. D-13.

12. National Archives, RG 393, Entry 674, District of Santa Fe, New Mexico, Letters Received, December 1861–March 1865.

13. National Archives, RG 393, Headquarters, Department of New Mexico, Letters Received, 1862, Microfilm Publication M1120 Roll 15, File No. C-30.

14. National Archives, RG 393, Entry 674, District of Santa Fe, New Mexico, Letters Received, December 1861–March 1865.

15. National Archives, RG 393, Headquarters, Department of New Mexico, Unregistered Letters Received, 1862–63. Microfilm Publication M1120 Roll 29.

16. National Archives, RG 393, Entry 733, Southern District of New Mexico, Letters Sent, August 1861–May 1862.

17. Ibid.

18. National Archives, RG 393, Entry 674, District of Santa Fe, New Mexico, Letters Received, December 1861–March 1865.

19. National Archives, RG 393, Headquarters, Department of New Mexico, Letters Received, 1862, Microfilm Publication M1120 Roll 15, File No. C-37.

20. National Archives, RG 393, Entry 674, District of Santa Fe, New Mexico, Letters Received, December 1861–March 1865.

21. National Archives, RG 393, Headquarters, Department of New Mexico, Letters Received, 1862, Microfilm Publication M1120 Roll 15, File No. A-12.

22. National Archives, RG 393, Entry 674, District of Santa Fe, New Mexico, Letters Received, December 1861–March 1865.

23. National Archives, RG 393, Headquarters, Department of New Mexico, Unregistered Letters Received, 1854–61, Microfilm Publication M1120 Roll 28.

24. National Archives, RG 393, Entry 674, District of Santa Fe, New Mexico, Letters Received, December 1861–March 1865.

25. Ibid.

26. Ibid.

27. Ibid.

28. Ibid.

29. National Archives, RG 393, Headquarters, Department of New Mexico, Unregistered Letters Received, 1862–63, Microfilm Publication M1120 Roll 29.

30. Ibid.

31. National Archives, RG 393, Headquarters, Department of New Mexico, Letters Received, 1862, Microfilm Publication M1120 Roll 15, File No. A-19.

32. National Archives, RG 393, Headquarters, Department of New Mexico, Letters Received, 1862, Microfilm Publication M1120 Roll 15, File No. A-21. This letter was evidently dictated by Captain Aragon but written in a fine hand, by an educated English-speaking person.

33. National Archives, RG 393, Headquarters, Department of New Mexico, Letters Received, 1862, Microfilm Publication M1120 Roll 15, File No. C-52.

34. National Archives, RG 393, Headquarters, Department of New Mexico, Unregistered Letters Received, 1862–63, Microfilm Publication M1120 Roll 29.

35. Ibid.

36. National Archives, RG 393, Entry 674, District of Santa Fe, New Mexico, Letters Received, December 1861–March 1865.

37. National Archives, RG 393, Entry 115, Eastern District of New Mexico, Letters Received, March 1862.

38. Ibid.

Chapter 12

1. The Library of Congress, Manuscript Division, Microfilm Edition of the Records of the Confederate States of America, Vol. 58 (Reel No. 32).

2. Ibid.

3. Documentos de Ciudad Juárez, 1862, vol. 1. In Archives of the Ayuntamiento of Ciudad Juárez 1861–1864, reel 64, Letters Received, frame 0188, University of Texas at El Paso Library.

4. The Library of Congress, Manuscript Division, Microfilm Edition of the Records of the Confederate States of America, Vol. 58 (Reel No. 32).

5. The Library of Congress, Manuscript Division, Microfilm Edition of the Records of the Confederate States of America, Untitled letterbook of diplomatic correspondence, C.S.A., Department of State, Vol. 11 (Reel No. 10).

6. The Library of Congress, Manuscript Division, Microfilm Edition of the Records of the Confederate States of America, Vol. 58 (Reel No. 32).

Chapter 13

1. National Archives, RG 393, Entry 3183, Military Department of New Mexico, Miscellaneous Records, 1850–66.

2. National Archives, RG 393, Entry 735, Southern District of New Mexico, Letters Received, October 1861–August 1862.

3. Ibid.

4. National Archives, RG 393, Headquarters, Department of New Mexico, Letters Received, Microfilm Publication M1120 Roll 16, File No. F1 of 1862.

5. Corrections and annotations in the list below are from National Archives, RG 94, Records of the Adjutant General's Office, 1780s–1917, Preliminary Inventory 17, Entry 729, "Union Battle Reports," "Report of the Killed and Wounded at the Battle of Valverde, New Mexico," "List of Prisoners Taken by the Confederate Troops in New Mexico," filed with N87 1862 AGO.

6. *Santa-Fe Gazette*, May 10, 1862, 2.

7. *San Antonio Herald*, May 3, 1862, 2.

Chapter 14

1. By reference to Ovando Hollister's *Boldly They Rode* (1863; repr., Lakewood, Colo.: The Golden Press Publishers, 1949), this was generally known as Kozlowski's Ranch.

2. Miller just told us that Second Lieutenant William Marshall was killed, accidentally, which is what happened. Perhaps he meant to say Captain Cook was wounded.

3. *The Pueblo Chieftain* (Pueblo, Colo.), Sept. 29, 1907, 10. I am very grateful to Mr. Ed Simonich of Pueblo, Colorado, for locating and copying this article.

4. National Archives, RG92, Consolidated Correspondence File 1794–1915, "Pigeons Ranch, N.M.," Book 48, M430.

5. National Archives, RG92, Entry 225, Consolidated Correspondence File 1794–1915, "Pigeons Ranch, N.M.," in box 817.

6. National Archives, RG393, Headquarters, Department of New Mexico, Unregistered Letters Received, 1862–63, Microfilm Publication M1120 Roll 29.

7. Ibid.

8. National Archives, RG 94, Records of the Adjutant General's Office, 1780s–1917, Preliminary Inventory 17, Entry 729, "Union Battle Reports," Battle Report No. 56 1/2/116. The spellings of names have, where necessary, been corrected to conform with the spellings shown in William C. Whitford's *Colorado Volunteers in the Civil War.* However, in several instances, as with Slauson, Hotchkiss, and Kimball, it would appear that the spellings in Chivington's report are more probably the correct ones, and in these cases the original spellings have been retained.

9. *San Antonio Herald*, May 24, 1862, 1. Where necessary, the spellings of names have been corrected to conform with the spellings given in Martin H. Hall's *Confederate Army of New Mexico*.

Chapter 15

1. National Archives, RG 393, Headquarters, Department of New Mexico, Letters Received, File No. G-35 of 1862, Microfilm Publication M1120 Roll 16, 1862E-L.

2. National Archives, RG 393, Headquarters, Department of New Mexico, Unregistered Letters Received, 1862–63, Microfilm Publication M1120 Roll 29.

3. National Archives, RG 393, Entry 733, Southern District of New Mexico, Letters Sent, August 1861–May 1862.

4. Ibid.

5. Ibid.

6. Ibid.

7. Ibid. Steele's note has not been found. There is no copy of it in his letterbook.

8. National Archives, RG 94, Letters Received by the Office of the Adjutant General, Main Series, 1861–1870, File No. 191-N-AGO-1862, Microfilm Publication M-619 Roll 122, 1862I-294N. In 1971, the National Archives examined the file that contains the original copy of this letter. They reported that the undated issue of *The Mesilla Times* mentioned in this postscript was not there. This newspaper was probably separated from the letter at Fort Craig or Santa Fe, and subsequently discarded or lost. It would have been one of the latest issues of *The Mesilla Times*, because Donald S. Frazier (in *Blood and Treasure: Confederate Empire in the Southwest* [College Station: Texas A&M University Press, 1995], 197), indicates that Baylor had returned to Texas by the end of March 1862.

9. National Archives, RG 393, Headquarters, Department of New Mexico, Letters Received, 1862, File No. A-30, Microfilm Publication M1120 Roll 15, 1862A-D.

10. National Archives, RG 393, Entry 733, Southern District of New Mexico, Letters Sent, August 1861–May 1862.

11. Ibid.

12. National Archives, RG 393, Headquarters, Department of New Mexico, Unregistered Letters Received, 1862–63, Microfilm Publication M1120 Roll 29.

13. National Archives, RG 393, Headquarters, Department of New Mexico, Letters Received, 1862, File No. C-302, Microfilm Publication M1120 Roll 15, 1862A-D.

14. National Archives, RG 393, Headquarters, Department of New Mexico, Letters Received, 1862, File No. C-215, Microfilm Publication M1120 Roll 15, 1862A-D.

15. National Archives, RG 393, Entry 735, Southern District of New Mexico, Letters Received, October 1861–August 1862.

16. National Archives, RG 393, Headquarters, Department of New Mexico, Unregistered Letters Received, 1862–63, Microfilm Publication M1120 Roll 29.

17. National Archives, RG 393, Entry 734, Southern District of New Mexico, Letters Sent, July–September 1862.

18. Ibid. The enclosures have not been found.

19. Ibid.

20. National Archives, RG 393, Letters Sent by the Ninth Military Department, the Department of New Mexico, and the District of New Mexico 1849–1890, Vol. 8 (12 NMex) Jan.–Sept. 1862, Microfilm Publication M-1072 Roll 2.

21. National Archives, RG 393, Entry 735, Southern District of New Mexico, Letters Received, October 1861-August 1862.

Chapter 16

1. National Archives, RG 109, War Department Collection of Confederate Records, Compiled Military Service Records, Col. William Steele, Seventh Regiment, Texas Cavalry.

2. National Archives, RG 109, War Department Collection of Confederate Records, Chapter II, Vol. 270, Letters Sent, General William Steele's Command.

3. National Archives, RG 109, War Department Collection of Confederate Records, Compiled Military Service Records, Confederate Staff Files, Thomas P. Ochiltree.

4. There is some confusion in the dates. May 12, 1862, was a Monday. Assuming that the council did meet for the second time on May 15, this date was a Thursday.

5. *The Tri-Weekly Telegraph* (Houston, Tex.), Aug. 27, 1862, 2.

6. There is no record of this officer in Martin H. Hall's *Confederate Army of New Mexico*.

7. National Archives, RG 109, War Department Collection of Confederate Records, General and Staff Officers' Files, Gen. Henry H. Sibley. Baylor's letter, dated March 17, may be seen in chapter 10.

8. National Archives, RG 109, War Department Collection of Confederate Records, Chapter II, Vol. 270, Letters Sent, General William Steele's Command. Herbert commanded a locally raised battalion; see Donald S. Frazier, *Blood and Treasure*.

9. Ibid.

10. Ibid. Alderete probably refers to Pablo Alderete from the Rio Bonito country; see chapter 9. He evidently led a local company, of which we have no other evidence. Such units served for short periods on both sides, but were never mustered in.

11. Ibid.

12. Not identified. The writer was probably referring to Capt. William H. Cleaver.

13. *The Tri-Weekly Telegraph* (Houston, Tex.), Aug. 18, 1862, 2, col. 3. The author of this letter was probably Jo. A. Kirgan; see Martin H. Hall's *Confederate Army of New Mexico*, 252.

14. *San Antonio Weekly Herald,* July 12, 1862, 2, col. 3.

15. National Archives, RG 109, War Department Collection of Confederate Records, Chapter II, Vol. 270, Letters Sent, General William Steele's Command.

16. *The Semi-Weekly News* (San Antonio, Tex.), July 21, 1862, 2, col. 1. Captain Gustav Hoffmann commanded Co. B, Seventh Regiment, Texas Mounted Volunteers; see Martin H. Hall, *The Confederate Army of New Mexico,* 231–32.

17. National Archives, RG 109, War Department Collection of Confederate Records, Compiled Military Service Records, Col. John R. Baylor, Second Regiment Texas Cavalry.

References

Publications

Alberts, Don E.
1983   "The Battle of Peralta." *New Mexico Historical Review* 58(4): 369–79.
1984   *Rebels on the Rio Grande: The Civil War Journal of A. B. Peticolas.* Albuquerque: University of New Mexico Press.
1998   *The Battle of Glorieta: Union Victory in the West.* College Station: Texas A&M University Press.

Anderson, Hattie M., ed.
1929   "With the Confederates in New Mexico during the Civil War—Memoirs of Hank Smith." *Panhandle-Plains Historical Review* 2: 65–97.

Armstrong, A. F. H.
1961   "The Case of Major Isaac Lynde." *New Mexico Historical Review* 36(1): 1–35.

Barbaras, Richard, and Cassandra Richard
1980   "Sibley's Retreat." *Rio Grande History* No. 11: 2–3. Las Cruces: New Mexico State University.

Baylor, George Wythe
1996   *Into the Far, Wild Country: True Tales of the Old Southwest.* El Paso: Texas Western Press.

Beers, Henry Putney
1968   *Guide to the Archives of the Government of the Confederate States of America.* Washington, D.C.: U.S. Government Printing Office.

Bethel, Elizabeth
1957   *Preliminary Inventory of the War Department Collection of Confederate Records* (Record Group 109). Washington, D.C.: National Archives and Records Service.

Bloom, Lansing B., ed.
1930   "Confederate Reminiscences of 1862." *New Mexico Historical Review* 5(3): 315–24.

Brophy, A. Blake
1968   "Fort Fillmore, N.M., 1861: Public Disgrace and Private Disaster." *The Journal of Arizona History* 9(4): 195–218.

Brown, William O., Jr., and Richard C. K. Burdekin
2000   "Turning Points in the U.S. Civil War: A British Perspective." *The Journal of Economic History* 60(1): 216–31.

Chivington, John M.
1958   "The First Colorado Regiment." *New Mexico Historical Review* 33(2): 144–54.

Colton, Ray C.
1959   *The Civil War in the Western Territories.* Norman: University of Oklahoma Press.

Curry, W. Hubert
1979   *Sun Rising on the West, The Saga of Henry Clay and Elizabeth Smith.* Crosbyton, Tex.: Crosby County Pioneer Memorial.

Drumm, Stella M., ed.
1926   *Down the Santa Fe Trail and into Mexico: The Diary of Susan Shelby Magoffin, 1846–1847.* New Haven: Yale University Press.

Edrington, Thomas S., and John Taylor
1998   *The Battle of Glorieta Pass: A Gettysburg in the West, March 26–28, 1862.* Albuquerque: University of New Mexico Press.

Everly, Elaine, Alice Haynes, Maizie Johnson, Sarah Powell, Harry Schwartz, John Scroggins, Aloha South, and Evelyn Wade
1973   *Preliminary Inventory of the Records of United States Army Continental Commands, 1821–1920 (Record Group 393),* Vols. 1–4. Washington, D.C.: National Archives and Records Service.

Faulkner, Walter A., ed.
1951   "With Sibley in New Mexico; The Journal of William Henry Smith." *West Texas Historical Association Year Book* 27: 111–42. Abilene: West Texas Historical Association.

File, Lucien A.
1965   *Directory of Mines of New Mexico.* State Bureau of Mines and Mineral Resources, Circular 77. Socorro: New Mexico Institute of Mining and Technology.

Finch, L. Boyd
1969   "Sherod Hunter and the Confederates in Arizona." *The Journal of Arizona History* 10(3): 137–206.

1996   *Confederate Pathway to the Pacific: Major Sherod Hunter and Arizona Territory, C.S.A.* Tucson: The Arizona Historical Society.

Frazier, Donald S.
1995   *Blood and Treasure: Confederate Empire in the Southwest.* College Station: Texas A&M University Press.

Gracy, David B., II, ed.
1964   "New Mexico Campaign Letters of Frank Starr, 1861–1862." *Texas Military History* 4(3): 169–88.

Graham, Stanley S.
1972   "Campaign for New Mexico, 1861–1862." *Military History of Texas and the Southwest* 10(1): 5–27.

Grinstead, Marion Cox
1993   *Destiny at Valverde: The Life and Death of Alexander McRae.* Socorro, N.M.: The Socorro Historical Society.

Haas, Oscar, trans.
1963   "The Diary of Julius Giesecke, 1861–1862." *Texas Military History* 3(4): 228–42.

Hall, Martin Hardwick
1956   "Colonel James Reily's Diplomatic Mission to Chihuahua and Sonora." *New Mexico Historical Review* 31(3): 232–42.
1958a   "The Journal of Ebenezer Hanna." *Password* 3(1): 14–29.
1958b   "The Formation of Sibley's Brigade and the March to New Mexico." *Southwestern Historical Quarterly* 61(3): 383–405.
1959   "The Skirmish at Mesilla." *Arizona and the West* 1(4): 343–51.
1960a   "The Baylor-Kelley Fight: A Civil War Incident in Old Mesilla." *Password* 5(3): 83–90.
1960b   *Sibley's New Mexico Campaign.* Austin: University of Texas Press.
1962   "Albert Sidney Johnston's First Confederate Command." *The McNeese Review* 13: 3–12.
1967   "Native Mexican Relations in Confederate Arizona, 1861–1862." *The Journal of Arizona History* 8(3): 171–78.
1968a   "Planter vs. Frontiersman: Conflict in Confederate Indian Policy." In *Essays on the American Civil War,* ed. William F. Holmes and Harold M. Hollingsworth, 45–72. Austin: University of Texas Press.
1968b   "Negros with Confederate Troops in West Texas and New Mexico." *Password* 13(1): 11–12.
1976   "An Appraisal of the 1862 New Mexico Campaign: A Confederate Officer's Letter to Nacogdoches." *New Mexico Historical Review* 51(4): 329–35.
1978   *The Confederate Army of New Mexico.* Austin: Presidial Press.
1979   "The Taylor Letters: Confederate Correspondence from Fort Bliss, 1861." *Military History of Texas and the Southwest* 15(2): 53–60.
1981   "The Court-Martial of Arthur Pendleton Bagby, C.S.A." *East Texas Historical Journal* 19(2): 60–67.

Heyman, Max L.
1959   *Prudent Soldier: A Biography of Major General E. R. S. Canby, 1817–1873.* Glendale, Calif.: Arthur H. Clark Co.

Hollister, Ovando J.
1949   *Boldly They Rode.* 1863. Reprint, Lakewood, Colo.: The Golden Press, Publishers.

Hord, Ruth Waldrop, ed.
1978   "The Diary of Lieutenant E. L. Robb, C.S.A., from Santa Fe to Fort Lancaster, 1862." *Permian Historical Annual* 18 (December): 59–80. Odessa, Tex.: Permian Historical Society.

Hunter, John Warren
1926   "Fighting with Sibley in New Mexico." *Frontier Times* 3(12): 9–15.
        Apparently reprinted from *Hunter's Magazine*, Vol. 1, November 1910.
        Reprinted as "A Raft Voyage down the Rio Grande" in *Frontier Times*,
        November 1951, 33–40.

Josephy, Alvin M., Jr.
1991   *The Civil War in the American West.* New York: Alfred A. Knopf.

Kajencki, Francis C.
1987   "The Battle of Glorieta Pass: Was the Guide Ortiz or Grzelachowski?" *New
        Mexico Historical Review* 62(1): 47–54.

Kerby, Robert Lee
1958   *The Confederate Invasion of New Mexico and Arizona, 1861–1862.* Los Angeles:
        Westernlore Press.

Ketchum, Richard M., ed.
1960   *The American Heritage Picture History of The Civil War.* New York:
        American Heritage Publishing Co.

Library of Congress, Manuscript Division
n.d.   Finding Aid to the Records of the Confederate States of America ("Pickett
        Papers"). Washington, D.C.: Library of Congress.

McKee, James Cooper
1960   *Narrative of the Surrender of a Command of U.S. Forces at Fort Fillmore, New
        Mexico, July 1861.* 3d. ed., 1886. Reprint, Houston, Tex.: Stagecoach Press.

McMaster, Richard K., and George Ruhlen
1960   "The Guns of Valverde." *Password* 5(1): 20–34.

Meketa, Charles, and Jacqueline Meketa
1987   "Heroes or Cowards? A New Look at the Role of Native New Mexicans at
        the Battle of Valverde." *New Mexico Historical Review* 62(1): 33–46.

Meketa, Jacqueline Dorgan, ed.
1986   *Legacy of Honor: The Life of Rafael Chacon, a Nineteenth-Century New
        Mexican.* Albuquerque: University of New Mexico Press.

Miller, Darlis A.
1979   "Hispanos and the Civil War in New Mexico: A Reconsideration." *New
        Mexico Historical Review* 54(2): 105–23.
1983   "Military Supply in Civil War New Mexico." *Military History of Texas and
        the Southwest* 16(3): 177–97.
1989   *Soldiers and Settlers: Military Supply in the Southwest, 1861–1885.*
        Albuquerque: University of New Mexico Press.

Mills, W. W.
1962   *Forty Years at El Paso, 1858–1898.* El Paso: Carl Hertzog.

Mumey, Nolie, ed.
1958   *Bloody Trails along the Rio Grande: A Day-by-Day Diary of Alonzo Ferdinand
        Ickis.* Denver: Old West Publishing Company.

Munden, Kenneth W., and Henry Putney Beers
1962   *Guide to Federal Archives Relating to the Civil War.* Washington, D.C.: U.S.
        Government Printing Office.

Noel, Theophilus
1961   *A Campaign from Santa Fe to the Mississippi, Being a History of the Old Sibley
        Brigade.* 1865. Reprint, Houston, Tex.: Stagecoach Press.

Owsley, Douglas W.
1994   *Bioarchaeology on a Battlefield: The Abortive Confederate Campaign in New
        Mexico.* Museum of New Mexico Office of Archaeological Studies
        Archaeology Notes 142. Santa Fe: Museum of New Mexico.

Pendell, Lucille H., and Elizabeth Bethel
1949   *Preliminary Inventory of the Records of the Adjutant General's Office.* Preliminary
        Inventory No. 17. Washington, D.C.: National Archives and Records
        Service.

Perrine, David P.
1981   "The Battle of Valverde, New Mexico Territory, February 21, 1862."
        In *Civil War Battles in the West*, ed. LeRoy H. Fischer, 26–38.
        Manhattan, Kans.: Sunflower University Press.

Rittenhouse, Jack D., comp.
1961   *New Mexico Civil War Bibliography.* Houston, Tex.: Stagecoach Press.

Samuels, Peggy and Harold
1995   *Remembering the Maine.* Washington, D.C.: Smithsonian Institution Press.

Simmons, Marc
1970   "Horse Race at Fort Fauntleroy: An Incident of the Navajo Wars." *La Gaceta*
        5(1): 3–13. Santa Fe: El Corral de Santa Fe Westerners.
1987   *The Battle at Valley's Ranch.* Sandia Park, N.M.: San Pedro Press.

Stanley, F. [Father Stanley Crocchiola]
1960   *The Civil War in New Mexico.* Denver: The World Press.

Tate, Michael L.
1987–1988 "A Johnny Reb in Sibley's New Mexico Campaign: Reminiscences of
        Pvt. Henry C. Wright, 1861–1862." *East Texas Historical Journal* 25(2):
        20–33; 26(1): 23–35; 26(2): 48–60.

Taylor, John
1995   *Bloody Valverde: A Civil War Battle on the Rio Grande, February 21, 1862.*
        Albuquerque: University of New Mexico Press.

Teel, T. T.
1956   "Sibley's New Mexico Campaign—Its Objects and the Causes of Its
        Failure." *Battles and Leaders of the Civil War* 2: 700. New York: Thomas
        Yoseloff.

Thompson, Jerry D.
1971   *Colonel John Robert Baylor: Texas Indian Fighter and Confederate Soldier.* Hill
        Junior College Monograph in Texas and Confederate History, No. 5.
        Hillsboro, Tex.: Hill Junior College.

1972   "Mexican-Americans in the Civil War: The Battle of Valverde." *Texana* 10(1):
       1–19.
1983   "The Vulture Over the Carrion: Captain James 'Paddy' Graydon and the
       Civil War in the Southwest." *The Journal of Arizona History* 24(4): 381–404.
1987   *Henry Hopkins Sibley: Confederate General of the West.* Natchitoches, La.:
       Northwestern State University Press.
1990   *Westward the Texans: The Civil War Journal of Private William Randolph Howell.*
       El Paso: Texas Western Press.
1991a "The Gallinas Massacre and The Death of Captain James Graydon."
       Password 36(1): 5–22.
1991b *From Desert to Bayou: The Civil War Journal and Sketches of Morgan Wolfe
       Merrick.* El Paso: Texas Western Press.
1992a *Desert Tiger: Captain Paddy Graydon and the Civil War in the Far Southwest.*
       Southwestern Studies Series No. 97. El Paso: Texas Western Press.
1992b "Drama in the Desert: The Hunt for Henry Skillman in the Trans-Pecos,
       1862–1864." *Password* 37(3): 107–26.
1994   "The Civil War Diary of Major Charles Emil Wesche." *Password* 39(1):
       37–47.
1998   "'Gloom over Our Fair Land'; Socorro County during the Civil War." *New
       Mexico Historical Review* 73(2): 99–119.
1999   "An Indian Superintendent at the Battle of Valverde: The Civil War
       Letters of James L. Collins." *Southwestern Historical Quarterly* 103(2):
       215–29.

Torrez, Robert J.
1988   "The San Juan Gold Rush of 1860 and Its Effect on the Development of
       Northern New Mexico." *New Mexico Historical Review* 63(3): 257–72.

United States Government Printing Office
1880–1901 *The War of the Rebellion: A Compilation of the Official Records of the Union
       and Confederate Armies.* 128 vols. Washington, D.C.

Walker, Charles S.
1933   "Causes of the Confederate Invasion of New Mexico." *New
       Mexico Historical Review* 8(2): 76–97.

Weidenmier, Marc D.
2000   "The Market for Confederate Cotton Bonds." *Explorations in Economic
       History* 37(1): 76–97.

Whitford, William Clarke
1963   *Colorado Volunteers in the Civil War: The New Mexico Campaign in 1862.*
       1906. Reprint, Boulder, Colo.: Pruett Press.

Wike, John W.
1952   "Colors, Colors, Who's Got the Colors: An Episode in the History of
       the Seventh Infantry." *Military Collector and Historian* 4(4): 91–92.

Wilson, John P.
1975   "Retreat to the Rio Grande: The Report of Captain Isaiah N. Moore." *Rio
       Grande History* 2(3&4): 4–8. Las Cruces: New Mexico State University.

1987   *Merchants, Guns, and Money: The Story of Lincoln County and Its Wars.* Santa
        Fe: Museum of New Mexico Press.
1989   "The End of Sibley's New Mexico Campaign." *La Crónica de Nuevo
        México,* Issue No. 28: 2–4. Santa Fe: Historical Society of New Mexico.
1993   "Whiskey at Fort Fillmore: A Story of the Civil War." *New Mexico Historical
        Review* 68(2): 109–32.
1999   "The Civil War at the Pima Villages." Chapter 10 in "Peoples of the
        Middle Gila: A Documentary History of the Pimas and Maricopas."
        Unpublished MS.

Wright, Arthur A.
1964   *The Civil War in the Southwest.* Denver: Big Mountain Press.

Manuscripts and Microfilms

The Library of Congress, Manuscript Division
    Microfilm Edition of the Records of the Confederate States of America
        ("Pickett Papers"), 70 reels.
        Vol. 11 (Reel No. 10)
        Vol. 24 (Reel No. 14)
        Vol. 58 (Reel No. 32)

National Archives and Records Administration
    RG 75. Records of the Bureau of Indian Affairs.
        Letters Received by the Office of Indian Affairs, 1824–1880.
            M-234, rolls 550, 551.
    RG 92. Records of the Office of the Quartermaster General.
        Consolidated File, Fort Fillmore, New Mexico.
        Entry 225, Consolidated Correspondence File 1794–1915, "Pigeons
            Ranch, N.M." In box 817.
        Consolidated Correspondence File 1794–1915, "Pigeon's Ranch, N.M."
            Book 48, M430.
    RG 94. Records of the Adjutant General's Office, 1780s–1917.
        Letters Received, 1861. Report No. 613C 1861, F/W 591P 1861, folder 2.
        Letters Received by the Office of the Adjutant General (Main Series),
            1861–1870. M-619, rolls 42, 122.
        Preliminary Inventory 17 Entry 729, "Union Battle Reports": (1) "Report
            of the Killed and Wounded at the Battle of Valverde, New Mexico."
            (2) "List of Prisoners Taken by the Confederate Troops in New
            Mexico." (3) Battle Report No. 56 ½/116.
    RG 109. War Department Collection of Confederate Records.
        Chapter II, vol. 270. Letters Sent, Gen. William Steele's Command,
            March 1862–May 1863.
        Compiled Military Service Records, Col. John R. Baylor, Second
            Regiment Texas Cavalry.
        Compiled Military Service Records, Confederate Staff Files, Thomas P.
            Ochiltree.

Compiled Military Service Records, Col. William Steele, Seventh
    Regiment Texas Cavalry.
Compiled Service Records of Confederate Soldiers Who Served in
    Organizations from the State of Texas. M-323, roll 182.
General and Staff Officers' Files, Gen. Henry H. Sibley.
RG 123. Records of the United States Court of Claims.
    General Jurisdiction Case No. 1883, *William S. Grant v. The United
    States*, folder unnumbered.
RG 153. Records of the Office of the Judge Advocate General (Army).
    File No. 107, Case of Major Isaac P. Lynde, 1861–62.
RG 249. Records of the Commissary General of Prisoners.
    Federal Prisoners, 1861–65 [E107], Miscellaneous List No. 436.
RG 393. Records of United States Army Continental Commands, 1821–1920.
    Headquarters Records of Fort Union, New Mexico, Letters Received,
        June–August 1861.
    Letters Sent by the Ninth Military Department, the Department of
        New Mexico, and the District of New Mexico 1849–1890. M-1072,
        rolls 2, 13.
    Registers of Letters Received, and Letters Received by Headquarters,
        Department of New Mexico, 1854–1865. M-1120, rolls 13, 14, 15,
        16, 28, 29.
    Vol. I Entry 3183, Military Department of New Mexico, Miscellaneous
        Records, 1850–66.
    Vol. I Entry 3662, Miscellaneous Records of the Column from California,
        Claim of Messrs. White and Noyes, Pima Villages, 1862.
    Vol. III Entry 89, Central District of New Mexico, Letters Received,
        1862.
    Vol. III Entry 111, District of Fort Craig, New Mexico, Letters
        Received, August 1861.
    Vol. III Entry 115, Eastern District of New Mexico, Letters Received,
        March 1862.
    Vol. III Entry 674, District of Santa Fe, New Mexico, Letters Received,
        December 1861–March 1865.
    Vol. III Entry 733, Southern District of New Mexico, Letters Sent,
        August 1861–May 1862.
    Vol. III Entry 734, Southern District of New Mexico, Letters Sent,
        July–September 1862.
    Vol. III Entry 735, Southern District of New Mexico, Letters Received,
        October 1861–August 1862.

University of Texas at El Paso Library
    Microfilm of the Archives of the Ayuntamiento of Ciudad Juárez 1861–1864,
    reel 64.

Newspapers

Daily Alta California (San Francisco, Calif.). June 29, Aug. 10, 1862.

Daily Conservative (Leavenworth, Kans.). Oct. 19, 1861.

The Daily Picayune (New Orleans, La.). Aug. 27, Nov. 1, 1861.

Dallas Herald (Dallas, Tex.). Aug. 28, 1861.

Galveston News (Galveston, Tex.). Aug. 20, 1861.

The Pueblo Chieftain (Pueblo, Colo.). Sept. 29, 1907.

Quincy Daily Whig and Republican (Quincy, Ill.). Mar. 5, 1862.

St. Louis Post-Dispatch (St. Louis, Mo.). Mar. 21, 1887.

San Antonio Herald (San Antonio, Tex.). May 3, May 24, 1862.

San Antonio Weekly Herald (San Antonio, Tex.). July 12, 1862.

Santa-Fe Gazette (Santa Fe, N.M.). Sept. 14, 28, 1861; May 10, 1862.

The Semi-Weekly News (San Antonio, Tex.). July 21, 1862.

Socorro Bullion (Socorro, N.M.). Sept. 1, 1883.

The Tri-Weekly Telegraph (Houston, Tex.). Nov. 1, 1861; May 12, 28, June 6,
    Aug. 18, 27, 1862.

The Weekly Texas State Gazette (Austin, Tex.). Feb. 15, 1862.

Index